A N S W E R I N G
J E W I S H
O B J E C T I O N S
to
J E S U S

Michael L. Brown is a Jewish believer in Jesus and has a Ph.D. in Near Eastern Languages and Literatures from New York University. He is president of the FIRE School of Ministry in Concord, North Carolina and has served as a visiting professor at Trinity Evangelical Divinity School and Fuller Theological Seminary. He has written over fifteen books and is a contributor to the *Oxford Dictionary of Jewish Religion*.

ANSWERING JEWISH OBJECTIONS *to* JESUS

Volume 4

New Testament Objections

MICHAEL L. BROWN

BakerBooks

a division of Baker Publishing Group
Grand Rapids, Michigan

Published by Baker Books
a division of Baker Publishing Group
P.O. Box 6287, Grand Rapids, MI 49516-6287
www.bakerbooks.com

Printed in the United States of America

Library of Congress Cataloging-in-Publication Data
Brown, Michael L., 1955–
    Answering Jewish objections to Jesus : new testament objections / Michael L.
Brown.
        p.   cm.
    Includes bibliographical references (p.   ) and indexes.
    ISBN 10: 0-8010-6426-0 (pbk.)
    ISBN 978-0-8010-6426-5 (pbk.)
    1. Apologetics. 2. Jews—Conversion to Christianity. 3. Jesus Christ—Messiahship. I. Title.
    BV4922.B76 2006
    239—dc21   99-046293

To Nancy,
my bride of thirty years,
and my best friend in this world

Contents

Preface

After debating a rabbi in Montreal in September 2005, I was interviewed by a correspondent for a local college newspaper who asked me how I got involved in debates like this. His question actually gave me pause for thought. How, in fact, did I become a specialist in Messianic Jewish apologetics? How did I end up debating Orthodox Jewish rabbis, professors, and anti-missionaries? What prompted me to devote so many years of my life to answering Jewish objections to Jesus?

The answer is really quite simple: The rabbis left me no choice, speaking to me earnestly when I first believed in Jesus—beginning in early 1972, shortly after I had been transformed from a rebellious, proud, heroin-shooting, rock-drumming, Jewish sixteen year old into a fervent, clean-living, God-fearing believer—and continuing to interact with me for years thereafter, discussing the Scriptures with me, challenging the veracity of my beliefs, urging me to reconsider my views, telling me that if I really knew Hebrew, I would never believe in Jesus, seeking to point out all kinds of errors in the New Testament writings, sharing books and resources with me that they hoped would cause me to embrace traditional Judaism.

I am eternally grateful to each and every one of these sincere, Jewish leaders for their efforts! Their well-intended challenges only forced me to dig deeper—on my knees, with the Scriptures opened, seeking God for his truth, in continued dialogue with these rabbis and with Jewish scholars, in college and university classrooms until I had earned a Ph.D. in ancient Semitic studies, and, since the era of the Internet, in online discussion groups and on anti-missionary websites.

It is because of the challenges of these first rabbis that my faith was ultimately strengthened, although, to be totally candid, when I really decided to follow the evidence wherever it led, I was not sure how deeply my beliefs would be challenged. As it turns out, after many years of intensive study of the Scriptures—including the New Testament documents, which are constantly attacked by the anti-missionaries—the result has been a greater appreciation for the God who inspired these writings and for the Messiah whose story they told. It is for good reason that Yeshua said to the Jews who believed in him, "If you hold to my teaching, you are really my disciples. Then you will know the truth, and the truth will set you free" (John 8:31b–32). How liberating the truth really is! As I stated on numerous occasions, Yeshua's followers have nothing to fear, since they are on the side of truth—which means they are backed by the One who cannot lie, the living embodiment of Truth.

This volume, devoted entirely to answering Jewish objections to the New Testament, was originally planned to be part of volume 3 in this series, but it became clear that I had left far too much material to be covered in one volume. (As originally planned, volume 3 was to cover Messianic prophecy objections, New Testament objections, and objections based on traditional Judaism.) And so, in the preface to volume 3, I explained that there would be a fourth volume that would cover the last two sections, namely, New Testament objections and objections based on traditional Judaism. However, when I completed the writing of volume 4, the manuscript came to more than 650 pages, and because such a lengthy volume would have been unwieldy, it was agreed that there would have to be a *fifth* volume, devoted exclusively to traditional Jewish objections. (I express my great appreciation to Baker Books for their tremendous flexibility and understanding in this project, one which has continued for almost ten years from its inception and has expanded and changed several times along the way.)

Upon completion, then, the series will total more than 1,500 pages, but I believe that most all of the objections treated are worthy of serious responses, and I have more than received the rewards for my labor in numerous ways: first, in the delight of the deeper discovery of God's truths, which, in turn, have produced a greater delight in my Redeemer; second, in the many reports received of Jewish believers in Jesus whose faith was strengthened—or recovered—through the volumes; third, in the testimonies of Jewish people coming to faith in Jesus through these writings; fourth, in the reports of Gentile Christians whose faith and understanding have been enriched. How can I thank God for such kindness?

To recap what has been published to date, volume 1 dealt with general and historical objections (covering thirty-five objections in all, numbered respectively as 1.1–1.19 and 2.1–2.16). Volume 2 dealt with theological objections (twenty-eight in all, numbered as 3.1–3.28). Volume 3 dealt with thirty-nine major objections to the Messianic prophecies (numbered as 4.1–4.39), this current volume treats thirty-four key objections to the New Testament (5.1–5.34), many of which address numerous issues within each objection, and volume 5 will deal with eighteen key objections raised by traditional Judaism, dealing in particular with the Oral Law (6.1–6.18; for a preview of the questions that will be addressed in volume 5, go to www.realmessiah.org).

To briefly summarize the material treated in this series, *general objections* boil down to the perception that, "Jesus is not for Jews! Our religion is Judaism, not Christianity. No true Jew would ever believe in Jesus." *Historical objections* tend to be more substantial and deal with the very purpose of the Messiah (in other words, the claim that the role of the Messiah was to bring peace to the world) or the alleged failure of the church ("Christian" anti-Semitism; the state of the "church" worldwide, including divisions and scandals). The heart of these objections is: "Jesus cannot be the Messiah because we are obviously not in the Messianic age."

Theological objections cut to the heart of the differences between traditional Judaism and the Messianic Jewish/Christian faith. They revolve around: the nature of God (the Trinity, the deity of Jesus, the person of the Holy Spirit); the nature of man and the need for salvation; sin and the means of atonement. In sum, these objections claim that "the religion of the New Testament is a completely foreign religion which is not only un-Jewish, but is also unfaithful to the Hebrew Bible."

The *objections based on Messianic prophecies* arise from traditional Judaism's rejection of our standard Messianic prophetic "proof texts," either denying that they have anything to do with Jesus, claiming that they have been mistranslated, misquoted, or taken out of context by the New Testament authors or traditional Christian apologists, or arguing that none of the *real* Messianic prophecies—the so-called "provable" prophecies—were ever fulfilled by Jesus. In short, these objections say: "We don't believe Jesus is the Messiah because he didn't come close to living up to the biblical description of the Messiah."

Jewish *objections to the New Testament* can be broken down into several categories: The New Testament misquotes and misinterprets the Old Testament, at times manufacturing verses to suit its purposes; the genealogies of Jesus given by Matthew and Luke are hopelessly contradictory (at best) and entirely irrelevant anyway; the New Testament is filled with historical and factual errors (especially Stephen's speech!); the teachings of Jesus are impossible, dangerous, and un-Jewish (and Jesus as a person was not so great either); the New Testament is even self-contradictory. To sum up rather bluntly: "Only a fool would believe in the divine inspiration of the New Testament."

Finally, *objections based on traditional Judaism* are founded on two key points: (1) "Judaism is a wonderful, fulfilling, and self-sufficient religion. There is no need to look elsewhere." (2) "God gave us a written and an unwritten tradition. We interpret *everything* by means of that oral tradition, without which the Bible makes no sense." (For further background to the history of these objections, see volume 1, introduction.)

Each of the volumes follows a similar format. I begin with a concise statement of the objection, followed by a concise answer to the objection, which is then followed by an in-depth answer, including citations of important sources as needed, also considering possible objections to our answers. For those interested in more detailed discussion, substantial endnotes have been provided, although in this volume, because of the breadth of the material cited—which required well over five hundred endnotes—I have not attempted to be exhaustive in my citations.

I have dedicated this study to my precious wife, Nancy, my extraordinary companion and friend of more than thirty years, a lover of truth without compromise. May the prayers she has prayed out of a broken heart before God be answered in keeping with his glory and majesty and power. It's time!

Michael L. Brown
August 14, 2006

Note on citations and sources: Rabbinic literature is cited using standard conventions (e.g., the letter "m." before a Rabbinic source means "Mishnah" while "b." stands for "Babylonian Talmud"). When there was a difference in the numbering of biblical verses between some Christian and Jewish versions, the Jewish numbering was put in brackets (e.g., Isa 9:6[5]). Bear in mind, however, that the actual verses are identical; only the numbering is different. Also, in keeping with the stylistic conventions of the publisher, all references to deity are lowercase. However, in keeping with traditional Jewish conventions, other words (such as Rabbinic, Temple, and Messianic) have been capitalized. Unless otherwise noted, all emphasis in Scripture quotations is my own.

PART 5

OBJECTIONS BASED ON THE NEW TESTAMENT

5.1. The New Testament misquotes and misinterprets the Old Testament. At times it manufactures verses to suit its purposes.

There is no truth to this claim. You must remember that all the New Testament authors were Jews—with one probable exception—and they were sometimes writing to Jewish readers who knew their Scriptures well. To manufacture, misquote, or misinterpret verses from the Tanakh would be absolutely self-defeating. The fact is, these authors spent much time meditating on the Tanakh, and you would be amazed to see just how insightful their quotations and interpretations are, not to mention how much they are in keeping with the ancient Jewish methods of scriptural hermeneutics.

You need to keep in mind that your very objection points to something of great significance: *The New Testament authors are constantly quoting and referring to the Hebrew Scriptures*. That was their Bible, their primary source of authority, the foundation of their faith. As noted in volume 1 (239, n. 160), the pages of the New Testament are filled with citations from the Hebrew Scriptures, with as many as three hundred direct quotations from the Tanakh and several thousand allusions to the Hebrew Bible in the New Testament. In fact, some scholars claim that *almost one out of three verses* in the New Testament—2,500 out of a total of 8,000 verses—contains an Old Testament quote or general allusion, while, quite solidly, it can be demonstrated that "more than ten percent of the New Testament text is made up of citation or direct allusions to the Old Testament."[1] More than 10 percent! The Book of Revelation, the last book of the New Testament, contains 404 verses, most of which (as many as 331 verses) are drawn from the imagery of the Hebrew Scriptures, although Revelation hardly ever directly quotes a specific verse from the Tanakh. All this indicates how deeply the Hebrew Scriptures are intertwined in the New Covenant Scriptures.[2]

New Testament and Judaic literature scholar Craig Evans summarized the situation well:

> The theology of the NT is fundamentally indebted to, and a reflection of, major OT themes, images, and language. There is simply no significant element in NT theology that is not in some way a development of a tradition or theology expressed in the sacred writings that eventually came to be what Christians call the Old Testament (OT), Jews call the Tanakh, and scholars call the Hebrew Bible (HB).[3]

Not surprisingly, with so many quotes and references drawn from the Tanakh by different authors writing with different styles, not every citation will follow the same format or be based on the same principle of interpretation. This, of course, is the case as well in Rabbinic literature (e.g., the Talmud) and the Dead Sea Scrolls (abbreviated DSS): Not all citations from the Hebrew Bible in these writings follow an identical pattern. (This is actually a massive understatement!) To mention just a few of the ways that the Scriptures are cited in ancient Jewish literature, some of the citations reflect something as minor as a play on words, others are primarily homiletical (i.e., midrashic), while others play a foundational role, with the Scripture verse supporting a major doctrinal or legal point. To illustrate some of these principles, we turn to the Dead Sea Scrolls, the Rabbinic writings, and then the New Covenant Scriptures.

New Testament and Semitic scholar Joseph Fitzmyer observed that there are four major ways in which verses from the Tanakh were cited in the writings from Qumran, each of which has a parallel in the New Testament writings, pointing once again to the Jewishness of those writings. Fitzmyer calls the first class of quotations "The Literal or Historical Class," which he describes as citations "in which the Qumran author quotes the Old Testament in the same sense in which it was used in the original writing,"[4] citing seven examples, including CD 7:8–9 which quotes Numbers 30:17. For a New Testament example, Fitzmyer cites, among others, John 6:31 quoting Psalm 78:24.

The next grouping of citations is labeled "The Class of Modernized Texts," meaning those texts,

> in which the words of the Old Testament refer to a specific event in their original context, but which are nevertheless vague enough in themselves to be used by the Qumran author of some new event on the contemporary scene. In other words, the same *general* sense of the Old Testament is preserved, but it is applied to a new subject. . . . In this class of quotations one normally finds the Old Testament quoted in the same way it is

found in the original context, without modification or deliberate changing of it. A new reference or a new dimension, however, is given to it in the way it is quoted.[5]

In the Qumran *pesharim* (biblical interpretations), Fitzmyer finds such citations to be "abundantly attested."[6] Among other texts, for example, he cites CD 1:13–14, quoting Hosea 4:16. For a New Testament parallel, compare Matthew 4:15–16, citing Isaiah 9:1–2[8:23–9:1], where Fitzmyer notes:

> No less than the Qumran authors, the New Testament writers considered their history to be guided by the hand of God. But for the New Testament authors his word spoken through the prophets and writers of the Old Testament had already seen fulfillment in the new events and situations of the early Christian history. Due to the predominantly backward glance of the New Testament writers, which we have already noted, the number of such modernized texts in the New Testament is considerably greater.[7]

The next class of quotations is called "Accommodated Texts," which, Fitzmyer explains, "has in common with the [Modernized Texts] the application of the text to a new situation or subject. However, it differs in that the Old Testament text in this case is usually wrested from its original context or modified somehow to suit the new situation."[8] He cites twelve examples of this from Qumran, including 1QS 8:13–16, quoting Isaiah 40:3 (for more on this, see below). For a New Testament example cited by Fitzmyer, compare Ephesians 4:8, citing Psalm 68:18[19].

Fitzmyer calls the fourth and final class of quotations "The Eschatological Class of Texts," described as such because "they usually express in the Old Testament context a promise or threat about something still to be accomplished in the *eschaton*, which the Qumran writer cites as something still to be accomplished in the new *eschaton* of which he writes."[9] He cites ten passages in this category, including CD 7:10–12, quoting Isaiah 7:17. Among the examples he cites from the New Testament is Romans 12:19, citing Deuteronomy 32:35. As for the relative paucity of these types of citation in the New Testament, Fitzmyer observes that it occurs less frequently than in the Qumran writings, suggesting,

> this is probably due again to the fact that Christian writers were more often looking back at the central event in which salvation had been accomplished rather than forward to a deliverance by Yahweh, which seems to characterize the Qumran literature.[10]

To summarize, the use of the Tanakh in the New Covenant Writings finds many parallels with the usage of the Tanakh in the Qumran writings, in keeping with Jewish methods of biblical interpretation dating back to the first century (and even earlier). In other words, a biblically literate Jew living in the first century of this era would not find the New Testament citations of Scripture to be outlandish in the least. Rather, both the substance and style of the quotes would be very familiar to him. The same can be said of the use of the Scripture in the later, Rabbinic writings. Let's analyze a representative—but tiny—sampling of the Rabbinic use of Scripture, looking at the first few pages of Berachot, the opening tractate of the Babylonian Talmud.

(1) On 2a (the Talmud always starts on p. 2), the end of Deuteronomy 6:7 is cited ("when you lie down and when you get up") to explain why the Mishnah first deals with reciting the Shema in the evening before dealing with reciting it in the morning; alternatively, Genesis 1:5b is cited ("And there was evening, and there was morning—the first day") as another possible supporting verse. Are these scriptural "proofs"? Hardly, but they are part of the supporting discussion. (2) Leviticus 22:7 is then cited to explain at what time the priests can partake of their portion of the offering. As rendered in the NJPSV, the meaning is straightforward, simple, and completely unambiguous: "As soon as the sun sets, he shall be clean [Hebrew, *we-taher*]; and afterward he may eat of the sacred donations, for they are his food." Surprisingly, the Talmud raises the question as to whether the meaning of *we-taher* is "he [the man] shall be clean," which is the universal understanding of the text in virtually all ancient and modern versions, or "it [the day] shall be clean" (as if it meant "clear"), meaning that the sun has set. As stated, the fact that this discussion occurs at all is surprising, but it is startling that it is the latter meaning ("the day is clear") that the Talmud eventually accepts, basing its final decision on that understanding (see 2b, "the meaning of *we-taher* is the clearing away of the day"). This is totally contrary to the meaning of the Torah text.[11]

(3) Nehemiah 4:15–16 [4:21–22 in most English versions] are cited as a hint (*zeker*) rather than a proof (*ra'ayah*) that the appearance of the stars was the mark of nighttime. (4) On 3b, Judges 7:19, which makes reference to "the middle watch," is cited to support the view that there are three watches in the night (meaning that the night is divided into three four-hour periods). Psalm 119:62 and 119:148 are then cited to prove that there are actually *four* watches in the night. A simple review of these verses from Psalm 119 would indicate that, at first glance, they do not demand such an understanding, but that is how the Talmudic rabbis interpret them. (5) Psalm 119:147, Proverbs 7:9, and 1 Samuel

30:17 are then brought into the discussion to determine the meaning of the word *nesheph* ("evening" or "morning"?), followed by a discussion of Exodus 11:4, with the goal of determining exactly when midnight occurred. (6) On 3b–4a, there is a *misquotation* of a biblical text, the Talmud confusing two different individuals with similar names. To cite this in full, "R. Joseph says: What verse [may be cited in support of this]? 'And after Ahithofel was Jehoiada, the son of Benaiah, and Abiathar; and the captain of the King's host was Joab,' [1 Chron. 27:34]" but, as noted in the Soncino Talmud footnote, "The [Talmudic] text here has 'Benaiah, the son of Jehoiada', who is mentioned in II Sam. XX, 23."[12] Yet the quote in the Talmud is from 1 Chronicles 27:34, which says that "Ahithophel was succeeded by *Jehoiada son of Benaiah* [not Benaiah son of Jehoiada, as written in the Talmudic citation]. . . ." The Talmud apparently got Jehoiada son of Benaiah confused with the better-known Benaiah son of Jehoiada, and for centuries, that reading has been preserved.[13] If we continue reading for several more pages, we find plays on words, a very common method of using the Scriptures in Rabbinic literature.

Now, this is just a sampling from the first few pages of the Talmud, pages which are certainly reflective of the Talmudic use of the Hebrew Scriptures, but already we found: (1) verses cited to support positions which barely relate to the discussions at hand; (2) verses cited in somewhat contrived ways to support various positions; (3) a verse cited, discussed, and ultimately interpreted contrary to its clear, contextual meaning; (4) a verse that is actually misquoted, with key names being reversed; (5) plays on words, with no attempt to elucidate the primary (or, original) meaning of the text.[14]

Do I write this to demean the Talmud? Absolutely not. Rather, my purpose is to illustrate that: (1) Jewish interpretation and use of Scripture in the first five-plus centuries of this era was much more free-flowing than our contemporary, historical-grammatical approach. (2) Verses from the Tanakh could be cited on many different levels and for many different purposes. (3) Editorial or copyist errors could easily creep into the texts. (4) The use of the Hebrew Bible in the New Covenant Scriptures is completely in line with the Jewish interpretive methods of the day, with this one caveat: In many ways the use of the Tanakh in the New Testament is more restrained, contextual, and sober than its use in the Rabbinic writings.

An analysis of the use of the Tanakh in the Dead Sea Scrolls, representing Jewish biblical interpretation contemporaneous with and immediately prior to the New Testament period, offers further support for this position.[15] This was the conclusion of Robert H. Gundry, a respected

Christian scholar who painstakingly analyzed the citations from the Tanakh found in Matthew's Gospel—the Gospel most frequently attacked for alleged misuse of the Tanakh—comparing Matthew's usage of the Hebrew Scriptures with that of the early Rabbinic writings and the Dead Sea Scrolls. What he found was that "Matthean hermeneutics were not atomizing—in contrast to Qumran and rabbinical literature."[16] In other words, it was Matthew who cited verses from the Hebrew Bible with more care for their original context than either the Rabbinic writings or the Dead Sea Scrolls!

Orthodox Jewish journalist and author David Klinghoffer, speaking of the citations from the Tanakh in the early chapters of Matthew, wrote:

> Pointing out the imprecision of proof texts like these, one feels almost unsporting. It's too easy. Yet it is with these that the New Testament begins its first attempt at a narration of the life of the Christian Messiah. Whoever the first educated Jews were to have these prophetic verses cited to them, whether in Jesus' lifetime or later, they could have reacted only with puzzlement and disbelief. As the song says, "Is that all there is?"[17]

To the contrary, to many educated Jews of his day, Matthew's use of Scripture was both legitimate and sensible, regardless of whether the evidence was accepted or not, and statements such as Klinghoffer's actually betray ignorance of either ancient Jewish usage of Scripture or the thoroughly Jewish nature of Matthew's use of Scripture—or both.[18]

Many Jewish readers through the centuries have also felt a deep kinship with Matthew's style of interpretation (for a well-known example, see vol. 1, 150). It is because of this that W. D. Davies and Dale C. Allison Jr., the learned scholars who produced the most exhaustive, technical, and linguistically detailed commentary on Matthew to date (totaling over 2,300 pages!), recognized the depth of Matthew's hermeneutics, stating:

> Matthew was not above scattering items in his Greek text whose deeper meaning could only be appreciated by those with a knowledge of Hebrew. Indeed, it might even be that Matthew found authorial delight in hiding 'bonus points' for those willing and able to look a little beneath the gospel's surface.[19]

Those differing with this conclusion would do well to work through the massive scholarly data presented in their commentary before begging to differ. Rather than Matthew (and the other New Testament authors) being superficial, it is actually the criticisms of Matthew (and the other New Testament authors) that are superficial.[20]

In some of the objections that follow (see 5.2–5.5), we will carefully analyze some of the better known quotations in Matthew and Hebrews. Here, we will look at some general issues of importance before examining some verses from other parts of the New Testament, as well as some less-cited quotations in Matthew. After reviewing the evidence, it should be readily apparent to you that some of the claims of the antimissionaries are quite bizarre, if not somewhat deceptive. Typical are the remarks of Rabbi Tovia Singer:[21]

> Moreover, in an effort to distance Christians from a compelling Jewish message, the founders and defenders of Christianity methodically altered selected texts from the Jewish scriptures. This rewriting of *Tanach* was not done arbitrarily or subtly. The church quite deliberately tampered with the words of the Jewish scriptures in order to bolster their most startling claim which is: The Old Testament foretold of no messiah other than Jesus of Nazareth. With this goal in mind, missionaries manipulated, misquoted, mistranslated, and even fabricated verses in *Tanach* in order to make Jesus' life fit traditional Jewish messianic parameters and to make traditional Jewish messianic parameters fit the life of Jesus. . . .
>
> The King James Version and numerous other Christian Bible translations were meticulously altered in order to produce a message that would sustain and advance church theology and exegeses. This aggressive rewriting of biblical texts has had a remarkable impact on Christians throughout the world who unhesitatingly embrace these twisted translations. . . .[22]

Of course, it is easy for anyone with solid biblical foundations to refute and dismiss such charges—in fact, it is tempting to simply ignore this kind of rhetoric—and it is only fair to ask what Singer would have said had he been criticizing the *Rabbinic* use of Scripture. Without a doubt, serious students of the Scriptures who will read this accusation that the New Testament authors "manipulated, misquoted, mistranslated, and even fabricated verses" from the Hebrew Bible will only shake their head in pity and disbelief. Still, I'm aware that there are many seekers of truth with limited knowledge in these areas, and so it is worthwhile to take the time to refute such extreme claims.

We must first understand that the Tanakh existed in a number of different textual forms in Jesus' day, including several Hebrew texts (reflecting different versions of the original), some Aramaic versions (in written or oral form, reflecting different translations and paraphrases of the original), and at least one Greek version (again, reflecting a translation of the original). This means that when a New Testament author was quoting from the Scriptures, he might have drawn from any number of *recognized, Jewish* biblical sources. This would be like a rabbi preaching to his congregation today and translating directly from the Hebrew or quoting from one of the modern Jewish translations of the Tanakh into English or paraphrasing the text based on Rabbinic interpretations. In all these cases he would be following common Jewish practices, and, in most cases, even if the specific wording differed between the versions he might be using, the overall meaning would be the same. All this is regularly done by rabbis communicating in a language other than Hebrew or by pastors communicating in a language other than Hebrew (for the Old Testament) and Greek (for the New Testament), and all of it has validity.

"But that's where you're wrong," you object. "You see, there is only one true and original Tanakh, and it's in Hebrew, the Masoretic text, not in any translation. Plus, when the New Testament authors quote from one of the other versions you speak of—like the Greek Septuagint or the Aramaic Targum—they *do* change the meaning of the verse itself."

I'm glad you raised these points. Let's take a more careful look at these issues.

There are many good reasons to believe that God has caused the text of the Bible—both the Tanakh and the New Covenant Scriptures—to be preserved with the utmost care. No documents from the ancient world have been preserved with such accuracy as have the manuscripts of the Bible (see below, 5.6). Still, we do not have *one* authoritative copy of the Scriptures; rather, we have thousands of copies, not all of which agree with each other in totality. With regard to the Tanakh, it is a misnomer to speak of "*the* Masoretic text" as if there was one authoritative, definitive, final text of the Hebrew Scriptures that was preserved unsullied through the centuries. Rather, there is a *Masoretic textual tradition* consisting of several thousand manuscripts which are in remarkable harmony but still contain thousands of minor discrepancies.[23] In addition to this, the Dead Sea Scrolls preserve four different textual traditions—I'm speaking here of *Hebrew* textual traditions—some of which agree letter for letter with the tradition we call the Masoretic tradition, others of which differ at many points.[24] Yet on some occasions, scholars have shown clearly that it is the *variant* tradition found in the Scrolls that is the most accurate and the Masoretic tradition that is faulty!

To give just one example, in 1 Samuel 1:24, the Masoretic textual tradition (abbreviated MT) tells us that when Hannah went to dedicate her son Samuel to the work of the Lord, she brought with her *three bulls*, an ephah of flour, and a skin of wine. However, the next verse says that they slaughtered *the bull*. What happened to the other bulls? Why this reference to only one bull? The answer is simple: There was only one bull involved, as the Hebrew text of 1 Samuel preserved in the Dead Sea

Scrolls (DSS) indicates (confirmed also by the Greek Septuagint), telling us in verse 24 that Hannah brought with her one *three-year-old* bull (cf. Gen. 15:9, where Abram was commanded by the Lord to offer up some three-year-old animals). This fits the context perfectly and makes complete sense: She brought a three-year-old bull and sacrificed it at the Tabernacle. The differences in the Hebrew texts are minimal, and on a doctrinal level, there is nothing significant about those very minor differences. Nonetheless, in this case, the evidence clearly suggests that the MT does not preserve the original wording whereas the DSS and the Septuagint (abbreviated LXX) do.

This phenomenon, of course, is of real importance when discussing the usage of the Hebrew Bible in the New Testament since, (1) the New Testament authors sometimes cite texts reflecting the MT (or another ancient biblical Hebrew tradition, as reflected in the DSS); (2) at other times—quite frequently, in fact—they cite the Septuagint, which would be logical when writing for an audience that read and understood Greek and for whom the Septuagint was their Bible; (3) still other times, they make their own translation or paraphrase from the Hebrew original (remember: the authors of the New Testament wrote in Greek—with only rare, possible exceptions—so they would have to translate the Hebrew text or else use a Greek translation);[25] and (4) there are times when the authors cite texts reflecting the interpretation preserved in the Aramaic Targums. So, while it would be easy to jump to conclusions and accuse the New Testament writers of misusing the Tanakh, a closer look proves the opposite: They drew on their biblical heritage in many varied and rich ways without changing the essential meaning of the original text.

Interestingly, Abraham Ibn Ezra, one of the greatest of the medieval Rabbinic exegetes, made this important observation about the prophets of Israel: "The prophets do not preserve the exact wording when they repeat something. They only preserve its substance. For that is what is important. . . . There are many other such instances . . . [and] many other additions and omissions in the [second version of the] decalogue. The intelligent person will understand why this is so."[26] The same can be said of the New Testament authors: They too preserve the substance of the original, often with unique and penetrating insights, without always preserving the exact wording.[27] As to the accuracy of the citations of the New Testament authors, Evans correctly observes:

> The multiformity of the biblical text must be taken into account when studying OT quotations and allusions in the NT and in other writings of late antiquity. What at first may appear to be an inaccurate quotation, or a quotation of the LXX, itself thought to be an inaccurate translation of

the underlying Hebrew, may in fact be a quotation of a different textual tradition.[28]

Here are a few examples:

- In Isaiah 6:10, the prophet is commissioned to a ministry of hardening his people, lest upon seeing, hearing, and understanding "it [i.e., the nation] repents and is made well" (my translation). This verse is quoted in Mark 4:12, where the Gospel author follows the rendering found later in the Aramaic Targum, "and *they* repent and be *forgiven*," the highlighted words representing interpretive variations from the Hebrew (cf. also the Syriac Peshitta, and note that the LXX's literal *kai iasomai autous* was not followed by Mark).[29] This, then, is an example of a New Testament author following a tradition similar to that found in the Aramaic Targum—which was the translation that was later read in the synagogues—and in doing so, he interprets the text with fairness, not altering its fundamental meaning.[30]

- Matthew 8:16 describes the miracles of healing that took place at the Messiah's hands, stating in 8:17 that this fulfills what was written in Isaiah 53:4, which Matthew translates, "He took up our infirmities and carried our diseases." Here he does not cite the Septuagint, which spiritualized the verse in Isaiah ("He himself bore our sins and was pained because of them") nor does his translation agree with the paraphrase found in the Targum, which also spiritualized the Hebrew ("Then for our sins he will pray and our iniquities will be forgiven because of him"). Rather, he translated the Hebrew literally, emphasizing the reality of its fulfillment in Yeshua.[31]

- The LXX is cited with great frequency by the authors of the New Testament since Greek was the most widely spoken language of the day, common to both Jews and Gentiles, and the LXX would be the translation of the Hebrew Scriptures to which most of the readers would have access. (Remember, however, that the LXX was a *Jewish* translation of the Tanakh by Greek-speaking Jews and was only subsequently adopted by Christians. It was *not* a later Gentile translation!)[32] In many cases, the differences between the LXX and the MT are minute; in many other cases, the wording changes but the overall meaning is not altered.[33] A good example is found in Mark 1:3, with reference to John the Immerser, quoting Isaiah 40:3. He is described as: "a voice of one calling in the desert, 'Prepare the way for the Lord, make straight paths for him.'" (See also Luke 3:4.) The problem here is that the MT of Isaiah 40:3 reads, "A voice of one calling: 'In the desert prepare the way for the Lord; make straight in the wilderness a highway for our God.'" So, the New Testament text speaks of "one calling in the desert, 'Prepare the way of the Lord,'" while the MT speaks of, "A voice of one calling: 'In the desert prepare the way for the Lord.'" Why the discrepancy? Very simply, Mark and Luke are quoting the LXX, which reads just as it is cited here in the Gospels. And in reality, there is no conflict in meaning, since both refer to preparing a way for the Lord in the desert, the LXX also placing the speaker there. No one reading the LXX would have accused the translators of "manipulating, misquoting, or mistranslating" the Hebrew, to use the words of the anti-missionaries. And it is not without significance that the DSS used the Hebrew of Isaiah 40:3 in almost the identical way, explaining why the Qumran community felt called "to go into the desert to prepare there the way of Him, as it was written, 'in the desert make ready the way of . . . Make straight in the wilderness a highway for our God'" (1QS 8:13–14).[34]

- Hebrews 1:6 reads, "And again, when God brings his firstborn into the world, he says, 'Let all God's angels worship him.'" The citation is from Deuteronomy 32:43, but when you check the MT, you find that these words do not exist. Does that mean that the author of Hebrews made this up? Certainly not! What would be the purpose of citing a nonexistent verse? Why draw attention to something that is not there? Of course, scholars have known for many centuries that Hebrews 1:6 was simply quoting the LXX. What they only learned last century was that this reading was also attested in the DSS in Hebrew, and so the author of Hebrews was citing a verse that was attested in both a Hebrew biblical manuscript and a Jewish, Greek translation well before the first century of this era.

- There are also examples of homiletical interpretations (or free-form uses of the biblical text), similar to the midrashic usage found in later Rabbinic literature. A good example of this is found in Romans 10:6–8, based on Deuteronomy 30:12–14, with a possible reference to Psalm 107:26. The text in Romans reads: "But the righteousness that is by faith says: 'Do not say in your heart, "Who will ascend into heaven?"' (that is, to bring [Messiah] down) 'or "Who will descend into the deep?"' (that is, to bring [Messiah] up from the dead). But what does it say? 'The word is near you; it is in your mouth and in your heart,' that is, the word of faith we are proclaiming." So Paul, noticing the emphasis on the nearness of God's Word, specifically with reference to *mouth* and *heart*, applies the verse to "the word of faith," with specific reference to confessing Yeshua as Messiah *with the mouth* and believing in him *with the heart* (see Rom. 10:9–10). In similar fashion, the Talmudic rabbis interpreted Deuteronomy 30:12–14 in terms of their own system of belief, first stating the Torah was no longer in heaven, as if that meant that God would no longer give legal revelation from heaven, and interpreting the references to having the Word in one's heart and mouth as if it were referring explicitly to the oral Torah (for more on this, see vol. 5, 6.1, 6.9). Both Paul and the Talmudic rabbis, then, homiletically interpreted well-known verses in the Torah, and both methods are valid within their own systems of belief, without serving as exegetical or doctrinal "proofs." Thus, Joseph Klausner, one of the original professors of the Hebrew University, wrote, "It would be difficult to find more typically Talmudic expositions of Scripture than those in the Epistles of Paul,"[35] citing this text in Romans 10 as a prime example.

- As observed in *Hard Sayings of the Bible*: "Sometimes New Testament writers chose a particular version because it made the point they wanted to make, much as preachers today sometimes choose to quote from translations which put a passage in such a way that it supports the point they want to make. For example, when we read Ephesians 4:8 we discover that it reads differently than Psalm 68:18 in English. This is not because Paul used the Septuagint, for in this case that translation agrees with our English Bibles. Instead, Paul appears to have used one of the Aramaic translations (called a Targum). In many Jewish synagogues the Scriptures were first read in Hebrew and then translated into Aramaic, for that is the language the people actually spoke. Paul would have been familiar with both versions, and in this case he chose to translate not the Hebrew but the Aramaic into Greek. The Hebrew text would not have made his point."[36]

- On certain occasions, the New Testament speaker or author will insert some additional words to explain or apply the text he is quoting. So, in Acts 2:17, Peter cites Joel 2:28[3:1], which in the MT reads, "And afterward, I will pour out my Spirit on all people. . . ." Yet Peter quotes it as saying, "In the last days, God says, I will pour out my Spirit on all people. . . ." This was obviously quite intentional, indicating to the hearers that, not only was Joel's prophecy being fulfilled, but that the season in which it was being fulfilled was the season of the "last days," meaning, the inbreaking of the Messianic age, a concept that certainly would have been in keeping with the message of Joel.

Such examples could easily be multiplied, but those already cited provide a representative sampling, indicating again that the use of the Hebrew Scriptures in the New Covenant Writings is both fair to the original text and in keeping with Jewish interpretive methods of the day. The summary given in *Hard Sayings of the Bible* bears repeating:

> What [the authors of the New Testament] are doing is teaching New Testament truth and showing that the Old Testament supports the point that they are making. In general this is true, even though they did not have the relatively accurate and carefully researched texts of the Old Testament that we have today. When they appear to be "wrong" (allowing that they interpreted the Old Testament differently then than we do now), we must remember (1) that it could be that they may indeed have a better reading for the text in question than we have in our Bibles and (2) that the Spirit of God who inspired the Old Testament text has every right to expand on its meaning.[37]

The comments of professor John Wenham are also relevant:

> We have . . . no right to demand of believers in verbal inspiration that they always quote Scripture verbatim, particularly when the Scriptures are not written in the native language of either writer or reader. As with the word preached, we have a right to expect that quotations should be sufficiently accurate not to misrepresent the passage quoted; but, unless the speaker makes it clear that his quotation is meant to be verbatim, we have no right to demand that it should be so. In the nature of the case, the modern scholarly practice of meticulously accurate citation, with the verification of all references, was out of the question.[38]

Before looking at some of the New Testament citations that are most frequently attacked as erroneous (this will be done in 5.2–5.5; for the famous virgin birth prophecy, see vol. 3, 4.3), we will look at more examples of verses from the Tanakh that are allegedly misquoted in the New Testament, using these as test cases to see whether there is truth to the claims of the anti-missionaries that the New Testament misquotes and/or misuses the Hebrew Scriptures. My intent in doing so is not to prove that it is possible to come up with all kinds of ingenious ways to cover up errors and inaccuracies in the Messianic Scriptures (commonly called the New Testament). To the contrary, my intent here is to evaluate the data with honesty and integrity, allowing you to draw your own conclusions. And I will do this in an evenhanded manner, seeing if there is a plausible answer to the apparent problem, rather than attacking the objection in a hostile manner, since that often produces very superficial discussion. (For more on this, see the appendix in vol. 5, "Unequal Weights and Measures.")

We will now look at three passages from the Tanakh that are cited (or appear to be cited) with some key changes (or misunderstandings) in the New Testament: first, Isaiah 59:20, cited in Romans 11:26–27, then Zechariah 9:9, cited in Matthew 21:5, and, finally, the famous words of the Shema, the prayer of confession found in Deuteronomy 6:4–5, with 6:5 apparently cited in Matthew 22:37.

In Romans 11:26–27, Paul pens these famous words, "And so all Israel will be saved, as it is written: 'The deliverer will come from Zion; he will turn godlessness away from Jacob. And this is my covenant with them when I take away their sins.'" In these verses, Paul quotes from the Book of Isaiah, primarily from Isaiah 59:20, but with allusion also to 59:21 and 27:9. The problem is in the phrase "The deliverer will come from Zion," whereas the Hebrew reads, "The redeemer will come to [or for] Zion."[39] Did Paul misquote or misunderstand the Hebrew text?

One logical answer would be that he was simply quoting from the LXX, but in this case, that answer will not do, since the LXX reads, "The redeemer will come for Zion," which is an equally legitimate reading of the Hebrew *letsiyon*. But that is not what Paul wrote. Was he wrong, then? Actually, it is very superficial to suggest that he wrongly quoted the text, since the reading of either the MT or the LXX would support his argument well in that he is quoting a promise in the Tanakh that speaks of Israel's final redemption at the time of the Messiah's return. So, either the MT's "The redeemer will come to Zion," or the LXX's "for Zion" would work well. Why then didn't Paul use either of these texts?

W. B. Wallis suggested many years ago that Paul's understanding of the Hebrew *letsiyon* (which consists of the preposition *lamed*, meaning, "to, for," and the proper noun *tsiyon*) reflected a largely unrecognized nuance of *lamed*, meaning "from," with apparent support from Ugaritic (an important Semitic language) and biblical Hebrew as well.[40] Further research into this grammatical argument, however, has indicated that such a meaning is highly improbable and, accordingly, this proposal should be dropped.

A better explanation is that Paul, in keeping with his Pharisaical heritage (see the quote from Klausner, cited above, and see further, below, 5.26), conflated two passages, namely, Isaiah 59:20 and Psalm 14:7a (= 53:7a), which reads, "Oh, that salvation for Israel would come out of [or from] Zion! When the LORD restores the fortunes of his people, let Jacob rejoice and Israel be glad!" (Cf. also Psalm 20:2: "May he send you help from the sanctuary and grant you support from Zion.") Both Isaiah 59:20 and Psalm 14:7 are passages speaking of national redemption/salvation for Israel, both speak of Zion and Jacob, and both contain the root *shuv*, meaning turn back, repent, restore. So Paul, in a very sophisticated use of Scripture, blends the themes of the passages together, citing parts of both accurately, indicating that Israel's salvation would ultimately come from Zion, which could either mean from the heavenly Zion to the earthly Zion, or from the Messiah who will rule and reign from Zion after his return to Zion.

An interesting parallel to this can be found in the Siddur, the Jewish prayerbook, where a similar conflation of verses is found, beginning with Psalm 20:2, "May [the LORD] send you support from Zion" and continuing with Isaiah 59:20–21, the promise that the redeemer will come to Zion (see *ArtScroll Siddur*, 153–55).[41]

Matthew's use of part of Zechariah 9:9 has also received much attention, often in a derogatory way, with the claim sometimes made that he did not understand Hebrew poetic parallelism. The verse in Zechariah reads:

> Rejoice greatly, O Daughter of Zion!
> Shout, Daughter of Jerusalem!
> See, your king comes to you,
>   righteous and having salvation,
>   gentle and riding on a donkey,
>   on a colt, the foal of a donkey.

Matthew actually merges part of Isaiah 62:11 with his citation of Zechariah 9:9 (specifically, the words, "Say to the Daughter of Zion," which is followed by, "See, your Savior comes!" which is very close to Zechariah 9:9). And so Matthew quotes "the prophet" to say:

> Say to the Daughter of Zion,
>   "See, your king comes to you,
>   gentle and riding on a donkey,
>   on a colt, the foal of a donkey."
>
> Matthew 21:5

None of this presents any problem at all and actually speaks of Matthew's fluency in the Scriptures as opposed to his ignorance of the Scriptures. The alleged problem is found in the preceding verses which, according to Matthew 21:4, fulfill Zechariah's prophecy. The narrative states:

> As they approached Jerusalem and came to Bethphage on the Mount of Olives, Jesus sent two disciples, saying to them, "Go to the village ahead of

you, and at once you will find a donkey tied there, with her colt by her. Untie them and bring them to me. If anyone says anything to you, tell him that the Lord needs them, and he will send them right away." . . . The disciples went and did as Jesus had instructed them. They brought the donkey and the colt, placed their cloaks on them, and Jesus sat on them.

Matthew 21:1–3, 6–7

What was Zechariah actually predicting? Was he speaking of two animals, a donkey and her colt, or was he using Hebrew parallelism, referring to a donkey, namely, a colt, the foal of a donkey?[42] Without question, it is the latter, as New Testament scholar D. A. Carson rightly notes: "The Hebrew, of course, refers to only one beast: the last line is in parallelism with the next-to-the-last line and merely identifies the 'donkey' (line 3) as a colt (a young, male donkey)."[43] Certainly, even to someone ignorant of Hebrew, it is clear that Zechariah was *not* prophesying that Israel's king would come riding *both* a donkey and her colt at the same time. Moreover, "it is quite unreasonable to suggest that Matthew, who demonstrably had a good command of Hebrew (cf. Gundry, *Use of Old Testament*, 198), added the extra animal to fit a text he radically misunderstood."[44]

"But," you say, "Matthew clearly misread Zechariah, which is why he drew attention to the two animals—in contrast with Mark and Luke, who only spoke of one donkey, namely a young animal that had never been ridden—and, quite preposterously, Matthew specifically claims that Jesus rode on both the donkey and her colt."

Let's deal with the second part of your objection first. We cite Carson once more, commenting on the words, "Jesus sat 'on them.'" He explains, "Not a few critics take the antecedent of 'them' to be the animals and ridicule the statement. But as Plummer remarks, 'The Evangelist credits his readers with common sense.'"[45] Common sense indeed! Matthew 21:7 states, "They brought the donkey and the colt, placed their cloaks on them, and Jesus sat on them"—meaning, *he sat on the cloaks*, which were placed on the colt, not that he somehow managed to ride the donkey and colt at the same time, like some rodeo showman.

As for Matthew's understanding of the parallelism of Zechariah 9:9, a few comments are sufficient: (1) It is clear from other biblical citations in Matthew's work that he understood Hebrew well; see, for example, his citation of Isaiah 53:4a in Matthew 8:17, referenced above. This makes it highly unlikely that he would grossly misunderstand Zechariah's words. Moreover, his whole point, in harmony with the other Gospel accounts, is that Jesus rode a colt, in accordance with Zechariah 9:9. (2) Matthew is the one Gospel author of whom the tradition exists that he wrote his book in Hebrew, implying that it was then translated into Greek (see vol. 5, 6.15, for further discussion; some scholars accept that there was a Hebrew Matthew but argue that the Greek shows no signs of being a translation and, hence, is an independent work).[46] This tradition would also underscore the unlikelihood that Matthew, who may have *written* his account in Hebrew, misunderstood Zechariah. (3) It is possible that Matthew, in keeping with a style attested in later Rabbinic Midrash, found a hyperliteral meaning of Zechariah 9:9, just as some Rabbinic interpretation of the verse also found a reference to *two animals*.[47] This would mean that Matthew, just like the rabbis, chose to read the text in a hyperliteral manner, either for homiletical purposes or here, as a hyperliteral fulfillment of the prophetic text. That is to say, *even if* Matthew understood Zechariah 9:9 to refer to two animals, he probably did so intentionally (rather than through misunderstanding), and in doing so, he was in good company with the later Rabbinic interpreters. So much for Matthew's ignorance![48]

What about Matthew 22:37? There Matthew has Yeshua say that the first and greatest commandment is to "Love the Lord your God with all your heart and with all your soul and with all your *mind*," whereas the Shema, the fundamental prayer of confession in Judaism, says, "Love the Lord your God with all your heart and with all your soul and with all your *strength*." How could any literate Jew, even a barely literate Jew, get this wrong? It was one thing for Mark to add the word "mind" to the phrase, as cited in Mark 12:30, "Love the Lord your God with all your heart and with all your soul and with all your *mind* and with all your *strength*." An expansion like that, especially for the purposes of clarification—specifically, that God required our total devotion, mind and heart (both contained in the Hebrew *levav*, used in Deut. 6:5), soul and strength—is not problematic. What appears to be problematic is that Matthew, reducing the number of nouns to three, seems to have left out the wrong one (i.e., he should have left out *mind*, not *strength*). Again, it is argued, that even a Jewish child living in Matthew's day would have caught this.[49]

The very force of this objection, however, is its greatest weakness. How could *Matthew*, a man literate in the Scriptures with a clear knowledge of Hebrew, have made this mistake, especially in light of the fact that his book was directed to Jews? It is one thing to question his use of the Tanakh (see above, and cf. 5.2–5.4); it is another thing to accuse him of getting something as fundamental as this completely wrong. To make that case, one would have to argue that Matthew was actually a Gentile, a position widely dismissed by scholars for many good reasons.[50] To the contrary, even here in Matthew 22:37 there is a possible indication that

Matthew had the Hebrew text in mind, since he does not follow Mark or the LXX here, both of which use the preposition *ek*, literally, "out of," to render the Hebrew preposition *be*, "in, with." Instead, he substitutes the Greek preposition *en*, which corresponds to the Hebrew, pointing again to his familiarity with the text.[51]

What then is the solution to this apparent slip on Matthew's part? First, it is possible that the twice-daily recitation of the Shema, including Deuteronomy 6:5, which is assumed by the time of the final compilation of the Mishnah at the end of the second century C.E., had not yet been rigidly fixed in Yeshua's day. As Foster notes, after examining the evidence for the recitation of Deuteronomy 6:5 at the beginning of the first century C.E.,

> . . . while Deuteronomy 6:4–5, as part of the biblical text, was known in both the Hasmonean and Herodian periods (and presumably throughout all of the postexilic era), it had not at that time attained the prominence that was to be ascribed to it from the third century onward as part of the twice-daily creedal affirmation of a fundamental tenet of the Jewish faith.[52]

If this is true, then it would not have been so striking—or sacrilegious!—for Matthew to have varied the words slightly, seeing that they were not yet part of a fixed, daily liturgical formula and, after all, Jesus is simply responding to a question about religious obligation in which Scripture truths form the basis for his answer. More specifically, the Talmud in b. Ber 21b asks whether the recitation of both Deuteronomy 6:4 and 6:5 was mandated by the Torah or if verse 4 was a Torah obligation and verse 5 only a Rabbinic obligation, in which case it would have become fixed later in time. The conclusion there is that the recitation of verse 5 was a Rabbinic obligation, and it is verse 5 that Jesus is quoting here.[53]

Second, there are translation variants in the LXX to Deuteronomy 6:5, with some rendering the Hebrew *levav* with the Greek *kardia*, heart, and others with *dianoia*, mind, but both of these terms are used in Matthew's text.[54] However, since Mark used the Greek word *ischus* to translate the Hebrew *me'od*, strength, whereas the LXX used *dunamis*, it appears that Matthew, writing in Greek (or, translating and paraphrasing from a Hebrew original into Greek), was removing the one word from Mark's account that did not occur in the LXX while returning to the threefold emphasis found in the Hebrew. (Remember that Mark used four nouns while the MT and LXX each used three; Matthew, then, is returning to the proper threefold emphasis.) Interestingly, after analyzing all this in detail, Foster concluded:

This decision could not have been undertaken by a person who did not possess linguistic competence in both Hebrew and Greek, as well as a knowledge of the Hebrew biblical text. It is far more plausible to think of a native Jew having gained competence in Greek in addition to his native language, than to suggest the opposite possibility. . . .

Matthew 22:37 does not reflect an ignorant Gentile author who erred in his presentation of a fixed liturgical text. Rather, it reveals the opposite, an ethnically Jewish evangelist who dealt sensitively and conservatively in transmitting a text that had become part of the dominical tradition of his community, but in the sources which Matthew received deviated from both the structure and contents of the biblical tradition. The redactional reworking of the sources shows a sophisticated editor who attempted to produce greater conformity with existing biblical tradition but also did not wish to deviate from this well-known Jesus saying in too radical a fashion. Surely this is the work of a highly trained Jewish scribe.[55]

It is true that some medieval Hebrew manuscripts of Matthew 22:27 read "with all your heart," etc., while others read "with all your heart, all your soul, and all your strength," which might even point to an original reading, thus "correcting" our extant Greek manuscripts of Matthew 22:37. That, however, is quite speculative, and Foster's observations sufficiently answer the charge that Matthew was ignorant of Hebrew and/or Jewish custom of the day. (For further thoughts on Matthew's knowledge of Scripture, see below, 5.4.)

Let us now, in the next four objections, move on to some of the more prominent claims of "Scripture-twisting" in the New Covenant Scriptures.

5.2. According to Matthew 2:15, when the little boy Jesus, along with Joseph and Mary, fled to Egypt to escape from Herod, this "fulfilled what the Lord had said through the prophet: 'Out of Egypt I called my son.'" But Matthew only quoted the second half of the verse in Hosea. What the prophet really said was this: "When Israel was a child, I loved him, and out of Egypt I called my son." The verse has to do with Israel, not Jesus, and it is recounting a historical event, not giving a prophecy. And you claim that Matthew was inspired. Hardly!

When Matthew quoted the second half of Hosea 11:1, he took
for granted that his Jewish readers would know the whole
verse. (Remember that many of Matthew's intended readers
knew large portions of the Hebrew Scriptures by heart, and
quoting just part of a verse was a common Jewish practice of
the day.) What he was saying was clear: Just as it happened
to Israel, God's national "son," so also it happened to Jesus,
God's Messianic Son, and the ideal representative of the nation. Both were called out of Egypt in their childhood.

It is very common—often the norm—in the Talmud and Rabbinic
literature to cite a key part of a verse, sometimes even a short phrase,
even though it is the whole verse that is under discussion. Matthew, a
Jew well-versed in the Hebrew Bible, was writing to fellow Jews, also
presumably well-versed in their Scriptures, and the last thing he was
trying to do was pull the wool over the eyes and ears of his readers. The
very thought of it is ludicrous, since, even if they did *not* know the whole
verse by heart, they could eventually look the verse up or ask someone
who had memorized the text. Soon enough, if his citation really was
erroneous, someone would have quickly challenged his reading, and
within days—or even hours—Matthew would have been exposed and his
book of Good News (= Gospel) would have been discarded as an unreliable fraud. So, the belief, all too common among anti-missionaries, that
Matthew tried to trick his readers by only quoting part of the verse is
patently absurd.[56] To the contrary, "Matthew expects all his readers to
understand the primacy of Scripture and the centrality of Christ's mission in Scripture; but *he expects his more sophisticated readers to catch
his allusion to Israel's history as well.*"[57]

Thus, Matthew finds many important parallels between Israel's formative, early years and the early years and formative ministry of the
Messiah, also couching his writing in very Jewish/biblical terms from the
opening words: *biblos geneseōs*, the Greek words being the equivalent of
the Hebrew expression *seper toledot* (as in Gen. 5:1; see the Septuagint
[LXX]) or *seper yuhasin* (the Rabbinic way of introducing a genealogy).
This is not a standard Greek expression but rather a Hebraic one, indicating that his intended audience is clearly Jewish—especially literate
Jews. Note also that Matthew does not follow the LXX here, which
translates Hosea 11:1b with "children" rather than "son." Rather, he
translates directly from the Hebrew.[58]

As we continue to read, we notice in the opening chapters that there
are several parallels between both Moses and the Messiah as well as
Israel and the Messiah (this is called "Messianic typology"):

- There was an edict to kill all the Israelite baby boys at the time Moses was born (Exod. 1:15–22), just as there was an edict to kill all the Jewish baby boys in Bethlehem at the time Yeshua was born (Matt. 2:16–18).
- Israel in its infancy went into Egypt, just as Jesus did (Gen. 46:1–7; 47:27—Israel; Exod. 4:19—Moses; Matt. 2:13–15—Jesus), and then both were called out of Egypt back to the Promised Land (Exod. 3:8; Matt. 2:21; note also the parallels between "those who were seeking your life are dead" in Exod. 4:19 [NRSV]—Moses to go into Egypt; Matt. 2:20—Joseph to bring Jesus out).
- "By leaving 'at night,' Joseph's family made their route of departure impossible to trace; the language might also evoke Jewish readers' memory of Exodus 12:31."[59]
- Israel crossed the Jordan River while Jesus was immersed in the Jordan River (Joshua 3; Matt. 3:13–15; in both cases, these were "rites of passage"; it is also possible that the Jordan parallels the Red Sea).
- Israel was called God's son, and Jesus was called God's Son (see, e.g., Exod. 4:22; Matt. 3:17; 17:5).
- Israel was tested for forty years in the wilderness, while Jesus was tempted for forty days in the wilderness, actually quoting the Book of Deuteronomy three times when rebuking Satan (Matt. 4:4, quoting Deut. 8:3; Matt. 4:7, quoting Deut. 6:16; Matt. 4:10, quoting Deut. 6:13; remember that Deuteronomy was the book composed at the end of Israel's wilderness wanderings).
- Just as Israel received the Torah, God's authoritative instruction, at the foot of Mount Sinai, so also, when Yeshua began to give the people his holy instruction, he too ascended a mountain and gathered his disciples there (see Matt. 5:1–2).

All this indicates just how deeply this period of Israel's history was in Matthew's mind: Israel going into Egypt, Moses' birth, Israel coming out of Egypt, receiving the Law, being tested in the wilderness, crossing the Jordan. Therefore, with good reason, he looked to Hosea 11:1 as a prophetic parallel to the early years of the Messiah: As it happened to Israel, God's son, so also it happened to the Messiah, God's Son. As professor Craig Keener summarized:

Matthew builds almost every paragraph from the genealogy to the Sermon on the Mount around at least one text in the Old Testament, explaining some event of Jesus' life from Scripture. In context Hosea 11:1 refers plainly to the Israelites leaving Egypt in the exodus; Matthew applies this text to Jesus because Jesus epitomizes and fulfills Israel's history (Matt. 1:1).[60]

Amazingly, anti-missionary author Michoel Drazin claims that Matthew not only misquoted Hosea here, but that he borrowed the historical account from the life of Krishna! He writes: "When Krishna was born, his father is said to have fled with him from the governor, who sought the infant's life. . . . The New Testament transferred this legend to Jesus."[61] While such claims are so bizarre as to be laughable, they point to the extremely skewed view that some ultra-Orthodox Jews (and many anti-missionaries) have about Yeshua and the New Testament. Their level of mistrust and suspicion is extremely high, to put it mildly. As we have seen in the case of Matthew's quotation of Hosea, neither the mistrust nor suspicion are merited in the least. To the contrary, those who take the time to explore the spiritual riches of Matthew's writings will not be disappointed, and they will find their intellects enriched as well.[62] Suffice it to say that you will be on infinitely more solid ground if you trust Matthew than if you trust the anti-missionaries.

5.3. Matthew 2:23 says that when Jesus moved to the town of Nazareth, this "fulfilled what was said through the prophets: 'He will be called a Nazarene.'" There's only one problem. The prophets never said this! Matthew actually made it up.

If you'll look closely at the text, you'll see that Matthew does not use his normal quotation formula for citing verses from the Hebrew Bible. Normally he would say something like, "to fulfill what was spoken through the prophet," making reference to a specific text in a specific prophetic book. In 2:23 he says, "so that what had been spoken through the prophets might be fulfilled," indicating that he is dealing with a theme (or play on words) that occurs in several prophetic books as opposed to only one text in a specific prophetic book. With this in mind, it's not difficult to see the sections from the Tanakh that Matthew had in mind. As always with Matthew, his insights are deep.

More than any New Testament author, Matthew makes constant reference to the Hebrew Bible when describing the life, death, and resurrection of Yeshua (see also immediately above, 5.2). Every major event that took place in the Messiah's life took place "to fulfill what was said" through a specific prophet in the Tanakh. God had laid it out in advance! Matthew uses this form of speech frequently (see Matt. 1:22; 2:15; 2:17; 4:14; 8:17; 12:17; 13:35; 21:4; 27:9). Now, in almost every instance, Matthew makes reference to *one particular* prophet or prophecy, unless he is referring to several events that took place in the life of Jesus. In that case reference is made to "the Scriptures" (plural) being fulfilled (Matt. 26:54) or it is explained that certain things occurred "that the writings of the prophets [plural] might be fulfilled" (Matt. 26:56; see also Luke 24:44). Also, every time he makes reference to a specific prophetic utterance, he follows it with the word "saying," indicating a direct quote from the Tanakh. But in Matthew 2:23, we read that when Jesus and his family settled in Nazareth, "So was fulfilled what was said *through the prophets*: 'He will be called a Nazarene.'"[63] (Remember that there were no quotation marks in the original text, and so it is misleading to have them in our English translations, since it gives the impression that there is a direct citation.) From looking at this formula, we can see clearly that Matthew was not looking at one particular prophecy (he refers to "the prophets" and omits the word "saying"). Rather, he had in mind a *theme* or *common thread* found in several prophetic books. The question is: What exactly was he thinking of? Which texts and which themes?[64]

Bearing in mind that Matthew's use of the Tanakh was the fruit of much careful thought and reflection, and remembering that he shows a clear knowledge of the Hebrew text of Scripture (see above, 5.1; cf. also 5.4), we would do well to look for two things: First, is there a play on words that caught his attention? (As we saw above, 5.1, this was very common in Jewish biblical interpretation.) Second, is there a related Messianic theme? The answer to both questions is yes, and the key again is *context*. In Matthew 1:23, reference is made to Isaiah 7:14, while in Matthew 4:12–16, reference is made to Isaiah 9:1–2[8:23–9:1]. And these chapters are part of an important Messianic section in Isaiah (chapters 7–11), culminating with the major Messianic prophecy in Isaiah 11 which begins with these words: "A shoot will come up from the stump of Jesse; from his roots a Branch will bear fruit" (Isa. 11:1). And what is the Hebrew word used here for "Branch"? It is *netser*, a form closely related to the Hebrew word for Nazareth.[65]

This is important for several reasons: First, it shows us that Matthew had the entire Messianic section of Isaiah 7–11 in view when he quoted prophecies regarding Yeshua's birth (Isa. 7:14; see vol. 3, 4.3) and early life (Isa. 9:1–2[8:23–9:1] and 11:1). Second, it gives us a clear link to the word Nazareth. Third, it ties in with the well-known concept of the Messiah being called "the Branch" (elsewhere with the Hebrew word *tsemach*; see Jer. 23:5; 33:15; Zech. 3:8; 6:12; cf. also Isa. 4:2; in Rabbinic literature, as well as in the Dead Sea Scrolls, the Messiah was sometimes referred to as *netser*, and there is a Talmudic story—speaking disparagingly of Jesus—in which one of his disciples is called *netser*).[66] Fourth, both in the context of Isaiah 11:1 and in the lowly reputation of Nazareth, it ties in with the humble origins of the Messiah (see also Isa. 53:1–3; and cf. vol. 3, 4.11; the lowly reputation of Nazareth is reflected in Nathanael's words in John 1:46a upon hearing the claim that the Messiah was a man from Nazareth. As paraphrased in *The Message*, he exclaimed, "Nazareth? You've got to be kidding.")[67] Therefore, rather than being something that Matthew made up—as if he would have fooled his Jewish readers anyway!—this verse reminds us of how insightful Matthew was in opening up the true meaning of the Tanakh.[68] And this should come as no surprise to us: He was taught by the Messiah himself! (See Luke 24:44–45.)

Finally, as noted by other scholars, Ezra 9:10–12 provides an interesting parallel to Matthew 2:23, since Ezra, while praying and repenting, says to the Lord:

> For we have disregarded the commands you gave through your servants the prophets when you said, "The land you are entering to possess is a land polluted by the corruption of its peoples. By their detestable practices they have filled it with their impurity from one end to the other. Therefore, do not give your daughters in marriage to their sons or take their daughters for your sons. Do not seek a treaty of friendship with them at any time, that you may be strong and eat the good things of the land and leave it to your children as an everlasting inheritance."

The problem, of course, is that these exact words are not found anywhere in the prophetic books in the Tanakh, yet Ezra claims to be quoting the Lord's word spoken through the prophets. Was Ezra making this up? Was he intentionally falsifying things so as to delude the people? Or, since he was quoting these words to God in prayer, was he trying to delude the Lord? Putting sarcasm aside, it is clear that he was summarizing and paraphrasing the consistent message of God's prophets—notice that he refers to "prophets" in the plural just as Matthew did—even though it would appear at first glance that this was a literal quotation (see further Deut. 11:8–9; Isa. 1:19; Ezek. 37:25; and cf. Lev. 18:24–26; Deut. 7:1–6; 2 Kings 17; 23:8–16; Ezek. 5:11). Of course, someone could argue that Ezra was quoting from some lost prophetic books, but then we could just as well argue that Matthew was doing the same! To do so in either case is completely unnecessary. Ezra was simply restating the consistent message of the prophets in his own words; Matthew was making reference to a common Messianic theme, one which caught his attention through an interesting play on words—a wonderfully perceptive and rich interpretation.[69]

Putting yourself in Matthew's shoes—he was an eyewitness of the Messiah's teaching, miracles, death, resurrection, and ascension—and then looking back at the Hebrew Bible through his eyes, with the understanding that everything that was written in the Tanakh ultimately pointed towards the Messiah, discovering insights such as these must have been a further source of inspiration. God so wonderfully laid out his redemptive plan in advance!

5.4. Matthew 27:9–10 is totally confused. First Matthew quotes part of a prophecy from Zechariah, then he says it comes from Jeremiah, and then he takes the whole thing totally out of context. What a mess!

Allow me to respond to your objection with a question of my own: If you were a traditional Jew and found a similar citation in the Talmud—not with reference to Yeshua, but with reference to some halakhic or haggadic subject—would you say that it was "totally confused," or would you say that it was a difficult passage but one that could certainly be resolved through careful study? No doubt, you would say that it could be resolved. In fairness, then, let me show you how these verses in Matthew can also be explained through careful study, looking at the deeper themes of his book and not just at this one passage in isolation. Once again, you will see that Matthew is anything but confused in his reading of the Tanakh.

I want to be totally candid with you. Before I examined this passage in depth, I was also confused by the citation, wondering, "What in the world was Matthew thinking? Was he really that free with his use of the Scriptures?" However, the more I looked into the quotation, beginning with the Hebrew text of Zechariah 11:13, the more impressed I was with his insights. I was pleasantly surprised by what I found!

I'm fully aware, of course, that some liberal scholars who have studied Matthew's *Besorah* (Hebrew for gospel or good news) have accused him of handling the Tanakh in a superficial or even pedestrian way (see above, 5.1–5.3, for examples of such charges). Others who have studied his work meticulously have come to very different conclusions, and the verdict of two of the top Matthew scholars in the world today bears repeating, especially since both have been highly conversant in ancient Jewish studies and neither of them have been "fundamentalists." As noted above, professors Davies and Allison wrote:

> Matthew was not above scattering items in his Greek text whose deeper meaning could only be appreciated by those with a knowledge of Hebrew. Indeed, it might even be that Matthew found authorial delight in hiding 'bonus points' for those willing and able to look a little beneath the gospel's surface.[70]

Let's take a look beneath the surface and see what we can learn about Matthew's methodology here in Matthew 27:1–10. The text records that, after some of the Jewish leaders had decided to put Yeshua to death, Judas Iscariot was struck with remorse over his betrayal of his Master, returning the thirty silver coins he had received in payment from the chief priests and elders, saying to them, "I have sinned, for I have betrayed innocent blood" (see 27:1–4; and take note of that phrase, "innocent blood"). His words were greeted with indifference, so Judas threw the money into the Temple and then went out and hung himself (27:5). Matthew 27:6–10 then continues the narrative, including the key citation from "Jeremiah" (I have highlighted the text, below):

> The chief priests picked up the coins and said, "It is against the law to put this into the treasury, since it is blood money." So they decided to use the money to buy the potter's field as a burial place for foreigners. That is why it has been called the Field of Blood to this day. *Then what was spoken by Jeremiah the prophet was fulfilled: "They took the thirty silver coins, the price set on him by the people of Israel, and they used them to buy the potter's field, as the Lord commanded me."*

What are the main problems with this citation? First, the text seems to come from Zechariah 11:11–13 rather than anywhere in Jeremiah, yet Matthew cites it as coming from Jeremiah. Second, there is no reference to a potter's field in the text in Zechariah. Third, the original context of Zechariah does not seem to relate to the actions of Judas. Let's review these objections in the order they have been presented, summarizing the best solutions to the apparent problems. For those wanting to study this question further, there are lengthy treatments that already exist.[71]

Did Matthew get Zechariah and Jeremiah confused? Some have speculated that there was a scribal error in transmission (due to the close

spelling of the names in Greek) or that the original text did not mention a specific prophet's name (as attested in some manuscripts), but
there is little evidence to support these proposals. Others have argued
that Matthew simply forgot who said what. This, however, is untenable
for a number of reasons: (1) As we have seen clearly, he was a careful student of the Tanakh and would hardly make such an error. (2)
Even those who are not convinced that Matthew knew the Scriptures
that well must remember that he did not just sit down and write his
Gospel on the fly from memory one day, so the idea that he just had a
momentary mental slip and never corrected it is also highly unlikely,
to say the least. (3) It has been observed that the passage quoted here
"shows evidence of receiving the author's close attention,"[72] again making it difficult to believe that he then wrongly identified the source. In
fact, we will see that Matthew translated directly from the Hebrew. He
would have hardly gotten the name of the book wrong! (4) The formula
introducing this Scripture citation varies from the general quotation
formula used in Matthew, but it is identical to that of Matthew 2:17,
the only other passage where Jeremiah is cited directly. This too points
to premeditation and care.

What then is the solution? It would appear that, while quoting primarily from Zechariah, Matthew was pointing the reader to a key passage (or theme) in Jeremiah as well, one that tied in with the point he
wanted to make. Thus, to draw this to the reader's attention, he made
reference to Jeremiah, since the reference to Zechariah would be obvious. Similar, although not identical to this, is Mark's citation from both
Isaiah and Malachi, but the introductory comment in Mark 1:2a says, "It
is written in Isaiah the prophet," the next verses then citing Isaiah and
Malachi in succession (Mark 1:2b–3). In the case before us in Matthew
27, the blending of texts and concepts is more subtle, but it is certainly
there. What Mark and Matthew also have in common between them is
that they cite the more prominent prophet when making reference to
two prophetic texts, in the former, to Isaiah, in the latter, to Jeremiah.
We will return to the question of which text(s) in Jeremiah Matthew had
in mind when we put all the pieces together in concluding our answer
to this objection.

What about the potter's field? Let's first deal with the issue of the potter.
In the NIV, Zechariah 11:13 reads, "And the LORD said to me, 'Throw it
to the potter'—the handsome price at which they priced me! So I took
the thirty pieces of silver and threw them into the house of the LORD
to the potter." In the NJPSV, however, it reads, "The LORD said to me,
'Deposit it in the treasury.' And I took the thirty shekels and deposited
it in the treasury in the House of the LORD," with a note that the mean-

ing of some of the words, including "treasury" is uncertain. Why this discrepancy? The Masoretic textual tradition (MT) reads *ha-yotser*, the potter, but some textual and interpretive traditions understood this to be the equivalent of *ha-'otsar*, the treasury (cf. Rashi; Radak), or, *ha-'otser*, the keeper of the treasury (cf. Targum; Rashi). Within the Tanakh, however, the word *yotser* never means treasury (or, treasurer) but rather potter, and the text literally says: "Throw it (not, "Deposit it") to the potter . . . And I threw it into the house of the Lord to the potter." The Septuagint (LXX), however, understood *ha-yotser* to refer to the furnace (as if from "smelter"), a possible but otherwise unattested usage of this noun in the Tanakh.

Which version, then, did Matthew follow? Did he cite the LXX here, as he often does elsewhere? No. Did he follow the tradition reflected later in the Targum? No, although we cannot be sure that this interpretive tradition was already known in his day. What about the tradition reflected in the Syriac Peshitta, which was close to the Targum as well? No, he did not follow (or know) that tradition. Instead, he translated directly from the Hebrew, rendering *ha-yotser* as "the potter," but with the addition of one detail (that, in hindsight, made tremendous prophetic sense): The money that was cast into the house of the Lord *for the potter* was actually used to buy *the potter's field*. In other words, as noted below, this was not a matter of Matthew creating a story to fit the biblical text, as if his secret agenda was to make it look as if Jesus fulfilled the prophecies. Rather, as Carson noted, "when we examine Matthew's quotation clause by clause, we can see impressive reasons for holding that the narrative does not grow out of the prophecy. . . ."[73]

Certainly, Matthew was well aware of the tragic events involved in his Master's betrayal, events which included: (1) the price of the shepherd (a term used by Jesus to describe himself) being set at thirty pieces of silver; (2) those thirty pieces of silver being thrown into the house of the Lord by a despondent Judas; and (3) that money then being used to purchase the potter's field. With all this in mind, this text in Zechariah could not help but jump to his attention. To quote Zechariah 11:13 once again: "And the Lord said to me, 'Throw it to the potter'—the handsome price at which they priced me! So I took the thirty pieces of silver and threw them into the house of the Lord to the potter." It is a very small jump, indeed, to move from "to the potter" to "to the potter, for his field." (For additional comments on the interpretation of this passage, see below.)

And yet there is more, and this is where we need to give Matthew the credit he is due. Why did he make reference to Jeremiah? Wasn't this prophecy close enough, especially given its somewhat cryptic nature, even in its original context? Obviously, any reader familiar with the Scriptures would have known that the verse itself was drawn from Zechariah, not Jeremiah, so, as we pointed out, above, there must be something else to which Matthew was pointing. It would seem then, in light of all the potential texts in Jeremiah, that Matthew was most likely pointing to Jeremiah 19:1–13, where the prophet is commanded by the Lord to "buy a clay jar from a potter" (*yotser*) and to take it, in the presence of the elders and the priests, "to the Valley of Ben Hinnom, near the entrance of the Potsherd Gate," proclaiming a word of solemn judgment on Jerusalem: "This is what the Lord Almighty, the God of Israel, says: Listen! I am going to bring a disaster on this place that will make the ears of everyone who hears of it tingle" (19:1–3). Jeremiah was then to smash the potter's jar and say: "This is what the Lord Almighty says: I will smash this nation and this city just as this potter's jar is smashed and cannot be repaired" (Jer. 19:11).

Tragically, Jeremiah lived to see this prophecy fulfilled, with the Temple of the Lord and the city of Jerusalem demolished by the Babylonians. And note carefully 19:4: Not only would God destroy Jerusalem because of its idolatry, but also because "they have filled this place with the blood of the innocent"—the very phrase on Judas's lips in Matthew 27:4: "I have betrayed innocent blood." And it was this blood money that was used to buy the potter's field, henceforth called the Field of Blood. And to whom did Judas make this confession, and who was it that decided to use the blood money to buy the potter's field? It was "the chief priests and the elders" (27:3b). Shades of Jeremiah 19:1! Notice also that Jeremiah, after breaking the potter's jar, declares, "They will bury the dead in Topheth [in the Valley of Ben Hinnom] until there is no more room" (Jer. 19:11b), while the potter's field in Matthew 27 became used "as a burial place for foreigners" (27:7). "As a result," Michael Knowles points out, "whereas both were formerly associated with potters, they now carry names connoting bloodshed ('Valley of Slaughter'; 'Field of Blood')."[74]

What then was Matthew saying? He was saying, "Remember the potter! Remember the blood guilt! Remember Jeremiah's prophecy about the destruction of our city and Temple! It happened just as he said it would. And today there is even greater blood guilt with even greater consequences. We have betrayed God's Son. We have given the Messiah over to death. Judgment is near!" By citing Zechariah, with allusion to Jeremiah, he made his point quite powerfully, not to mention profoundly.[75]

As D. P. Senior notes: "The explicit details which have been fulfilled are spelled out in the words of [Zechariah], but it is the tragic tone of

Jeremiah's prophecy that colors the accomplishment of God's will in a moment of betrayal and truth."[76] Knowles also finds evidence that Matthew was making a direct comparison between Jesus and Jeremiah, both of whom were rejected and mistreated by their own people, and both of whom prophesied the destruction of Jerusalem and the Temple. And, just as Matthew pointed to the slaughter of the innocent boys of Bethlehem in Matthew 2:16–18, quoting from Jeremiah 31:15 and using the identical introductory formula in 2:17 and 27:9a, so also here, at the climax of Messiah's mission, innocent blood is being shed. As Knowles explains:

> In 27:9–10 Matthew sees in what is probably the most perfidious act of opposition to the messiah in his Gospel—Jesus' betrayal by one of his closest disciples—not only the fulfillment of prophecy in general but also a link to the words of Jeremiah in particular. Indeed, the fact that the entire fulfillment quotation is given under the name of Jeremiah characterizes the whole as typical of that prophet. Without question, the fulfillment quotation provides the climax and focal point for Matthew's narrative: the messiah is sold for the price of a slave, with Judas's belated attempt to redress the wrong demonstrating both a recognition of his own guilt and the complicity of those who refuse what they themselves acknowledge to be "the price of blood." In this way Matthew demonstrates Jesus' innocence at the expense of the other participants' guilt and responsibility. And all this is seen to be fulfilled in the words ascribed deliberately, albeit enigmatically, to the prophet Jeremiah.[77]

But was Zechariah really prophesying the betrayal of the Messiah? It is true that both the New Testament and the Rabbinic writings cite several passages from Zechariah with reference to the Messiah. As noted in the *Jewish Study Bible*:

> Many ancient readers found in Zechariah numerous references to messianic times. As expected, some early Christian readers understood them in christological terms (see, for instance Mark 14.27 and Zech. 13.7; Matt. 27.9 and Zech. 11.12–13; John 19.37 and Zech. 12.10; John 12.15 and Zech. 9.9). Rabbinic Judaism interpreted many of these texts in relation to a messianic time still to come (e.g., Zech. 3.8; 6.12 in the Targum; in relation to Zech. 6:12 see *Num. Rab.* 18.21; for Zech. 9:9 see *Gen. Rab.* 56.2, 98.9; and for Zech. 12.10 as pointing to the Messiah from the House of Joseph, see *b. Sukkah* 52a).[78]

That being said, the question remains: Is there Messianic significance to Zechariah 11:12–13? Let's see how some of the classical Rabbinic commentators interpret this verse, after which we can ask again: Was

Matthew justified in citing this with reference to the betrayal of Yeshua, the Good Shepherd who laid down his life for the sheep?
According to Rashi:

12 And they weighed out My hire, thirty pieces of silver. [Targum] Jonathan paraphrases: And they performed My will with a few men. There were a few good men among them, such as the craftsmen and the sentries, Daniel, Hananiah, Mishael, Azariah, and Ezekiel. But I do not know how to explain the expression here of thirty pieces of silver exactly, except that *kesep* is an expression of desire. Our Sages, too, explained it this way in Chullin (92a). They brought proof from (Prov. 7:20), "The bundle of the desirable ones He took in His hand." The thirty they explained in the following manner: There are forty-five righteous men in every generation. They brought proof from (Hosea 3:2), "a *homer* of barley and a *letek* of barley"—fifteen righteous in Babylon and thirty in Eretz Israel. It is said: "And I took the thirty pieces of silver, and I cast them into the house of the Lord in Eretz Israel." The number thirty is explained by the Midrash Aggadah (Cf. Genesis Rabbah 49:3, Pesikta d'Rav Kahana 88a), that our father Abraham was promised that no generation would have fewer than thirty righteous in men, the number of (Gen. 15:8): "So shall your seed be." The word *yihyeh* has the numerical value of thirty.

Does this sound somewhat far-fetched? Rashi continues:

13 And the Lord said to me: Cast it to the keeper of the treasury like *ha'otser* the keeper of the treasury. Said the Holy One, blessed be He, to the prophet: Write, and leave over these and their righteousness to be preserved for the end of the seventy years of the Babylonian exile. The Temple shall be built by them. Now what is the treasury? [Cf. below] **the stronghold of glory** My Temple, the stronghold of My glory. **of which I stripped them** of which I stripped them so that they should no longer have glory. . . . My explanation is similar to Jonathan's translation. I have seen many variant versions of the explanation of this prophecy, but I cannot reconcile those with the text.

The *Living Nach* conveniently summarizes some of the other, major Rabbinic commentators:

—**thirty pieces of silver.** This was the standard wage for a shepherd in those days (*Metzudoth*). The 30 pieces allude to the 30 righteous people who are alive in every generation (Rashi, *Metzudoth*). According to Malbim, the 30 righteous individuals of Zechariah's generation gave their lives to sanctify God's Name. In this way they "paid" God to continue protecting the Israelites despite their wickedness.

—**Deposit it.** God commanded Zechariah to store away the merit of the 30 righteous individuals alluded to in the previous verse (see preceding note) until the future, when, in that merit, the Third Temple will be built (*Metzudoth*). Or, God commanded the prophet to have the images of the 30 righteous individuals who died sanctifying God's Name engraved on the silver coins [citing Malbim and others]

—**treasury.** (Radak on 11:[13]; *Metzudoth*.) The Hebrew word *yotzer*, which begins with the letter *yod*, and usually means "craftsman." However, this is one of the cases where a *yud* is used interchangeably with an *aleph*, making the word *otzar*, "treasury" (Rashi, Radak). Or, "keeper of the treasury" (Targum, Rashi).

Malbim, however, interprets *yotzer* to mean "craftsman": God figuratively commands Zechariah to bring the 30 silver talents to a coin minter, for him to engrave the image of the 30 righteous individuals.[79]

As odd as all this seems (remember, these are not simply midrashic applications that are being made from the text; these are *interpretations* of the text by the leading Rabbinic commentaries), the rendering of the Orthodox Jewish *Stone Edition* of the Tanakh adds one more twist, translating part of Zechariah 11:13 with, "Throw it to the treasurer of the Precious Stronghold," explaining in the note, "The Temple. By throwing the deeds of these thirty righteous people into the Temple, Zechariah symbolized that the Temple would be rebuilt because of their merits."

Contrast all this with Matthew's citation: First, he accurately translates *yotser* with potter, adding that it was the potter's field that was bought by the coins; second, he explains thirty silver coins to mean thirty silver coins, as opposed to the deeds of thirty righteous people or the faces of these thirty righteous people engraved on the coins; third, he refers the text to the actual betrayal of the Good Shepherd (see 11:4–9), the principle difference being that in Zechariah it was the prophet, as the shepherd, who acted out the symbolic vision of his own betrayal, whereas in Matthew 27 it was Judas who literally committed the act; fourth, the larger context in Zechariah is fraught with Messianic imagery, including 9:9, the prophecy of the Messianic king coming meek and lowly, riding on a colt; 12:10, where repentant Israel looks to the one whom they have pierced; 13:7, where God calls for the sword to strike the one who is his close companion, resulting in the scattering of the sheep (cf. the translation of the *Living Nach*, "O sword, rouse yourself against My shepherd and against My colleague—declares the God of hosts.");[80] and 14:1–21, which is Messianic from beginning to end. Matthew knew exactly what he was doing, and with complete justification cited this passage with reference to the Messiah's betrayal for thirty pieces of silver, also pointing to the profound parallels with Jeremiah.

Really now, who could honestly say that Matthew got this wrong but the Rabbinic commentaries, just cited, got it right? And is it any wonder that the Targum removes all reference to the thirty coins in this verse? According to Targumic scholar Bruce Chilton, the Targum here "omits the reference to 'thirty pieces of silver' at 11:12, to 'the potter' at 11:13 (cf. Matt. 27:3–10), and to 'him whom they have pierced' at 12:10 (cf. John 19:37; Rev. 1:7)"—all with the intent of removing these references that were pointed to by the New Testament authors.[81]

Far from this being an example of exegetical confusion, it is an example of inspired interpretation, perhaps inspired by the Messiah himself (see Luke 24:44–46), and rather than exposing Matthew's weakness in the Word, it reveals his depth.

Later, at 5.14, we address the objection that the New Testament writers reconstructed the life of Jesus to fit the Messianic prophecies (an objection, of course, that completely contradicts the claim that he actually fulfilled none of the prophecies; see below, 5.15; vol. 3, 4.32–4.33). In terms of the prophecy under discussion here, Carson offers a wise response to the critical scholars who also espouse the view that the life of Jesus was rewritten to conform to the prophecies:

> Many scholars hold that Matthew presents as history a number of "fulfillments" that did not happen. Rather he deduces that they must have happened because his chosen OT texts predict, as he understands them, that such events would take place. To this there are two objections. First, the more complex and composite a quotation (as here), the less likely is it that the "fulfillment" was invented. It is far easier to believe that certain historical events led Matthew to look for Scriptures relating to them. . . . Second, when we examine Matthew's quotation clause by clause, we can see impressive reasons for holding that the narrative does not grow out of the prophecy. . . . To give but one instance, the "thirty silver coins" (v. 3) are mentioned in Zechariah 11:13; but Mark speaks of betrayal money without mentioning Zechariah. Even if Mark does not specify the amount, the *fact* that Judas had been paid became well known, independent of any Christian interpretation of Zechariah 11:12–13; and it is not unreasonable to suppose that the *amount* of money also became common knowledge.[82]

You might say, "Well, I've heard your arguments and I'm not convinced that Matthew got it right. If he was trying to get me to believe in Jesus through this citation, it hasn't worked."

Actually, Matthew was not trying to "prove" to his readers that Yeshua had to be the Messiah based on this one citation from Zechariah and Jeremiah. Rather, as an eyewitness to Messiah's glory and as one convinced by the testimony of Scripture that Yeshua, indeed, was the Messiah of Israel, he then wrote his account to share this Good News with his Jewish people (and other interested readers), looking back at the Tanakh and seeing remarkable prophecies and allusions and hints and types and shadows of what was to come.[83] He carefully observed Jesus' life, he carefully studied the Tanakh, and there before his eyes, on many different levels, he saw some of the key events foretold and foreshadowed, without thinking for a moment that each of these foreshadowings constituted a "proof." This would be similar to the Rabbinic teaching that there are seventy facets to the Torah, but not all of them carry legal authority and certainly not all of them are to be interpreted in the same way.

Listen once more to Carson:

> What must not be overlooked is that, unlike any other broad, hermeneutical category used by the Jews, NT approaches to the OT are steeped in a salvation-historical perspective that finds in the sacred text entire patterns of prophetic anticipation (see esp. on 2:15; 5:17–20; 8:17; 11:11–13; 13:34–35). In this sense Matthew sees in Jeremiah 19 and Zechariah 11 not merely a number of verbal and thematic parallels to Jesus' betrayal but a pattern of apostasy and rejection that must find its ultimate fulfillment in the rejection of Jesus, who was cheaply valued, rejected by the Jews, and whose betrayal money was put to a purpose that pointed to the destruction of the nation (see on 15:7–9; 21:42).[84]

Insights such as these on the part of Matthew are hardly superficial or confused. Rather, they only appear to be off base when read superficially, critically, or with wrong presuppositions. So then, rather than ask, "Does this citation prove that Jesus is the Messiah?," ask instead, "If he is the Messiah and if he did fulfill everything that had to be fulfilled at that time, was it legitimate for Matthew to turn back and look at the whole Bible and find spiritual parallels and Messianic foreshadowings throughout Israel's history and throughout the words of the prophets?" The answer is yes, without a doubt. And I repeat a statement made above, 5.1: The interpretations of Matthew are sober and restrained in comparison with later Rabbinic interpretation. In fact, as I have interacted with some extremely Orthodox or Chasidic Jews who have discovered that Yeshua is our Messiah, I have been amazed to see some of the "proofs" they have come up with in the Tanakh. Why? It is because that is how they have been reading Scripture all their lives—finding references to

Torah or some halakhic principle or mystical insight in every letter, word, and phrase—and now that they encountered Moshiach, they see him everywhere in Scripture too. To repeat once more: Matthew is quite restrained in comparison!

This, then, was the perspective of Matthew and his fellow authors who penned the Messianic Scriptures. Messiah *did* come at the time appointed by the *peshat* (that is, the plain, historical sense) of Scripture and he *did* fulfill what had to be fulfilled during that phase of his mission—again, according to the plain, historical sense of the Tanakh—and he continues to accomplish that mission—once again, according to the plain, historical sense of the Tanakh (see vol. 1, 2.1; vol. 3, 4.32–4.33, for more on this). And so, the New Testament authors started with that reality: Messiah has come in accordance with the true and literal meaning of the Hebrew Scriptures, announced by angels and confirmed by miracles, and based on that reality, they then turned to their Bible and saw prophecies and allusions and types of the Messiah throughout the Scriptures, just as the rabbis saw references to the Torah everywhere in the Scriptures, even where those references were entirely midrashic or allegorical. To repeat: Yeshua's followers did not try to prove his Messianic credentials by means of midrashic interpretations; rather, having seen him teach Torah, perform miracles, die, rise from the dead, ascend to heaven, and then immerse them in the Holy Spirit, and recognizing that he fulfilled the essential qualifications for the Messiah's mission at that point in time—in accordance with the plain meaning of the Scriptures!—they adorned their message with midrashic allusions and illustrations. Even in doing this, however, they were led by the Spirit, who also inspired the authors of the Tanakh. And so, just as traditional Jews trust the methodology and interpretation of the Talmudic sages, I trust the methodology and interpretation of the followers of Jesus the Messiah and, when read through fair-minded and not caustically critical eyes, the spiritual riches are there to behold.

5.5. Hebrews 10:5 is one of the worst examples of New Testament Scripture-twisting. The writer quotes from Psalm 40, where the psalmist says, "You have opened my ears," but he applies it to Jesus and *changes* the words to read, "A body you have prepared for me." Could you imagine anything more dishonest?

> Actually, the writer to the Hebrews was simply quoting from the Septuagint—the Greek version of the Scriptures made by and for Greek-speaking Jews—as he generally does throughout his book. In this particular case, the exact meaning of the original Hebrew is somewhat unclear, and the Septuagint offered an interpretive rendering. So, neither the Septuagint nor Hebrews were in the least bit dishonest or misleading. Also, it's interesting that Hebrews does not major on the part of the verse that was supposedly changed but puts the emphasis on other parts of the quote.

Anti-missionary Tovia Singer writes, "Notice how King David's original words, 'but my ears You have opened' have disappeared entirely in the Hebrews quote. Instead, this New Testament author replaced this expunged clause with the words 'But a body you have prepared for Me.' This is a startling alteration of the Jewish scriptures."[85]

Is there any truth to this charge? Aside from the fact that such a practice would be totally self-defeating—as I have stressed repeatedly, first-century Jewish readers would have been quick to spot the creation of a nonexistent verse or the wholesale changing of an existing text—it would make no sense: Why would the author of Hebrews completely change the text of a verse from a favorite section of the Bible (viz., the Psalms), knowing full-well that at least some of his readers would know the verse in Hebrew? It would be like a political leader speaking today to an audience of educated Americans and saying to them, "As Patrick Henry said, 'Give me poverty or give me birth!'" Who would he be fooling with this? And what would his point be? There would be none.

This is underscored when we remember that the author of Hebrews was writing to Jewish *believers* and was not trying to convince them of something. In other words, he was just opening up the Scriptures to them, giving them insight and instruction to build their faith. All the more then is it absolutely preposterous to think that he would "erase" the original wording and replace it with his own.

Why then does the citation of Psalm 40:6[7] in Hebrews 10:5 read differently than most translations of the Hebrew text? The answer is simple: The Hebrew expression there is somewhat obscure, and the Septuagint (LXX), which was quoted in Hebrews, offered an interpretative rendering of the text. That's it! No Scripture-twisting, no manipulating of the text, no sleight of hand. Just a simple quotation from the Greek Bible used by Greek-speaking Jews in that day, consistent with the pattern of the author of Hebrews, who quotes from the LXX throughout his book.[86] And this striking rendition of the original text fit well into the general theme of Hebrews 10, so it was especially suitable to quote it here. This would be just like a preacher today looking for a specific translation of a particular verse that would best suit his sermon needs. If the translation was reliable and really brought out his point well, he would probably use it. All of us who regularly quote the Scriptures, teach from the Scriptures, or preach from the Scriptures have done similar things, and there is nothing wrong or dishonest about it, provided that the translation is faithful and reliable.

Anti-missionaries, however, would say that in the case under discussion here, the translation was *not* faithful and reliable. According to Rabbi Bentzion Kravitz of Jews for Judaism, it is an open-and-shut case:

> Hebrews 10:5 of the New Testament, when quoting Psalm 40, claims that G-d replaced animal sacrifices with the death of the Messiah, by stating that, *"sacrifices and offerings You have not desired, but a **body** You have prepared for Me."* However, the original quote from Psalm 40:6 does not say this; it says, *"sacrifices and meal offerings You have not desired; My **ears** You have opened."* This refers to G-d's desire that we listen to Him, as it says, *"Behold!—to obey is better than sacrifice."* (1 Sam. 15:22)[87]

What Rabbi Kravitz fails to note is that the Hebrew text in Psalm 40:6 (v. 7 in Hebrew texts) is not totally clear, containing an interesting phrase that can be roughly translated, "you have dug out ears for me." What does this actually mean and how should it be properly translated? Consider for a moment the renderings of these contemporary *Jewish* translations. The Orthodox Jewish *Stone Edition* translates this as, "You opened ears for me," which makes good sense in English but fails to explain why such an unusual Hebrew idiom would be used. (The Christian NIV tentatively renders, "but my ears you have pierced," reminding us that the verb really does not mean "open.") The NJPSV renders with, "You gave me to understand . . . ," noting, "Meaning of Heb. uncertain." That's quite a jump from a literal translation! Similarly, the commentary of Martin S. Rozenberg and Bernard M. Zlotowitz translates, "You have made me aware." (What would an anti-missionary say of *these* translations? Where is the dishonest motivation here?) Rozenberg and Zlotowitz then explain, "lit[erally] 'Ears you have dug for me,' i.e., He unstopped the ears so he could hear clearly God's declaration and obey it. To just listen and not act is like having the ears stopped."[88] (This is similar to the interpretation of Rashi and Metsudat David; cf. also Ibn Ezra.)

Again, however, we need to ask, Why is the Hebrew verb in question (*k-r-h*, normally "dig"; cf. Exod. 21:33, and see Midrash Tehillim 40:4) used in the context of opening up or unstopping ears? Commentators and lexicographers have no easy answer to this question, since the usage is quite unique.[89]

In any case, regardless of one's specific interpretation of the Hebrew phrase, the point I'm making is obvious: The text is difficult, both Jewish and Christian translators have struggled to bring out its meaning, and, just as some modern Jewish versions paraphrase the text in an attempt to explain it, so also the oldest Jewish version, the Septuagint, paraphrased it in an attempt to explain it, translating with "a body you have prepared for me."[90] And it was this translation—which I remind you again was the oldest and most widely used *Jewish* translation in the ancient world—that the author of Hebrews quoted, nothing more, nothing less.[91] Note also that the emphasis in the next verses in Hebrews 10:8–9 is put on the words from Psalm 40 concerning which there is no dispute:

> First he said, "Sacrifices and offerings, burnt offerings and sin offerings you did not desire, nor were you pleased with them" (although the law required them to be made). Then he said, "Here I am, I have come to do your will." He sets aside the first to establish the second.

It is only in verse 10 that reference is made to Yeshua's "body," but not even as part of the previous quote. That's not where the emphasis was being placed.

The verdict of Franz Delitzsch, the highly respected Old Testament, Semitic, and Rabbinic scholar is sober and sound. He stated that it is "impossible that the writer of our epistle should have himself accommodated the translation of the original to the facts of the New Testament history; such alterations and accommodations of the received [Hebrew] text, or its Septuagint translation, being unknown to writers of the New Testament."[92] Anti-missionaries may *accuse* the New Testament writers of such practices, imputing all kinds of deceitful and devious motivations to them, but biblical scholars know better.

Earlier, we quoted the words of Abraham Ibn Ezra, one of Judaism's most revered biblical commentators, to the effect that, "The prophets do not preserve the exact wording when they repeat something. They only preserve its substance. For that is what is important. . . ."[93] That is exactly what the writer to the Hebrews did here and in doing so, was in good Jewish company, in particular, with the ancient Jewish translators, paraphrasers, and teachers of Scriptures—such as those behind the LXX and the Targums.[94]

5.6. The New Testament is full of historical inaccuracies.

> Actually, where the New Testament accounts can be veri-
> fied or checked by external, contemporary sources, they are
> consistently accurate. (If they can't be verified or checked,
> and they bear the marks of good history writing—which they
> do—how can anyone claim that they are inaccurate?) So,
> the real question is: What contemporary historical records
> are there that contradict the New Testament authors? In
> point of fact, there are none. It should also be pointed out
> that out of all ancient documents, the New Testament was
> the best preserved.

This objection has been treated fairly and fully in other, more general studies, such as those cited in what follows, and I encourage readers who are interested in a more in-depth treatment to study those sources, since this volume is directed in particular to *Jewish objections* to the New Testament. Nonetheless, it will be useful to provide a general response to this objection, offering some specific details in support. We will then consider two, specifically Jewish objections that have been raised against the trustworthiness of the New Testament before looking briefly at Stephen's speech as recorded in Acts 7.

First, let me share with you the story of Sir William M. Ramsay (1851–1939), famed as the once-skeptical New Testament scholar and archaeologist who became a staunch believer in the historical accuracy of the New Testament. He was educated in Scotland (University of Aberdeen) and England (Oxford University), during which time he became enamored with the extremely critical scholarship of the F. C. Baur school of Tübingen, Germany. As a result of this, in 1890, he embarked on a journey through the biblical lands in order to confirm the historical *errors* of the New Testament writers. To his great surprise, he found that, at point after point, archeological data and sound historical scholarship confirmed the *accuracy* of the New Testament authors, and he wrote several important volumes that are still used to this day.[95] Subsequent scholarship over the last century has brought further confirmation to Ramsay's writings. Ramsay explained:

> It was gradually borne upon me that in various details the narrative [of
> Luke in Acts] showed marvelous truth. In fact, beginning with a fixed
> idea that the work was essentially a second-century composition, and
> never relying on its evidence as trustworthy for first-century conditions,

I gradually came to find it a useful ally in some obscure and difficult investigations.[96]

In other words, historical details in Luke's writings helped provide Ramsay with reliable bearings for some of his other historical and archeological investigations. He concluded that, "Luke is a historian of the first rank; not merely are his statements of fact trustworthy; he is possessed of the true historic sense . . . this author should be placed along with the very greatest of historians."[97]

In refuting anti-missionary attacks on the reliability of the New Testament, Eric Snow provided three tests against which the New Testament's credibility could be tested: the bibliographical test, the internal evidence test, and the external evidence test.[98] Let's take these one at a time with specific application to the historical accuracy of the New Covenant Writings.

The bibliographical test. As Snow explains,

> The bibliographical test has two parts: First, on average, the more handwritten manuscript copies there are of an ancient historical document, the more reliable it is. [Second], the closer in time the oldest presently existing manuscript that has survived is to the original first copy (autograph) of the author, the more reliable that document is. That's because then less time is allowed for distortions to creep into the text by scribes down through the generations who are copying by hand (before, in Europe, Gutenberg's perfection of printing using moveable type by c. 1440).[99]

How does the New Testament score on this test? The highly respected biblical scholar F. F. Bruce summarizes the evidence:

> About the middle of the [nineteenth] century it was confidently asserted by a very influential school of thought that some of the most important books of the New Testament, including the Gospels and the Acts, did not exist before the thirties of the second century AD. This conclusion was the result not so much of historical evidence as of philosophical presuppositions. Even then there was sufficient historical evidence to show how unfounded these theories were, as Lightfoot, Tischendorf, Tregelles and others demonstrated in their writings; but the amount of such evidence available in our own day is so much greater and more conclusive that a first century date for most of the New Testament writings cannot reasonably be denied, no matter what our philosophical presuppositions may be.

So then, 150 years ago there were critical scholars claiming that "some of the most important books of the New Testament" did not even exist before roughly one hundred years after the death and resurrection of

Jesus. Archeological discoveries, however, coupled with sound scientific methodology, made this skeptical position untenable to the point that "a first century date for most of the New Testament writings cannot reasonably be denied, no matter what our philosophical presuppositions may be." Bruce continues:

> The evidence for our New Testament writings is ever so much greater than the evidence for many writings of classical authors, the authenticity of which no one dreams of questioning. And if the New Testament were a collection of secular writings, their authenticity would generally be regarded as beyond all doubt. It is a curious fact that historians have often been much readier to trust the New Testament records than have many theologians. Somehow or other, there are people who regard a "sacred book" as *ipso facto* under suspicion, and demand much more corroborative evidence for such a work than they would for an ordinary secular or pagan writing. From the viewpoint of the historian, the same standards must be applied to both. But we do not quarrel with those who want more evidence for the New Testament than for other writings; firstly, because the universal claims which the New Testament makes upon mankind are so absolute, and the character and works of its chief Figure so unparalleled, that we want to be as sure of its truth as we possibly can; and secondly, because in point of fact there is much more evidence for the New Testament than for other ancient writings of comparable date.

How interesting! If we were not dealing with a sacred text, and if, instead, "the New Testament were a collection of secular writings, their authenticity would generally be regarded as beyond all doubt." What then is the evidence? According to Bruce:

> There are in existence about 5,000 Greek manuscripts of the New Testament in whole or in part. The best and most important of these go back to somewhere about AD 350, the two most important being the Codex Vaticanus, the chief treasure of the Vatican Library in Rome, and the well-known Codex Sinaiticus, which the British Government purchased from the Soviet Government for £100,000 on Christmas Day, 1933, and which is now the chief treasure of the British Museum. Two other important early MSS in this country are the Codex Alexandrinus, also in the British Museum, written in the fifth century, and the Codex Bezae, in Cambridge University Library, written in the fifth or sixth century, and containing the Gospels and Acts in both Greek and Latin.

How does this compare with the manuscript evidence from other ancient writings? If you are not familiar with this information, you are in for quite a surprise:

Perhaps we can appreciate how wealthy the New Testament is in manuscript attestation if we compare the textual material for other ancient
historical works. For Caesar's *Gallic War* (composed between 58 and 50 BC)
there are several extant MSS, but only nine or ten are good, and the oldest
is some 900 years later than Caesar's day. Of the 142 books of the Roman
History of Livy (59 BC–AD 17) only thirty-five survive; these are known
to us from not more than twenty MSS of any consequence, only one of
which, and that containing fragments of Books iii–vi, is as old as the fourth
century. Of the fourteen books of the *Histories* of Tacitus (c. AD 100) only
four and a half survive; of the sixteen books of his *Annals*, ten survive
in full and two in part. The text of these extant portions of his two great
historical works depends entirely on two MSS, one of the ninth century
and one of the eleventh. The extant MSS of his minor works (*Dialogue
de Oratoribus, Agricola, Germania*) all descend from a codex of the tenth
century. The History of Thucydides (c. 460–400 BC) is known to us from
eight MSS, the earliest belonging to c. AD 900, and a few papyrus scraps,
belonging to about the beginning of the Christian era. The same is true of
the History of Herodotus (c. 488–428 BC). Yet no classical scholar would
listen to an argument that the authenticity of Herodotus or Thucydides
is in doubt because the earliest MSS of their works which are of any use
to us are over 1,300 years later than the originals.

Did you catch that? The oldest reliable manuscripts from these important historical works date to 1,300 years after the originals were
written—1,300 years!—yet no respected historian would "listen to an
argument" questioning their authenticity. Bruce then explains:

But how different is the situation of the New Testament in this respect!
In addition to the two excellent MSS of the fourth century mentioned
above, which are the earliest of some thousands known to us, considerable
fragments remain of papyrus copies of books of the New Testament dated
from 100 to 200 years earlier still. The Chester Beatty Biblical Papyri, the
existence of which was made public in 1931, consist of portions of eleven
papyrus codices, three of which contained most of the New Testament
writings. One of these, containing the four Gospels with Acts, belongs
to the first half of the third century; another, containing Paul's letters to
churches and the Epistle to the Hebrews, was copied at the beginning of
the third century; the third, containing Revelation, belongs to the second
half of the same century.
    A more recent discovery consists of some papyrus fragments dated by
papyrological experts not later than AD 150, published in *Fragments of an
Unknown Gospel and other Early Christian Papyri*, by H. I. Bell and T. C.
Skeat (1935). These fragments contain what has been thought by some
to be portions of a fifth Gospel having strong affinities with the canonical
four; but much more probable is the view expressed in *The Times Liter-*

ary Supplement for 25 April 1935, "that these fragments were written by someone who had the four Gospels before him and knew them well; that they did not profess to be an independent Gospel; but were paraphrases of the stories and other matter in the Gospels designed for explanation and instruction, a manual to teach people the Gospel stories."

Earlier still is a fragment of a papyrus codex containing John 18:31–33, 37–38, now in the John Rylands Library, Manchester, dated on palaeographical grounds around AD 130, showing that the latest of the four Gospels, which was written, according to tradition, at Ephesus between AD 90 and 100, was circulating in Egypt within about forty years of its composition (if, as is most likely, this papyrus originated in Egypt, where it was acquired in 1917). It must be regarded as being, by half a century, the earliest extant fragment of the New Testament.

A more recently discovered papyrus manuscript of the same Gospel, while not so early as the Rylands papyrus, is incomparably better preserved; this is the Papyrus Bodmer II, whose discovery was announced by the Bodmer Library of Geneva in 1956; it was written about AD 200, and contains the first fourteen chapters of the Gospel of John with but one lacuna (of twenty two verses), and considerable portions of the last seven chapters.

This is extraordinary. Contrary to the evidence from the classical writings in which the major manuscripts postdate the original autographs by more than a millennium, there are fragments of the New Testament preserved in manuscripts dating back to just a few decades after the writing of the original, with major manuscripts dating to within one to two centuries.

Yet there is more evidence for the reliability of the New Testament documents:

Attestation of another kind is provided by allusions to and quotations from the New Testament books in other early writings. The authors known as the Apostolic Fathers wrote chiefly between AD 90 and 160, and in their works we find evidence for their acquaintance with most of the books of the New Testament. In three works whose date is probably round about AD 100—the "Epistle of Barnabas," written perhaps in Alexandria; the *Didache*, or "Teaching of the Twelve Apostles," produced somewhere in Syria or Palestine; and the letter sent to the Corinthian church by Clement, bishop of Rome, about AD 96—find fairly certain quotations from the common tradition of the Synoptic Gospels, from Acts, Romans, 1 Corinthians, Ephesians, Titus, Hebrews, 1 Peter, and possible quotations from other books of the New Testament. In the letters written by Ignatius, bishop of Antioch, as he journeyed to his martyrdom in Rome in AD 115, there are reasonably identifiable quotations from Matthew, John, Romans, 1 and 2 Corinthians, Galatians, Ephesians, Philippians, 1 and 2 Timothy, Titus, and possible allusions to Mark, Luke, Acts, Colossians, 2 Thessalonians, Philemon, Hebrews, and 1 Peter. His younger contemporary, Polycarp, in a letter to the Philippians (c. 120) quotes from the common tradition of the Synoptic Gospels, from Acts, Romans, 1 and 2 Corinthians, Galatians, Ephesians, Philippians, 2 Thessalonians, 1 and 2 Timothy, Hebrews, 1 Peter, and 1 John. And so we might go on through the writers of the second century, amassing increasing evidence of their familiarity with and recognition of the authority of the New Testament writings. So far as the Apostolic Fathers are concerned, the evidence is collected and weighed in a work called *The New Testament in the Apostolic Fathers,* recording the findings of a committee of the Oxford Society of Historical Theology in 1905.

Nor is it only in orthodox Christian writers that we find evidence of this sort. It is evident from the recently discovered writings of the Gnostic school of Valentinus that before the middle of the second century most of the New Testament books were as well known and as fully venerated in that heretical circle as they were in the Catholic Church.[100]

Again, this evidence is quite striking, to say the least. Not only did the early followers of Jesus, writing between 90–160 c.e. show "acquaintance with most of the books of the New Testament," quoting many passages in their writing, but even heretical leaders were using these books "before the middle of the second century." This means that the collection of books we read today in what is commonly called "the New Testament" is the same collection that was read and revered 1,900 years ago.

Scholars who evaluate evidence such as this are called "textual critics," as Bruce explains:

The study of the kind of attestation found in MSS and quotations in later writers is connected with the approach known as Textual Criticism. This is a most important and fascinating branch of study, its object being to determine as exactly as possible from the available evidence the original words of the documents in question. It is easily proved by experiment that it is difficult to copy out a passage of any considerable length without making one or two slips at least. When we have documents like our New Testament writings copied and recopied thousands of times, the scope for copyists' errors is so enormously increased that it is surprising there are no more than there actually are. Fortunately, if the great number of MSS increases the number of scribal errors, it increases proportionately the means of correcting such errors, so that the margin of doubt left in the process of recovering the exact original wording is not so large as might be feared; it is in truth remarkably small. *The variant readings about which any doubt remain among textual critics of the New Testament affect no material question of historic fact or of Christian faith and practice.*

To sum up, we may quote the verdict of the late Sir Frederic Kenyon, a scholar whose authority to make pronouncements on ancient MSS was second to none:

"The interval then between the date of original composition and the earliest extant evidence become so small to be in fact negligible, and the last foundation for any doubt that the Scriptures have come down to us substantially as they were written has now been removed. Both the authenticity and the general integrity of the books of the New Testament may be regarded as finally established."[101]

How then do the New Testament writings pass the bibliographic test? With flying colors! In fact, in comparison with all other ancient books written in Greek or Latin, if the New Testament writings scored an A+, using the same criterion, the best of the other books would barely pass the test. For those who would point to the care with which the Tanakh has been copied and preserved through the centuries—and I certainly concur that God has superintended the careful preservation of his entire Word, both the Tanakh and the New Covenant Writings—a comparison with the New Testament is also enlightening. Until the discovery of the Dead Sea Scrolls in the middle of the last century, the oldest complete manuscript of the Tanakh dated from the tenth century c.e.—in other words, more than 1,300 years after the writing of the last book! This is because older manuscripts were buried or hidden away, but the fact remains that the oldest known complete manuscript was quite late.

Of course, the scribes were meticulous in their writing habits, providing counts of every letter, word, and sentence at the end of their work, also counting the middle letter, word, and sentence just to verify their accuracy. I certainly thank God for the jealousy with which this was done! Yet when the Dead Sea Scrolls were discovered, they provided evidence of: (1) Hebrew manuscripts which agreed with the later Masoretic tradition letter for letter (these manuscripts were not for complete books but for fragments); (2) Hebrew manuscripts showing a more full spelling of words (similar to the older, British spelling of words like "colour" and "favour" as opposed to our American spelling) and a less precise scribal style; (3) Hebrew manuscripts which agreed in part with the Septuagint tradition; (4) Hebrew manuscripts (of parts of the Torah) which agreed in part with the tradition preserved in the Samaritan Pentateuch (see also, above, 5.1).

So, the Hebrew Bible was not preserved without variant readings and traditions either (not to mention the thousands of very minor variations found within the Masoretic tradition), and scholars working with the Hebrew Scriptures also engage in the science of textual criticism, just as do scholars of the Greek Scriptures.

What this means for a twenty-first-century reader of the New Testament is simply this: You can be totally confident that the books you are reading are the books that were written more than 1,900 years ago and there is no issue of substance affected by any textual variants.

The internal evidence test. Snow explains the second of his three tests for credibility:

> The internal evidence test involves analyzing the document itself for contradictions and self-evident absurdities. How close in time and place the writer of the document was to the events and people he describes is examined: The bigger the gap, the less likely it is reliable.[102]

How do the books of the New Testament score on this test? First, it is clear that the authors, who, for the most part, claimed to be eyewitnesses of the events they recorded, give clear evidence to their close proximity to the public ministry, death, and resurrection of the Messiah, along with the subsequent events that transpired over the course of the next two to three decades. With regard to the Gospel accounts, New Testament scholar Craig Keener pointed out:

> On the continuum between more and less careful writers, the writers of the Gospels are among the most careful. . . . The first Gospels were written when eyewitnesses were still in positions of authority in the church and oral tradition could be checked, and this supports their reliability; biographies of roughly contemporary characters were normally far more accurate than those concerning heroes of the distant past.[103]

In the case of the New Testament, the writers show a strong familiarity with the places, customs, and even language of the day, on several occasions making reference to Aramaic sentences spoken by Yeshua (see Mark 5:41; 7:34; 15:34), on other occasions using Hebrew or Aramaic expressions that would not have been understandable to a later, more distant audience (for these words on the lips of Jesus, see, e.g., Matthew 5:22 [*raka, geenna*]; 6:24 [*mamōnas*]; Mark 14:36 [*abba*]; also Matthew 27:6 [*korbanas*]; Luke 1:15 [*sikera*]; John 5:2 [*bēthzatha*]; John 19:13 [*Gabbatha*]; Mark 10:51; John 20:16 [*rabbouni*]), and often providing details about geographical location or local customs or events (see, e.g., Matt. 27:6–8 [Field of Blood]; Mark 11:1; Luke 19:29; John 1:28; 11:18 [Bethany]; John 5:2–4 [Pool of Bethesda]; Luke 13:1–4 [Galilean blood mixed with sacrifices and tower of Siloam]; John 19:13 [Stone Pavement]; Luke 24:13 [Emmaus seven miles from Jerusalem]; John 11:18 [Bethany less than two miles from Jerusalem]; John 4:4–6 [location of Jacob's well]). All this points to the work of eyewitnesses.

Some scholars also point to the legal disputes that took place between Jesus and the Jewish religious leaders, disputes that would fit well into an early first-century context when Jewish law reflected more diversity and fluidity (see the arguments of Dr. John Fischer, presented in vol. 5, 6.15). It would have been difficult for later writers to have retrojected these disputes into their earlier cultural setting.

The New Testament historical books also bear other marks of accurate and honest accounts, such as: (1) The preserving of examples of the disciples' spiritual dullness and even failure (see, e.g., Matt. 16:22–23; 17:16–20, 24–27; 26:69–75; 28:17; Mark 4:40; 6:52; 8:17–21; Luke 8:25; 9:33, 46–50; 24:9–12; John 20:24–25). This is quite significant, given the fact that these men became the leaders of the new spiritual community, with Peter at the forefront. Yet it is Peter who is repeatedly singled out for his rash words and actions, while the other disciples are often seen as immature or struggling in their faith. This stands in stark contrast to other religious literature, including the apocryphal gospel accounts that turned some of these leaders into supermen. Even the Book of Acts, which shows how God mightily used Saul of Tarsus (Paul), points to a dispute that arose between him and Barnabas, without it being resolved (Acts 15:36–41). This is not the kind of stuff of which late, falsified legends are made, ones which smooth over difficulties like this. (2) There are sayings of Jesus preserved which could be taken to mean that his return was expected within the lifetimes of his disciples (see below, 5.22). This, of course, is not an accurate reading of the texts, but it is highly unlikely that a later, believing author would create such sayings and put them on the lips of the Savior. The very fact that they are recorded lends credence to their authenticity. (3) Although many outstanding miracles are recorded in the Gospels and Acts, they are marked by sobriety and lack of sensationalism, especially when compared to the apocryphal gospels. As noted by J. N. D. Anderson:

> And who can read about the appearance to Mary Magdalene, or the incident where the risen Christ joined two disciples on an afternoon walk to Emmaus, or the time when Peter and John raced each other to the tomb—who can read these stories and really think they're legend? They are far too dignified and restrained; they are far too true to life and psychology. The difference between them and the sort of stories you find in the apocryphal gospels of but two or three centuries later is a difference between heaven and earth.[104]

(4) The apparent contradictions preserved within the Gospels indicate that later authors or editors did not try to smooth things out and produce an airtight, perfectly harmonious narrative. Rather, traditions

were accurately preserved and written down, giving evidence to the differing perspectives of several eyewitnesses telling the same story. (For an extremely minor example, see Matthew 17:1 [cf. Mark 9:2], "*After six days* Jesus took with him Peter, James and John the brother of James, and led them up a high mountain by themselves," and Luke 9:28, "*About eight days after* Jesus said this, he took Peter, John and James with him and went up onto a mountain to pray" [my emphasis in both]. Two people could easily describe the same event with these two time frames, and no one would think that their whole story was skewed because of the differences in expression.)[105] And the apparent contradictions in the Gospels are by no means insuperable, especially when compared to some apparent contradictions in the Tanakh (see the appendix in vol. 5, "Unequal Weights and Measures," for more on this). As noted by Blomberg:

> The student who takes the time to read any three reliable historians' accounts of other ancient figures or events will frequently find much more variation among them than he encounters in the Synoptics [meaning, Matthew, Mark, and Luke]. All these observations [summarizing his earlier findings] add up to a strong case for the historical accuracy of the first three gospels. Those who disagree may be invited to reconsider their methodology and to reflect on the possibility that they are treating the biblical documents more harshly than is warranted.[106]

One fifth-century follower of Yeshua pointed out that there is an amazing overall harmony which exists in the Gospel accounts of our Messiah. He stated that any apparent discrepancies which might be noticed could be explained only if we understood that each of the eyewitnesses was accurately reporting what he saw and heard. Thus, if we ourselves were there at the time the event occurred, we would see how perfectly all the pieces of the puzzle fit together to form one clear picture of the life and teaching of the Son of God. Therefore, rather than being evidence of poor memory and lies, the different perspectives of the various New Covenant authors help us realize just how accurate their accounts really were.

To summarize: Based on the internal evidence test, the New Testament scores very well once again, and those who put their trust in the veracity of its witness have every reason to feel secure.[107]

The external evidence test. Snow defines this third of his three tests for credibility as follows:

> The external evidence test checks the document's reliability by comparing it to other documents on the same subjects, seeing whether its statements

differ from theirs. Archeological evidence also figures into this test, since many Biblical sites and people can be confirmed by what archeologists have dug up in the Middle East and the Mediterranean Basin.[108]

It was this test that led to the transformation in the thinking of Sir William Ramsey, discussed above, who went from cynic to committed believer *based on archeological and historical evidence*. Because this has been treated at such length in other studies, I will only provide the smallest sampling of material, focusing on the medical doctor Luke, who was responsible for writing the Gospel account that bears his name along with the Book of Acts and is, therefore, the primary historian of the New Covenant Writings. As Eric Snow points out, other scholars have learned that "whenever Luke could be checked, he has repeatedly proven to be correct."[109]

"But," you say, "I've actually heard the opposite, specifically with regard to Luke. According to what I've read, Luke really messes things up badly, especially in the opening chapters of his book. In fact, when he talks about the birth of Jesus, he's got the Roman names and dates confused."

Actually, there are some critics who hold to this position, and liberal commentators have often stated this freely. A more careful investigation, however, yields different results. As an example, then, of how the external evidence test in no way disproves the New Testament writings, here are some specific details provided by F. F. Bruce that deal with the very objection you are raising:

The reference in Luke 2:2 to Quirinius as governor of Syria at the time of the birth of Christ (before the death of Herod the Great in 4 bc) has frequently been thought to be an error, because Quirinius is known to have become imperial legate of Syria in ad 6, and to have supervised in that year the enrolment mentioned in Acts 5:37, which provoked the insurrection led by Judas of Galilee. But it is now widely admitted that an earlier enrolment, as described in Luke 2:1 ff., (a) may have taken place in the reign of Herod the Great, (b) may have involved the return of everyone to his family home, (c) may have formed part of an Empire wide census, and (d) may have been held during a previous governorship of Quirinius over Syria.

(a) Josephus informs us that towards the end of Herod's reign (37–34 bc) the Emperor Augustus treated him "more as a subject than as a friend," and that all Judaea took an oath of allegiance to Augustus as well as to Herod. The holding of an imperial census in a client kingdom (as Judaea was during Herod's reign) is not unparalleled; in the reign of Tiberius a census was imposed on the client kingdom of Antiochus in eastern Asia Minor.

(b) The obligation on all persons to be enrolled at their domiciles of origin, which made it necessary for Joseph to return to Bethlehem, has been illustrated from an edict of AD 104, in which C. Vibius Maximus, Roman prefect of Egypt, gives notice as follows: "The enrolment by household being at hand, it is necessary to notify all who for any cause whatsoever are away from their administrative divisions to return home in order to comply with the customary ordinance of enrolment, and to remain in their own agricultural land."

(c) There is scattered evidence of the holding of enrolments in various parts of the Empire between 11 and 8 BC, the papyrus evidence in the case of Egypt being practically conclusive.

(d) There is good inscriptional evidence that when Quirinius took up office in Syria in AD 6 this was the second occasion on which he served as imperial legate. The first occasion was when he commanded an expedition against the Homanadensians, a mountain tribe of Asia Minor, some time between 12 and 6 BC. But our evidence does not state expressly in which province he was imperial legate at this earlier date. Sir William Ramsay argued that the province was Syria. We have, however, a continuous record of governors of Syria for those years, which leaves no room for Quirinius; Ramsay suggested that he was appointed as additional and extraordinary legate for military purposes. On the other hand, a good case has been made out for believing that his first term of office as imperial legate was passed in Galatia, not in Syria. The question is not yet finally decided, but it may be best to follow those commentators and grammarians who translate Luke ii. 2 as "This census was before that which Quirinius, governor of Syria, held."

Another supposed mistake has been detected by some in Luke iii. 1, where Lysanias is said to have been tetrarch of Abilene (west of Damascus) in the fifteenth year of Tiberius (AD 27–28), whereas the only Lysanias of Abilene otherwise known from ancient history bore the title of king and was executed by order of Mark Antony in 34 BC. Evidence of a later Lysanias who had the status of tetrarch has, however, been forthcoming from an inscription recording the dedication of a temple "for the salvation of the Lords Imperial and their whole household, by Nymphaeus, a freedman of Lysanias the tetrarch." The reference to "the Lords Imperial"—a joint title given only to the Emperor Tiberius and his mother Livia, the widow of Augustus—fixes the date of the inscription between AD 14 (the year of Tiberius' accession) and 29 (the year of Livia's death). On the strength of this and other evidence we may well be satisfied with the verdict of the historian Eduard Meyer, that Luke's reference to Lysanias is "entirely correct."[110]

Similar examples could be cited at length, but this much can be said for the external evidence test: In many cases, it has proved strong enough to convert skeptics; in all cases, it is strong enough to support the faith of a serious-minded, thinking believer.[111]

Before closing this section, which, again, is intended to be representative rather than comprehensive, we will examine briefly three charges often brought by Jews who do not believe in Yeshua: First, that the picture of Pontius Pilate is completely at odds with historical facts and that it has been falsified so as to make the Jews look like the killers of Christ. Second, in keeping with the theme of Jewish culpability, the New Testament writers went out of their way to make the Jews look bad by changing other key historical facts, seen even within the New Testament itself. Third, that the New Testament can make no claim to historical reliability in light of the many errors in Stephen's speech.

As for the first argument, Orthodox rabbi Shmuley Boteach, a prolific author, well-known media figure, and my debating opponent for several years, expressed this view with passion in one of our debates:

> Pontius Pilate, according to every modern and ancient historian, was the cruelest Proconsul the Romans ever put into Judea. . . . a man described by King Agrippa in a letter to the Emperor Caligula [as], "A man who harbors acts of violence, plunderings, abuses, provocations, corruption, continual murders of persons untried, uncondemned, never ending unbelievable cruelties gratuitous and most grievous inhumanity."
>
> Philo, one of the most important figures of the entire ancient world, speaking about Pilate says, "[He] was an unbending and recklessly hard character, famous for corruptibility, violence, robberies, ill treatment of the people, grievances, continued execution without any form of trial, endless and intolerable cruelties."
>
> . . . If you don't believe me about the nature of Pontius Pilate, read Luke 13:1, where it is related that Pilate massacred huge groups of Galileans who were worshiping in the Temple. Of course, Jesus was a Galilean.
>
> Read Josephus, who says that Pilate was so cruel that he had to be recalled by Rome in the year 36, because a Samaritan prophet had gained a large following and brought them up to a holy mountain, and Pilate slaughtered all 4,000 of them. Can you imagine how cruel you have to be for the ancient Romans to consider you cruel?[112]

Yet, according to the Gospels, he is seen as vacillating, wanting to let Jesus go free, being swayed by a dream from his wife in which she was convinced of Jesus' innocence, finally bowing to the will of the hostile Jewish crowd. (For a discussion of Matthew 27:25, see vol. 1, 154–56.) How should we respond to this apparent discrepancy?

In the just-cited excerpt from my debate with Rabbi Boteach, I responded as follows:

Let's take a moment and ask the question, Is the New Testament picture of Pilate accurate?

Never does the New Testament exonerate him. Acts 4[:27] plainly says that he was involved in Jesus' death. All of the early church creeds—they don't mention the Jews—they say "He suffered under Pontius Pilate." Paul, the alleged one that had all the stories wrong, he says again in 1 Timothy 6[:13] that Jesus stood firm before Pilate.

The picture of Pilate in the New Testament is tremendously accurate. What did we hear [from Rabbi Boteach]? We heard that [Pilate] hated the Jewish leadership, so the Jewish leadership says, "We want Jesus to be turned over to death." So what does Pilate do but oppose the leadership because he hates them—the very thing that you would expect him to do. This guy is so calloused that he says "go ahead and scourge him" even though he thought Jesus was innocent. Scourging would just about kill you. Pilate was convinced Jesus was innocent. His wife had a dream and got spooked and it spooked him. That can happen in a household—can't it? Pilate was dealing with the Son of God—he'd never met anyone like him.

Even though Pilate believed he was innocent, he still said to go ahead and crucify him. Not only so, but we know from the historical record that Pilate had different problems with the Jewish leadership because of his violence. There were several protests against him to Rome. The New Testament does not say he was moved with compassion, nor that he cared about Jesus. He was afraid there was going to be an uproar. He didn't want more trouble under his rule. Even Roman leaders were expected to keep the peace. It makes perfect sense. Some of the top New Testament scholars in the world, who have written massive volumes, going through in detail the accounts of the death of Jesus—say they are accurate and that the portrayal of Pilate is accurate. They also note that sometimes the more power someone has the more weak they are on the inside, and Jesus confronted that in Pilate, and he did not know how to handle it.[113]

Consider also the comments of D. A. Carson, from which I drew some of my thoughts:

Extrabiblical sources portray Pilate as a cruel, imperious, and insensitive ruler who hated his Jewish subjects and took few pains to understand them (e.g., Jos. Antiq. XVIII, 35 [ii.2], 55–62 [iii.12], 177–78 [vi.5]; War II, 169–77 [ix.2–4]; Philo, *ad Gaium* 38; cf. Hoehner, *Herod Antipas*, pp. 172–83). He stole korban (see on 15:5) money to build an aqueduct; and when the population of Jerusalem rioted in protest, he sent in soldiers who killed many. He defiled Jerusalem more than once (cf. Luke 13:1). These known facts about Pilate are often thought to render the Gospel accounts incredible, for here Pilate is portrayed as weak, ineffectual, and cowardly, judicially fair enough to want to release Jesus but too cowardly to stand up to the Sanhedrin's browbeating tactics. This transformation of Pilate's character, it is claimed, results from the evangelists' desire to exculpate the Romans and condemn the Jews.[114]

In defense of the biblical witness, he explains:

1. Modern psychology helps us understand that the weak, insecure, selfish man elevated to a position of authority may become despotic and insensitive. Thus the evidence about Pilate may be complementary rather than disjunctive.
2. Pilate hated the Jews and especially the Jewish leaders. In the crisis forced on him by the Sanhedrin, though he may have seemed to be *for* Jesus, in reality he was probably *against* the Sanhedrin. His final decision betrayed no trace of sympathy for the Sanhedrin; rather, the Jews' threat (John 19:12) could well have intimidated so corrupt a man at any point in his career.
3. Jesus was not the criminal or guerrilla fighter with which Pilate was familiar. Jesus' silence and poise, the wisdom of his brief answers, and the dreams of Pilate's wife ([Matt. 27:]19) may have prompted less drastic action than Pilate usually took.
4. Arguably, [Matthew 27:]24 does not exculpate Pilate or reserve exclusive blame for the Jews (see on vv. 24–25). Instead, as in v. 35, Matthew uses irony to say that no one connected with this crisis could escape personal responsibility.
5. Both the Sanhedrin trial and the trial before Pilate were necessary for capital punishment. Without the Sanhedrin, Pilate would never have taken action against Jesus unless he had become convinced Jesus was a dangerous Zealot leader; without Pilate the Sanhedrin might whip up mob violence against Jesus, but not a legally binding death sentence (cf. John 18:31).[115]

As to the charge that the New Testament writers reconstructed key events to make the Jews look bad—even murderous—I quote again from the pointed comments of Rabbi Boteach from our debate:

Just to show that there are major changes—this is just one famous example: 2 Corinthians [11:32–33], Paul himself writes, that when he was in Damascus, "the governor under King Aretas guarded the city of Damascus in order to seize me, but I was let down in a basket through a window in the wall, and I escaped his hand." So Paul says that the pagan king of Syria wanted him dead because he was subversive. Look at how the exact same story is retold in Acts 9:22–25. . . . "But Saul increased all the more in strength and confounded the Jews who lived in Damascus by proving that Jesus was the Christ. When many days had passed, the Jews plotted to kill him, but his disciples took him by night and let him down over the wall, lowering him in a basket." The original story by Paul is, the pagan king who is a vassal of Rome wants him dead. As soon as it is rewritten . . . it is the Jews who want him dead. Well surprise, surprise!

Then we have a similar story in Mark 12:28, where Jesus is teaching, and the Sadducees ask him a question. He gives a good response: "and one of the Scribes (Pharisees) came up and heard them disputing with one another, and seeing that Jesus answered them well" [it's a very positive story] "he said, 'Master, which commandment is the greatest of all?'" So Jesus said, "Love your God with all your heart and all your soul." And the Scribe said to him, "You are right, teacher. You have truly said that he is one and there is no other but he." It demonstrates a very warm relationship between Jesus and the Pharisees.

Jesus ends the exchange by saying, "You are not far from the Kingdom of Heaven."

Look at how the exact same exchange is retold in Matthew 22:33: "The crowd heard Jesus and they were astonished at his teaching. But when the Pharisees heard that he had silenced the Sadducees" [now it's already contentious] "they came together" [now they are plotting—the Pharisees were always plotting against Jesus] "and one of them, a lawyer, asked him a question to test him." It's the exact same story, but gone is the warm, friendly exchange. Now the Rabbis are in a debate, trying to prove that Jesus is an ignoramus.

This is clear-cut editing of earlier stories, especially because we know Mark was the first Gospel and Matthew came after. This is clear-cut editing just to make the Rabbis look bad.[116]

Regarding these last comments, what then is the explanation to Mark 3:6, which states that, after Jesus healed on the Sabbath and rebuked the religious leaders publicly, "Then the Pharisees went out and began to plot with the Herodians how they might kill Jesus"? It seems that Mark was quite aware of these conflicts too! See also Mark 7:1–13, which contains a very strong rebuke of the Pharisees; 8:11–12, which recounts an attempt by the Pharisees to test Jesus; 8:15, with a warning against the "yeast" of the Pharisees (and that of Herod); and 10:2–9, yet another account of the Pharisees trying to test Jesus. Matthew and Mark agree! (If you simply read the accounts in full in Mark 12 and Matthew 22, you will see that here too, they are in agreement, each one providing some additional, complimentary details, with Matthew simply emphasizing that this interaction did, in fact, take place in the midst of a somewhat hostile dialogue.)

What about the discrepancies between Acts 9:22–25 and 2 Corinthians 11:31–32? Do these point to an intentional rewriting of the accounts? Certainly not. First, Paul himself makes reference to conflicts he had with his own Jewish people in this very same chapter in 2 Corinthians, stating just a few verses earlier, "Five times I received from the Jews the forty lashes minus one" (11:24; see also 11:26, "in danger from my own countrymen"). He is hardly glossing over the persecution he endured from his people! For related statements in his writings, see especially 1 Thessalonians 2:14 (cf. vol. 1, 164–67, for more on this verse).

Why then didn't Paul implicate the Jewish opposition in 2 Corinthians 11:31–32, as Luke did? Could it be that Luke changed things? Actually, the two accounts work together perfectly well, with Acts 9 explaining 2 Corinthians 11. That is to say, there would have been little reason for King Aretas (and/or his governor) to have wanted to apprehend Paul if he had not been stirring up trouble of some kind. It would appear, then, that as his preaching stirred up heavy opposition from some of the Jews there, to the point of creating dissension, this came to the attention of the king and/or governor, who then wanted him arrested. At the same time, Luke records that the Jewish opposition wanted him dead and watched the gates carefully to guard against his escape, hence, his exit from the city with the help of a basket lowered through a break in the wall. Is this so hard to believe? Is this some kind of insuperable contradiction? Is this a major proof of later, anti-Jewish editing? I doubt it would hold much weight in a court of law.

On a separate note, I find it interesting that no one accuses the New Testament of being anti-Semitic when it speaks of Saul of Tarsus violently opposing the faith and persecuting followers of Jesus to their death, even though Saul was a Jew. Why then is it accused of being anti-Semitic when it states that *other Jews* wanted *Saul's* death once he became a believer? (For more on the question of anti-Semitism in the New Testament, see below, 5.20, and, more fully, vol. 1, 2.6–2.8.)

Finally, we turn to Stephen's speech before the Sanhedrin, one which is supposedly riddled with historical error. How could this be possible for this Jewish man who, according to Acts, was "full of faith and of the Holy Spirit" (Acts 6:5) and "full of God's grace and power" (6:8) and of whom it is recorded that the Jews who opposed him "could not stand up against his wisdom or the Spirit by whom he spoke" (6:10)?

Their answer is quite simple: First, some of the contradictions are only apparent such as Acts 7:14, where Stephen says, "Joseph sent for his father Jacob and his whole family, seventy-five in all," whereas "Genesis 46:27 (MT) sets the figure at seventy (i.e., sixty-six plus Jacob, Joseph, and the latter's two sons)."[117] This, however, presents no difficulty, and, as has often been pointed out, "Genesis 46:27 in the LXX, for example, does not include Jacob and Joseph but does include nine sons of Joseph in the reckoning, thereby arriving at 'seventy-five souls' all together who went down to Egypt. And with this number both Exodus 1:5 (LXX) and 4QExod^a at 1:5 agree."[118] So then, a Hebrew, biblical scroll from Qumran along with the LXX both counted the number at seventy-five rather than seventy, so Stephen was in good company with his figures here. This is hardly an error!

Second, as Orthodox Jewish professor James Kugel has noted, Stephen, in common with other contemporary Jews, was also drawing on a rich exegetical tradition that had been growing within his nation for several centuries, and some of that tradition is reflected in Stephen's comments;[119] and third, just because he was anointed and empowered by the Spirit did not mean that he was reciting history by infallible, divine inspiration! As one who holds to the inerrancy of Scripture, I believe that Luke accurately related what Stephen said, and that Luke's record was inspired by God and without error. But on what basis should I believe that Stephen got every detail right in his wide-ranging historical presentation, especially if some of the apparent contradictions seemingly reflect variant Jewish traditions? (To be sure, there are some scholars who argue that every apparent discrepancy can be fully resolved, but, as stated, I see no reason to argue for this here.)

Yes, it is true that Stephen's "face was like the face of an angel" (Acts 6:15) while he was speaking and that, before he was killed, it is recorded that he, "full of the Holy Spirit, looked up to heaven and saw the glory of God, and Jesus standing at the right hand of God" (7:55). But does this mean that he used perfect grammar when he spoke, or that when he quoted the Scriptures, he did not paraphrase the text? Of course not! Rather, it means that God was mightily with him as he called our people to account, pointing out our historic sins against the Spirit—with exactitude and precision—and calling our leadership to account for their rejection of the Messiah. The Spirit was backing that message, and if there were any errors in his presentation in terms of the details of some peripheral accounts—and again, this is debatable—it is remarkable that Acts records things just as he said them, without glossing over the difficulties. I challenge any critic to demonstrate that Stephen's speech had to be infallible in all historic details simply because he was a man anointed by God in his ministry.

I find it interesting that Kugel, formerly a professor at Yale but now teaching at the Orthodox Jewish Bar Ilan University in Israel, did not emphasize the apparent discrepancies in Stephen's account—and his purpose was decidedly *not* apologetic. Rather, he concluded that:

> Much more could be said about the exegetical background of this speech; indeed, a thorough treatment of the subject could, without exaggeration, fill a book. The angel who "spoke to [Moses] at Mount Sinai" (Acts 7.38 RSV),

"law as delivered by angels" (7.53 RSV), and a great many other of Stephen's exempla might likewise be shown to reflect other well-known exegetical motifs. [Kugel is speaking here of Jewish, exegetical motifs.][120]

To offer one specific example, Kugel treats Stephen's statement in 7:14–16 that is commonly cited as a clear error on his part. Again, there are those who claim that the error can be resolved, but Kugel is not one of them. Rather, he finds the larger issue raised by Stephen there to be grounded in contemporary Jewish traditions:

> All this is to say that, in however garbled a form, the references in Acts 7:14–16 to the removal of Jacob and "our fathers" reflects a substantial body of already existing extrabiblical material. "Our fathers" refers specifically to Joseph's brothers, whose bodies were removed before his but sometime after the transfer of Jacob's last remains to Hebron. Indeed, it is certainly significant that the same phrase, "our fathers," occurs in the first Qumran document cited above [namely, 4Q545 *Visions of Amram*], apparently in the same sense.[121]

Thus, even in Stephen's often-criticized speech, there is more going on than meets the eye, and that based on ancient *Jewish* interpretive traditions.

To return, then, to the larger objection, namely, that the New Testament is full of historical inaccuracies, those who put their trust in its record can rest assured that this is not the case, while those who are still questioning will find plenty of additional, confidence-building evidence in the works cited in this section.

The bottom line is this: Some of the greatest minds this world has ever seen have devoted their entire lives to the careful study of the New Testament text and some of history's greatest skeptics have attacked it. There is nothing new that today's critics will discover. The New Covenant has endured the test of time. It continues to be worthy of our faith.

5.7. None of the important historical writers of the period—Roman or Jewish—make mention of Jesus. It's questionable whether he even existed.

No reputable scholar in the world denies that Jesus existed. You might as well as deny the existence of George Washington or Julius Caesar. As for Roman and Jewish historians, there are important ancient testimonies from key authors who write of Jesus as well as his early followers. You might also be surprised to know that almost all of these sources tell us more about Jesus than they do about any contemporary Rabbinic leaders. Does this mean that these famous rabbis never existed?

Yohanan ben Zakkai was one of the key leaders of the early Rabbinic movement, and, without a doubt, one of the greatest of the Tannaim.[122] In fact, Rabbinic tradition recognizes him as the successor of Hillel, who declared that he was "the father of wisdom" and "the father of coming generations" (y. Nedarim v., end, 39b). According to a famous account preserved in the Talmudic writings (see b. Gittin 56b; cf. also Lamentations Rabbah i. 5; Avot de Rabbi Nathan iv.), during the Jewish war with Rome in 67–70 C.E., after his calls for his countrymen to surrender were not heeded, he was smuggled out of Jerusalem in a casket. He was then brought to Roman leadership who allowed him to make a new start in Yavneh, thereby laying the foundations of Rabbinic Judaism. Not surprisingly, Rabbinic literature has much to say about this influential leader, who according to the *Jewish Encyclopedia*, "felt the fall of his people more deeply than any one else, but—and in this lies his historical importance—he did more than any one else to prepare the way for Israel to rise again."[123]

Interestingly, not a word is spoken about him in any external sources—neither Jewish nor Roman. The primary Jewish historian of the day, Flavius Josephus, himself a Pharisee, does not mention Rabbi Yohanan, despite providing the most detailed account of the Jewish war and the fall of Jerusalem. If anyone should have written about him, it is Josephus, but he did not. And there is a not a single Roman source that corroborates the Rabbinic accounts about this highly esteemed rabbi, despite the Talmudic claim that he, like Josephus, prophesied that Vespasian would become emperor and that the Romans would defeat the Jews, and that he received permission from Vespasian himself to establish an academy in Yavneh upon fulfillment of his predictions. Despite this, not a Roman historian mentions him.

Should we therefore claim that Yohanan ben Zakkai did not exist? How absurd! All the more absurd is it to claim that Jesus did not exist, especially in light of the historical evidence that explicitly speaks of him.[124] Since numerous scholarly monographs have been written on this subject, showing clearly that Jesus was written about by key historians in the ancient world, both Gentile and Jewish, I will only summarize the evidence here:[125]

From the classical writings (those of the ancient Greek and Latin writers), we have the following attestations:

- Later writers report that the Greek historian Thallus, who wrote in approximately 55 C.E., claimed that the darkness at the time of Jesus' crucifixion was caused by a solar eclipse.[126]
- Pliny the Younger (ca. 61–113 C.E.), both a senator and prominent lawyer in Rome who adjudicated the trials of many Christians, sending some to their execution, began to have doubts about the whole process, asking counsel from the emperor Trajan. In Letter 96 of Book 10 of his writings, he speaks of false Christians who willingly "reviled Christ" and others who admitted to having gathered for early morning worship and singing "a hymn to Christ as if to a god."[127]
- Suetonius, whose full name was Gaius Suetonius Tranquillus (ca. 70–ca. 140 C.E.) was a Roman writer and lawyer. In his book *The Deified Claudius*, he writes that, "[Claudius] expelled the Jews from Rome, since they were always making disturbances because of the instigator Chrestus."[128] Obviously, to Suetonius, "Christos" in Greek was a name of no significance, and he mistakenly understood it to be "Chrestos."[129]
- Cornelius Tacitus, the greatest of the Roman historians (ca. 56–120 C.E.?) made specific reference to Jesus in his *Annals*, the last of his historical works. In describing the great fire that ravaged Rome in 64 C.E., he had occasion to refer to people "whom the crowd called 'Chrestians'"—an obvious misunderstanding of the name "Christians" by the crowd—then explaining, "The founder of this name, Christ, had been executed in the reign of Tiberius by the procurator Pontius Pilate."[130]
- Other less important classical writers also speak of the historical Jesus, including Mara bar Serapion, writing sometime after 73 C.E., who speaks of Jesus as the "wise king" of the Jews;[131] Lucian of Samosata (ca. 115–ca. 200 C.E.), who writes of "that one whom they still worship today, the man in Palestine who was crucified because he brought this new form of initiation into the world," also referring to him as "that crucified sophist";[132] and Celsus, writing after 175 C.E., whose work attacking Christianity was largely preserved in Origen's famous *Contra Celsum*, and who speaks of Jesus as a magician.[133]

As summarized by professor Robert E. Van Voorst:

First, we note a significant variety of witnesses to Jesus in classical authors. The famous Roman writers on history and imperial affairs have taken pride of place: Suetonius, Tacitus, and Pliny the Younger. On the other end of the spectrum, the comparatively unknown writers Mara and Thallos have also contributed their voices. Philosophic opponents to Christianity such as Lucian and Celsus have also written about Christ. These writers have a range of opinion: from those perhaps sympathetic to Christ (Mara); through those moderately hostile (Pliny) and those fully hostile but descriptive (Tacitus, Suetonius); to those not interested in description, but who vigorously attack Christianity and in the process attack Christ (Lucian and Celsus). A variety of languages is also notable: Latin, the official language of Rome; Greek, both a common literary language and the language of trade; and Syriac, a main language of the eastern Mediterranean. Together, they speak of a variety of topics about Jesus' teachings, movement, and death. And they know that Jesus is worshiped by Christians, which they relate to his founding of a movement.[134]

This is certainly an adequate body of testimony.

As to the question of why there are not even *more* references to Jesus in the classical writings, Van Voorst suggests that for the Roman historians, "Christ" did not become much of an issue to them until Christianity became more of a pressing concern. As to why there were not more *contemporary* references to Jesus in the classical authors, Van Voorst points to several factors: First, the works of most of the classical historians contemporary with Jesus "have almost completely perished."[135] Second, "historical interpretation of events was not the 'instant analysis' we have become accustomed to, for better or worse, in modern times."[136] In other words, these writers were historians, not news reporters, and the more prominent the author, the more reluctant was he to be the first to recount the historical events. Rather, he preferred to look back at the reports of lesser historians and then to write a more major history. Third, "Roman writers seem to have considered Christianity an important topic only when it became a perceived threat to Rome."[137] Fourth, "Romans had little interest in the historical origins of other groups, especially 'superstitions,'" and for these Roman writers, Christianity to them was just another Eastern superstition.[138] In any case, what *should* be stressed is that a number of key classical writers, in a fairly consistent way, attest to a man known as Christ who lived and died in Palestine and who founded a whole new religious movement.

In Jewish literature, it is well known that Josephus wrote about John the Immerser, Jesus, and Jacob (James) the brother of Jesus. It is equally well known, however, that virtually all extant manuscripts of the relevant portions of his writings contain later, Christian interpolations.

The question is: Are these reports total and complete forgeries, or are they embellishments of the actual words of Josephus? The scholarly consensus, both Jewish and Christian, points to the latter, recognizing that Josephus did, in fact, have something to say about Jesus. The statements largely recognized as authentic are found in his *Antiquities* 20.9.1 §200, where he speaks of the high priest Annas bringing Jacob (James), whom he calls "the brother of Jesus called Christ,"[139] before the Sanhedrin, and, more significantly, in *Antiquities* 18.3.3 §63–64, where, in all extant manuscripts, he speaks about Jesus at length, and with some level of admiration. According to what has been called the neutral reconstruction of the text, the passage, now greatly abbreviated from its later form, reads:

> Around this time lived Jesus, a wise man. For he was a worker of amazing deeds and was a teacher of the people who gladly accept the truth. He won over both many Jews and many Greeks. Pilate, when he heard him accused by the leading men among us, condemned him to the cross, [but] those who had first loved him did not cease [doing so]. To this day the tribe of Christians named after him has not disappeared.[140]

A Slavonic manuscript of Josephus also has him referring to Jesus in his *Jewish War* 5.5.4 §214; *Jewish War* 5.5.2 §195; and *Jewish War* 6.5.4, replacing §313, but these are generally recognized as interpolations.[141] As for the lengthier statement just quoted, the question is not whether Josephus wrote about Jesus; the question is how much he wrote. Regardless of how that question is answered, the fact remains that the most important Jewish historian of the first century of this era did write about Jesus.[142]

As for the Rabbinic writings, there are numerous *possible* references to Jesus, under the name of Balaam, Ben Stada, or "a certain one," but there is dispute about whether they really do refer to him (see, e.g., b. Shabbat 104b; t. Shabbat 11:15; b. Sanhedrin 67; t. Sanhedrin 7:16; m. Sanhedrin 10:2; m. Abot 5:19; b. Gittin 56b–57a; b. Sanhedrin 106b; m. Yebamot 4:13; b. Yoma 66d; t. Yebamot 3:3–4; b. Sanhedrin 106a; b. Hagigah 4b; note that a good number of scholars, including traditional Jews, do believe that many—or even most—of these passages do refer to Jesus, and that in extremely negative and derogatory terms).[143] There are also clear references to a certain "Yeshu,"[144] but either the Talmud has its chronology totally amiss, placing him in different centuries more than a hundred years apart (see b. Sanhedrin 107b; b. Sotah 47a, placing him during the time of King Jannaeus, who died in 76 B.C.E.; note also y. Hagigah 2:2; y. Sanhedrin 23c), or else at least one of the references does not speak of Jesus (it is, however, possible, that the Talmudic editors did, in fact, make such a chronological error). In these various accounts, Jesus is seen, among other things, as a deceiver, idolater, and apostate, but, to repeat, it is uncertain as to how many of these texts, if any, intended to speak of Jesus of Nazareth.

Having said this, there are some definite references to Jesus in the Talmud (always spelled Yeshu), most prominently the following account:

> "On the eve of Passover they hanged Jesus [Yeshu] the Nazarene. And a herald went out before him for forty days, saying, 'He is going to be stoned, because he practiced sorcery and led Israel astray. Anyone who knows anything in his favor, let him come and plead in his behalf.' But, not having found anything in his favor, they hanged him on the eve of Passover" (b. Sanh. 43a; t. Sanh. 10:11; y. Sanh. 7:16, 67a).[145]

This same passage from b. Sanh 43a also states that "Jesus practiced magic and led Israel astray" (b. Sanh 43a; cf. t. Shabbat 11:15; b. Shabbat 104b), making reference to five of his disciples, although only some of their names agree with their New Testament counterparts, pointing to the Talmud's vague and largely erroneous recollection of the details surrounding the life and death of Jesus. There is also a negative reference to "Jesus of Nazareth" in b. Sanh 103a; cf. b. Berakhot 17b) and there are negative references to some of his followers in the early Tannaitic literature, notably as having the power to heal, but that is not germane to the question at hand (see, e.g., t. Hul 2:22–23).[146]

Also of significance to traditional Jews, despite its late date, is the testimony of Moses Maimonides (1135–1204). In its original form (before being edited because of Catholic Church censors), Maimonides, in his law code, speaks of "Jesus of Nazareth who aspired to be the Messiah and was executed by the court," going on to explain why he could not be the Messiah but how, despite the false nature of their teachings, Christianity and Islam would still help prepare the world for the knowledge of the one true God (Hilchot Melachim 11:4).

For a religious Jew, this settles the question, since both the Talmud and Maimonides state clearly that Jesus lived and was put to death.[147] In fact, for a traditional Jew the *existence* of Jesus has never been questioned. Rather, the question has been, Who is he, really? And that question remains relevant for each and every reader, both Jewish and Gentile: Do you know for sure who he is?

Here is something worth considering. According to Isaiah 53:2, the origins of the Messiah, called in this passage the servant of the Lord (see vol. 3, 4.5–4.17), are described in the most humble terms:

He grew up before him like a tender shoot,
and like a root out of dry ground.
He had no beauty or majesty to attract us to him,
nothing in his appearance that we should desire him.

The passage then goes on to speak of his rejection, suffering, and death, before pointing to his resurrection and ending with this divine promise in 53:12:

Therefore I will give him a portion among the great,
and he will divide the spoils with the strong,
because he poured out his life unto death,
and was numbered with the transgressors.
For he bore the sin of many,
and made intercession for the transgressors.

Do you realize that this is exactly what has happened, not just in terms of Yeshua's life on earth, which began in total obscurity, seeing that the Son of God was born in a stable and grew up as a carpenter's son, but in terms of the larger picture of the development of his Messianic movement? That too started in obscurity as far as the Roman world was concerned, being ignored rather than revered and receiving scorn rather than admiration, while his followers were often mocked, imprisoned, and killed. How could this man and this movement impact the world?

Amazingly, as an extraordinary testimony to the power of Yeshua's life, death, and resurrection, his movement continues to impact the world—quite impressively—to this very hour. The one whom a modern historian could characterize as "a marginal Jew"[148]—in terms of his earthly life—has become the most influential figure in human history, as captured in these well-known words that describe this "one solitary life."

Here is a man who was born in an obscure village, the child of a peasant woman. He grew up in another village. He worked in a carpenter shop until He was thirty. Then for three years He was an itinerant preacher.

He never owned a home. He never wrote a book. He never held an office. He never had a family. He never went to college. He never put His foot inside a big city. He never traveled two hundred miles from the place He was born. He never did one of the things that usually accompany greatness. He had no credentials but Himself. . . .

While still a young man, the tide of popular opinion turned against him. His friends ran away. One of them denied Him. He was turned over to His enemies. He went through the mockery of a trial. He was nailed upon a cross between two thieves. While He was dying His executioners gambled for the only piece of property He had on earth—His coat. When He was dead, He was laid in a borrowed grave through the pity of a friend.

Nineteen long centuries have come and gone, and today He is a centerpiece of the human race and leader of the column of progress.

I am far within the mark when I say that all the armies that ever marched, all the navies that were ever built; all the parliaments that ever sat and all the kings that ever reigned, put together, have not affected the life of man upon this earth as powerfully as has that one solitary life.[149]

With this, I rest my case.

5.8. Modern scholars are in complete agreement that the Gospels portray a mythical Jesus. There is very little that we can really know about his life.

> The real myth is that we cannot know anything certain about the life of Jesus! The issue is one of presuppositions. Those scholars who are skeptical about knowing anything certain about the life of Jesus presuppose that the Gospel accounts are not reliable, just as they presuppose that the accounts in the Hebrew Bible about Abraham, Moses, or David are not reliable. The same scholars who deny the resurrection of Jesus also deny the exodus from Egypt. In any case, a strong case can actually be made for the historical reliability of the New Testament accounts.

This objection, along with several others addressed in this section, is not specifically Jewish and has been treated at length in other books and monographs, so we will not treat it at length here. For a more full response to the related criticism that the New Testament writings are not historically accurate, see above, 5.6; for refutation of the idea that there is no historical support for the existence of Jesus in sources outside of the New Testament, see 5.7. Those wishing to pursue this matter further will profit from the writings of the following scholars: Craig Blomberg, *The Historical Reliability of the Gospels* (see above, 5.6); Michael J. Wilkins and J. P. Moreland, eds., *Jesus Under Fire: Modern Scholarship Reinvents the Historical Jesus* (Grand Rapids: Zondervan, 1996); Luke Timothy Johnson, *The Real Jesus: The Misguided Quest for the Historical Jesus and the Truth of the Traditional Gospels* (San Francisco: HarperSanFrancisco, 1997); Ben Witherington, *The Jesus Quest: The Third Search for the Jew from Nazareth* (Downers Grove, IL:

InterVarsity, 1997); N. T. Wright, *The Challenge of Jesus: Rediscovering Who Jesus Was and Is* (Downers Grove, IL: InterVarsity, 1999). For a debate between a leading critical scholar and a leading conservative scholar, see Paul Copan, ed., *Will the Real Jesus Please Stand Up? A Debate Between William Lane Craig and John Dominic Crossan* (Grand Rapids: Baker, 1998). For a useful compendium of essays on all sides of the debate, see James D. G. Dunn and Scot McKnight, eds., *The Historical Jesus in Recent Research* (Winona Lake, IN: Eisenbrauns, 2005).

For those who are unfamiliar with the debate in question, I will offer some food for thought. First, for the most part, Jewish scholars dealing with the Gospels, as compared to liberal scholars, are far more inclined to take the historical accounts there seriously. For further discussion of this, see below, 5.26. Second, to a great extent, the whole debate is a matter of presuppositions. In other words, with rare exception, scholars who claim that the Gospels are unreliable in their portrayal of Jesus are those who come *predisposed* to that point of view or who studied under professors who were so inclined. Thus it is no coincidence that most of the scholars in the well-known Jesus Seminar were trained by a small group of liberal scholars sharing the same nihilistic views. Little wonder that their conclusions were also nihilistic. As Luke Timothy Johnson noted,

> What becomes clear from scanning the academic training of the participants [of the Jesus Seminar] is that they overwhelmingly come from a cluster of graduate programs in New Testament that have in recent decades championed the sort of methodological and ideological stances reflected in the Seminar's work. Forty of the seventy-four fellows listed by the *Five Gospels* [one of the major publications of the Jesus Seminar] received their doctorates from five schools: fourteen from Claremont, nine from Vanderbilt, eight from Harvard, five from Chicago, and four from Union Theological Seminary.[150]

Again, little wonder that they came to such skeptical conclusions, most famously, concluding by vote that Jesus only said 18 percent of what the Gospels attributed to him! As Johnson pointed out, "Like a great deal of Gospel criticism, [the Seminar] began with the assumption that the Gospels are not accurate histories but are narratives constructed out of traditional materials with literary art and theological motives."[151]

Taking this even further, Johnson notes that there is an agenda behind the work of the Jesus Seminar and, in particular, professor Robert Funk, who has led the Seminar since its inception:

The Seminar has, to a great extent, carried out the agenda set for it by Funk's keynote address at the first meeting in 1985, as reported in the Seminar's publication *Forum* 1/1 (1985) under the title "The Issue of Jesus." Funk there begins with a complaint against the established church: "The religious establishment has not allowed the intelligence of high scholarship to pass through pastors and priests to a hungry laity" (p. 8). More specifically, he objects to the way television evangelists have "preyed on the ignorance of the uninformed." He sees the work of the Seminar, therefore, as spelling "liberty for . . . millions."[152]

With an agenda like this, where is the objective scholarship? Johnson's critique, then, is certainly deserved:

> From the start, then, we see that the agenda for the Seminar is not disinterested scholarship, but a social mission against the way the church controls the Bible, and the way in which the church is dominated by a form of evangelical and eschatological theology—that is, a theology focused on both the literal truth of the Gospels and the literal return of Jesus—that Funk finds intolerable. It is important to note from the start that Funk does not conceive of the Seminar's work as making a contribution to scholarship but as carrying out a cultural mission.[153]

And it is the Jesus Seminar, due to its popularity and public presence, that has put forth the idea that the Jesus of the Gospels is mythical.[154] To repeat: So much for objective scholarship!

Third, the same scholarly assumptions that call into question the veracity of the New Testament witness also call into question—more radically still—the veracity of the Hebrew Scriptures, rejecting many (if not most) of the pivotal events recorded there as myths and fables. Again, this is largely a matter of presuppositions and methodology, and skeptical scholars tend to find ample confirmation for their skepticism while conservative scholars tend to find ample confirmation for their conservatism. How true it is that you will find what you are looking for! A key difference, however, is pointed out by Blomberg, who asks, "If the trustworthiness of the gospels represents a verdict which careful historical analysis can yield regardless of the confessional perspectives, why do so many still resist this conclusion?"[155] In other words, if the application of sound and scientific historical methodology results in positive conclusions as to the historicity of the Gospels, regardless of one's presuppositions or beliefs, why aren't critical scholars more willing to accept this?

Blomberg addresses this head on, noting that, on both sides of the debate, there are presuppositions:

Too often conservatives summarily dismiss skeptical studies as merely developing the logical inferences of invalid assumptions. To be sure, this allegation has some force, but few works are so consistently deductive that they contain no discussion of hard data for others to take the time to sift through. Similarly, more radical critics regularly charge conservatives with concluding only what their beliefs about Jesus and the Bible already permit. This charge is also occasionally valid. . . . The crucial difference, however, is that this research [referring to the research underlying his book] has self-consciously tried to avoid presupposing the infallibility of Scripture or the deity of Christ, but has merely attempted to follow the standard methods of historical enquiry. It derives from a willingness to consider the possibility that these traditional beliefs might have to be abandoned if historical investigation were to demonstrate them to be unwarranted. No such demonstration has yet appeared. On the other hand, the critical scholarship which has abandoned these very beliefs virtually never considers where its investigations might lead if it questioned *its* starting-point and took seriously the possibility of the divine origin of Scripture and of Jesus.[156]

So then, while conservative scholars are often willing to look at both sides of the debate and consider the possibility of the negative and positive evidence, realizing the high stakes involved if the negative position proved true, liberal scholars generally do not even consider the possibility that God inspired the writing of the Gospels and that their depiction of Yeshua is accurate in full.

Of course, it is impossible to *prove* to a skeptical reader that the Gospel's depiction of Jesus is accurate, just as it is impossible to *prove* to a skeptical reader that God spoke to Israel on Mount Sinai (for discussion of this event and its implications, see vol. 5, 6.11). This much, however, can be offered to the serious seeker: (1) The Gospels are presented as historical accounts, replete with historical and cultural detail, inviting honest investigation. (2) The more archeological evidence that is discovered, the more confirmation these accounts receive, and to the extent that the Gospels can be placed against the cultural background of the day—especially the Jewish background—the more they ring true. (3) These accounts were largely written by eyewitnesses, some of whom gave their lives for their Messiah or, at the least, suffered serious persecution and hardship for their beliefs. How many willful concocters of myths are then willing to suffer and die for the myths they created? (4) The movement that Jesus began continues to this day, growing at a faster rate than at any time in history (see vol. 1, 91–93), and the vast majority of these new adherents to the faith hold to the truth of the Gospel accounts, having experienced the atoning power of Jesus' death and the reality of his resurrection and ongoing life. While all these people could merely be dismissed as religious fanatics or, less disparagingly, as naïve and misled sheep, it is also possible that their beliefs are true, *confirming* what is written in the Gospels. That is to say, they are living witnesses of the fact that "Jesus Christ is the same yesterday and today and forever" (Heb. 13:8).

If you are truly open-minded and in search of the truth, this is a possibility that you do not want to exclude, and the monographs cited at the beginning of this response will help you sort through the issues involved. I would also encourage you to read the Gospels for yourself, carefully and prayerfully, asking God to show you the truth, keeping an open heart and an inquisitive mind. Many of those who are staunch defenders of the faith started in this very place of open and honest searching. Jeremiah 29:13, spoken to the Jewish people long ago, remains true to this day.[157]

5.9. Jesus was not born of a virgin. In fact, we have traditions that actually tell us who Jesus' real father was—and it wasn't Joseph! Anyway, the idea of a god being born to a virgin is just one of several pagan myths that made its way into the New Testament.

> The fact of the virgin birth was something that made the ministry of Jesus harder, not easier. You try telling someone that your Master and Teacher was born of a virgin! Almost everyone thought that Joseph was his real father, and it was known that Joseph was a descendant of David, something which could have only helped, not hurt, Jesus' cause. If not for the virgin birth being a fact—and one which was also foreshadowed in the Hebrew Scriptures—the New Testament writers would have never created such a story. As for the virgin birth being a borrowed pagan myth, could you tell me which pagan myth you are referring to? There is none!

Let's get away from the Bible for a moment and think about this whole subject in contemporary, real-life terms. Let's say that you were a chaste young man engaged to be married to a lovely young woman. Both of you were virgins, committed to having no sexual relations until your wedding night. One day your fiancée comes to you and says, "I'm pregnant—but I haven't slept with anybody. I'm still a virgin! Trust me. An angel appeared to me in a vision and told me that I would become pregnant by the Holy Spirit and give birth to the Messiah." What would you say? Probably something like, "Right, and my name is Santa Claus and my pet dog is actually a reindeer." Such a reaction would be perfectly understandable!

Now, take a look at this New Testament account which I cite here to underscore the fact that the concept of a virgin birth was hardly an easy pill to swallow:

> Here is how the birth of Yeshua the Messiah took place. When his mother Miryam was engaged to Yosef, before they were married, she was found to be pregnant from the *Ruach-HaKodesh* [the Holy Spirit]. Her husband-to-be, Yosef, was a man who did what was right; so he made plans to break the engagement quietly, rather than put her to public shame. But while he was thinking about this, an angel of *Adonai* [the Lord] appeared to him in a dream and said, "Yosef, son of David, do not be afraid to take Miryam home as your wife; for what has been conceived in her is from the *Ruach-HaKodesh*. She will give birth to a son, and you are to name him Yeshua, [which means '*Adonai* saves',] because he will save his people from their sins." . . .
>
> When Yosef awoke he did what the angel of *Adonai* had told him to do—he took Miryam home to be his wife, but he did not have sexual relations with her until she had given birth to a son, and he named him Yeshua.
>
> Matthew 1:18–21, 24–25 JNT

The virginal conception of the Messiah came as quite a shock to Miriam and Joseph. And after their marriage, Joseph still had no relations with Miriam until after Jesus was born—not the easiest thing for a newly married couple. But these were sacred, supernatural times.

You might be saying to yourself, "Look, the fact is that there was no way to prove that she was a virgin. Maybe Joseph's dream was just an example of wishful thinking on his part." That's an interesting idea, but it's not accurate. According to the Torah, there *was* a way to prove one's virginity. The Book of Deuteronomy states:

> If a man takes a wife and, after lying with her, dislikes her and slanders her and gives her a bad name, saying, "I married this woman, but when I approached her, I did not find proof of her virginity," then the girl's father and mother shall bring proof that she was a virgin to the town elders at the gate. The girl's father will say to the elders, "I gave my daughter in marriage to this man, but he dislikes her. Now he has slandered her and

said, 'I did not find your daughter to be a virgin.' But here is the proof of my daughter's virginity." Then her parents shall display the cloth before the elders of the town, and the elders shall take the man and punish him. They shall fine him a hundred shekels of silver and give them to the girl's father, because this man has given an Israelite virgin a bad name. She shall continue to be his wife; he must not divorce her as long as he lives.

If, however, the charge is true and no proof of the girl's virginity can be found, she shall be brought to the door of her father's house and there the men of her town shall stone her to death. She has done a disgraceful thing in Israel by being promiscuous while still in her father's house. You must purge the evil from among you.

Deuteronomy 22:13–21[158]

So, if Joseph doubted his wife's account, even after the dream, he could have simply gone ahead immediately with the marriage (which, in fact, he did), slept with Miriam, and then checked to see whether she had bled.[159] After all, if she had slept with another man, she would have been guilty of a terrible sin, and there is no way in the world that Joseph would have wanted to go ahead with the marriage. This was not modern America, after all! It would have been unthinkable for a godly man like Joseph to have married a nonvirgin. (In today's terms, think of how you would feel if your son—your wonderful, dear son—came home and told you he was going to marry a stripper who had already been married and divorced five times and who was currently pregnant with the child of another man.)

But there was no reason for Joseph to have any doubts. God abundantly confirmed the supernatural character of the child who was born to them, both in his infancy (to the continued amazement and awe of Joseph and Miriam), then at age twelve, then throughout his public ministry, culminating with his resurrection from the dead. (For the early years, see Matt. 2:1–11; Luke 1:39–55; 2:8–51.) There was no reason for Yeshua's mother or father or any of his disciples to question his virgin birth in the least, while there were plenty of reasons to believe it without doubt.[160] It explained how the Son of God could be born into the world and yet still be fully human as well. (See vol. 2, 3.1–3.4 for the Messiah's divine nature; for the virgin birth being foreshadowed in the Hebrew Bible, see vol. 3, 4.3.)

Of course, you still might say, "Maybe this whole virgin birth story was just a cover-up for adultery. Who knows what rumors were circulating?" Actually, we *do* know one of the most common rumors that circulated: "This man is just the son of Joseph the carpenter. Who does he think he is? He's just a regular, neighborhood guy like us, and we know his whole family!" *That* is what the people were saying:

> "Isn't this the carpenter's son? Isn't his mother called Miryam? and his brothers Ya'akov, Yosef, Shim'on and Y'hudah? And his sisters, aren't they all with us? So where does he get all this?" And they took offense at him. But Yeshua said to them, "The only place people don't respect a prophet is his home town and in his own house."
>
> Matthew 13:55–57 JNT

> All spoke well of him and were amazed at the gracious words that came from his lips. "Isn't this Joseph's son?" they asked.
>
> Luke 4:22

> Philip found Nathanael and told him, "We have found the one Moses wrote about in the Law, and about whom the prophets also wrote—Jesus of Nazareth, the son of Joseph."
> "Nazareth! Can anything good come from there?" Nathanael asked.
> "Come and see," said Philip.
>
> John 1:45–46

> At this the Jews began to grumble about him because he said, "I am the bread that came down from heaven." They said, "Is this not Jesus, the son of Joseph, whose father and mother we know? How can he now say, 'I came down from heaven'?"
>
> John 6:41–42

The fact is, the primary reason that some later, Jewish traditions began to circulate the scurrilous myth that Miriam committed adultery with a Roman soldier[161] was *because* of the virgin birth account in the Gospels. In other words, because the New Testament taught that Joseph was *not* the real father of Jesus, later protagonists seized upon this and tried to turn it into a mockery. The only hint of this within the Gospel accounts themselves is found in John 8:41, based on which Bruce Chilton wrote, "The charge that he was illicitly conceived plagued Jesus all his life. Even far from his home, during disputes in Jerusalem after he had become a famous teacher, Jesus was mocked for being born as the result of fornication (John 8:41). The people of his own village called him 'Mary's son,' not Joseph's (Mark 6:3)."[162] While this is somewhat of an overstatement—seeing that it overlooks the bulk of the New Testament evidence—it underscores the fact that the virgin birth is hardly the kind of story you would want to make up! Of course, this does not conclusively prove the truthfulness of the Gospel accounts, but it remind us again that the virgin birth account is hardly something that the Messiah's followers would choose to invent.

What of the question of the New Testament borrowing a pagan myth here? First, it is interesting to note that in all the major cults and world religions that have arisen in the last 1,900 years, I am not aware of any of them which claim that their founder or leader was born of a virgin. This is quite important, since many of the cults and false religions try to pattern themselves after the Bible, using Scripture to disguise their new, twisted beliefs. Thus, modern cults use terms such as "Christ-consciousness" and "new birth," often claiming that their leaders are a new incarnation of Jesus or are a manifestation of God in the flesh. Yet none of them claim that their "anointed" leader was born of a virgin! And, unfortunately for the cults, while some of their founders were expected to rise from the dead, none of them ever succeeded. In reality, none of these deluded men or women resembled Jesus in any way, shape, size, or form.[163] And while they were foolish enough to think they could even rise from the dead—that's pretty foolish!—they were not foolish enough to claim that they were virgin born. This should make you think again before skeptically rejecting the New Testament account.

Second, the whole notion of a pagan myth being borrowed is not accurate. Simply stated, there are no pagan or Jewish parallels to such a virginal conception. As documented in the massive, technical commentary on Matthew by W. D. Davies and Dale C. Allison Jr., "Conception without a male element in some form, parthenogenesis in the strict sense, does not seem to be attested. . . . None of the proposed parallels, either pagan or Jewish, seemingly accounts for the story we find in the NT."[164] While there are myths about gods or angels taking on human form and having sex with a woman, who then conceives, none of these resembles the Gospel accounts in the slightest.[165] As Keener emphasizes,

> Yet most alleged parallels to the virgin birth (see Allen 1977: 19; Soares Prabhu 1976: 5–6; cf. Grant 1986: 64) are hopelessly distant, at best representing supernatural births of some kind (Barrett 1966: 6–10; Davies and Allison 1988: 214–15; Hagner 1993: 17; even further are ancient biological views, e.g., *Arist. Generation of Animals* 3.6.5; *Ep. Arist.* 165). Certainly pagan stories of divine impregnation, which typically involve seduction (e.g., *Ovid Metam.* 3.260–61) or rape (*Ovid Metam.* 3.1–2) bear no resemblance to a virgin birth.[166]

As for such crude, "parallel" accounts, the fact is that you have rough, pagan "parallels" to the biblical creation account, the biblical flood account, and even the account of baby Moses in the Nile River, some of which provide closer parallels to the biblical accounts than the alleged parallels to the Messiah's virgin birth. The "parallel" stories only make the biblical accounts shine all the more brightly.[167]

According to professor Raymond Brown, one of the world's leading New Testament scholars and a man who is by no means a fundamentalist believer,

> it is difficult to explain how the idea [of the virgin birth] arose if not from fact. Many parallels for a virginal conception have been suggested from world religions, from paganism, and from pre-Christian Judaism; but they are not really satisfactory . . . and there is little reason to believe that most of them would have been known or acceptable to early Christians.[168]

All in all, there is no good reason to question the reliability of the New Testament account of the virgin birth of Jesus. If you will study the Scriptures carefully, especially regarding the divine nature of the Messiah, you will see that his supernatural birth makes perfect sense (vol. 3, 4.3). And when you make the wonderful discovery that even now, Jesus is alive and well, bringing his Father's will to pass throughout the earth, you will *know* that the New Testament account of his virgin birth is gospel truth. You may have dismissed it all your life—as if the Messiah's supernatural birth were a Catholic myth—but you will find it to be a powerful, biblical truth, one of the great treasures of the Jewish faith.

Oddly enough, some anti-missionaries claim that the New Testament authors as a whole didn't seem to know about Yeshua's virgin birth.[169] This is easily refuted: First, Matthew and Luke describe it at length, devoting a good part of two chapters in each of the accounts to describe this important event (see Matthew 1–2; Luke 1–2). Second, neither Mark nor John speak of his birth or early years, but Mark calls Yeshua the Son of God—in fact, that is the opening statement of his Gospel (see Mark 1:1)—and John calls him the divine Word made flesh (John 1:1–18). While these terms aptly describe the virgin-born Messiah, they can hardly be applied to a mere mortal man. Third, Paul's statement in Romans 1:3–4 is consistent with a belief in the virgin birth, while it is difficult to explain otherwise. He calls Jesus God's "Son, who as to his human nature was a descendant of David, and who through the Spirit of holiness was declared with power to be the Son of God by his resurrection from the dead: Jesus [the Messiah] our Lord." So, Paul understands Jesus to be both David's son and God's Son, consistent with the New Testament witness. Notice also Paul's well-known statement in 1 Timothy 3:16 that Yeshua "appeared in a body." This is not how you speak of someone who was born naturally! Now, when we recognize that Matthew, Luke, Mark, John, and Paul account for more than 95 percent of the New Testament, it's clear that the notion that the New Testament authors were ignorant of the virgin birth is totally unsupportable.[170]

5.10. The genealogies of Jesus given by Matthew and Luke are hopelessly contradictory.

There do appear to be some contradictions in these genealogies, just as there appear to be contradictions in some of the genealogies in the Hebrew Scriptures. But there are very reasonable answers that resolve the conflicts without having to advance any far-fetched or implausible theories. Common sense would also tell you that the followers of Jesus, who were totally dedicated to demonstrating to both Jews and Gentiles that he was truly the Messiah and Savior, would not preserve and pass on two impossibly contradictory genealogies. In fact, this very suggestion directly contradicts the common objection that the New Testament authors rewrote the accounts of the Gospels in order to make Jesus look like he was the Messiah (see below, 5.14). The reality is that they accurately reported the story of his life and were careful to include two important genealogies in presenting the account of his ancestry and birth.

With all the objections raised against the genealogies in Matthew and Luke (see further 5.11, below), one could easily surmise that these were the Achilles' heel of the Christian faith, an embarrassment to the Messianic credentials of Jesus. Actually, these genealogies are given pride of place in both Matthew and Luke, serving to *underscore* Yeshua's Messianic qualifications.[171] Matthew introduces his whole account with a genealogy, beginning with the words, "A record of the genealogy of Jesus [the Messiah] the son of David, the son of Abraham" (Matt. 1:1), while Luke inserts the genealogy at a crucial point in his book (immediately after Yeshua's immersion in water, when the Holy Spirit came upon him and the voice from heaven identified him as the Son of God, and immediately before his trial in the wilderness), tracing the Messiah's ancestry all the way back to Adam (see Luke 3:21–4:2). The genealogies were both strategic and informative, and Matthew and Luke preserved them for two main reasons: (1) They supported Jesus' Messianic credentials; (2) they were true!

Nonetheless, an unbiased reading of the two accounts does raise questions, since there appears to be a number of contradictions between the two accounts, some major and some minor. Let's look at the two lists in close proximity, in descending order (i.e., from the earliest in time to the latest, beginning with David, after which the variations begin). I will underline the key names where potential discrepancies could exist.

Matthew: David, Solomon, Rehoboam, Abijah, Asa, Jehoshaphat, Jehoram, Uzziah, Jotham, Ahaz, Hezekiah, Manasseh, Amon, Josiah, Jeconiah, Shealtiel, Zerubbabel, Abiud, Eliakim, Azor, Zadok, Akim, Eliud, Eleazar, Matthan, Jacob, Joseph, Jesus.

Luke: David, Nathan, Mattatha, Menna, Melea, Eliakim, Jonam, Joseph, Judah, Simeon, Levi, Matthat, Jorim, Eliezer, Joshua, Er, Elmadam, Cossam, Addi, Melki, Neri, Shealtiel, Zerubbabel, Rhesa, Joanan, Joda, Josech, Semein, Mattathias, Maath, Naggai, Esli, Nahum, Amos, Mattathias, Joseph, Jannai, Melki, Levi, Matthat, Heli, Joseph (?), Jesus.

The most obvious difference between the genealogies is that Matthew lists twenty-six names between David and Jesus while Luke lists forty-one names, but this is not uncommon in genealogies (even in the Bible), where one list might contain more prominent names, skipping over generations (as if to say, "Tom is the ancestor of Bill," rather than, "Tom is the father of Bill") and the other list might contain every name. (Matthew's complete genealogy cites forty-one names; Luke's, seventy-one names.) As noted by professor Walter Kaiser Jr. in the *Hard Sayings of the Bible*,

No one has studied this phenomenon more closely than the late William Henry Green in his April 1890 article in *Bibliotheca Sacra* entitled "Primeval Chronology." For example, Green demonstrates that the same high priestly line of Aaron appears in 1 Chronicles 6:3–14 and Ezra 7:1–[5], but it has twenty-two generations and names in Chronicles, while Ezra only has sixteen names. When the two lists are placed side by side, it is clear that Ezra deliberately skipped from the eighth name to the fifteenth name, thereby abridging his list, but in a way that was legitimate within the traditions of Scripture. This is exactly what is illustrated in the lists in Matthew. In fact, Ezra 8:1–2 abridges the list even further, seemingly implying that a great-grandson and a grandson of Aaron, along with a son of David, came up with Ezra from Babylon after the captivity! Now that is abridgment! Of course, Ezra was only indicating the most important persons for the sake of this shorter list.[172]

In keeping with this, Matthew begins his book with reference to Yeshua being "the son of David" and the "son of Abraham," where "son of" can only mean "descendant of." It is also clear that Matthew, either for mnemonic purposes or out of symbolism with the numeric value of the name David, which is fourteen in Hebrew, chose to group his list in fourteens (see Matt. 1:17). So, the difference in the number of names is not an issue of concern at all, especially when we realize that, in all likelihood, there would be a variation in the total number of generations over a period of centuries since not everyone would have the same life span.

What of the fact that Matthew traces Yeshua's line through Solomon, son of David, while Luke traces him through Nathan, son of David? If these are two different genealogies, Matthew giving us the ancestry of Joseph, Yeshua's earthly father, through Solomon, and Luke giving us the ancestry of Miriam, Yeshua's mother, through Nathan, then there is no problem. (For the argument that the Messiah had to be a descendant of Solomon, see below, 5.11.) So this, too, presents no concern.

Things appear to be complicated, however, when we get to Shealtiel, the father of Zerubbabel. Both geneaologies list these same two names consecutively, but according to Matthew, Jeconiah (Jehoiachin) is the father of Shealtiel, whereas according to Luke, Shealtiel's father is Neri. How can this be explained? (For the argument that Yeshua is disqualified as being Messiah because he comes through the so-called cursed line of Jeconiah, see below, 5.12.)

One suggestion is that they are *not* the same people. Glen Miller summarizes the evidence for this:

- They have different parents
- They have different children.
- They are descended from different sons of David.
- Their chronological placements on a time line could differ by as much as a CENTURY! (depending on how the omissions in Matthew are accounted for, and on what the average age of child-bearing was).

THE ONLY THING THEY HAVE IN COMMON ARE THEIR NAMES!

This can hardly be a strong argument for their identity:

1. Zerubbabel was a common name from the early Persian period (539–331 BC), as shown by cuneiform inscriptions from Babylonia (see *ZPEB*, V. 1057).

2. The genealogies themselves have numerous names that repeat WITHIN the genealogy (e.g. Joseph, Mattathias, Judah) without being the same individuals; these names could also be common names.

3. The names in the genealogies are standard, common, everyday names. We have NUMEROUS people named Levi, Amos, Nahum, etc., in the

OT accounts. There is just NO REASON to associate the S[healtiel] + Z[erubbabel] of Luke with the S[healtiel] + Z[erubbabel] of Matthew. (And even the pattern of S[healtiel]-followed-by-Z[erubbabel] doesn't carry much weight—families often honored prominent people this way.)

What this means is that the S[healtiel] + Z[erubbabel] of Matthew are the S[healtiel] + Z[erubbabel] of Jeremiah, and that the S[healtiel] + Z[erubbabel] of Luke (whose genes DO reach to Jesus) are a different set, descended from Nathan and not through Solomon-thru-Jeconiah.[173]

If Miller is correct—and there is no *conclusive* evidence that can be raised against his position, only that it is highly unlikely that two pairs of men with the same names, listed in the same consecutive order in both genealogies, refer to two different pairs of men—then there is no contradiction at all. If Miller is not correct, the matter is still easily resolved, a key hint being found in 1 Chronicles 3:17–19, which states that Pedaiah and Shealtiel were among the sons of Jehoiachin (Jeconiah) and that Pedaiah was the father of Zerubbabel. Elsewhere, however, Zerubbabel is always known as the "son of Shealtiel" (see, e.g. Ezra 3:2; Neh. 12:1; Hag. 1:1), just as Matthew records (see Matt. 1:12). The standard answer given for this apparent contradiction within the Tanakh is that this was a case of levirate marriage (see Deut. 25:5–10; see also Gen. 38:8–9), in which "the widow of a childless man could marry his brother so that a child of the second marriage could legally be considered as the son of the deceased man in order to perpetuate his name. In a genealogy the child could be listed under his natural or his legal father."[174] In the case of Zerubabbel, it would appear that his biological father was Pedaiah, the younger brother of Shealtiel who died childless. Pedaiah then married the widow of Shealtiel, in accordance with the laws of levirate marriage, and his firstborn son, Zerubbabel, was counted as the son of his deceased brother, Shealtiel, to "build up his brother's family line" (Deut. 25:9).

What does this have to do with the possible contradiction between Matthew and Luke? If, in fact, they are referring to the same Shealtiel and Zerubbabel, with Matthew listing Jeconiah as Shealtiel's father (in accordance with 1 Chron. 3:17) and Luke listing Shealtiel's father as Neri, it is certainly possible that there was also a levirate marriage (or adoption) in the case of Shealtiel's father as well, but this is only speculation and can neither be proved nor disproved.

Supporting the view, however, that Luke is speaking of a different Shealtiel and Zerubbabel than Matthew (along with Ezra, Nehemiah, and Haggai) is the fact that Luke carefully reviewed and compared his sources (Luke 1:1–4) before compiling his account and he had at his disposal at least the genealogy of 1 Chronicles 3 as well as, possibly, the genealogy found in Matthew 1. Why then deviate from these sources unless he was referring to different people, people who were not mentioned in either 1 Chronicles 3 or Matthew 1? Conversely, if they were the same people, why record their names with a different father for Shealtiel unless Luke was convinced that his records were also accurate and that it was proper to refer to both Neri and Jeconiah as the father of Shealtiel, just as the Hebrew Bible refers to both Pedaiah and Shealtiel as the father of Zerubbabel?

Lest this seem like special pleading, I remind you that the possible contradictions found in these two genealogies are less difficult to resolve than similar problems found in the Tanakh. Not surprisingly, the section in *Hard Sayings of the Bible* entitled "Why Don't Bible Genealogies Always Match Up?" spends most of its time dealing with genealogical problems *in the Hebrew Bible*. Even some of the most forthright biblical narratives present problems that must be carefully analyzed and interpreted lest errors in understanding arise. Consider, for example, Genesis 11:26 that states, "After Terah had lived 70 years, he became the father of Abram, Nahor and Haran." Kaiser notes:

> It would appear that [Terah] lived 70 years and then had triplets born to him (Gen 11:26). His total life span was 205 years (Gen 11:32). However, something does not add up, for Abram left Haran after his father died (Gen 12:4; Acts 7:4), but he was only 75 years old at the time and not 135, which he should have been had the figures been intended in a way that current usage would approve! Hence, had we added up the numbers in this part of the genealogy, we would already be 60 years in error, for the text must have meant that Terah "began having children when he was 70 years old," but that Abram was actually born when his father was 130 and not when he was 70. He was not the eldest son, but his name is given first because he was the most significant figure.[175]

It appears, then, that the birth of Abram did not happen in accordance with the simplest reading of Genesis 11:26—and this is just one, minor example. More difficult is the account of Saul and David recorded in 1 Samuel. According to 1 Samuel 16:14–23, Saul requested that Jesse send his son David to him to play the harp to relieve him of the torment he was suffering and Saul became enamored with David: "Saul liked him very much, and David became one of his armor-bearers. Then Saul sent word to Jesse, saying, 'Allow David to remain in my service, for I am pleased with him'" (1 Sam. 16:21–22). Yet sometime after this, when David went out to fight against Goliath in battle, Saul had no idea who he was:

> As Saul watched David going out to meet the Philistine, he said to Abner, commander of the army, "Abner, whose son is that young man?"
> Abner replied, "As surely as you live, O king, I don't know."
> The king said, "Find out whose son this young man is."
> As soon as David returned from killing the Philistine, Abner took him and brought him before Saul, with David still holding the Philistine's head.
> "Whose son are you, young man?" Saul asked him.
> David said, "I am the son of your servant Jesse of Bethlehem."
>
> 1 Samuel 17:55–58

Critical scholars claim that this discrepancy reflects the fact that there were different stories about how David and Saul became connected, and a later editor weaved them together in one story. (Obviously, he didn't do too good of a job in smoothing out the contradictions!) Some conservative scholars have suggested that Saul simply had a memory lapse, due to his ongoing mental problems. Rashi offers a different interpretation to verse 55: "Our Rabbis said: Did he not recognize him? Is it not stated: 'And he became his weapon bearer' (supra [1 Sam.] 16:21)? But, (rather this is the explanation): he saw him behaving in a kingly manner." (This is followed by further Talmudic amplification.) Certainly, someone could accuse Rashi and the Talmudic rabbis of special pleading too, but they are simply looking for a solution to an apparent contradiction with the presupposition that the Scriptures are accurate and true. The same opportunity to resolve apparent contradictions should be given to those who take the New Testament accounts seriously as well.

In point of fact, there are far more problems to address in the genealogies found in the Hebrew Scriptures than are found here in Matthew and Luke, although, in a certain sense, the stakes are higher with the New Testament account, since it presents to us the lineage of the Messiah. Still, traditional Jews who believe that the Tanakh is accurate must wrestle with the genealogies in, for example, 1 Chronicles, while intellectual integrity would require that we use the same standards to evaluate the genealogies in the Hebrew Scriptures as we use in evaluating the New Testament records. With this in mind, the comments of the conservative Old Testament scholar Carl Friedrich Keil bear repeating. Speaking of the genealogies in 1 Chronicles, he observed that

> in regard to their plan and execution, these genealogies are not only unsymmetrical in the highest degree, but they are in many cases fragmen-

tary. In the tribe of Judah, besides the descendants of Dàvid, 1 Chron 3, two quite independent genealogies of the families of Judah are given, in 1 Chron 2 and 1 Chron 4:1–23. The same is the case with the two genealogies of the Levites, the lists in 1 Chron 6 differing from those in 1 Chron 5:27–41 [6:1–15] surprisingly, in 6:16, 20, 43, 62, Levi's eldest son being called Gershom, while in 1 Chron 6:1 and 1 Chron 23:6, and in the Pentateuch, he is called Gershon. Besides this, there is in 1 Chron 6:35–38 a fragment containing the names of some of Aaron's descendants, who had been already completely enumerated till the Babylonian exile in 1 Chron 5:29–41 [6:3–15]. In the genealogies of Benjamin, too, the family of Saul is twice entered, viz., in 1 Chron 8:29–40 and in 1 Chron 9:35–44. The genealogies of the remaining tribes are throughout defective in the highest degree. Some consist merely of an enumeration of a number of heads of houses or families, with mention of their dwelling-place: as, for instance, the genealogies of Simeon, 1 Chron 4:24–43; of Reuben, Gad, half Manasseh, 1 Chron 5:1–24; and Ephraim, 1 Chron 7:28–29. Others give only the number of men capable of bearing arms belonging to the individual fathers'-houses, as those of Issachar, Benjamin, and Asher, 1 Chron 7:2–5, 7–11, 40; and finally, of the longer genealogical lists of Judah and Benjamin, those in 1 Chron 4:1–20 and in 1 Chron 8 consist only of fragments, loosely ranged one after the other, giving us the names of a few of the posterity of individual men, whose genealogical connection with the larger divisions of these tribes is not stated.

By all this, it is satisfactorily proved that all these registers and lists have not been derived from one larger genealogical historical work, but have been drawn together from various old genealogical lists which single races and families had saved and carried with them into exile, and preserved until their return into the land of their fathers; and that the author of the Chronicle has received into his work all of these that he could obtain, whether complete or imperfect, just as he found them. Nowhere is any trace of artificial arrangement or an amalgamation of the various lists to be found.[176]

I would encourage any of you who still believe that the genealogies of Matthew and Luke are hopelessly contradictory, despite the simple, workable solutions presented here, to resolve all the issues that arise in the comparative study of the genealogies in the Tanakh before claiming that there is no solution to the New Testament accounts. You can rest assured that by the time you get back to Matthew and Luke, you will find the few apparent contradictions quite easy to resolve.

All this being said, it is certainly ironic that the same people who often claim that the New Testament writers rewrote the story of Yeshua's life to create the (allegedly false) impression that the events of his life corresponded to biblical prophecy (see below, 5.14) also claim that two of the principle authors—in fact, the primary "historians" of the New Testament—preserved two hopelessly contradictory and self-defeating genealogies, Matthew starting his book with his ancestral record and Luke giving a special place in his book to a lengthy genealogical record. Added to this is the supposition that the editors and copyists carefully preserved and passed on these contradictory accounts—and not one early church leader ever thought of changing this. Now this is special pleading.[177]

One final comment is in order, and it has to do with the question of whether there were reliable, genealogical records that could have been used to prove Davidic descent in Matthew's day. The answer is certainly yes, as Carson explains:

> After Zerubbabel, Matthew relies on extrabiblical sources of which we know nothing. But there is good evidence that records were kept at least till the end of the first century. Josephus (*Life* 6[1]) refers to the "public registers" from which he extracts his genealogical information (cf. also Jos. *Contra Apion* I, 28–56 [6–10]). According to Genesis R 98:8, Rabbi Hillel was proved to be a descendant of David because a genealogical scroll was found in Jerusalem. Eusebius (*Ecclesiastical History* 3.19–20) cites Hegesippus to the effect that Emperor Domitian (A.D. 81–96) ordered all descendants of David slain. Nevertheless two of them when summoned, though admitting their Davidic descent, showed their calloused hands to prove they were but poor farmers. So they were let go. But the account shows that genealogical information was still available.[178]

And while it is true that, even today, there are Jews who claim that they can prove their Davidic descent—something that would be necessary for a Messianic claimant—solid, genealogical proof was far more certain two thousand years ago, especially before the destruction of the Temple and the dispersion of our people through the centuries, than it is today. This then, is one more reason why the New Testament accounts should be taken seriously.[179]

5.11. The Messiah is David's son. If Jesus were really born of a virgin, then Joseph was not his father and he is really not a descendant of David, even according to Matthew's genealogy. And if you claim that Luke's genealogy is that of Mary, Jesus still doesn't qualify, since the genealogy in Luke goes through David's son Nathan, whereas

the Messianic promises must go through David's son Solomon. Therefore, Jesus cannot be the Messiah.

Obviously, you don't believe in the virgin birth, otherwise you wouldn't be raising this objection. Therefore, you believe that the disciples invented the myth of the virgin birth—a myth totally unique in the history of religion (see above, 5.9)—even though you argue that this "myth" completely undercut their claim that Jesus was the son of David. Wouldn't this be totally self-defeating? As we demonstrated above (see again, 5.9), no one would make up an account like this, especially when the people in Jesus' hometown thought he was the son of Joseph (and therefore a descendant of David) while the crowds hailed Jesus as the son of David when he entered Jerusalem. To the contrary, it is the truth of the virgin birth that explains the unique Messianic qualifications of Yeshua—both the son of David and yet greater than David—while his actual, physical descent from David is also taught in the New Testament. As for the Messiah having to come through Solomon, that is not correct according to the Scriptures or even according to some Rabbinic tradition.

The Jews for Judaism website summarizes the principle objections to the Messianic credentials of Yeshua based on the genealogies in Matthew and Luke:

According to the Jewish Bible, the Messiah must be a descendant of King David. (Jeremiah 23:5, 33:17; Ezekiel 34:23–24) Although the Greek Testament traces the genealogy of Joseph (husband of Mary) back to David, it then claims that Jesus resulted from a virgin birth, and, that Joseph was not his father. (Matt. 1:18–23) In response, it is claimed that Joseph adopted Jesus, and passed on his genealogy via adoption.

There are two problems with this claim:

a) there is no Biblical basis for the idea of a father passing on his tribal line by adoption. A priest who adopts a son from another tribe cannot make him a priest by adoption;

b) Joseph could never pass on by adoption that which he doesn't have. Because Joseph descended from Jeconiah (Matt. 1:11) he fell under the curse of that king that none of his descendants could ever sit as king upon the throne of David. (Jeremiah 22:30; 36:30).

To answer this difficult problem, apologists claim that Jesus traces himself back to King David through his mother Mary, who allegedly descends from David, as shown in the third chapter of Luke. There are four basic problems with this claim:

a] There is no evidence that Mary descends from David. The third chapter of Luke traces Joseph's genealogy, not Mary's.

b] Even if Mary can trace herself back to David, that doesn't help Jesus, since tribal affiliation goes only through the father, not mother. Cf. Num. 1:18; Ezra 2:59.

c] Even if family line could go through the mother, Mary was not from a legitimate Messianic family. According to the Bible, the Messiah must be a descendant of David through his son Solomon (II Sam. 7:14; I Chron. 17:11–14, 22:9–10, 28:4–6) The third chapter of Luke is useless because it goes through David's son Nathan, not Solomon. (Luke 3:31)[180]

d] Luke 3:27 lists Shealtiel and Zerubbabel in his genealogy. These two also appear in Matthew 1:12 as descendants of the cursed Jeconiah. If Mary descends from them, it would also disqualify her from being a Messianic progenitor.[181]

Let's tackle these points one at a time. As we do, you will see that none of them have any substance and all of them can easily be refuted. (The next answer, 5.12, deals specifically with objections [b] and [d], namely, the issue of descent through "the cursed Jeconiah.")

The first claim is that "there is no Biblical basis for the idea of a father passing on his tribal line by adoption." Actually, that is not an issue in these genealogies since: (1) A good case can be made for Luke's genealogy coming through Yeshua's mother, Miriam, in which case he would be a blood descendant of David (more on that point shortly). (2) A good case can be made for genealogical descent through a woman when there were no male heirs (again, we will return to this point shortly). (3) The Messiah was both David's son—and therefore a physical descendant—and yet David's lord—and therefore more than just a physical descendant.[182] Let's take this up in a little more depth before returning to the question of genealogical descent through the mother.

In Sanhedrin 98a, the Talmud asks an important question: Will the Messiah, the son of David, come with the clouds of heaven, as indicated in Daniel 7:13–14, or will he come riding on a donkey, as written in Zechariah 9:9? The Talmud says if we are worthy, he will come in the clouds, but if we are unworthy, he will come riding on a donkey.[183] The problem is that the Hebrew Scriptures do not present these two events as either-or options. Rather, they are both explicit prophecies that must be fulfilled (see also the discussion in vol. 1, 2.1). How then can these two opposing statements be reconciled? The New Covenant Scriptures provide us with the solution. The virgin birth is the key!

The Gospels make two things perfectly clear: The Messiah is the son of David and the Messiah is greater than David, both earthly and heavenly. These facts are also seen through a careful reading of the Tanakh. First, there are prophecies that are universally recognized as Messianic which indicate that the Messiah was to be "the son of David" (see, e.g., Isa. 11:1–16; sometimes the Messiah is actually called "David"; cf. Ezek. 34:23). Second, the Tanakh indicates that the Messiah would be highly exalted and greater than David, as recognized also by certain Rabbinic traditions (see vol. 2, 3.22). Daniel 7:13–14, cited above by the Talmud, teaches that the Messiah will be a heavenly figure who will be served and worshiped by all peoples and nations, sitting enthroned in the heavens. Another important passage is Psalm 110, beginning with the well-known words, "YHWH said to my lord, 'Sit at My right hand . . .'" (NJPSV). Although some Rabbinic commentaries dispute that David wrote this about the Messiah, other Rabbinic sources (e.g., Midrash Tehillim 2:9; 18:29) follow the Messianic interpretation, indicating that they had no trouble with David calling the Messiah "lord" or "master" (this interpretation was so common that it is presupposed by the New Testament; see further vol. 3, 4.29). There are also Rabbinic traditions that speak of the Messiah's preexistence and his heavenly dialogues with God, indicating that he was not your everyday, run-of-the-mill, physical descendant of David (see vol. 2, 3.22).[184] Note also the midrash to Isaiah 52:13, which states that the Messiah, who will come forth out of David, will be higher than Abraham, lifted up above Moses, and loftier than the ministering angels (see Yalqut Shim'oni 2:571).[185]

How then could the Messiah be David's son and yet in some sense be preexistent and greater than David? It is only through his virgin birth. His earthly father Joseph was a descendant of David and in the royal line, while it appears from the New Testament record that his mother, Miriam (Mary), was also a descendant of David.[186] As Keener observes,

> There is little doubt that Jesus' family historically stemmed from Davidic lineage: all clear early Christian sources attest it (e.g., Rom 1:3); Hegesippus reports a Palestinian tradition in which Roman authorities interrogated Jesus' brother's grandsons for Davidic descent (Euseb. *H.E.* 3.20); Julius Africanus attests Jesus' relatives claiming Davidic descent (*Letter to Aristides*); and, probably more significantly, non-Christian Jewish polemicists never bothered to try to refute it (Jeremias 1969: 291).[187]

The same authors who speak clearly of the virgin birth of Yeshua speak just as clearly of his being a son of David (cf., e.g., Matt. 1:1, 17–25; 9:27, 21:9, etc.; note that Matthew breaks his genealogy down to three groups of fourteen, which is also the numeric equivalent of the name David in Hebrew).[188] They found no contradiction here. And this leads to an important question for consideration: Given the unique nature of the Messiah—the son of David and yet greater than David—could you present a more scriptural scenario than the one offered in the Gospels? His mother's husband—they were espoused before Jesus was conceived—and the man who in all respects outside of literal begetting functioned as his earthly father, was in the line of legal heirs to the throne, going back to David. His mother Miriam, whose bloodline he continued, was a descendant of David. Once you see God's hand in all this, it becomes awe-inspiring, the kind of thing the human mind would never invent. The Messiah is David's son and David's lord, descended from the earthly king and yet descended from the heavenly throne, earthly and yet transcendent, able to fully identify with us in our humanity and weakness yet bearing the divine nature and able to save us fully from our sins. Thus, after Yeshua's immersion in water, Luke 3:22b records that a voice came from heaven saying, "You are my Son, whom I love; with you I am well pleased," while the very next verse states, "Now Jesus himself was about thirty years old when he began his ministry. He was the son, so it was thought, of Joseph, the son of Heli" (Luke 3:23). The Messiah, then, was the Son of God and the son of man.

This whole argument, of course, is greatly weakened if the Messiah's descent cannot be traced through Miriam and if she is not, in fact, in the legitimate Messianic line from David.[189] Thus Jews for Judaism claims that, "There is no evidence that Mary descends from David. The third chapter of Luke traces Joseph's genealogy, not Mary's." This is simply not true, and there *is* evidence for this being Miriam's (Mary's) genealogy, although a healthy scholarly debate exists on the subject. First, there is no sign of any debate about the Davidic lineage of Yeshua in any of the early sources, suggesting that Miriam's Davidic background was well known. Second, Luke 1:32, recounting Gabriel's words to Miriam, makes good sense if she was a descendant of David, since she is being informed that the son to be conceived within her *as a virgin* will inherit the throne of his father David: "He will be great and will be called the Son of the Most High. The Lord God will give him the throne of his father David." Third, the fact that the New Testament preserves two different genealogies lends support to the view that one is Joseph's and the other is Miriam's. Why preserve and supply two seemingly contradictory genealogies? Fourth, the Greek construction of Luke 3:23 certainly allows for the genealogy to be that of Miriam, stating, in effect, that Yeshua was thought to be the son of Joseph but was actually the (grand)son of Heli.[190] This would be in harmony with some of the genealogical evidence from the Tanakh, as seen immediately below. Fifth, there is no evidence that proves that the genealogy is *not* Miriam's. In light of all the arguments that can be mustered to support Luke's genealogy as coming through Miriam, unless conclusive evidence can be raised to the contrary, then the case for Davidic descent through Miriam must be considered as a strong possibility, if not probability.

As noted above, however, Jews for Judaism has an answer for this as well: "Even if Mary can trace herself back to David, that doesn't help Jesus, since tribal affiliation goes only through the father, not mother. Cf. Num. 1:18; Ezra 2:59."[191] Once more, this statement only tells part of the story, since the Hebrew Bible actually provides us with two examples that offer relevant parallels to the Messiah's bloodline being traced through his mother. First, in terms of inheritance, the Torah teaches that if a man dies, leaving no sons but only daughters, the inheritance is passed on through the daughters and their husbands, provided that they marry within the tribe (see Num. 27:1–11; 36:1–12).[192] Thus, the daughter's inheritance is joined with her husband's. While this does not deal with genealogy, it does deal with the passing on of family inheritance through a daughter, certainly a related concept.[193] This is further confirmed by Ezra 2:61 (= Neh. 7:63), which makes reference to "Barzillai (a man who had married a daughter of Barzillai the Gileadite and was called by that name)."[194]

In the case of Jesus, Miriam also married within the same tribal family, since Joseph was a Judahite and, more specifically, a descendant of David. In fact, according to U. Holzmeister,[195] this is how Luke's genealogy should actually be understood as that of Miriam, but in connection with Joseph. As explained by John Nolland, who favors this proposal,

> Holzmeister argues that Mary was an heiress (i.e., had no brothers) whose father Eli, in line with a biblical tradition concerned with the maintenance of the family line in cases where there was no male heir (Ezra 2:61 = Neh 7:63; Num 32:41 cf. 1 Chr 2:21–22, 34–35; Num 27:3–8), on the marriage of his daughter to Joseph, adopted Joseph as his own son. Matthew gives Joseph's ancestry by birth, Luke that by adoption.[196]

Regardless of whether this proposal is accepted, it is clear that Luke's genealogy through Yeshua's mother, Miriam, is of direct relevance to the objection at hand.

Second, 1 Chronicles 2:34–36 states, "Sheshan had no sons—only daughters. He had an Egyptian servant named Jarha. Sheshan gave his daughter in marriage to his servant Jarha, and she bore him Attai. Attai was the father of Nathan, Nathan the father of Zabad. . . ." Do you see it? Sheshan's genealogy continues through his daughter's children, all of whom bear good Israelite names rather than Egyptian names, despite Jarha's Egyptian background.[197] The genealogy continues through the daughter's children! Both of these examples—inheritance and genealogy—are helpful here, since Miriam and Joseph's pedigrees together provide Jesus with a legitimate line to the throne, without, however, making him a mere descendant of David.

It is also interesting to note the genealogical record found in 1 Chronicles 2:13–16:

> Jesse was the father of Eliab his firstborn; the second son was Abinadab, the third Shimea, the fourth Nethanel, the fifth Raddai, the sixth Ozem and the seventh David. Their sisters were Zeruiah and Abigail. Zeruiah's three sons were Abishai, Joab and Asahel.

Why no mention of Zeruiah's husband, the father of Abishai, Joab, and Asahel? Or did these brothers have different fathers, perhaps through their mother's widowhood and remarriage? Scripture gives us no indication. What is clear, however, is that in this genealogy as well as throughout the Hebrew Scriptures, they are only known as the "sons of Zeruiah." Notice these phrases: "Joab son of Zeruiah" (2 Sam. 2:13, plus twelve more times); "Abishai son of Zeruiah" (1 Sam. 26:6, plus five more times); "The three sons of Zeruiah were there: Joab, Abishai and Asahel" (2 Sam. 2:18); "these sons of Zeruiah" (2 Sam. 3:39); "you sons of Zeruiah" (2 Sam. 16:10; 19:22). It seems clear that Zeruiah's importance as the mother of these mighty men in David's army was well known. But, for our purposes, it is more important to notice that she, and not the father, is cited in the genealogical record.

Even these answers, however, do not satisfy the anti-missionaries. They raise one further objection, one that is intended to be the *coup de grace*: "Even if family line could go through the mother, Mary was not from a legitimate Messianic family. According to the Bible, the Messiah must be a descendant of David through his son Solomon (II Sam. 7:14; I Chron. 17:11–14, 22:9–10, 28:4–6) The third chapter of Luke is useless because it goes through David's son Nathan, not Solomon. (Luke 3:31)." Of all the objections raised, this is actually the easiest to refute, on the basis of both Scripture and even Rabbinic tradition. (Is this the reason that Jews for Judaism did not say, "According to the Bible *and* Rabbinic tradition"?)

Let's review each of the passages cited, beginning with 2 Samuel 7:14 in its larger context. Here, Nathan the prophet is giving David a promise from the Lord:

> When your days are over and you rest with your fathers, I will raise up your offspring to succeed you, who will come from your own body, and I will establish his kingdom. He is the one who will build a house for my Name, and I will establish the throne of his kingdom forever. I will be his father, and he will be my son. When he does wrong, I will punish him with the rod of men, with floggings inflicted by men. But my love will never be taken away from him, as I took it away from Saul, whom I removed from before you. Your house and your kingdom will endure forever before me; your throne will be established forever.
>
> 2 Samuel 7:12–16

First Chronicles 17:11–14 is a parallel passage to the verses we just read in 2 Samuel 7. Note carefully the language used about Solomon: "I will establish his kingdom. . . . I will establish his throne forever. . . . I will set him over my house and my kingdom forever; his throne will be established forever" (1 Chron. 17:11b, 12b, 14). What glorious promises! This is repeated once more in 1 Chronicles 22:10b, "And I will establish the throne of his kingdom over Israel forever." There was, however, a divine condition clearly laid out: "I will establish his kingdom forever if he is unswerving in carrying out my commands and laws, as is being done at this time" (1 Chron. 28:7). Was Solomon unswerving in carrying out God's commands and laws? Hardly! The scriptural record is very clear:

> King Solomon, however, loved many foreign women besides Pharaoh's daughter—Moabites, Ammonites, Edomites, Sidonians and Hittites. They were from nations about which the LORD had told the Israelites, "You must not intermarry with them, because they will surely turn your hearts after their gods." Nevertheless, Solomon held fast to them in love. He had seven hundred wives of royal birth and three hundred concubines, and his wives led him astray. As Solomon grew old, his wives turned his heart after other gods, and his heart was not fully devoted to the LORD his God, as the heart of David his father had been. He followed Ashtoreth the goddess of the Sidonians, and Molech the detestable god of the Ammonites. So Solomon did evil in the eyes of the LORD; he did not follow the LORD completely, as David his father had done.
>
> On a hill east of Jerusalem, Solomon built a high place for Chemosh the detestable god of Moab, and for Molech the detestable god of the Am-

monites. He did the same for all his foreign wives, who burned incense and offered sacrifices to their gods.

1 Kings 11:1–8

There were serious consequences to Solomon's ugly sin:

The LORD became angry with Solomon because his heart had turned away from the LORD, the God of Israel, who had appeared to him twice. Although he had forbidden Solomon to follow other gods, Solomon did not keep the LORD's command. So the LORD said to Solomon, "Since this is your attitude and you have not kept my covenant and my decrees, which I commanded you, I will most certainly tear the kingdom away from you and give it to one of your subordinates. Nevertheless, for the sake of David your father, I will not do it during your lifetime. I will tear it out of the hand of your son. Yet I will not tear the whole kingdom from him, but will give him one tribe for the sake of David my servant and for the sake of Jerusalem, which I have chosen."

1 Kings 11:9–13

Solomon did *not* meet God's conditions, and his throne was *not* established forever. The Word of God states this clearly. There are even some Rabbinic traditions which claim that Solomon was banished from the throne during his lifetime; see y. Sanh 2:6; cf. also b. Meg 11b: "Is there not Solomon?—He did not retain his kingdom [till his death]," explained by Rashi to mean, "He did not complete his kingship, for he was expelled," with reference to his comments at b. Gittin 68b, where he states that Solomon did not return to his throne. How then can the anti-missionaries claim that Solomon's throne was established forever when, in reality, some Rabbinic traditions claim he did not even finish out his rule on that throne? To the contrary, it is the throne of David that remains established forever.

Gerald Sigal, writing for Jews for Judaism, is either unaware of these biblical truths or fails to recognize the weight of them, arguing that the kingship was not taken from Solomon the way it was taken from Saul:

How did God take the kingdom from Saul? The right to the kingship terminated with Saul's death. No son of Saul ever sat on or had a right to the throne. But Solomon's descendants, with the exception of one branch of the family, would never lose their right to the throne. The punishment for disobedience would be chastening at the hands of men but not the termination of the monarchical right. It is God's unconditional promise that the posterity of David, specifically that of Solomon, will possess the

kingship forever. God assures that there will always be a male of paternal
Solomonic descent with the right to reign upon David's throne.[198]

Sigal, however, completely misses the point, looking primarily at
the promise of divine chastisement laid out in 2 Samuel 7:14 while
overlooking the statement in 1 Chronicles 28:7 that Solomon's throne
would only be established forever *if* he followed God's commands un-
swervingly, which he certainly did not. The fact is, Solomon's throne
was not established forever, David's throne was! And while it is true
that descendants of Solomon continued to sit on David's throne—it
was only logical that the son of a king would be the next king—this
was because of the unconditional promises given to David (in contrast
with Saul), not the conditional promises given to Solomon, which
he violated. And, following the exile of the Davidic monarchy in 586
B.C.E., there was not a hint that future kings would have to trace their
lineage through Solomon. He flagrantly sinned against the requirements of the Lord!

I find it interesting that the anti-missionaries not only fail to deal with
1 Chronicles 28:7, they virtually always ignore the categorical statement
found in 1 Kings 9:4–9 where God speaks directly to Solomon, warning
him plainly:

> As for you, if you walk before me in integrity of heart and uprightness, as
> David your father did, and do all I command and observe my decrees and
> laws, I will establish your royal throne over Israel forever, as I promised
> David your father when I said, "You shall never fail to have a man on the
> throne of Israel."
>
> But if you or your sons turn away from me and do not observe the com-
> mands and decrees I have given you and go off to serve other gods and wor-
> ship them, then I will cut off Israel from the land I have given them and will
> reject this temple I have consecrated for my Name. Israel will then become a
> byword and an object of ridicule among all peoples. And though this temple
> is now imposing, all who pass by will be appalled and will scoff and say,
> "Why has the Lord done such a thing to this land and to this temple?" People
> will answer, "Because they have forsaken the Lord their God, who brought
> their fathers out of Egypt, and have embraced other gods, worshiping and
> serving them—that is why the Lord brought all this disaster on them."

The divine threat here is so emphatic that Hebrew scholar Ziony Zevit
claims that God actually refused Solomon's request in 1 Kings 8:25–26
for an unconditional guarantee. In that passage Solomon prayed this
very promise back to the Lord—namely, that David would never fail to
have a man on the throne of Israel. Here the Lord says to him that there

are conditions, and the breaking of those conditions could actually result in the exile of the people and the destruction of the Temple.[199] Thankfully, God was determined to keep his long-term promises to David, but nothing was guaranteed to Solomon or his posterity. Such a pledge simply does not exist anywhere in the Bible.[200]

The Hebrew Scriptures are absolutely clear on this. Thus, there is not one single reference in the Bible to "the throne of Solomon" but many references to "the throne of David." See 2 Samuel 3:10; 1 Kings 2:12, 24, 45; Isaiah 9:7[6], in a decidedly Messianic context; Jeremiah 17:25; 22:2, 30; 29:16; 36:30. Why? Because Solomon's throne was not established forever, David's was! All subsequent Judean kings sat on David's throne, not Solomon's. Similarly, there is not a single biblical reference to a future king who will be from the line of Solomon or will be called a son of Solomon or come from the seed of Solomon, while there are important references to a future king who will be from the line of David or called a son of David or come from the seed of David.[201] Why? Because Solomon's throne was not established forever, David's was! Quite simply, there are no unconditional promises to Solomon to raise up royal heirs from his lineage, nor was there a requirement that the Messiah had to trace his lineage through Solomon. The Messianic line was promised to David, not Solomon. See also the promises given to David in the Psalms:[202]

> You said, "I have made a covenant with my chosen one,
>   I have sworn to David my servant,
> 'I will establish your line forever
>   and make your throne firm through all generations.'"
>
> Psalm 89:3–4

> Once for all, I have sworn by my holiness—
>   and I will not lie to David—
> that his line will continue forever
>   and his throne endure before me like the sun;
> it will be established forever like the moon,
>   the faithful witness in the sky.
>
> Psalm 89:35–37

> The LORD swore an oath to David,
>   a sure oath that he will not revoke:
> "One of your own descendants
>   I will place on your throne—
> if your sons keep my covenant
>   and the statutes I teach them,

> then their sons will sit
> on your throne for ever and ever."
>
> Psalm 132:11–12

God made no such promises to Solomon. That's why God spoke through the prophets about David and about his throne and his line, but never—not once!—about Solomon:

> For this is what the LORD says: "David will never fail to have a man to sit on the throne of the house of Israel." . . .
> . . . This is what the LORD says: "If you can break my covenant with the day and my covenant with the night, so that day and night no longer come at their appointed time, then my covenant with David my servant—and my covenant with the Levites who are priests ministering before me—can be broken and David will no longer have a descendant to reign on his throne."
>
> Jeremiah 33:17, 20–21

> But if you are careful to obey me, declares the LORD, and bring no load through the gates of this city on the Sabbath, but keep the Sabbath day holy by not doing any work on it, then kings who sit on David's throne will come through the gates of this city with their officials. They and their officials will come riding in chariots and on horses, accompanied by the men of Judah and those living in Jerusalem, and this city will be inhabited forever.
>
> Jeremiah 17:24–25

Notice again the wording of this passage: Kings will "sit on David's throne"—not Solomon's throne. In similar fashion, a godless Judean king was told that "none of his offspring will prosper, none will sit on the throne of David [not Solomon!] or rule anymore in Judah" (Jer. 22:30, discussed below, 5.12; see also Jer. 36:30). David's heirs sat on the throne of David, not the throne of Solomon, and whatever glorious intentions the Lord had for his servant Solomon, they were virtually wiped out through his gross idolatry and disobedience.[203] To whom much is given, much is required! It remained for Yeshua the Messiah to fulfill the promises given to David: "He will be great and will be called the Son of the Most High. The Lord God will give him the throne of his father David, and he will reign over the house of Jacob forever; his kingdom will never end."[204] To this day, his kingdom is growing and expanding, and it will continue forever without interruption or abatement. To reiterate, the witness of the Scriptures is absolutely clear on this point: The throne of David, not Solomon, was established forever, and the Messiah had to be a descendant of David, not Solomon. As the nineteenth-century-commentator Malbim explained, the unconditional promises did not continue through the offspring of David's grandchildren (meaning, the sons of Solomon); those were only conditional.[205]

You ask, "But haven't the rabbis always taught what Jews for Judaism states, namely, that, 'According to the Bible, the Messiah must be a descendant of David through his son Solomon'?" Absolutely not. Such a statement is not found in the Talmud or Law Codes—not once!—and there is not the slightest evidence that, for example, when Rabbi Akiva proclaimed Bar Kochba to be the Messiah in 132 c.e., he claimed that he was a descendant of Solomon. Why? It was simply not an issue. In the same way, in the early 1990s when the followers of the Lubavitcher Rebbe, Menachem Schneerson, claimed that he was the Messiah, they did not major on an (alleged) claim that he was a descendant of Solomon. Being an alleged descendant of David was sufficient in their eyes. Why? *Because in most Rabbinic thought, descent through Solomon was not considered a requirement for the Messiah.*[206]

Throughout Rabbinic literature, the only time the phrase *ben sh'lomo* (son of Solomon) occurs is with reference to Rehoboam, his immediate offspring (see, e.g., Numbers Rabbah 23:13; b. Megillah 31b; b. Nedarim 40a). Outside of this, in the whole of Talmudic literature, the phrase "son of Solomon" does not occur a single time. Why? Because it had no significance at all, whereas the phrase "son of David" became synonymous with the Messiah. (This is very common in Rabbinic literature; see, e.g., Genesis Rabbah 97; Exodus Rabbah 25:12; b. Yoma 10a; b. Sukkah 52 a–b; b. Sanhedrin 97a–98b; this usage is reflected in the New Testament as well; see Matt. 9:27; 12:23; 15:22; 20:30–31; 21:9, 15; 22:42; with parallels in Mark and Luke.) The Messiah was to be the son of David, not necessarily the son of Solomon, because David's throne was established forever, not Solomon's.

It is therefore highly significant for a traditional Jew that Moses Maimonides, one of *the* leading voices in Rabbinic Judaism, omitted any reference to the Messiah's supposed need to be of Solomonic descent in his authoritative law code called the Mishneh Torah, speaking of it in his Book of Commandments, which is less authoritative than his Mishneh Torah.[207] In his oft-quoted section dealing with the Messiah, he simply stated, "If a king will arise from the House of David . . ." (Hilchot Melachim 11:4). As one ultra-Orthodox rabbi pointed out to me, "The fact that he did not mention Solomonic descent in his law code meant that it was not that important a concept to him." This statement, which is in keeping with the scriptural evidence (which is really enough in itself), is reinforced by the fact that the Talmud refers to the Messiah as the son of David but never the son of Solomon, while not a single authoritative statement in traditional Judaism makes the claim that the Messiah must be a descendant of Solomon. It is therefore not surprising that such an argument was not raised in the sharp medieval polemics between Judaism and Christianity, nor was it raised in the classic anti-Christian work known as *Hizzuk Emunah*, "Faith Strengthened," considered the granddaddy of anti-missionary works.[208]

And yet there is one more objection that is raised, namely 2 Kings 11:1 (see 2 Chron. 22:10) where we read that, "When Athaliah the mother of Ahaziah saw that her son was dead, she proceeded to destroy the whole royal family," her goal being to take over the throne by eliminating any potential heirs, yet she killed only the male members of the royal family, not the female members. From this the anti-missionaries argue that legitimate Davidic descent can only come through a male, otherwise Athaliah would have sought to kill the Davidic women as well. But that is to read more into this event than is warranted, since Athaliah was only trying to wipe out immediate, potential heirs to the throne, meaning either sons or siblings of the king. This is the most likely meaning of the "whole royal family." In this way, she could proclaim herself queen. So, her goal was not to try to thwart all future promises to the house of David—why would she be thinking about that?—but to secure the throne for herself, since the normal pattern was for the son or sibling of a king to become the next king. That direct line of royal succession, however, was broken more than 2,500 years ago.[209]

As to the notion that, theoretically, she should have killed David's female descendants as well (or, at least, Solomon's), that would imply that she thought through all the issues of genealogy and inheritance involving descent through women (discussed above), which is a ludicrous and baseless assumption. Moreover, it fails to address the fact that there was a specific reason that the Messiah had to be virgin born, namely, so he could be both the son of David and the Son of God, David's descendant and David's lord, as explained above. This too would have had no relevance at all to Athaliah's murderous deeds, deeds which had only one goal, and that was to secure the throne for herself at that moment. Having stated this, however, we should note that the New Testament does put emphasis on the fact that Yeshua's earthly, adoptive father was also a son of David, thereby placing Yeshua in the royal line through Joseph as well, since in all respects aside from conception—in the one, unique time in human history that such a thing took place—Joseph, a descendant of the ancient royal line of David, was the father of Yeshua.[210]

The bottom line is this: If, in fact, Jesus was supernaturally conceived by the will and power of God—as we believe without hesitation or doubt—making the Lord his heavenly Father, then technical, pseudo-legal objections to his lineage are dubious. God brought the Messiah into the world—in one sense David's son, in another sense David's lord—and this alone fulfills the promise of the Tanakh and answers the "either-or" problem raised in the Talmud. It would be the height of absurdity to say, "Jesus cannot be the Messiah because he was supernaturally conceived by the Spirit and God is his real Father." With "objections" like this, who needs proofs?

5.12. Jesus cannot be the Messiah because he is a descendant of King Jehoiachin. God cursed both this king and his offspring, saying that none of his descendants would ever sit on the throne of David.

There are some Bible teachers who argue that only Jesus is qualified to be the Messiah because of the curse on Jehoiachin. In other words, it is argued that the Messiah should have come through the royal line of Jehoiachin but that king's descendants were disqualified from sitting on the throne. Therefore, it is only through the virgin birth that the curse of Jehoiachin's descendants can be bypassed. In reality, however, there is no need to raise this argument, since the curse on Jehoiachin may only have referred to his own sons and, more importantly, the Hebrew Bible gives strong indications that he repented and the curse was reversed. This understanding of the text is actually confirmed by Rabbinic tradition.

According to Matthew 1:12, Yeshua's genealogy is traced through Jeconiah (a nickname for Jehoiachin). He was the son of Jehoiakim and the grandson of Josiah, reigning for just three months before being exiled by king Nebuchadnezzar of Babylon (see 2 Kings 24:6–17). Of him it was said by the Lord, "Record this man as if childless, a man who will not prosper in his lifetime, for none of his offspring will prosper, none will sit on the throne of David or rule anymore in Judah" (Jer. 22:30). How then could the Messiah be traced through his lineage? According to John McTernan and Lou Ruggiero, "The messianic line runs from David to

Solomon to Rehoboam to Jeconiah to Zerubbabel to the Messiah. There is no place in the Bible which shows the curse on the kingly line has been lifted. Because of the curse, anyone born of a human father and [*sic*] claims to be the Messiah will have the curse of Jeconiah to block such a claim. The Messiah of Israel cannot have a human father."[211] Of course, I fully affirm the supernatural, virginal conception of the Messiah and, as noted above (see 5.9), this helps explain how the Messiah can be both earthly and heavenly, the son of David and yet David's lord. In terms of the curse on Jehoiachin, however, there is no need to point to the necessity of the virgin birth since: (1) there is, in fact, solid scriptural evidence that the curse was reversed; and (2) the curse may only have applied primarily to Jehoiachin's immediate descendants.[212] Let's take a look at the passage in Jeremiah 22 in greater depth.

As I noted in my commentary on Jeremiah concerning Jehoiachin:

> A command is given (v. 30) in the pl. (*kitbû*, write!) to record that he will be *'arîrî*, childless (see Gen 15:2, and note esp. Lev 20:20–21, where being *'arîrî* is a curse for an unauthorized union), yet v. 28 spoke of his offspring while 1 Ch 3:16–17 states that he had seven sons. The explanation for this is found in the rest of v. 30, which should be understood in light of the presumed ardent hope and desire of the people of Judah—in their land and in exile—that this son of David, or one of his sons, would be restored to the throne. God says it will not happen, the emphasis being on "his lifetime" (in which he'll not succeed) and the lifetimes of his sons, none of whom would reign on the throne, making it as if he was childless (so NIV). In keeping with this, the divine promises to the line of David are not renewed until the days of Zerubbabel, his grandson (see Hag 2:20–23, and . . . Jer 52:31–34).[213]

Note further the comment of evangelical scholar Walter Kaiser Jr., who observes,

> According to 1 Chronicles 3:16–17, Jehoiachin had seven descendants. These, however, were hauled off into Babylon and there, according to an archaeological finding on a Babylonian tablet in the famous Ishtar Gate, all seven were made eunuchs. In this manner, Jehoiachin became "as if childless," as no man of his seed prospered, nor did any sit on David's throne.[214]

Similarly, Jeremiah commentator John Bright explains: "The figure is that of a census list. Jehoiachin is to be entered as childless since, as far as throne succession was concerned, he was as good as that."[215]

You may wonder, "Is it really that simple? Is this whole thing of a lasting curse on Jehoiachin's descendants an exaggeration?" Let's take a look at Jeremiah 36:30, a passage that is rarely cited in these discussions, but one that is quite relevant, since in Jeremiah 36:30, it is prophesied of Jehoiakim—the father of Jehoiachin!—that, "He will have no one to sit on the throne of David." But his son Jehoiachin *did* sit on David's throne, reigning for three months and still this prophecy was recorded as true. What then did this prophecy mean? It certainly did not mean that there was a curse on all of Jehoiakim's future descendants, nor did it mean that none of his sons would sit on the throne at all. Rather, the fact that Jehoiachin did sit on David's throne for three months meant that any reign of any of Jehoiakim's sons would be fleeting at best, completely devoid of the blessing of God.[216] Yet the language of Jeremiah 36:30 is very similar to the language of Jeremiah 22:30. On what basis do we press the meaning of the latter so far beyond the meaning of the former? And on what basis do we make the pronouncement against Jehoiachin one that would last for all time when the context points primarily to a curse on his immediate offspring?

In reality, however, we don't even need to debate these points at all, since the Tanakh gives two important pieces of evidence that point to: (1) Jehoiachin's repentance and (2) the subsequent removal of any generational curse.

The first piece of evidence is found in Jeremiah 52:31–34 which describes the special favor that was shown to Jehoiachin after decades in prison in exile:

> In the thirty-seventh year of the exile of Jehoiachin king of Judah, in the year Evil-Merodach became king of Babylon, he released Jehoiachin king of Judah and freed him from prison on the twenty-fifth day of the twelfth month. He spoke kindly to him and gave him a seat of honor higher than those of the other kings who were with him in Babylon. So Jehoiachin put aside his prison clothes and for the rest of his life ate regularly at the king's table. Day by day the king of Babylon gave Jehoiachin a regular allowance as long as he lived, till the day of his death.

In light of the divine fury directed against Jehoiachin in Jeremiah 22:24–29, this reversal of circumstances is quite striking, suggesting a change of heart in the king. For the Talmudic rabbis and their successors, there was little doubt: Jehoiachin had repented! Further, explicit evidence was provided in Haggai 2:20–23, speaking of Zerubbabel, the grandson of Jehoiachin, who became the governor of Judah after the return from exile:

The word of the LORD came to Haggai a second time on the twenty-fourth day of the month: "Tell Zerubbabel governor of Judah that I will shake the heavens and the earth. I will overturn royal thrones and shatter the power of the foreign kingdoms. I will overthrow chariots and their drivers; horses and their riders will fall, each by the sword of his brother.

'On that day,' declares the LORD Almighty, 'I will take you, my servant Zerubbabel son of Shealtiel,' declares the LORD, 'and I will make you like my signet ring, for I have chosen you,' declares the LORD Almighty."

Note carefully these words in Haggai 2:23: "'I will take you, my servant Zerubbabel son of Shealtiel,' declares the LORD, 'and I will make you like my signet ring, for I have chosen you.'" Now compare this promise with the threat against Jehoiachin in Jeremiah 22:24: "'As surely as I live,'" declares the LORD, 'even if you, Jehoiachin son of Jehoiakim king of Judah, were a signet ring on my right hand, I would still pull you off.'" Do you see it? The Lord told Jehoiachin that even if he were as close to God and as personal to him as the signet ring on his own hand, he would be cast off—and he was. Two generations later, the Lord tells his grandson, "I will make you like my signet ring, because I have chosen you." Without a doubt, the curse was reversed and favor was restored.

Based on these texts, Rabbinic literature is filled with references to Jehoiachin's repentance and his subsequent restoration, the final evidence being the promise to his grandson Zerubbabel. See, for example, the commentary of Radak to Jeremiah 22:30, who follows the Talmud and midrashic writings in using this example to extol the power of repentance, namely, "Great is the power of repentance, which can nullify a decree and nullify an oath" (see also b. R. H. 17b, for further statements on the power of repentance; see also the comments of Shelah; cf. also t. Niddah 70b; see further Netivot Olam b, 163; Hiddushei Aggadot, 1:118). There are actually many statements in the Rabbinic writings that speak of Jehoiachin's repentance and the reversal of any curse, as illustrated by this lengthy citation from Pesikta deRav Kahana 24:11.[217]

I accepted the repentance of Jeconiah: shall I not accept your repentance? A cruel decree had been imposed upon Jeconiah: Scripture says, *This man Coniah is a despised, shattered image ('ṣb)* (Jer. 22:28), for Jeconiah, according to R. Abba bar Kahana, was like a man's skull (*'ṣm*) which once shattered is utterly useless, or, according to R. Helbo, like a wrapper of reed matting that dates are packed in, which, once emptied, is utterly useless. And Scripture goes on to say of Jeconiah: *He is a vessel that none reaches for with delight (ibid.),* a vessel, said R. Hama bar R. Hanina, such as a urinal; or a vessel, said R. Samuel bar Nahman, such as is used for drawing off blood. [These comments on Jeconiah derive from] R. Meir's statement: The Holy One swore that He would raise up no king out of Jeconiah king of Judah. Thus Scripture: *As I live, saith the Lord, though Coniah the son of Jehoiakim . . . were the signet on a hand, yet by My right, I would pluck thee hence* (Jer. 22:24), words by which God was saying, explained R. Hanina bar R. Isaac, "Beginning with thee, Jeconiah, I pluck out the kingship of the house of David." It is to be noted, however, that the Hebrew for "pluck thee" is not as one would expect '*tkk*, but the fuller and less usual '*tknk*, which may also be rendered "mend thee"—that is, mend thee by thy repentance. Thus in the very place, [the kingship], whence Jeconiah was plucked, amends would be made to him: [his line would be renewed].

R. Ze'era said: I heard the voice of R. Samuel bar Isaac expounding from the teacher's chair a specific point concerning Jeconiah, but I just cannot remember what it was. R. Aha Arila asked: Did it perhaps have some connection with this particular verse—*Thus saith the Lord: Write ye this man childless, a man [who] will not prosper in his days* (Jer. 22:30)? "Yes, that's it!" said R. Ze'era. Thereupon R. Aha Arila went on to give R. Samuel bar Isaac's interpretation of the verse: In his days Jeconiah, so long as he is childless, will not prosper, but when he has a son, then he will prosper by his son's prosperity.

R. Aha bar Abun bar Benjamin, citing R. Abba bar R. Papi, said: Great is the power of repentance, which led God to set aside an oath even as it led Him to set aside a decree. Whence the proof that a man's repentance led Him to set aside the oath He made in the verse *As I live, saith the Lord, though Coniah the son of Jehoiakim were the signet on a hand, yet by My right, I would pluck thee hence* (Jer. 22:24)? The proof is in the verse where Scripture says [of one of Jeconiah's descendants] *In that day, saith the Lord of hosts, will I take thee, O Zerubbabel . . . the son of Shealtiel . . . and will make thee as a signet* (Haggai 2:23). And the proof that a man's repentance led God to set aside a decree He issued in the verse *Thus saith the Lord: Write ye this man childless*, etc. (Jer. 22:30)? The proof is in the verse where Scripture says, *The sons of Jeconiah—the same is Asir—Shealtiel his son*, etc. (1 Chron. 3:17). R. Tanhum bar Jeremiah said: Jeconiah was called *Asir*, "one imprisoned," because he had been in prison ('*asurim*); and his son called "Shealtiel" because he was like a sapling, newly set out (*hustelah*), through whom David's line would be continued.

R. Tanhuma said: Jeconiah was called *Asir*, "imprisoned," because God imprisoned Himself by His oath in regard to him; and Jeconiah's son was called Shealtiel, "God consulted," because God consulted the heavenly court, and they released Him from His oath.[218]

So, this Rabbinic text—in homiletical, not literal fashion, based on a statement in the Talmud in b. Sanh 38a—goes so far as to claim that God asked the heavenly court to release him from his oath against Jehoiachin! That's how firmly entrenched this king's repentance was in the minds of the rabbis. More importantly, there is explicit scriptural support for the position that any curse against Jehoiachin's posterity was lifted, as the Messianic promises are renewed in his grandson Zerubbabel. It is therefore only fitting that the Messiah's genealogy be traced through Jehoiachin.

There is, however, one final question that needs to be asked, and this one is for the anti-missionaries, since they commonly cite the curse on Jehoiachin as proof that Jesus could not be the Messiah. The argument of Jews for Judaism, cited above (5.11), is typical: "Luke 3:27 lists Shealtiel and Zerubbabel in his genealogy. These two also appear in Matthew 1:12 as descendants of the cursed Jeconiah. If Mary descends from them, it would also disqualify her from being a Messianic progenitor." My question, then, is this: Are these anti-missionaries unfamiliar with all the ancient Rabbinic traditions that state that the curse was reversed?[219] That would be hard to imagine, since these Rabbinic texts are quite well known and some of the anti-missionaries are educated rabbis. Why then do they advance an argument that flies in the face of Rabbinic tradition? That would be like a Christian advancing an argument that contradicted the teachings of the New Testament. Could it be that it is quite hypocritical for some anti-missionaries to raise the charge of deception or dishonesty against Messianic Jews when, in reality, this is a charge by which they should examine themselves? After all, if an organization is called Jews for Judaism, shouldn't it be expected to represent the position of traditional Judaism rather than to attempt to refute the Christian position by any and all means? For lovers of truth, this is certainly something to consider.

5.13. Jesus did work some miracles, but they were not by God's power. We have traditions that tell us he learned magical arts in Egypt.

Aside from the fact that it is highly unlikely—to say the least!—that someone could raise the dead and open the eyes of people born blind by demonic or magical power (these were the kinds of miracles that Jesus performed, and they demonstrated the power of God, not the power of demons), the idea that Jesus learned magical arts in Egypt has as much factual or historical support as the claim that Santa Claus delivers gifts through the chimney on Christmas Eve. In fact, the Talmudic account that claims that a certain "Jesus" practiced magic actually places that "Jesus" in the wrong century! Also, the miracles of Jesus resulted in multitudes of Jews praising and worshiping the God of Israel, to whom Jesus pointed all people. To this day, around the world, genuine miracles take place as followers of Jesus simply pray to the God of Abraham, Isaac, and Jacob in the name of Yeshua the Messiah. This is hardly magic!

For the most part, it is only a small number of extremely fundamentalist Jews who take an objection like this seriously, but since it has been raised, we will take a moment to refute it.

We made reference (above, 5.7) to various Talmudic traditions that referred to a certain "Yeshu" (Jesus) who lived during several different centuries, concluding that either the Talmud was talking about two (or more) different people or that it was totally confused in its chronology.[220] The text in question here, b. Sanh 107b, dates this Yeshu to the reign of King Jannaeus, 104–78 b.c.e. So, if this was actually supposed to talk about the Yeshua of the Gospels, it is off by a hundred years. This would be similar to placing Ronald Reagan in the Civil War. How seriously would you take a history book that alleged that, while Reagan was president during the Civil War in the 1860s, he held secret meetings with Martian leaders who gave him counsel? Well, that's how seriously this Talmudic account should be taken, and only the most staunch and unscholarly Jews would even try to defend its contents as truthful and accurate.

For the record, here is the full account as rendered in the Soncino edition of the Talmud in footnote 17 to b. Sanh 107b. (It is found in the footnotes because it had been removed from the text by censors.)

What of R. Joshua b. Perahjah?—When King Jannai slew our Rabbis, R. Joshua b. Perahjah (and Jesus) fled to Alexandria of Egypt. On the resumption of peace, Simeon b. Shetach sent to him: 'From me, (Jerusalem) the holy city, to thee, Alexandria of Egypt (my sister). My husband dwelleth within thee and I am desolate.' He arose, went, and found himself in a certain inn, where great honour was shewn him. 'How beautiful is this Acsania!' (The word denotes both inn and innkeeper. R. Joshua used it in the first sense; the answer assumes the second to be meant.) Thereupon (Jesus) observed, 'Rabbi, her eyes are narrow.' 'Wretch,' he rebuked him, 'dost thou thus engage thyself.' He sounded four hundred trumpets and excommunicated him. He (Jesus) came before him many times pleading, 'Receive me!' But he would pay no heed to him. One day he (R. Joshua) was reciting the Shema', when Jesus came before him. He intended to receive him and made a sign to him. He (Jesus) thinking that it was to repel him, went, put up a brick, and worshipped it. 'Repent,' said he (R. Joshua) to him. He replied, 'I have thus learned from thee: He who sins and causes others to sin is not afforded the means of repentance.' And a Master has said, 'Jesus the Nazarene practised magic and led Israel astray.'[221]

You might say, "But doesn't the end of this text explicitly say that is talking about Jesus the Nazarene?"

The answer, of course, is yes it does, which points to how confused the whole account is—not to mention completely absurd—and why no reputable scholar defends it today.

You might still ask, "But shouldn't we have an answer for these charges? After all, they have been raised."

Yes, they have been raised, but there is no more need to defend Yeshua against such slanderous charges than it is necessary to provide scholarly documentation showing that, contrary to accounts in periodicals like the *National Enquirer*, Elvis Presley and Adolph Hitler are *not* alive today. Perhaps also the Jewish leadership should be required to provide scholarly documentation refuting every libelous charge that has come against them. Perhaps the rabbis should be required to prove that they do not make Passover matzah every year using the blood of Christian children whom they kidnap and crucify. Perhaps the Israeli leadership should be required to demonstrate that Jews are actually humans and not the "sons of monkeys and pigs." (For more on this, see my chapters, "Lies! Lies! Lies!" and "Bigotry and Biased Reporting," in *Our Hands Are Stained with Blood*.)

The fact is that, during his lifetime, Jesus was vilified and slandered, so there's no surprise that this continues to happen today. God himself is vilified and slandered to this day, so there's no surprise that such ridiculous charges are made against his Son. However, for those wanting a proper assessment of mythical accounts such as the one just quoted—I say mythical if they are alleged to describe the Jesus of the Scriptures— the verdict pronounced by professor Solomon Schechter in 1898, with reference to the medieval collection of anti-Jesus myths called *Toledot Yeshu*, stands true. He stated, "All the so-called Anti-Christiana collected by medieval [Jewish] fanatics, and freshed up again by modern ignoramuses, belong to the later centuries, when history and biography had already given way to myth and speculation."[222]

In stark contrast with all this are the miracles of the Messiah, who would not put on a show just to demonstrate his power, repeatedly refusing to give a miraculous sign to those who tested him (see, e.g., Matt. 12:38–42; 16:1–4). He even rebuked those who asked for such a sign, saying, "A wicked and adulterous generation looks for a miraculous sign, but none will be given it except the sign of Jonah" (Matt. 16:4). But he was moved with compassion to heal the sick and raise the dead, and his miracles brought glory and attention to his Father, God (for more on this, see vol. 2, 3.4). In fact, following the pattern of Moses and other great prophets in Israel's history, the miracles were part of the divine validation for their mission (see, e.g., Exod. 4:1–9, 29–31; 1 Kings 18).

As I wrote in *Israel's Divine Healer*:

> In the OT, Yahweh's healings were perceived as acts of mercy and grace, reflective of his goodness, and worthy of praise (see, e.g., Pss 6:2[3] and Ps 103, which have as their background healing from serious illness; . . . cf. also Php 2:27). So also, it is noted several times that Jesus healed out of compassion, stated most broadly in Matthew 14:14: "When Jesus landed and saw a large crowd, he had compassion on them and healed their sick." The following individual cases of healing or resurrection out of compassion (always *splanchnizomai*) are also recorded: the leper (Mk 1:40–42); the two blind men (Mt 20:29–34, in response to their cries for mercy; cf. Mk 9:22, and the request for compassion ["take pity on us"] from the father of the demon-possessed boy); the bereaved widow (Lk 7:11–15). In similar fashion, Jesus fed the five thousand and the four thousand because he was moved by compassion for them (Mk 6:34, 8:2), and it was because of his compassion for the crowds—like sheep without a shepherd—that he urged his disciples to petition the Lord of the harvest to send forth laborers into his harvest field (Mt 9:36–37). Thus these supernatural healings were not merely authenticating signs of his divinity or Messiahship . . . ; rather, they reflected the very heart of God towards sick and suffering humanity.
>
> Based on this observation, one gains insight into the character of the Father: Jesus healed and delivered because God was with him (Ac 10:38). In curing the paralytic on the Sabbath, he was only doing what he saw his Father doing (Jn 5:16–20); in fact, it was the miracles themselves that gave proof to the fact that the Father was in him and he in the Father (Jn 10:38). Thus Jesus could say to his detractors, "Do not believe in me unless I do what my Father does" (Jn 10:37); and to Philip he could pointedly ask, "Don't you know me, Philip, even after I have been among you such a long time? Anyone who has seen me has seen the Father. . . . The words I say to you are not just my own. Rather, it is the Father living in me, who is doing his work. Believe me when I say that I am in the Father and the Father is in me; or at least believe on the evidence of the miracles themselves" (Jn 14:9–11).
>
> As expressed elsewhere in the epistles, Jesus was "the radiance of God's glory and the exact representation of his being" (Heb 1:3a), "the image of the invisible God" (Col 1:15a)—both in power and in love. Through his words and deeds, his life and death, he made God known to humanity (Jn 1:18).[223]

So then, far from practicing magic and leading Israel astray, he ministered in the power of the Spirit and brought many Jews and Gentiles into an intimate relationship with the God of Israel. For a typical picture of the Son of God in action in New Testament times, see Matthew 15:30–31, and notice carefully the results of the miracles (my emphasis):

> Great crowds came to him, bringing the lame, the blind, the crippled, the mute and many others, and laid them at his feet; and he healed them. The people were amazed when they saw the mute speaking, the crippled made well, the lame walking and the blind seeing. *And they praised the God of Israel.*

What else would you expect? The crowds continue to praise the God of Israel because of Jesus the Messiah until this very day.

5.14. Jesus didn't fulfill any of the Messianic prophecies. We know that the New Testament writers actually reconstructed the life of Jesus so as to harmonize it with certain predictions made by the prophets.

We have demonstrated elsewhere that Jesus, in fact, did fulfill all the Messianic prophecies that had to be fulfilled before the Second Temple was destroyed in the year 70 c.e. We have also shown the historical reliability of the Gospels. But there is a problem with your whole objection. It is self-contradictory! Why would the New Covenant writers intentionally rewrite the events of Yeshua's life so as to make him fulfill predictions that were not really Messianic? If the prophecies which they quoted were really non-Messianic (or, if they had to be wrenched out of context to be used), then why did they "make" Yeshua's life conform to them? I should also point out that there is not an ounce of verifiable evidence that you can provide to support your claim.

In volumes 1 and 3, we demonstrated that Yeshua fulfilled all the prophecies that had to be fulfilled before 70 c.e., that he is the only possible candidate who can qualify to be Israel's Messiah, that, in his ongoing work throughout the earth today, he continues to fulfill Messianic prophecy, and we can therefore be confident that he will return and establish God's kingdom on the earth, bringing to completion the

Messianic mission (see vol. 1, 2.1; vol. 2, 3.24). In this current volume, we addressed the question of the textual and historical reliability of the New Covenant Writings (see 5.1, 5.6). These two facts, namely, that Yeshua *did* fulfill the requisite prophecies and that the New Testament authors *were* historically and textually reliable, completely undermine the current objection, one that is based on speculation and not on the evidence of any written, ancient texts.

In light of the cumulative evidence presented elsewhere in this series, there is no need to respond to this objection at length. I will, however, offer three further considerations in support of the reliability of the New Testament accounts.

First, we know that Yeshua died a violent death at the hands of the Romans—this is verified by external sources as well as internal evidence—and that his death was understood by his followers to be an atoning sacrifice for the sins of the world, in accordance with the biblical prophecies (see also vol. 2, 3.15). Some of these prophecies also mentioned that this servant of the Lord who would offer his life as an 'asham, a guilt offering, would be rejected and misunderstood by his own people (see Isa. 53:3–5) before being a light to the Gentiles, who would put their trust in him on a global basis (see Isa. 49:3–7; note also 42:1–7; 52:13–15). Now, it is one thing to argue that the New Testament writers, despondent and disappointed over Yeshua's death, reconstructed the events of his life to make it look as though prophecy was being fulfilled. But how do you explain the fact that, to this day, Yeshua is fulfilling these very prophecies? And if he is not fulfilling them, who is? A more logical possibility is that Jesus *did* suffer and die and rise, just as the prophets foretold and just as the New Testament records, which is why his Messianic mission continues to make progress to this day, with multitudes finding healing and redemption through him, just as the prophets foretold (see especially Isa. 53:5–6).

Second, it is clear that the authors of the Gospels accurately recorded the events of Jesus' life since they make no effort to deny that he was born (and died) as King of the Jews (Matt. 2:2; 27:11, 29, 37), that there was clear, prophetic expectation that he would usher in a reign of peace (cf. Luke 2:8–14; 24:21; see also 1:68–75, cited below), and that the disciples were unable to understand why he had to suffer and die (see, e.g., Matt. 16:21–22). In fact, they were so baffled by this that they couldn't even understand what he meant when he said that he was going to rise from the dead! (See Mark 9:10, as Peter, James, and John came down with Jesus from the Mount of Transfiguration: "Jesus gave them orders not to tell anyone what they had seen until the Son of Man had risen from the dead. They kept the matter to themselves, discussing what 'rising from the dead' meant.") Not only so, but after his resurrection, they had basically lost all hope, even having a hard time believing those who saw Yeshua after he rose. (See also John 20:9, written *after* the resurrection but describing the time before the disciples had seen the risen Messiah: "They still did not understand from Scripture that Jesus had to rise from the dead.")

Now, if their goal was to rewrite the life of Jesus to make it conform to the prophecies of a suffering servant of the Lord, why portray his birth as fulfilling the prophecy of the Messianic king in Micah 5:2 (see Matt. 2:1–6)? Why have Zechariah, the father of John the Immerser, speak these words at the birth of his son?

> Praise be to the Lord, the God of Israel,
>   because he has come and has redeemed his people.
> He has raised up a horn of salvation for us
>   in the house of his servant David
> (as he said through his holy prophets of long ago),
>   salvation from our enemies
>   and from the hand of all who hate us—
> to show mercy to our fathers
>   and to remember his holy covenant,
>   the oath he swore to our father Abraham:
> to rescue us from the hand of our enemies,
>   and to enable us to serve him without fear
>   in holiness and righteousness before him all our days.
>
> Luke 1:68–75

Why not show that, from the start, Jesus was fulfilling a *different* set of prophecies, ones having to do with Messiah's suffering and death rather than his royal reign? And why make the whole issue of his death such a surprise, since, after all, Messiah's death on the cross is the very foundation of the New Testament faith? Why not give the disciples a little more credit? (In fact, since some of the Gospels were written by these very disciples, why didn't they give themselves a little more credit?) Why make Yeshua's death and resurrection something that could only be seen as fulfilling Scripture *after* the fact? Luke records that, after his resurrection, Yeshua said to his disciples:

> "This is what I told you while I was still with you: Everything must be fulfilled that is written about me in the Law of Moses, the Prophets and the Psalms."
>   Then he opened their minds so they could understand the Scriptures. He told them, "This is what is written: The [Messiah] will suffer and rise

from the dead on the third day, and repentance and forgiveness of sins will be preached in his name to all nations, beginning at Jerusalem. You are witnesses of these things."

Luke 24:44–48

So, the events came first—as unexpected as some of them were—and the realization of the fulfilled Scriptures came later. If you go back and read the accounts, you will see that this makes perfect sense.

Third, the connection between the event and its prophetic antecedent is not always clear, indicating that the events preceded the finding of the prophetic fulfillment, rather than the event being manufactured to fit the prophetic text.[224] Why, for example, would Matthew manufacture the idea that Yeshua came from Nazareth and find fulfillment for this in "the prophets" when there was no single explicit text that makes this claim (see above, 5.3)? Or why would Matthew, who clearly understood Hebrew (see above, 5.1–5.4), construct an alleged myth about Jesus' virginal conception when the Hebrew word 'almah did not unequivocally refer to a virgin (see vol. 3, 4.3)? (With reference to the events recorded in Matthew 27:1–10, see the comments of D. A. Carson, cited above, at the end of 5.4).

So, the textual evidence stands against this objection, logic stands against it, the witness of the biblical prophets stands against it, and *the very next objection stands against it*. This, however, should occasion no surprise, since it is not uncommon for two objections to cancel each other out. So much for the strength of these objections!

5.15. When Jesus failed to fulfill the prophecies, his followers invented the myth of his substitutionary death, his resurrection, and finally, his second coming, which, of course, they completely expected in his lifetime.

> In order to make this claim, you virtually have to rewrite the entire New Testament, since a central theme of those writings, from their earliest strata on, is that Jesus had to go to the cross and suffer and die and then rise from the dead. This was his sacred mission! And Jesus frequently taught about his departure from this world and his eventual return, also indicating that he would be away for a long time. Not only so, but his substitutionary death also

> helped explain a number of passages in the Tanakh that
> spoke of the vicarious suffering of God's righteous servant.
> Would you argue that the followers of Jesus also invented
> those passages?

Since this objection has no historical or textual support of any kind, to refute it is roughly equivalent to punching the air. The punch has substance, but there is nothing to hit! In fact, the only way someone can raise this objection is to presuppose that it is true, throw out the consistent testimony of almost the entire New Testament, and then simply state that the presuppositions are correct. That is to say, you have to presuppose that: (1) There were no biblical prophecies pointing to the Messiah's suffering which, of course, completely contradicts the objection that Yeshua's followers reconstructed his life to *fit* those very prophecies (see 5.14). (2) Jesus never spoke to his disciples (or the crowds) about going to the cross, dying, and rising from the dead—a theme that it is on his lips in each of the four Gospels—and that he never said that he was giving his life as a ransom for many. (3) The Messiah's Last Supper with the disciples, in which Jesus said that his body was about to be given for them and his blood about to be shed to inaugurate the new covenant, actually never took place, despite the fact that this meal, at the Lord's command, has been commemorated by Yeshua's followers from that time until today. (4) Jesus never rose from the dead, which would mean that the books of the New Testament—all of which either record this, refer to it, or recognize the resurrection as a historical fact—are 100 percent wrong 100 percent of the time about the most foundational element of their faith. It would also mean that every eyewitness testimony of his resurrection was either the result of hallucination, "mistaken identity," or fabrication. (5) Within days, all the disciples, without breaking ranks, overcame the shock and trauma of their Master's ignominious death; quickly came up with this fabricated account; developed a whole new theology to support it—although until that time they had never once entertained the idea—including the idea of a first and second coming (also finding ample Scripture to support all this); then went public with their message in a matter of weeks and withstood rejection, persecution, imprisonment, beatings, and even martyrdom, without backing down one inch. And this was just the start! (6) On top of all this, they not only created the myth of the second coming but then misunderstood the myth they created, wrongly believing it would happen in their lifetimes when, in fact, they were fully aware that they had made the whole thing up.

If you believe this, I have an exclusive contract for you on the Brooklyn Bridge. Buy it while it's available! I also have some information for you on a new website in which you can correspond directly with aliens.

All sarcasm aside, the whole objection has no more merit to it than the latest "Elvis is alive" headlines in the tabloids or the proverbial sale of the Brooklyn Bridge. Those still needing to understand more fully why this objection is itself a complete fabrication would benefit from reviewing 5.22, where we address the objection that Jesus was a false prophet who predicted his return during the lifetimes of his disciples; 5.6, where we point to the evidence for the historical reliability of the New Testament books; 5.14, where we demonstrate that the Gospel accounts were not rewritten so as to agree with key biblical prophecies; volume 1, 2.1, where we explain that the Messiah first had to make atonement for our sins before the Second Temple was destroyed in 70 c.e. before establishing his kingdom on the earth; volume 2, 3.23, where we give further biblical foundations for the concept of a suffering Messiah, along with biblical support for his first and second comings; and volume 3, 4.5–4.21, where we treat key passages such as Isaiah 52:13–53:12; Psalm 22; Daniel 9:24–27. That will be more than enough!

5.16. Do you want irrefutable proof that the authors of the New Testament didn't know what they were talking about? Well, look at Matthew 23:35, where Jesus states that the last martyr spoken of in the Hebrew Scriptures was Zechariah son of Berechiah. Actually, that was the name of the biblical prophet (see Zech. 1:1); the last martyr was Zechariah son of Jehoiada (see 2 Chron. 24:20–22). So, either Jesus, your alleged Messiah, didn't know his Bible, or else Matthew (or the final editor of his book) didn't know the Tanakh. Either way, this is a glaring error that cannot be ignored.

Actually, there are simple solutions to this apparent discrepancy which are totally reasonable and which completely resolve the problem. I should point out, however, that the force of your objection is exaggerated, since there are similar difficulties in some ancient Rabbinic citations of

Scripture, one of which also seems to confuse these two
Zechariahs. Do you therefore conclude that the ancient
rabbis didn't know what they were talking about?

Let's begin by reviewing the problem. In Matthew 23:35, Yeshua culminates his rebuke of the hypocritical religious leaders by stating, "And
so upon you will come all the righteous blood that has been shed on
earth, from the blood of righteous Abel to the blood of Zechariah son
of Berekiah, whom you murdered between the temple and the altar."
The reference, then, is to the first and last martyrs of the Hebrew Bible,
yet there is no record of Zechariah son of Berekiah, apparently referring to the author of the Book of Zechariah, being killed, while there
is a reference to another Zechariah being killed, and this one fits the
description given in Matthew 23:

> Then the Spirit of God came upon Zechariah son of Jehoiada the priest.
> He stood before the people and said, "This is what God says: 'Why do you
> disobey the LORD's commands? You will not prosper. Because you have
> forsaken the LORD, he has forsaken you.'"
> But they plotted against him, and by order of the king they stoned
> him to death in the courtyard of the LORD's temple. King Joash did not
> remember the kindness Zechariah's father Jehoiada had shown him but
> killed his son, who said as he lay dying, "May the LORD see this and call
> you to account."
>
> 2 Chronicles 24:20–22

Further confirmation for this account being the one to which Jesus
was referring comes from its location in 2 Chronicles, the last book of
the Hebrew Bible according to the order found in all Rabbinic Bibles. If
this order of the books existed in Yeshua's day, then the reference would
be all the more appropriate, speaking of righteous Abel, whose murder
was recounted in Genesis, the first book of the Tanakh, and Zechariah
son of Jehoiada, whose murder was recounted in 2 Chronicles, the last
book of the Tanakh.[225]
Is it possible that the biblical prophet Zechariah *was*, in fact, martyred
and that Jesus was referring to this? Of course, it is possible, since the
Bible does not record how he died. But there is no evidence to support
this view whereas the evidence pointing to Zechariah son of Jehoiada
is very strong. The same can be said for the suggestion that there was
another Zechariah son of Berechiah—in other words, someone other than
the biblical prophet—and that this Zechariah was martyred, but again,

there is no evidence of any kind to support this view, and it is clear that Jesus was pointing to a known event and a known figure.[226]

How then should this discrepancy be explained? One explanation is that Zechariah son of Jehoiada also bore the family name, "son of Berechiah," probably meaning "grandson of Berechiah." A farfetched explanation, you say? Actually, a virtually identical phenomenon occurs in the Targum to Lamentations 2:20, where the end of this verse, which in the Hebrew text reads, "Should priest and prophet be killed in the sanctuary of the Lord?" (ESV), is expanded in the Targum to make reference to the killing of "Zechariah son of Iddo the high priest and faithful prophet" in the Temple on the Day of Atonement. So, the Targum also "confuses" Zechariah son of Jehoiada with Zechariah the prophet, who is not only described as the "son of Berechiah, son of Iddo" (ESV) in Zechariah 1:1, 7 but, significantly, is described as Zechariah son of Iddo in Ezra 5:1 and 6:14 (these verses are written in Aramaic)—the name used in the Aramaic Targum for the Zechariah who was martyred in 2 Chronicles 24.[227]

In light of this, several points can be made: (1) Perhaps both the Targum and the New Testament got things wrong. This, of course, is an untenable position for followers of Jesus who believe in the reliability of the biblical text and for traditional Jews who believe in the reliability of the ancient Rabbinic traditions.[228] (2) It could be that the biblical prophet *was* martyred in the Temple, with both the New Testament and Targum bearing witness to this fact. While this is possible, it cannot be proven, seeing that it has no support in other sources while, conversely, the reference to Zechariah son of Jehoiada seems so clear. (3) It is possible that Zechariah son of Jehoiada was also known as Zechariah son of Berechiah. (A traditional Jew would argue that he was also known as Zechariah son of Iddo!) Again, this cannot be demonstrated, but it is possible, especially since we do not have his grandfather's name, and, as we have seen, in Ezra 5:1; 6:14, the prophet Zechariah is identified as the (grand)son of Iddo (NIV has "the descendant of Iddo") rather than the son of Berechiah.[229]

Another explanation is that, just as may have occurred in the Targum, an error crept into many of the New Testament manuscripts when a scribe substituted the more familiar name of Zechariah son of Berechiah for the less familiar name of Zechariah son of Jehoiada. Then, when later copyists found this error, they were reluctant to alter the text, seeing that they believed that it preserved the correct reading, whereas in actuality it contained a scribal error. Errors like this have crept into virtually all major, ancient sacred texts, and, for the most part, they can be identified through the science called textual criticism.[230] Thankfully, in the case of the New Testament, we have abundant manuscript evidence, more than in any other ancient book of any kind (see above, 5.1).

What then does the textual data suggest in the case of Matthew 23:35? The evidence is significant. First, there are some Greek manuscripts that preserve the reading "Zechariah son of Jehoiada." While these manuscripts are in the very clear minority, and while it is possible that they reflect a later scribal *correction* to the original text, their witness is still of interest. Second, and more importantly, there is a statement from Jerome, a leading Gentile Christian scholar (331–420 c.e.) stating that the Nazareans, referring to one of the original groups of Jewish followers of Yeshua, had a Hebrew text of Matthew that read here Zechariah son of Jehoiada; see Jerome's commentary to Matthew 23:35. Given the fact that there are numerous statements from the early church pointing to an original Hebrew Matthew—or, at the least, a Hebrew version used by some of the early Messianic Jews (see further, vol. 5, 6.15)—the comments of Jerome would point to the possibility that the original reading *was* Zechariah son of Jehoiada and that the error first occurred in the Greek text of Matthew.

Additional light can be shed on this from the reading preserved in a medieval Hebrew manuscript of Matthew known as the Shem Tob Matthew (see again vol. 5, 6.15). While most scholars dismiss this as a *translation* into Hebrew from the Greek, there is some evidence that, on occasion, it provides insight into the wording of a putative Hebrew original. And, on a less controversial level, it reminds us of how Hebrew writers commonly abbreviated Hebrew and Aramaic names and phrases. In the case of Matthew 23:35, the Shem Tob manuscript makes reference to Zechariah, followed by the slash that signifies a shortened phrase in Hebrew. (It is the rough equivalent of "etc." in English and is found throughout Rabbinic writings. Note also that the parallel passage in Luke 11:51 simply reads, "from the blood of Abel to the blood of Zechariah, who was killed between the altar and the sanctuary.") So, it is very possible that an early scribe copying the words "Zechariah son of Jehoiada" wrote instead, "Zechariah, etc." (or, simply, "Zechariah," as in Luke 11:51), which was later mistakenly filled out as "Zechariah son of Berechiah," erroneously becoming the dominant textual tradition. As stated above, once the wrong reading became widely known, it was assumed to be the original reading, thus perpetuating the error. (Something similar could well have occurred in the Targumic text just discussed.) In the case of Matthew 23:35, we have Greek manuscripts of Matthew as well as references to ancient Hebrew manuscripts of Matthew that may preserve the accurate, original reading.[231] This, then, would completely eliminate the problem.

Interestingly, anti-missionaries often attack this passage in Matthew with passion, making it a special object of their scorn.[232] This, of course, is not only inaccurate, it is unfair, seeing that these same anti-missionaries would never attack the Rabbinic writings for apparent errors of similar—or much worse—magnitude, such as that found in the Targum to Lamentations 2:20. To illustrate this more fully, I will cite three more examples.

What do the anti-missionaries say about Genesis Rabbah 64:5, where reference is made to Jezebel's persecution of the prophets in the day of Jeremiah's father Hilkiah? Jezebel and Hilkiah were separated by several centuries. The footnote to the Soncino English edition of the Midrash explains,

> The mention of Jezebel in this connection is an anachronism, as of course she lived many generations earlier. It is probable that the Midrash wishes to indicate that it was a dangerous time for prophets (as indeed we see in the account of Jeremiah's own life) and cites Jezebel as an illustration.

An anachronism indeed! Why don't the anti-missionaries heap ridicule on this text? Why don't they claim that the authors and editors of Midrash Rabbah, considered by tradition to be among the greatest sages of the Jewish people, didn't know the first thing about their own history?

And what about b. Ber 3b, discussed briefly above, that incorrectly cites a biblical text, stating, "And after Ahithofel was Jehoiada, the son of Benaiah, and Abiathar; and the captain of the King's host was Joab," whereas, "The text here has 'Benaiah, the son of Jehoiada', who is mentioned in II Sam. XX, 23."[233] But the quote is from 1 Chronicles 27:34, "Ahithophel was succeeded by Jehoiada son of Benaiah and by Abiathar. Joab was the commander of the royal army"! There apparently was a Jehoiada, his son Benaiah, and his son Jehoiada (cf. the standard commentaries to 1 Chron. 27:34, with reference to 1 Chron. 12:27–28). The Talmud apparently got Jehoiada, son of Benaiah confused with the much more common Benaiah son of Jehoiada.[234]

Finally, note b. Sanh 107b, where the Talmud, making reference to Gehazi, the servant of Elisha, states: "as it is written: Elisha went to Damascus." The problem, as noted in the Schottenstein Talmud (107b², n. 13) is that, "There is no such verse in Scripture. Rather, *II Kings 8:7* reads: *wayyabo' 'eliša' dammeseq, Elisha came to Damascus*," pointing out that this is the reading in both the Jerusalem Talmud and the compilation of Talmudic Aggadah called Ein Yaakov. (A marginal note in standard Talmud editions also draws attention to this misquotation.)

The error may be minor, but in all standard editions of the Babylonian Talmud, a misquotation from the Tanakh is perpetuated.[235]

Now, in all candor, I have no problem with Orthodox and ultra-Orthodox Jews attempting to explain these discrepancies, even in the most ingenious ways. Where I do have a problem is when unequal weights and measures are used and when one canon of criticism is used on one text while an entirely different one is used on another text (see the appendix in vol. 5, "Unequal Weights and Measures," for further discussion). Let us be consistent in our methodology![236] If we were, we would find that the apparent difficulties in the New Covenant Writings are far more easily resolved than the apparent difficulties in the Tanakh and, much more so, than those found in the Rabbinic writings, as noted in the appendix in volume 5.

5.17. The New Testament is self-contradictory (especially the Gospels)!

This subject has been addressed thousands of times in commentaries and books dealing with apparent contradictions in the Bible, and the same fair and honest methods that resolve problems like this in the Hebrew Scriptures also resolve similar problems in the New Covenant Writings.

I address this issue in the appendix to volume 5, "Unequal Weights and Measures," demonstrating the unfairness of using one canon of criticism when evaluating the veracity of accounts in the Tanakh while using another canon of criticism when evaluating the veracity of accounts in the New Testament. The fact is, there are apparent contradictions in both parts of the Bible. For those who give the benefit of the doubt to the biblical authors and editors and assume that they would not preserve and transmit impossibly self-contradictory accounts and doctrines, there are plausible answers. For those who are skeptical or downright hostile to these authors and editors, the answers are not plausible. Thus, my only request is for fairness, and in the case of a traditional Jew, before attacking the New Covenant Writings as self-contradictory, he or she should ask: "If I attacked the Tanakh the same way as I am attacking the New Testament, would it stand? And if I attacked the Talmud in this same way, would it stand?" The answers to both questions are the same: Absolutely not. As explained in the appendix to volume 5, if the anti-missionaries "would be honest with themselves, they would have to admit that, using the same canon of criticism on their own sacred texts, they would utterly shipwreck their own faith. In other words, if the New Testament would be disqualified by anti-missionary arguments in one hour, using those same arguments, the Tanakh would be disqualified in a matter of minutes and the Talmud in a matter of seconds!"

To give just one example out of scores—if not hundreds—that could be adduced, note how nonfundamentalist, Jewish scholars resolve an apparent contradiction in Rabbinic sources:

> How the views of the Tannaim concerning Gentiles were influenced largely by their own personal temper and the conditions of their age, is apparent from an analysis of the discussion on the meaning of Prov. xiv. 34, of which two versions are found: one in Pesik. 12b; the other in a baraita in B. B. 10b. According to the former, Eliezer, Joshua, and Eleazar b. 'Arak, under their master Johanan ben Zakkai; and Gamaliel, a certain Abin b. Judah, and Nehunya ben ha-Kana are the participants. In the latter version, Eliezer, Joshua, Gamaliel, Eleazar of Modi'im, and Nehunya ben ha-Kana are mentioned. It is probable that two distinct discussions, one under Johanan ben Zakkai and the other under Gamaliel, were combined, and the names and opinions confounded (see Bacher, "Ag. Tan." i. 38, note).[237]

Note the conclusion: "It is probable that two distinct discussions . . . were combined, and the names and opinions confounded." And this is a minor example. Much more serious contradictions occur throughout Rabbinic literature. Liberal scholars recognize them as the result of human imperfection; the most religious scholars have an answer for each and every contradiction—and I assure you that their answers are far more ingenious than anything you will find in New Testament apologetics!

As for the issue of alleged contradictions within the New Testament, because this has been addressed on so many different occasions, I will make several methodological points that are useful when studying apparent contradictions, followed by a brief listing of relevant books for further study.

1. Common sense would tell us that the authors or editors of the different biblical books (be they the books of the Tanakh or the New Testament) did not willfully or knowingly compose or pass on contradictory accounts, especially ones that contradicted themselves within a matter of verses. So, rather than claiming that the creation accounts in Genesis 1 and Genesis 2 are in obvious contradiction, it would be better to ask first how these accounts could be harmonized without doing violence to the text. The same principle, of course, should be applied to the Gospels.

2. Witnesses testifying at the scene of an accident or in a court case often give similar but not identical accounts of what happened. That's because they each see the event from their unique vantage point and through their individual perspective. In fact, when they all tell the same story in exactly the same way, their testimony is suspect! The same can be said of the Gospel authors: They all tell the same overall story—quite clearly and indisputably—with each providing unique details and insights.

3. Authors often have a particular point to get across or a specific emphasis they want to communicate. Putting two such accounts side by side could give the impression that they are contradictory when, in fact, they are complementary.

4. Just because one author gives added information (such as Matthew referring to two demonized men in 8:28–34 whereas Mark refers to only one in Mark 5:1–20) does not mean that his account is contradictory.

5. Sometimes the whole problem is our limited vantage point: that is to say, we simply don't have all the information before us, and if we did, many contradictions would be resolved. How many times have you been involved with a situation and concluded that a particular person was responsible or guilty despite their claims to innocence (this can happen with parents and their kids) until the rest of the story emerged, proving their innocence. Sometimes just having more facts is the key, and often, with ancient accounts, that's the very thing we don't have.

Here is just one example of how an apparent contradiction, in this case between Matthew 27:5 with Acts 1:18–19, may be nothing more than a lack of information.

> Matthew says Judas hanged himself; Acts, that "he fell headlong, his body burst open and all his intestines spilled out." This does not imply a disease, or that Judas tripped, as some have held. If Judas hanged himself; no Jew would want to defile himself during the Feast of Unleavened Bread by burying the corpse; and a hot sun might have brought on rapid decomposition till the body fell to the ground and burst open. Alternatively, one long tradition in the church claims Judas hanged himself from a tree branch that leaned over a ravine (of which there are many in the area); and when the branch broke, whether before or after he died, Judas fell to a messy end. We are not so much beset by contradictory accounts as by paucity of information, making it difficult to decide which of several alternatives we should choose in working out the complementarity of the two accounts.[238]

Similar examples could be multiplied throughout the pages of the Scriptures, but this is not the place to repeat what others have already treated at length. For further study, Eric V. Snow's apologetic volume, *A Zeal for God Not according to Knowledge: A Refutation of Judaism's Arguments against Christianity*, contains much useful information, since it provides direct answers to many of the specific charges of contradictions raised directly by the anti-missionaries. See especially pages 156–255, and note also pages 18–155. Gleason Archer's *Encyclopedia of Bible Difficulties* (Grand Rapids: Zondervan, 1982) remains very useful and is backed by Archer's multifaceted scholarship. Dealing with a somewhat broader scope of questions, the *Hard Sayings of the Bible* series is highly recommended (now available in one volume, and cited elsewhere in this study). Craig Blomberg's *The Historical Reliability of the Gospels*, discussed above, 5.6, is useful in this context as well.

For recent, scholarly commentaries on the Gospels that deal fairly with apparent contradictions, on Matthew, see the commentaries of D. A. Carson, Craig S. Keener, Donald A. Hagner, and John Nolland; for Mark, see the volumes by William L. Lane, R. T. France, Robert A. Guelich, and Craig A. Evans; for Luke, see the commentaries of Darrell Bock, Joel B. Green, I. Howard Marshall, and John Nolland; for John, see again D. A. Carson, and Craig S. Keener, as well as Leon Morris and Andreas J. Köstenberger. (This list is not meant to be comprehensive.)

For a critical edition of the harmony of the Gospels in Greek with full scholarly apparatus, see *Synopsis Quattuor Evangeliorum*, ed. Kurt Aland (Stuttgart: Deutsche Bibelgesellschaft, 1986); for an English edition, see *Synopsis of the Four Gospels*, ed. Kurt Aland (New York: United Bible Societies, 1982).

5.18. Matthew claims that when Jesus died on the cross, "the tombs broke open and the bodies of many holy people who had died were raised to life. They came out of the tombs, and after Jesus' resurrection they went into the holy city and appeared to many people" (Matt. 27:52–53). This is obviously complete nonsense, without any hint of historical support. If such an incredible event ever took place—something like "the night of the living dead" in ancient Jerusalem—someone would have recorded it.

> Someone did record it: Matthew! The question is, Do you
> believe what he wrote? Or, perhaps a better question is,
> Is this account credible? Could such a thing have hap-
> pened? The fact is, the death of the Messiah for the sins of
> the world was one of the most important events in world
> history. Why should it be surprising that such an event
> would be attended with all kinds of unusual phenomena?
> The whole account in Matthew may seem incredible, but
> it is hardly impossible.

Let's be honest about all this. I can't prove the event happened and
you can't prove it didn't, and those who believe in the reliability of the
New Testament—for a host of excellent reasons, including personal
experience—believe this account too. Those who don't believe the New
Testament will dismiss this as well.

But let's not end our discussion on that note. As a Jewish person, do
you believe that the sun stood still in Joshua 10:12–14? If so, based on
what evidence? No one else recorded that incredible event.[239] How about
Elijah calling down fire on Mount Carmel in 1 Kings 18, or better yet,
calling down fire on more than a hundred people in 2 Kings 1? Do you
believe those accounts? If so, I ask again, based on what evidence? No
one else recorded these incredible events.

But these are relatively small miracles. Let's look at something more
foundational and of much greater import. Do you believe that the exodus from Egypt took place? Now *that* was an event! Just think of it: Ten
devastating plagues on the most advanced civilization of the day. The
liberation and escape of as many as two million slaves. The parting of
the sea. . . . How extraordinary!

What did the ancient Egyptian historians have to say about an event
of this magnitude, one which literally shook their whole country? Not a
word. Not even a hint! What about other Egyptian writers, perhaps poets
or philosophers or religious authors? What did they have to say? Nothing there either! Does that mean that you do not believe in the exodus
from Egypt, one of the greatest events in world history, not to mention
biblical history? The only fair question to ask in terms of the historicity
of the event is: Is there archaeological or literary evidence that rules out
the possibility of the exodus having occurred? Are there hard, cold facts
that preclude it, rather than an argument from silence?

In terms of the account in Matthew's Gospel, there is certainly no
evidence against it, nor have any contrary accounts been preserved
(meaning, claims from ancient writers that deny that this resurrection took place). And, considering the fanciful stories that occur in the

later, nonscriptural Gospel accounts (that is, in the other stories that were written about Jesus and his followers by nonbiblical authors), it is remarkable to see how understated Matthew is in his writing (along with the other Gospel authors in the New Testament).[240] Not only so, but in light of other, biblical accounts, his report in Matthew 27 does seem credible. Consider, for example, 2 Kings 13:20–21:

> Elisha died and was buried.
> Now Moabite raiders used to enter the country every spring. Once while some Israelites were burying a man, suddenly they saw a band of raiders; so they threw the man's body into Elisha's tomb. When the body touched Elisha's bones, the man came to life and stood up on his feet.

What if this was recorded in the New Testament with regard to the bones of Paul? Would you believe it? It really is quite an account.

How about God's sign to Hezekiah that he would be healed? The Lord said, "'I will make the shadow cast by the sun go back the ten steps it has gone down on the stairway of Ahaz.' So the sunlight went back the ten steps it had gone down" (Isa. 38:8). Some scientists have noted that if this actually happened, it would throw the entire galaxy into chaos, yet God did it. As he said to Jeremiah, "I am the Lord, the God of all mankind. Is anything too hard for me?" (Jer. 32:27).

How about his sending an angel to kill 185,000 Assyrian soldiers in a single night? Again, I ask: If this was recorded in the New Testament would you believe it or would you scoff at it? Yet 2 Kings 19:35 records, "That night the angel of the Lord went out and put to death a hundred and eighty-five thousand men in the Assyrian camp. When the people got up the next morning—there were all the dead bodies!" And is there a specific record of this in the Assyrian annals? Do their historians make reference to it? Absolutely not.

I could go on and on with similar examples of extraordinary acts of divine power in the Hebrew Scriptures, none of which are recorded by any other writers, but I've said enough to make the point: There is no reason to believe that God could not have raised a number of people when Jesus died on the cross, and the fact that no one else recorded it does not disprove it in the least. (If you are a traditional Jew, may I also ask you what historical, external confirmation you have for some of the more far-fetched miracle accounts found in the Talmud, accounts which are passed on as literal and truthful?)

A few more comments will suffice. First, who else would have recorded this? Certainly not a Roman historian (see above, 5.7) and certainly not a later, Rabbinic author. Second, how many historical accounts do we have from that particular part of the world during that particular period of time? Almost none! Looking for additional historical confirmation of most of the events that took place then and there is like looking for a needle in a haystack. Third, there are some interesting theological dimensions relating to Messiah's atoning death and the resurrection of the dead.

To explain further, professor Samuel Tobias Lachs noted in his comment on Matthew 27:52–53: "That the dead will rise at messianic times is commonplace."[241] Other passages in the New Testament point to this event as well, speaking of the resurrection of the righteous taking place in conjunction with Yeshua's return (see 1 Cor. 15:50–52; 1 Thess. 4:13–17; cf. also Matt. 24:30–31; Rev. 11:15), an event in which countless millions of people will get out of their graves.

Professor John Nolland sees the importance of this in its connection with the events surrounding Messiah's death, all of which were quite striking and filled with divine portent (including the darkening of the sky for three hours during midday; a powerful earthquake; and the rending of the Temple curtain from top to bottom; see Matthew 27:45–51). Nolland writes,

> With the opening of the tombs . . . the eschatological potential of the earth being shaken and the rocks being split is now clearly activated. But Matthew makes it quite plain that he is concerned here with proleptic [meaning, anticipatory] manifestations of eschatological realities, not with the full substance of those realities (which has been sketched as the culmination of the sweep through the future offered in chaps. 24–25). Matthew seems to be saying that with the death of Jesus history has begun its final rush to the eschatological denouement. That which happens now in miniature is an intimation, an anticipation, of what is due to happen on a grand, even a cosmic, scale.[242]

In light of the fact that this was one of the most important events that took place in the history of the human race, as the Son of God took on our punishment so that we could be saved from our sins, an accompanying event of this kind is hardly unbelievable. To read Matthew's words firsthand:

> From the sixth hour until the ninth hour darkness came over all the land. About the ninth hour Jesus cried out in a loud voice, "*Eloi, Eloi, lama sabachthani?*"—which means, "My God, my God, why have you forsaken me?"
>
> When some of those standing there heard this, they said, "He's calling Elijah."

Immediately one of them ran and got a sponge. He filled it with wine vinegar, put it on a stick, and offered it to Jesus to drink. The rest said, "Now leave him alone. Let's see if Elijah comes to save him."

And when Jesus had cried out again in a loud voice, he gave up his spirit.

At that moment the curtain of the temple was torn in two from top to bottom. The earth shook and the rocks split. The tombs broke open and the bodies of many holy people who had died were raised to life. They came out of the tombs, and after Jesus' resurrection they went into the holy city and appeared to many people.

Matthew 27:45–53

As to what happened to those who were raised to life, Matthew says nothing, since he was not trying to satisfy curiosity seekers, and we can only conjecture as to what happened to them. (The most obvious choices are that they went right back to their graves, which is possible but unlikely; that they lived for some time longer, and then died again, just like others who were raised from the dead in the Scriptures; or that they were translated to heaven like Enoch and Elijah in times past, which might be the most plausible suggestion.)

You might say, "I would think that an event like this would have created quite a stir," and you would be absolutely right. Within a few days of his death, it was taken for granted that everyone in Jerusalem was talking about Jesus, especially when reports of his resurrection began to circulate (see Luke 24:17–24). Then, after spending many days with his disciples, he ascended to heaven in the presence of five hundred witnesses, sending the Spirit on his followers ten days later. Not surprisingly, when one of them (Peter, who was a fisherman by trade but had now been trained by the Master) delivered the message about Messiah's death and resurrection, in a single day three thousand believed. Something was happening indeed!

The real questions you must ask are: Did Jesus the Messiah die for the sins of Israel and the nations, meaning for your sins as well? Did he rise from the dead and ascend to heaven? Is he alive this day and seated at the right hand of the Father? Will he come one day in the clouds of heaven to reward the righteous and punish the wicked?

These are the essential issues you must decide. Once they are settled, you will trust Matthew as a reliable guide.

5.19. The teachings of Jesus are impossible, dangerous, and un-Jewish ("Hate your mother and

father," "Let the dead bury their own dead," "Give to whoever asks you," etc.). There's no way he should be followed.

> As the Messiah and Son of God, Yeshua had the right to make serious demands of his followers, in keeping with God's demands on Israel in the Hebrew Scriptures. Still, some of his teachings have been misunderstood—on occasion, ironically enough, because of a lack of appreciation for the Jewish background of his words—while there are parallel accounts in traditional Jewish literature, until this very day, calling for radical commitment to Torah study, often to the dismay of family and friends. If this is justifiable, how much more justifiable is a wholehearted commitment to the Messiah? Those who know him and follow can testify firsthand that his ways are ways of life and what he demands of us, in the end, is for our good.

Before looking at the teachings of Jesus in question, let's consider some relevant passages from the Tanakh.

When God revealed himself to his people at Mount Sinai, he made his demands totally clear:

> I am the Lord your God, who brought you out of Egypt, out of the land of slavery.
> You shall have no other gods before me.
> You shall not make for yourself an idol in the form of anything in heaven above or on the earth beneath or in the waters below. You shall not bow down to them or worship them; for I, the Lord your God, am a jealous God, punishing the children for the sin of the fathers to the third and fourth generation of those who hate me, but showing love to a thousand generations of those who love me and keep my commandments.
>
> Exodus 20:2–6

He tolerated no rivals and clearly identified himself as a jealous (or, as some translate it, zealous) God who would punish sin as well as bless obedience. Does anyone question his right, as God, to make such demands?

Just a few weeks later, when Moses learned that his people had committed idolatry while he was on the mountain with God, he laid down the gauntlet, calling for radical obedience:

Moses saw that the people were running wild and that Aaron had let them get out of control and so become a laughingstock to their enemies. So he stood at the entrance to the camp and said, "Whoever is for the LORD, come to me." And all the Levites rallied to him.

Then he said to them, "This is what the LORD, the God of Israel, says: 'Each man strap a sword to his side. Go back and forth through the camp from one end to the other, each killing his brother and friend and neighbor.'" The Levites did as Moses commanded, and that day about three thousand of the people died. Then Moses said, "You have been set apart to the LORD today, for you were against your own sons and brothers, and he has blessed you this day."

Exodus 32:25–29

Here Moses actually called for his Israelite brothers *to kill* their fellow Israelites, something that Jesus the Messiah never did.

Forty years later, Moses set forth these commands from the Lord:

If your very own brother, or your son or daughter, or the wife you love, or your closest friend secretly entices you, saying, "Let us go and worship other gods" (gods that neither you nor your fathers have known, gods of the peoples around you, whether near or far, from one end of the land to the other), do not yield to him or listen to him. Show him no pity. Do not spare him or shield him. You must certainly put him to death. Your hand must be the first in putting him to death, and then the hands of all the people. Stone him to death, because he tried to turn you away from the LORD your God, who brought you out of Egypt, out of the land of slavery. Then all Israel will hear and be afraid, and no one among you will do such an evil thing again.

Deuteronomy 13:6–11

I can only imagine what the anti-missionaries would say if a passage like this was found in the New Testament! Somewhat ironically, the Ask Moses website, in its contemporary rendition of the 613 commandments, claims that, based on this passage of Scripture, God commands the Jewish people:

36. Not to missionize an individual to idol worship—Deuteronomy 13:12
37. Not to love the missionary—Deuteronomy 13:9
38. Not to cease hating the missionary—Deuteronomy 13:9
39. Not to save the missionary—Deuteronomy 13:9
40. Not to say anything in his defense—Deuteronomy 13:9
41. Not to refrain from incriminating him—Deuteronomy 13:9[243]

As we will see shortly, Jesus taught love, not hatred, calling on his followers to overcome evil with good, yet here, those who would criticize his teachings as extreme and dangerous advocate hatred towards those who are considered missionaries of idolatry.[244]

Returning to the passage in Deuteronomy 13, as harsh as it may sound to modern ears, it reminds us that, in the truest sense of the word, following the Lord or following idols was literally a matter of life or death, and if family allegiance got in the way of allegiance to the Lord, that allegiance was sinful. Put another way, it was a call for radical loyalty and ruthless love.[245]

Now, with this in mind, let's look at some of the statements made by Yeshua to his followers that have sometimes been considered extreme, also remembering that he said—sometimes in these very same contexts—"He who receives you receives me, and he who receives me receives the one who sent me" (Matt. 10:40) and "He who does not honor the Son does not honor the Father, who sent him" (John 5:23b). If he is the Messiah—and I say "if" for the benefit of readers who are unsure about his claims—then he is God's representative on the earth, and the way we treat him is the way we treat God. Conversely, the demands he places on us are not his demands alone, but those of his Father.

In Matthew 10, after quoting the words of Micah that end with "a man's enemies will be the members of his own household" (see Matt. 10:34–36; these verses are also quoted in the Mishnah in a Messianic context; see m. Sotah 9:15), he then states: "Anyone who loves his father or mother more than me is not worthy of me; anyone who loves his son or daughter more than me is not worthy of me; and anyone who does not take his cross and follow me is not worthy of me" (Matt. 10:37–38). Certainly, as Messiah and King, as the living will of God on earth, his demands are not in the least bit extreme, especially when compared to the verses just cited from Exodus 32 and Deuteronomy 13. (Remember: The Hebrew Bible was the one and only Bible of the people at that time, so Yeshua's words would be evaluated based on those words of Scripture.) Doesn't the Lord have the right to demand that we love him more than anyone else? He doesn't have to stoop to our level and make deals. We are called to walk worthy of him.

If you are a traditional Jew, try replacing the word "me" in these verses from Matthew 10:37–38 with "Torah," and see if you agree with the sentiments expressed. Or, for any other reader, just imagine God the Father speaking these words from heaven. Who among us would say that they were extreme? And what of the Talmud's teaching that, according to the Torah, honoring the Sabbath takes precedence over honoring one's parents? (See b. Yeb 5b, where it is stated that if a parent told a child to cook for him or her on the Sabbath, they were not to be obeyed, and see further, below, for extreme examples of Rabbinic devotion.)

How about Luke 14:25–33? Those verses sound a bit more extreme. Note these in particular:

> Large crowds were traveling with Jesus, and turning to them he said: "If anyone comes to me and does not hate his father and mother, his wife and children, his brothers and sisters—yes, even his own life—he cannot be my disciple. And anyone who does not carry his cross and follow me cannot be my disciple. . . .
>
> ". . . In the same way, any of you who does not give up everything he has cannot be my disciple."
>
> Luke 14:25–27, 33

Certainly, we can see what the Messiah was doing here. He was sifting the crowds and seeking out real disciples among them, those to whom he could entrust his message, those who would be faithful by life or by death. It was easy to flock around a miracle worker—after all, what do you think drew the crowds?—but who among them would really pay the price of obedience? As Dan Harman once said, "So long as Jesus was misunderstood He was followed by the crowd. When they came to really understand Him, they crucified Him."[246] For good reason, he was not impressed with crowds, challenging them in radical ways to prove their obedience (see John 6). And certainly, in light of the rewards associated with following Jesus—forgiveness of sins, eternal life, entrance into the family of God and the kingdom of God, the opportunity to serve the Master and be close to him—the call to leave everything for him could hardly be considered extreme.

But what about his opening words? Was it right for him to demand that his followers hate their fathers, mothers, wives, children, brothers, sisters, and even their own lives? When rightly understood, the answer is yes, it was right for him to demand this—but I repeat, only when we rightly understand his words.

To begin with, we must remember that elsewhere in the Gospels, Jesus taught *against* hatred, saying:

> You have heard that it was said, "Love your neighbor and hate your enemy." But I tell you: Love your enemies and pray for those who persecute you, that you may be sons of your Father in heaven. He causes his sun to rise on the evil and the good, and sends rain on the righteous and the unrighteous. If you love those who love you, what reward will you get? Are not even the tax collectors doing that? And if you greet only your brothers,

what are you doing more than others? Do not even pagans do that? Be perfect, therefore, as your heavenly Father is perfect.

Matthew 5:43–48

(For Jesus' teaching against retaliation, see the verses that immediately precede those above, namely, Matthew 5:38–42.)

Teachings such as these, coupled with his extraordinary personal example, were written indelibly on the hearts of his followers. They remembered well that when he was being crucified he prayed, "Father, forgive them, for they do not know what they are doing" (Luke 23:34), which explains why the powerful Jewish preacher named Stephen, the very first martyr for the Messiah, said with his very last breath as he was being stoned to death by the enraged Jewish leadership, "Lord, do not hold this sin against them" (Acts 7:60). This is what Jesus taught and modeled! A man being murdered in cold blood prays that God would not hold the sin of murder against his murderers.

Based on Jesus' example, Peter gave counsel to slaves who suffered under unjust masters:

> . . . For it is commendable if a man bears up under the pain of unjust suffering because he is conscious of God. But how is it to your credit if you receive a beating for doing wrong and endure it? But if you suffer for doing good and you endure it, this is commendable before God. To this you were called, because Christ suffered for you, leaving you an example, that you should follow in his steps.
>
> "He committed no sin,
>   and no deceit was found in his mouth."
>
> When they hurled their insults at him, he did not retaliate; when he suffered, he made no threats. Instead, he entrusted himself to him who judges justly. He himself bore our sins in his body on the tree, so that we might die to sins and live for righteousness; by his wounds you have been healed. For you were like sheep going astray, but now you have returned to the Shepherd and Overseer of your souls.

1 Peter 2:19–25

Was this the man who advocated hate? Ask his emissary Paul, who was a hateful and violent man before encountering his risen Messiah. He wrote to the believers in Rome:

> . . . If it is possible, as far as it depends on you, live at peace with everyone. Do not take revenge, my friends, but leave room for God's wrath, for it is written: "It is mine to avenge; I will repay," says the Lord. On the contrary:

"If your enemy is hungry, feed him;
     if he is thirsty, give him something to drink.
     In doing this, you will heap burning coals on his head."
Do not be overcome by evil, but overcome evil with good.

Romans 12:18–21

This is what happens to those who are transformed by the Messiah. Hatred is replaced by love and evil is overcome by good.

As for the notion that Jesus wanted us to despise our parents, bear in mind that he rebuked the Pharisees for allowing one of their traditions to get in the way of the command to honor one's father and mother (see Matt. 15:1–9), and, while dying on the cross, he asked his disciple John (Yohanan) to care for his mother Miriam. (See John 19:26–27: "When Jesus saw his mother there, and the disciple whom he loved standing nearby, he said to his mother, 'Dear woman, here is your son,' and to the disciple, 'Here is your mother.' From that time on, this disciple took her into his home.")

So we ask again, What exactly did he mean when he called on us to hate our closest relatives and even our own lives? Is it possible that he was telling us that, if we wanted to follow him, we should go home and say to our parents, "I hate your guts!", and if you're married, say to your spouse, "I despise you!", and then call our brothers and sisters and say, "I just want you to know that I absolutely loathe you!", and then, to prove that we hate our own lives, go and commit suicide? Out of the hundreds of millions of people who have read these words, I have yet to hear of a single account of anyone coming to these conclusions. Even common sense tells us that this could not be what he meant, while the overall context indicates that he was ultimately saying that "nothing, not love for father or mother or even one's own life, in and of themselves, take precedence over loyalty to God."[247]

"But," you ask, "then why use the word 'hate'?"

There were two reasons. First, and most obviously, he was making an extreme point and he wanted it to be heard in extreme terms. Following him was not a game, and his words were not for the fainthearted or double-minded. Second, if we examine the usage of the word *hate* in the Hebrew Bible, it is sometimes used to speak of being "unloved," or "scorned" or "rejected." For example, in Deuteronomy 21:15–17, the New Jewish Publication Society Version (NJPSV) translates the Hebrew word "hate" (*s-n-'*) with "unloved" ("If a man has two wives, one loved and the other unloved, and both the loved and the unloved have borne him sons, but the first-born is the son of the unloved one . . ."). As professor Jeffrey Tigay explains in his commentary to Deuteronomy, "Literally the two Hebrew terms mean 'loved' and 'hated,' but in describing a husband's feelings toward his wives, they mean his favorite wife and any other, whether she is simply unfavored, the object of indifference, or disliked," pointing out that, "Arabic also terms the favorite and nonfavorite wives, respectively, 'beloved' and 'hated.'"[248]

Related to this is the usage of *hate* in terms of God's dealing with the nation of Edom (descended from Esau). Did the Lord actually loathe the people of that nation—every last one of them—while he adored and loved each and every descendant of Jacob? Most translations of Malachi 1:2–3, which use the words *love* and *hate* could lend support to that notion, which would mean that not a single descendant was a recipient of his love. The NJPSV here, representing some of the finest Jewish scholarship, was sensitive to this, translating: "I have shown you love, said the LORD. But you ask, 'How have You shown us love?' After all—declares the LORD—Esau is Jacob's brother; yet I have accepted Jacob and have rejected Esau. I have made his hills a desolation, his territory a home for beasts of the desert." Notice here that the verb for *hated* is translated with "rejected," and I remind you that it was Jewish scholars who had this insight. What Jesus, therefore, was saying was that in order to follow him, we would have to reject every other hold and every other tie, following him alone and giving our allegiance to him alone, just as God called on each Israelite—in much stronger terms—to be the first one involved in putting an idolatrous family member to death (see above). The demands of Jesus, on behalf of his Father, are certainly less radical than that.

There is also a significant parallel to Yeshua's words found in Deuteronomy 33:9, recounting the faithfulness of the Levites at Mount Sinai when they killed fellow Israelites who had committed idolatry, referenced above. The text states:

> He said of his father and mother,
>   "I have no regard for them."
> He did not recognize his brothers
>   or acknowledge his own children,
> but he watched over your word
>   and guarded your covenant.

What striking words! Many scholars believe that Yeshua had this verse in mind when he called on those who would follow him to "hate" their parents and siblings.

Notice also the thrice-repeated phrase in the passage from Luke 14, "he cannot be my disciple." That is to say, it is impossible; it will not work; it cannot happen. "If you still have other loves greater than me, if you still have other allegiances that compete with me, you won't make it." You could almost picture the coach of a gifted athlete or the teacher of a gifted musician making similar demands on them for a season of their lives, telling them that they will have to eat, breathe, and think their sport (or music), telling them that they can have no competing interests, telling them that if they want to make it to the top, they will have to live differently than others live. And people actually do this for sports or music or money or fame, none of which can be compared in a million lifetimes with the privilege of serving and knowing Yeshua. He demands absolute allegiance. Who can argue with that?

What is beautiful is that, when you come to know him, you learn that, through his gracious help, his yoke is easy and his burden is light, and in coming to him, we find rest for our souls (see Matt. 11:28–30). Indeed, he offers us the water of life (John 7:37), and he himself is the bread of life and the resurrection of life (John 6:35; 11:24–25). That's why Paul could say, "But the things that used to be advantages for me, I have, because of the Messiah, come to consider a disadvantage. Not only that, but I consider everything a disadvantage in comparison with the supreme value of knowing the Messiah Yeshua as my Lord. It was because of him that I gave up everything and regard it all as garbage, in order to gain the Messiah" (Phil. 3:7–8 JNT).

It should also be added that millions of people around the world can testify that their marriages were put back together through following Yeshua, that their family was healed, that they became much better moms and dads or sons and daughters or husbands and wives, and that their own lives took on new significance and meaning. (As much as I love to provide footnotes and documentation, I could safely say that the largest libraries in the world could not contain the accounts of those who, in this generation and in past generations, would add a hearty "Amen" to this statement.)

Having said all this, I reiterate that Messiah's words were definitely meant to be radical here, but: (1) they were spoken with a definite purpose (to separate the devoted disciples from the casual consumers);[249] (2) they must be heard against the larger context of the forgiving and loving example that Jesus set from city to city, right up to his death; (3) the word "hate" should be understood to mean "utterly reject the claims and hold of"; and (4) compared to calls for allegiance in the Tanakh, his demands were relatively mild.[250] After all, didn't both Ezra and Nehemiah order all Jews who had intermarried with non-Jewish women to divorce their wives—even if they had children together—and separate? (See Ezra 9–10; cf. also Neh. 13:23–27.)

Added to all this was the urgency of the hour. Our Messiah and King had arrived here in the fullness of time, and he only had a few short years to handpick and train a faithful band of followers to whom he could entrust the message of salvation. He was about to die on the cross and shed his blood as a payment for the sins of the world, and the message and even effects of his sacrificial love could have been lost had there been no one to tell the world. I repeat: This was not a game! As the centuries have gone by, his words continue to carry tremendous relevance, since it is still a weighty thing to belong to him and he still requires absolute obedience to him and his Father. To this day, there are Muslims and Hindus and people from other religions who come to Jesus at great personal cost—sometimes even the cost of their own lives—and these words of the Master make lots of sense to them. And, from our vantage point today, we have the ability to read his words in the context of the entire New Testament, leaving us no reason to misunderstand his intent.

More difficult, perhaps, is another set of demands found in Luke 9:57–62 (cf. also Matt. 8:18–22, which, quite significantly, occurs in the context of great crowds following him after he performed many miracles):

> As they were walking along the road, a man said to him, "I will follow you wherever you go."
> Jesus replied, "Foxes have holes and birds of the air have nests, but the Son of Man has no place to lay his head."
> He said to another man, "Follow me."
> But the man replied, "Lord, first let me go and bury my father."
> Jesus said to him, "Let the dead bury their own dead, but you go and proclaim the kingdom of God."
> Still another said, "I will follow you, Lord; but first let me go back and say good-by to my family."
> Jesus replied, "No one who puts his hand to the plow and looks back is fit for service in the kingdom of God."

In light of what we have presented so far, the first and the last demands don't seem particularly harsh. He was saying to the first prospective disciple, "Really? You really want to follow me? Well, don't expect to be staying at the Ritz Carlton!" To the last he was most likely detecting a level of halfheartedness or procrastination, telling him that he had no place for such attitudes. After all, the man was not leaving his family forever, and we read of other disciples like Matthew (Levi) leaving everything and following Jesus and then, subsequently—perhaps that same day—holding a "a great banquet for Jesus at his house" (see

Luke 5:27–29). In other words, he dropped what he was doing and now devoted himself to following Yeshua, but he did not simply walk away from his home and never come back.[251] Was it so essential that this man went back to his family at that moment? The illustration given by Jesus underscores the aspect of doublemindedness, drawing on the imagery of "the plowman concentrating on the furrow before him, guiding the light plow with his left hand while goading the oxen with the right. Looking away would result in a crooked furrow."[252] And I reiterate: This was the Messiah, the Son of God, and he had the right to make these demands. He was not trying to win a popularity contest! Years later, John spoke of, "That which was from the beginning, which we have heard, which we have seen with our eyes, which we have looked at and our hands have touched—this we proclaim concerning the Word of life" (1 John 1:1). Encountering the Messiah and becoming part of his band of disciples was no small thing!

Still, the second demand is the hardest to understand, and commentators have wrestled with it for years, especially since Jewish law recognized the great importance of burying one's dead (not to mention common decency). What was Jesus saying? Lachs simply (and correctly) explains Jesus to mean, "Although the burial of the dead is meritorious, especially for a child to bury a parent, the work of the kingdom has absolute priority."[253] But it is possible that, here too, the text is not quite as extreme as it might appear at first glance, and many possible interpretations have been offered. Matthew commentator John Nolland lists the following: (1) this disciple was seeking "permission to stay behind until his aging parent (presently still in good health?) dies," which would seem to be quite a stretch, but, if true, would explain Yeshua's strong rebuke; or (2) he was seeking "permission to remain to see out the secondary mourning period (perhaps a year after his death) which was terminated by a secondary burial of the bones," a custom unknown to most people today but one that actually existed in Jesus' day, as documented by B. R. McCane in 1990;[254] or (3) that he wanted "permission to remain long enough to bury a dead or dying father, or to see out the primary seven days of mourning."[255]

Whatever the correct view would be, Nolland's conclusion is sound:

Even the normal claims of pious duty to one's parents must, however, give place to a more pressing duty (just as Jewish tradition allowed the pressing duty of dealing with one's dead to override the performance of other commandments and duties). There is here an incredible statement of the self-importance on the part of Jesus, coupled with an acute sense of the urgency of the hour in which he was operating (cf. Mt. 3:10).[256]

So then, taking Yeshua's words at the most extreme, what he was demanding would be similar to the situation of soldiers in battle who cannot stop to bury or gather their dead because of the exigencies of war. It does not speak of a lack of honor but rather of a more pressing demand. It is also possible, however, in light of several alternate and viable interpretations, that this excuse actually was a subterfuge and that Jesus saw through it, not allowing this would-be disciple to procrastinate.

If you come from a traditional Jewish background, may I encourage you to not be too quick in passing judgment on the words and ways of Yeshua? Let me give you some examples of what is considered to be praiseworthy behavior among Rabbinic leaders. Consider this story recounted by one of the most revered figures in modern-day, ultra-Orthodox Judaism, Rabbi Elazar Menachem Man Shach, who died in 2005 well past one hundred years old. He recalls:

> One of the outstanding students of the Volozhin yeshivah was Yossele Peimer, who was sent by his mother to study under Rav Chaim after his father passed away. Yossele was both a remarkable *ilui* (genius) and a phenomenal *masmid* (diligent student), who studied tirelessly day and night.
>
> One day a letter reached Rav Chaim from Yossele's mother. She wrote that she was unable to manage the family store and support her small children by herself and requested that Yossele return home to help out. Rav Chaim put the letter away without delivering it to his student. A few weeks later a second letter arrived, in which the mother complained that her son had not yet come home to help her and had not even answered the previous letter. Rav Chaim also put this letter away undelivered.
>
> A few months passed and another letter arrived from Yossele's mother in which she related that a fire had burned down her shop and left the family totally destitute. She demanded Yossele come home and help his family in its time of desperation. Rav Chaim again put the letter aside and said nothing to the boy. Not long after, a letter arrived from an older sister, who wrote that the mother was desperately ill. She castigated her brother for his cruelty. Rav Chaim hid this letter as well.
>
> Finally, a letter arrived with the news that Yossele's mother had passed away. It contained a plea from the forlorn orphans begging their older brother to come home and feed them. Rav Chaim hid this letter with the rest.
>
> Several years passed and Yossele, who was by then the best *bachur* [student] in the yeshivah, found a very desirable *shidduch* [marriage arrangement]. Before leaving Volozhin to get married, he went to take leave of the *Rosh Yeshivah* [head of the yeshivah]. Only then did Rav Chaim give him the letters he had been holding all those years.

Upon reading them, Yossele rent his garments and then fainted, stunned by the loss of his mother and shocked that he had not been told about her death until now. When he revived, he asked Rav Chaim why such vital information had been kept from him all those years.

Rav Chaim answered, "You have to know that all this was the work of the Satan. The Satan saw that you were destined to be one of the *gedolei hador* [great leaders of the generation]. To prevent that from happening, he burned down a whole row of shops, killed your mother, and left your family orphaned and forsaken. All in order to force you to leave the yeshivah.

"Now," concluded Rav Chaim, "would you have wanted the Satan's plans to succeed? *Baruch Hashem* [Praise the Lord], we were able to get the better of him!"

In the course of time, Yossele—now renowned as Rav Yossel Slutzker—arranged *shidduchim* for his sisters with some of the leading Torah scholars of the time. As penniless orphans, they were able to find such fine husbands only because they were sisters of the famous *gaon* [brilliant scholar].[257]

I imagine that many of you reading this book will find this story to be shocking and even abhorrent, but it is recounted with great pride by Rabbi Shach as a fitting and even praiseworthy course of action by the head of the yeshiva. For those readers who find this account commendable, I ask you: How can you possibly criticize the verses we just read in the New Testament?

Or take this example from the life of Rabbi Akiva, probably the most illustrious figure in Talmudic Judaism:

When R. Simeon, the son of R. Akiva, fell ill, the father did not neglect his house of study, but arranged for his messengers to stand by [the sickbed].

The first messenger came and said, "He is very ill."
"Carry on!" said R. Akiva to his disciples.
The second came and said, "He is getting worse."
He had them resume their study of Torah.
The third came and said, "He is dying."
"Carry on!"
The fourth came and said, "He is gone."
Hearing this, R. Akiva rose, removed his tefillin, rent his clothes, and said to his disciples: "Up to now we were obliged to study Torah. From this moment on, you and I are obligated to honor the dead."[258]

Do I recount this story to malign Rabbi Akiva? Not at all. I recount it simply to ask: What if this account was found in the New Testament?

What if it was written there that one of the disciples of Jesus would not leave a teaching session of the Messiah while reports came of his son becoming very ill and then dying, only leaving when the son was finally dead—and then justifying his behavior? I cannot imagine how ugly the attack would be, yet here, when it refers to a Talmudic sage, a traditional Jew might justify it or even cite it as a meritorious example. This account also underscores the point, made above, that traditional Jews often make demands of themselves or others for the sake of Torah that, in some ways, are even more far reaching than those that Yeshua put on his disciples. And those of like faith praise them for it!

It should also be noted that *ba'alei teshuvah* (which refers to Jews who become observant later in life rather than having been observant all their lives) often come into serious conflict with their families over their newfound devotion. Professor Walter Riggans highlights this when addressing similar objections in his excellent book *Yeshua ben David*.

He first cites Reform rabbi and professor Dan Cohn-Sherbok, who takes issue with some of Jesus' demands, stating, "The renunciation of family bonds was regarded as a travesty of the created order."[259] Riggans then quotes anti-missionary Beth Moshe, who has this to say concerning a Christian sharing his or her faith with a Jewish person:

> Isn't he asking you to break the commandment of honoring father and mother? The missionary does not care what he leaves in the wake of his attempt to capture the soul of a son or daughter. Great unhappiness and mental anguish result because of apostasy. If this is the peace Christianity offers, it seems to be only for the convert, not for his family which is left in torment.[260]

Not only does Riggans expose this kind of rhetoric as "malicious nonsense," he also provides some telling examples from a different side of the story. He observes:

> The very same kind of phenomenon is also observable within the Orthodox Jewish world today, as [anti-missionary author Gerald] Sigal and others know only too well, although they are hardly likely to draw attention to it. Many examples could be cited from recent years of secularised, highly-assimilated Jewish people who have had some sort of transforming experience and become Orthodox Jews in their beliefs and lifestyle. Their new way of life, their new beliefs and their new set of values often do not meet with approval and acceptance by their families and friends; indeed not always by their spouses either.[261]

Riggans next quotes sociologist Janet Aviad in her well-known study of Jews who become Orthodox:

> Relations between parents and children are upset on several grounds. A baal teshuvah finds it difficult to eat in the home of his parents who do not observe the dietary laws of Judaism. He finds it difficult to spend the Sabbath and holidays with his parents who violate the religious prescriptions regarding their observance. In most cases, baalei teshuvah moved out of the homes of their parents and set up their own aparments.[262]

Riggans then asks, quite appropriately:

> Would Orthodox rabbis and other spokespersons want to argue that the Torah itself must now be disqualified from being an authentic gift from God, etc., because observing it can break up Jewish homes? Of course not! They would claim that this is, tragically, an almost predictable consequence of the modern situation where so many Jewish people prefer to go their own way rather than God's way. Such Jewish people will always oppose the witness to the God of Israel which *ba'alei teshuvah* bring with them. The Torah is not corrupt, they will say, just because conflict often comes in its wake in these circumstances.
>
> Quite so. And Christians maintain that Jesus is not corrupt just because conflict often comes in his wake in circumstances where a Jewish person discovers that Jesus is the Messiah.[263]

Not only is Riggans's point well-taken, but I could imagine Orthodox Jewish leaders pointing to a passage such as m. B. M. 2:11, which teaches that if the choice has to be made between giving attention to the lost property of one's father or giving attention to the lost property of one's Torah teacher, that of his teacher takes precedence since "his father brought him into this world, but his teacher who taught him wisdom brings him thereby into the world to come." (The exception to this ruling would be if his father was also a Torah scholar.) The same holds true in cases where both the father and teacher are carrying a physical burden; helping one's teacher comes before helping one's father. The same goes for ransoming one's father or teacher from captivity—yes, from captivity! Ransoming the teacher comes before ransoming the father, with the same caveat applying (i.e., the father can get ransomed first if he too was a Torah scholar; see further Talmudic explication of this in b. B. M. 33a.)[264] Could not this be considered extreme and contrary to the biblical command to honor one's father and mother?

Suffice it to say that, not only does the Messiah as Son of God and Redeemer of the human race have the authority to call his followers to radical obedience, but Jewish objections to this authority have no ground on which to stand, based on both the testimony of the Tanakh and the teachings of Rabbinic Judaism.

Let us now consider two of the teachings of Yeshua that are often singled out as being impossible or dangerous, beginning with Luke 6:27–32 (cf. also Matt. 5:38–42), where Jesus taught:

> But I tell you who hear me: Love your enemies, do good to those who hate you, bless those who curse you, pray for those who mistreat you. If someone strikes you on one cheek, turn to him the other also. If someone takes your cloak, do not stop him from taking your tunic. Give to everyone who asks you, and if anyone takes what belongs to you, do not demand it back. Do to others as you would have them do to you.

He then went on to explain:

> If you love those who love you, what credit is that to you? Even "sinners" love those who love them. And if you do good to those who are good to you, what credit is that to you? Even "sinners" do that. And if you lend to those from whom you expect repayment, what credit is that to you? Even "sinners" lend to "sinners," expecting to be repaid in full. But love your enemies, do good to them, and lend to them without expecting to get anything back. Then your reward will be great, and you will be sons of the Most High, because he is kind to the ungrateful and wicked. Be merciful, just as your Father is merciful.
>
> Luke 6:33–36

Before looking at a few of the so-called "impossible" aspects of these verses, let me encourage you to step back and take in the beauty and power of Messiah's words, and then to stop and consider how much radical change has been brought to this world by those who have sought to serve rather than be served, to give rather than receive, to bless rather than curse, to respond kindly rather than retaliate hurtfully (remember also the principles of Prov. 15:1; 25:15). There is no doubt that Yeshua was calling us to a higher way of living, one that could not be accomplished by mere human effort but that required the help of the Spirit. But that is the whole point of much of his teaching: "On your own, you won't make it, but in me and through me and with me, all things are possible!" (See, e.g., John 15:1–9; Matt. 19:26.)

As for the "impossible" nature of the teaching, the same can be said for some of the requirements that God gave to Israel. Consider, for example, the law of the seventh year Sabbath, where God commanded his people to let the land itself rest every seventh year (Lev. 25:2–7; as stated in vv. 4–5, "But in the seventh year the land is to have a sabbath of rest, a sabbath to the LORD. Do not sow your fields or prune your vineyards. Do not reap what grows of itself or harvest the grapes of your untended vines. The land is to have a year of rest."). Here, a whole nation had to depend on God for his miraculous supply, as seen later in this same chapter:

> Follow my decrees and be careful to obey my laws, and you will live safely in the land. Then the land will yield its fruit, and you will eat your fill and live there in safety. You may ask, "What will we eat in the seventh year if we do not plant or harvest our crops?" I will send you such a blessing in the sixth year that the land will yield enough for three years. While you plant during the eighth year, you will eat from the old crop and will continue to eat from it until the harvest of the ninth year comes in.
>
> Leviticus 25:18–22

How could the Jewish people let the land lie fallow once every seven years? This could destroy the agricultural base of the whole nation! God said that he would supply, and in this case, he said that he would do it in advance if his people would obey. (For traditional Jewish circumlocutions to get around following this commandment literally, especially in modern day Israel, see vol. 5, 6.1, 6.3–6.4.)

God also made demands on his people that were very difficult on the flesh—our carnally-oriented, unbelieving, human nature—most specifically, his requirement concerning the cancelling of debts in the seventh and then in the fiftieth year, the Year of Jubilee. Focusing again on the seventh-year legislation—which was actually less rigorous than the fiftieth-year jubilee, in which long-term slaves would be freed and indentured land returned to its original owners (Lev. 25:10–55)—God commanded:

> At the end of every seven years you must cancel debts. This is how it is to be done: Every creditor shall cancel the loan he has made to his fellow Israelite. He shall not require payment from his fellow Israelite or brother, because the LORD's time for canceling debts has been proclaimed. You may require payment from a foreigner, but you must cancel any debt your brother owes you. However, there should be no poor among you, for in the land the LORD your God is giving you to possess as your inheritance, he will richly bless you, if only you fully obey the LORD your God and are careful to follow all these commands I am giving you today. For the LORD your God will bless you as he has promised, and you will lend to many nations but will borrow from none. You will rule over many nations but none will rule over you.

> If there is a poor man among your brothers in any of the towns of the land that the Lord your God is giving you, do not be hardhearted or tightfisted toward your poor brother. Rather be openhanded and freely lend him whatever he needs. Be careful not to harbor this wicked thought: "The seventh year, the year for canceling debts, is near," so that you do not show ill will toward your needy brother and give him nothing. He may then appeal to the Lord against you, and you will be found guilty of sin. Give generously to him and do so without a grudging heart; then because of this the Lord your God will bless you in all your work and in everything you put your hand to. There will always be poor people in the land. Therefore I command you to be openhanded toward your brothers and toward the poor and needy in your land.
>
> Deuteronomy 15:1–11

Unfortunately, by Yeshua's day, the Jewish people were guilty of the very thing that this passage spoke against—namely, not giving loans to the poor as the seventh year drew near—and so Hillel devised a legal loophole called the *prosbul* in which the debt was not technically payable to the individual lender but to the court, for whom the seventh year release was said not to apply (for more on this, see below, 5.28 and vol. 5, 6.3–6.4). Was Hillel motivated by compassion for the poor in his actions? It appears so. Did he have the best intentions in mind for both rich and poor? Probably, he did. But it was a human way out of a divinely instituted problem, one which required faith and not legal ingenuity.

With this in mind, let's look again at Jesus' words in Luke 6:34–36, remembering also that a number of top scholars believe that Jesus began his public ministry in close proximity to the Year of Jubilee, and therefore to a time when debts would soon be cancelled and people would be less inclined to give loans (unless they took Hillel's easier way out). Jesus said: "And if you lend to those from whom you expect repayment, what credit is that to you? Even 'sinners' lend to 'sinners,' expecting to be repaid in full" (v. 34). Yes, everyone can do that, even unholy people. But you are called to something more! "But love your enemies, do good to them" (v. 35), which is also in harmony with Torah requirements; see Exodus 23:4–5: "If you come across your enemy's ox or donkey wandering off, be sure to take it back to him. If you see the donkey of someone who hates you fallen down under its load, do not leave it there; be sure you help him with it." (For a Talmudic analysis of this verse, one that would doubtless surprise a Christian reader, see b. B. M. 32b–33a.)

Jesus continues: "And lend to them [meaning, even your enemies] without expecting to get anything back. Then your reward will be great, and you will be sons of the Most High, because he is kind to the ungrateful and wicked. Be merciful, just as your Father is merciful" (Luke 6:35–36). Do you see it? Messiah is calling the Jewish people to do what the Father commanded in the Torah, to trust him and not be stingy, even to go beyond what is required and not to expect payment in return, assuring them that, in accordance with the promise in Deuteronomy 15, they would be blessed. Indeed, he promised abundance, just as his Father had previously promised: "Give, and it will be given to you. A good measure, pressed down, shaken together and running over, will be poured into your lap. For with the measure you use, it will be measured to you" (Luke 6:38).

So then, rather than this being a recipe for disaster and failure, it was a path to blessing: blessing to those in legitimate need, and blessing to those who gave—in terms of character transformation, growth in faith, and, ultimately, even increase in material goods.

You say, "But someone could take advantage of this teaching!" True, but the same could be said of the laws in Deuteronomy 15 and Leviticus 25. Seen, however, against that background, which is clearly the background to our passage in Luke (as well as, by extension, to the parallel passage in Matthew 5), we can readily understand that the same principles apply: The context speaks of those who are in legitimate need (the poor, in Deuteronomy 15, even if they are enemies, according to Luke 6) coming for a loan to those who have the power to give. Decisions would then be made based on the possibility of giving the money, as well as common sense or community customs or relevant legal guidelines or (in a Messianic context) the leading of the Spirit. The bottom line, however, is clear: Jesus calls his disciples to generosity, kindness, sacrificial giving, and deep faith. It *is* hard on the flesh—our selfish, human nature—but it is richly rewarding in the long run.

Interestingly, while it is not uncommon for anti-missionaries to attack some of these passages, it is often the Jewish background to the passage that elucidates its meaning. Note, for example, that Luke 6:29 states, "If someone strikes you on one cheek, turn to him the other also," but Matthew 5:39, which occurs in the context of legal retaliation (see Matt. 5:38!), provides an important detail: "But I tell you, Do not resist an evil person. If someone strikes you on the right cheek, turn to him the other also." Does this mean that if someone breaks into your home and tries to kill your spouse and your kids, you should sit idly by even if you could easily stop them, or, perhaps even turn your family over to the intruder to be brutalized? Does it mean that you don't call the police or offer any resistance? Of course not. The issue is one of legal retaliation, in this case, for being publicly shamed, which we know because of the words, "If someone strikes you on the right cheek," implying a backhanded slap against the face. That is to say, a right-handed orientation is assumed in similar legal cases, and, since a right-handed slap would strike the *left* cheek and a right-handed person would not strike with the left hand, being struck on the *right* cheek means being struck with the back of the hand.

As Nolland and others have noted, the Mishnah dealt with this very situation in m. B. K. 9:6. To summarize, "a slap with the back of the hand calls for twice the payment in recompense for other blows; in terms of dishonour it is on the same level as tearing an ear, plucking out hair, spitting on someone, pulling a cloak off, and loosing a woman's hair in public."[265]

Now, it must be remembered that the Mishnah was often dealing with actual laws and procedures, along with legal theory, just as a court today would get into great detail in terms of determining culpability and assessing fines and punishments. That is perfectly understandable as an ongoing application of Torah law. Yeshua, however, was saying to his disciples, "This is not for you. I'm calling you to something higher. When you are publicly shamed and have the right to exact payment, turn the other cheek. Make yourself vulnerable and don't try to fight your opponent on his terms. Step higher!" (See also 1 Cor. 6:1–8, in a related context.)

This, of course, was the pattern exemplified so selflessly in Messiah's sacrifice on the cross, which is why Jesus stopped Peter from trying to fight against those who were about to arrest his Master:

> "Put your sword back in its place," Jesus said to him, "for all who draw the sword will die by the sword. Do you think I cannot call on my Father, and he will at once put at my disposal more than twelve legions of angels? But how then would the Scriptures be fulfilled that say it must happen in this way?"
>
> Matthew 26:52–54

In terms of Yeshua's teachings in Luke and Matthew, when it is remembered that the goal of his words is to produce a transformation of our attitudes rather than to give us a set of specific laws, we can more readily follow his lead. Generally speaking, those who follow him and take his words seriously know just what he meant when he taught us to "turn the other cheek"—indeed, this has become a popular, widely used expression—without even understanding the legal background to the original context.[266] For the most part, it is only when those who are *not* Yeshua's followers try to force the application of these verses on those who *do* follow him that things get bizarre, as was the case when an anti-missionary rabbi once quoted them to me while we stood in front of a Jewish bookstore, insisting that I give him my car keys and car, which I did, just to go along with his game, although in the end, he would not take them. (This actually happened!)

Before closing this section, let's look at one more example of a supposedly dangerous and un-Jewish teaching. It is found in Matthew 5:27–30, where Jesus warns against adultery (see also Matt. 18:7–9; Mark 9:43, 45, 47–48).

> You have heard that it was said, "Do not commit adultery." But I tell you that anyone who looks at a woman lustfully has already committed adultery with her in his heart. If your right eye causes you to sin, gouge it out and throw it away. It is better for you to lose one part of your body than for your whole body to be thrown into hell. And if your right hand causes you to sin, cut it off and throw it away. It is better for you to lose one part of your body than for your whole body to go into hell.
>
> Matthew 5:27–30

Now, in all candor, having read and embraced these words for well over thirty years, and personally knowing countless thousands of believers in Jesus around the world who also know and embrace these words, it would never have dawned on me that they were "dangerous" or "un-Jewish." As for the basic thrust, their meaning is perfectly clear, as explicated by New Testament scholar D. A. Carson:

> Cutting off or gouging out the offending part is a way of saying that Jesus' disciples must deal radically with sin. Imagination is a God-given gift; but if it is fed dirt by the eye, it will be dirty. All sin, not least sexual sin, begins with the imagination. Therefore what feeds the imagination is of maximum importance in the pursuit of kingdom righteousness. . . . Not everyone reacts the same way to all objects. But if . . . your eye is causing you to sin, gouge it out; or at very least, don't look. . . . The alternative is sin and hell, sin's reward. The point is so fundamental that Jesus doubtless repeated it on numerous occasions. . . .[267]

As I noted in my book *Go and Sin No More*:

> There are few things more radical than amputation. Doctors only cut off hands and feet and legs as a last resort when all else has failed. They do it because they have no choice. If they don't, the infection will spread, destroying the whole body. So it's either one limb that goes or the whole body that dies. And once the amputation is done, it can't be undone.

Once the limb is severed it will never be used again. Yet Jesus tells us to amputate our hands or feet if they cause us to sin.

Of course, this is *spiritual* imagery that graphically explains the ruthless way in which we must deal with sinful tendencies and habits, so you can put the meat cleaver or hatchet away for now! But let's not weaken the force of Jesus' words. They are absolutely radical, totally extreme, completely final: "Cut off that hand and throw it away"—even it's your right hand, the hand that you rely on in your daily labor, the hand with which you write, your strong hand. Even that hand must go if it leads you into sin. The same goes for our eyes. . . . And notice that Jesus [in the parallel passages] spoke about three parts of the body: our hands, signifying what we do; our feet, signifying where we go; and our eyes, signifying what we see and desire.

. . . Yes, in human terms, this is quite a price to pay, but falling away from God is a far greater price to pay. And that's what Jesus was trying to illustrate. Losing a hand or foot in this world is tragic. But losing your soul in the world to come is a million times more tragic.[268]

In short—and quite clearly—he is telling us to deal ruthlessly with sin, lest sin deal ruthlessly with us. Isn't this plain? In reality, it is so plain that I could address the question of self-mutilation with tongue in cheek, telling readers to "put the meat cleaver or hatchet away for now."

"Well," you reply, "I still think it's a dangerous teaching. After all, someone might just go and gouge out their eye or chop off their hand!"

Actually, there's no reason to speculate. As of the year 2000, there were more than two billion professing Christians in the world. Let's say that fully half of them were not true Christians and/or were biblically illiterate, being unaware of these words. That would leave roughly *one billion* people who were familiar with this text and took it seriously. (If you like, cut that number in half; that still leaves five hundred million people.) If this teaching was so dangerous then surely, by now, we would be reading accounts of how this self-mutilation was taking place on a daily basis. Surely, with these words in circulation for almost two thousand years, we would have countless thousands (or even millions) of cases of attempted self-mutilation, with some of the most famous "saints" of the past missing an eye or a hand or a foot, and with pastors in every city having to preach special sermons on a regular basis, telling their parishioners *not* to cut off their offending body parts. Surely, hospital wards would have special sections for "Christian self-amputees."

But none of this happened, and personally, I have not heard of a single person who has actually tried to do this to himself or herself. Given the amount of deranged people in the world, some of whom claim to be religious, this is quite significant. Where is the pattern of abuse?[269]

An interesting historical anecdote is provided in the *Hard Sayings of the Bible*, describing what happened when the organized church, which stood *against* having a Bible in the language of the people (see vol. 5, 6.3–6.4, for observations on this) and did its best to prevent William Tyndale from making such a translation, was now faced with the fact that the Bible was available:

> Shortly after the publication of William Tyndale's English New Testament, the attempt to restrict its circulation was defended on the ground that the simple reader might mistakenly take such language literally and "pluck out his eyes, and so the whole realm will be full of blind men, to the great decay of the nation and the manifest loss of the King's grace; and thus by reading of the Holy Scriptures will the whole realm come into confusion." So a preaching friar is said to have declared in a Cambridge sermon; but he met his match in Hugh Latimer, who, in a sermon preached the following Sunday, said that simple people were well able to distinguish between literal and figurative terms. "For example," Latimer went on, "if we paint a fox preaching in a friar's hood, nobody imagines that a fox is meant, but that craft and hypocrisy are described, which so often are found disguised in that garb."
>
> In fact, it is not recorded that anyone ever mutilated himself because of these words in the Gospels.[270]

Yes, "simple people [are] well able to distinguish between literal and figurative terms." So much for the teaching being dangerous!

What about being "un-Jewish"? Well, if by "un-Jewish" you mean "un-Rabbinic," there too, I must categorically disagree in light of later Rabbinic parallels. The most obvious parallel is found in m. Nid 2:1, discussed in b. Nid 13a–b. The Mishnaic law states: "Every hand that makes frequent examination is in the case of women praiseworthy [meaning, examining the private parts, in order to check for ritual uncleanness] but in the case of men it ought to be cut off [for fear of masturbation]." The Talmud (i.e., the discussion of the Mishnah) continues: "Wherein [in this respect] do women differ from men?—Women [in this matter] are not sensitive, hence they are praiseworthy, but in the case of men who are highly sensitive [their hands] ought to be cut off."

Was this a literal precept to be carried out? Was there an epidemic of Jewish men cutting off their hands? I would think not! Then, presumably, it is to be taken metaphorically, in which case, although far less clear than Yeshua's teaching, it is certainly parallel—meaning that Yeshua's teaching is quite Jewish after all!

Surprisingly, despite the Rabbinic view that "eye for eye" in the Torah referred to equivalent monetary compensation (see vol. 5, 6.5), the Talmud actually records an instance where "Rav Huna had the hand cut off [of one who was accustomed to strike other people]" (b. Sanh 58b). Shades of Islamic law! This is not metaphorical language, this is an example of a Rabbinic leader having the hand of a repeat violent offender cut off. Yet Yeshua is criticized for giving an unmistakably metaphorical teaching?

Here is one last teaching from a Talmudic sage:

> R. Muna said in R. Judah's name: A drop of cold water in the morning and bathing the hands and feet [in hot water] in the evening is better than all the eye-salves in the world. He [R. Muna] used to say: If the hand [be put] to the eye [taken to mean an unwashed hand], let it be cut off; the hand to the nose, let it be cut off: the hand to the mouth, let it be cut off; the hand to the ear, let it be cut off; the hand to the vein [opened for blood letting], let it be cut off; the hand to the membrum, let it be cut off; the hand to the anus, let it be cut off; the hand to the vat, let it be cut off: [because] the [unwashed] hand leads to blindness, the hand leads to deafness, the hand causes a polypus.[271]

Did he mean this literally? If so, then I repeat my last statement: How then can the clear metaphorical teaching of Jesus be criticized as dangerous? If he meant it metaphorically—which I certainly hope was the case—then I ask, all the more so, How can you criticize the teachings of Jesus as either un-Jewish or dangerous? I should also point out that, whereas Jesus gave clear indications that his teaching was to be taken metaphorically, speaking in Matt. 18:8–9 of "enter[ing] life" (meaning, heaven, eternal life) maimed or crippled or missing an eye—because of cutting off or gouging out the offending body part, as if, in the resurrection, a maimed person would be resurrected maimed—R. Muna here gave no such indication.

Of course, I accept that for a Rabbinic Jew, there is an accompanying tradition that explains many of these passages. But for the follower of Yeshua, there is the testimony of the whole Bible, including all of Messiah's words that are recorded in the New Covenant Writings, along with the leading and anointing of the Spirit (see 1 John 2:20), along with common sense. In light of this, it is not surprising that his followers have *not* misunderstood his intent.

So, in summary, it can be said that: (1) some of the teachings of Jesus are only impossible for those who try to put them into practice without God's supernatural help, but that has clear precedent in the Hebrew Scriptures; (2) none of them are dangerous; and (3) in the best sense of the word, they are thoroughly Jewish, even going beyond the best of our people's traditions, which would be expected for our Messiah and King, the living exposition of Torah.

5.20. The New Testament is anti-Semitic. It is filled with negative references to the Jewish people, and it blames them for the death of Jesus.

The New Testament reflects internal tensions and differences between different groups of religious Jews—some of whom followed Jesus the Messiah, and some (or, most) of whom rejected him as Messiah. These writings are no more anti-Semitic than the Hebrew Scriptures where both God and the prophets call the people of Israel stiff-necked and obstinate rebels. It is also important to understand that the Greek word translated "Jews" can also mean Judeans or Jewish leaders, so that, in context, many of John's negative statements about "the Jews" are limited to specific groups or leaders. You might also be surprised to know that the New Testament has many wonderful things to say about the Jewish people, including God's present love and care for them and his promise of a very bright future for them. As for Jewish guilt in rejecting Jesus, I'm sorry to say that it is a shameful fact of our history that some of our religious leaders played a key role in turning him over to the Romans to be crucified. We as individual Jews should repudiate that error by embracing Jesus the Messiah. This is all addressed at length in volume 1, 2.8.

Since I treated this subject at length in volume 1, I refer the interested reader to what was written there. For convenience, a very short summary is provided here. After pointing out that anti-Semitism *predates* the New Testament (see vol. 1, 2.8) and that certain verses in the Tanakh, if wrongly interpreted, could be understood to be anti-Semitic (even from God's own mouth; see again vol. 1, 2.8), we then demonstrated the *Jewishness* of the New Testament along with clear parallels between the Tanakh and the New Covenant Writings in terms of their description of the Jewish people (see also above, 5.1), after which we dealt with the following misconceptions:

- In answer to the charge that "Matthew makes all Jews—for all generations—responsible for the death of Jesus" (see Matt. 27:24–25), we saw instead that: (1) some Rabbinic sources indicate that Jewish leadership played a role in the death of Jesus; (2) the wording of Matthew 27:25 refers only to taking responsibility for the death of Jesus, not calling down a lasting curse on the nation; (3) from a historical standpoint, the picture painted by Matthew is certainly plausible; and (4) in and of itself, there is nothing anti-Semitic about Matthew 27:25. The fact that it has been utilized by anti-Semites is a terrible tragedy, but certainly no fault of the New Testament itself. It should also be emphasized that this verse did not initially *cause* Jewish suffering; rather, its misuse provided an alleged theological *justification* for that suffering (see vol. 1, 154–56).

- In answer to the charge that "'The Jews' are consistently demonized in the New Testament, especially in the Gospel of John," we saw instead that "the (Jewish) Gospel of John is no more anti-Semitic than the (Jewish) Dead Sea Scrolls or the writings of the (Jewish) historian Josephus," and that the book primarily reflects inter-Jewish conflicts, with the word "Jews" often referring to the Jewish leadership as opposed to the people as a whole (see vol. 1, 156–60).

- In answer to the charge that "The Jewish religious leaders, especially the Pharisees, are depicted as snakes and vipers, hypocrites who are rotten to the core, and men worthy of damnation," we explained that the New Testament speaks well of certain Jewish leaders, some of whom were Pharisees, while rebuking the hypocrisy of many of the other leaders, just as the prophets of Israel often reserved their strongest words for the corrupt prophets and priests—in other words, for the hypocritical leaders in ancient Israel. Yeshua, our nation's last and greatest Prophet, was simply following in these footsteps, and the fact that later readers have branded all Pharisees as hypocrites is *not* the fault of our Messiah, anymore than the fact that later readers have branded all Jews as stiffnecked, based on the words of Moses and God himself in the Hebrew Bible, is the fault of Moses or the Lord (see vol. 1, 160–64).

- In answer to the charge that, "Paul told his Gentile readers that the Jews displease God, and that they are hostile to all men, that they killed both the prophets and the Messiah, and they are objects of God's wrath to the uttermost" (see 1 Thess. 2:14–16), we saw that Paul was *not* saying that all Jews were guilty of killing Jesus any more than he was saying that all Jews were guilty of killing the prophets or that all Jews were guilty of driving him out of city after city. Rather, in writing to Gentile believers in Thessalonica, Paul explained that, "You (believing) Thessalonians are suffering persecution from your own (unbelieving) countrymen just like we (believing) Jews are suffering persecution from our own (unbelieving) countrymen." So, just as it would be completely wrong to conclude that Paul was saying that all Thessalonians were wicked, so too it would be wrong to conclude that he was saying that all Jews were wicked. He is speaking of unbelieving Jews, the same audience whom the prophets rebuked, and it is even possible that he is speaking in particular about the prophet-persecuting Jews of Judea, rather than all Jews worldwide, as being hostile toward God (see vol. 1, 164–67).

- In answer to the charge that "The New Testament charges the Jews with deicide—killing God! No wonder Christians turned on them so violently," we pointed out that: (1) Jesus the Messiah died for our sins (see, e.g., 1 Cor. 15:3), that is to say, he willingly died for us, for the ungodly (see Rom. 5:6–8). (2) The New Testament authors indicate that the death of Jesus was ordained by God himself, referring to him as "the Lamb that was slain from the creation of the world" (Rev. 13:8). Thus, even when dealing with his fellow Jews regarding their complicity in Messiah's death, Peter could say, "This man was handed over to you by God's set purpose and foreknowledge" (Acts 2:23a). (3) It is acknowledged that both Jew and Gentile conspired against Jesus, even in the most pointed New Testament statements. (4) Even when he was being crucified, Jesus uttered the unforgettable words, "Father, forgive them, for they do not know what they are doing" (Luke 23:34), a sentiment reflected elsewhere in the New Testament writings (see, e.g., Acts 3:17–20). (5) The New Testament emphasizes both the human nature and the divine nature of the Messiah, speaking of him throughout the Gospels as a fully human Jewish rabbi who at the same time was the Son of God. Every time, however, that reference is made in the New Testament to the Messiah's death, divine nature is never emphasized in any of them. In fact, if anything is emphasized, it is humanity. Thus, the charge is simply, "You handed over the Messiah! You betrayed him!" The supposedly logical next step that you suggested—i.e., "Therefore you killed God!"—is never hinted at in the least anywhere in the New Testament. Read every line of every book, and you will not find the charge of deicide (see vol. 1, 167–70).

- In answer to the charge that "The real problem with the New Testament is the notion that God is finished with the Jewish people, that they are now the synagogue of Satan, having been replaced by Christians who are the true Jews and the New Israel," we explained that: (1) The New Testament never says that God is finished with Israel but rather promised that in the future, Israel would be fully restored. (2) Paul never taught that the church was the new Israel or that it replaced Israel. (3) The New Testament rebuke of faithless Jews is similar to prophetic rebukes in the Tanakh and even inter-Jewish disputes as reflected in documents such as the Dead Sea Scrolls (see vol. 1, 170–75).

Finally, we noted that, despite the bloody and violent history of anti-Semitism in the professing "church"—a "church" that we labeled hypocritical and false (see vol. 1, 2.4–2.7, and cf. my full-length study, *Our Hands Are Stained with Blood*)—Israel's best friends today are Bible believing Christians, precisely because a proper reading of the New Testament will produce *love* for Israel, not hatred. Again, for a much more complete, documented treatment, see volume 1, 2.8.[272]

5.21. The Jesus of the New Testament is hardly Jewish. In fact, he even refers to the Torah as "your Law"—precisely because it was not his own.

Jesus stated emphatically that he did not come to abolish the Law and the Prophets but rather to fulfill them, and the primary focus of his earthly ministry was on reaching the lost sheep of the house of Israel. In all his teaching, he made reference to the Hebrew Scriptures, even stating to the Jewish leaders that if they truly believed Moses, they would believe him. After his death and resurrection, his followers continued in this pattern, living as Torah-observant Jews and pointing back to the Tanakh to support the Messianic claims of Jesus. How then can you possibly argue that this very same Law was not his own?

The specific verses in question are John 10:34, where Jesus responds to the Jewish leadership by saying, "Is it not written in your Law, 'I have said you are gods'." Related to this is John 15:25, where Jesus, again speaking of the Jewish leadership, says to his disciples—who were all Jews—"But this is to fulfill what is written in their Law: 'They hated me without reason.'" Addressing this in volume 1 (242, n. 183), I noted:

Some would also point to verses such as John 10:34, where Jesus speaking to "the Jews" says, "Is it not written in *your Law*, 'I have said you are gods'?" [my emphasis], as if he was saying, "This is your Law, not mine!" However, such an understanding of this text is completely untenable for the following reasons: (1) Elsewhere in John, Jesus insisted that it was *the whole Bible* in general, and *the Law of Moses* in particular, that bore witness to him: "You diligently study the Scriptures because you think that by them you possess eternal life. These are the Scriptures that testify about me, yet you refuse to come to me to have life. . . . But do not think I will accuse you before the Father. Your accuser is Moses, on whom your hopes are set. If you believed Moses, you would believe me, for he wrote about me. But since you do not believe what he wrote, how are you going to believe what I say?" (John 5:39–40, 45–47; see also John 8:32, where *continuing in God's Word*—meaning the Hebrew Bible!—is the prerequisite for being a true disciple); (2) When dialoging with Jewish leaders, Jesus alluded to Moses as part of their shared heritage; see, e.g., John 3:14–16; 7:19–23; (3) Jesus' own disciples are credited with seeing him as the fulfillment of Moses and the prophets: "We have found the one Moses wrote about in the Law, and about whom the prophets also wrote—Jesus of Nazareth, the son of Joseph" (John 1:45); (4) The verse from "the Law" cited by Jesus in John 10:34 is actually from the Psalms (82:6), indicating that Jesus used "the Law" (i.e., "Torah") in the broader sense of the Scriptures as a whole, something which was quite common in Jewish usage. Certainly no one would argue that Jesus was rejecting *the Psalms* as something foreign and alien! Rather, what he was saying here would be the equivalent of one Christian minister saying to another, hypocritical minister, "Look at what is written *in your own New Testament*. You're not even living by your own book!"

The same arguments apply to John 15:25, which also contains a quotation from the Psalms, not the Torah, the sense again being highly ironic, as "the men who posed as the champions of the Law were fulfilling the prophecy concerning the enemies of God's servant."[273] Yeshua is saying to his disciples, "And it's written right in their very own Book!" A clear example of this can be found in John 8:17, where Jesus again says to the leaders, "In your own Law it is written that the testimony of two men is valid." That was his whole point: Look in your very own Bible! It supports what I am saying and doing. But I ask once more, is it conceivable that Jesus was disowning the Hebrew Bible and distancing himself from the prophets? Is it conceivable that he was saying to these men, his devoted Jewish followers, that the Hebrew Bible—and the Book of Psalms in particular—was no longer theirs?

After his resurrection, Luke records that Jesus took his disciples to them and gave them final instructions, during which time: "He said to them, 'This is what I told you while I was still with you: Everything must be fulfilled that is written about me in the Law of Moses, the Prophets and the Psalms.' Then he opened their minds so they could understand the Scriptures" (Luke 24:44–45). He was saying that the Tanakh in its entirety pointed to him, and that a proper understanding of the Law and the Prophets would only draw more attention to his Messianic mission. In truth it could be said that, more than any other Jew who ever lived, this Book was *his Book*. It is therefore not surprising that the Tanakh was *the* Bible of the Messiah's followers for several decades (before being completed with the New Covenant Writings) and that the primary songbook of these believers was the Book of the Psalms—the very portion of Scripture from which Jesus allegedly distanced himself, according to this objection. Hardly! (For "singing the psalms" among the early believers, see Eph. 5:19; Col. 3:16, and cf. Matt. 26:30; Acts 16:25; 1 Cor. 14:26, all of which mention "hymns," which might also refer to Psalms.)

With passion and enthusiasm the *shelichim* (apostles) continue to teach and preach out of the Hebrew Bible—*their* Bible!—as would be expected for followers of Jesus, the Jewish Messiah, not the founder of a new alien religion (cf., e.g., Acts 2:14–36; 13:13–41; in the writings of Paul, see, e.g., Rom. 16:25–27). See further the related discussion below, in 5.25–5.26, 5.28–5.29.

5.22. Jesus was a false prophet. He claimed that his apostles would live to see his return, a prediction he missed by two thousand years. He also predicted that not one stone in Jerusalem would be left standing when the Romans destroyed it. Well, have you ever heard of the Wailing Wall?

The reason the New Testament writers preserved the prophecies of Jesus was because they were so accurate. This is a matter of common sense. There would be no reason to preserve and perpetuate his words if they were obviously false. To state that he predicted that his apostles would live to see his return is to misunderstand the clear context of his words and again, it begs the question of why those very apostles would pass those words on to posterity if they were completely false. As for his prophecies concerning the fall of Jerusalem, they are so accurate that some critics have argued that they must have been written after 70 c.e., when the Temple was burned down and the city destroyed by the Romans. In other words, because these scholars don't believe in prophecy, they have to say that the words of Jesus were not really his at all but were written years later, after the fact. That's how accurate his prophecies actually were! As for alleged exaggerations or misstatements, it is commonly known that the prophets of Israel often used hyperbole in their predictions, declaring that the country would be totally destroyed without any inhabitants left whereas in reality the many parts of the country were badly damaged with many people going into exile—and no one called them false prophets. In comparison with the biblical prophets who went before him, Jesus' prophecies show only the slightest hint of hyperbole, and if the use of hyperbole makes him a false prophet, then great prophets like Jeremiah and Ezekiel must also be called false prophets.

Let's first consider whether Jesus told his disciples that they would live to see his return, a question which could easily arise from two main texts, namely, Matthew 24:34 (with parallels) and Matthew 16:27–28 (with parallels). In Matthew 24, after Yeshua told his disciples that the Temple would be destroyed, they asked him, "When will this happen, and what will be the sign of your coming and of the end of the age?" (Matt. 24:3). He then began to answer their question, which really had two parts to it: (1) When will the Temple be destroyed? (2) What will be the sign of your coming and of the end of the age? In the minds of the disciples, these two events were one and the same. Jesus knew otherwise.

In any case, he began to explain to them what was coming on the immediate horizon—namely, great persecution and deception, terrible war and destruction—along with what was coming on the distant horizon—namely, his return in the clouds of heaven.[274] In the midst of this teaching, he said to the disciples, "Even so, when you see all these things, you know that it is near, right at the door. I tell you the truth, this generation will certainly not pass away until all these things have happened" (Matt. 24:33–34). From this statement, some scholars and critics have claimed that Jesus was predicting that *those very disciples*—"this generation"—would be alive when he returned. Yet these same critics will tell us that these words of Jesus were written down and preserved *by the next generation*. What a strange contradiction!

Actually, it is not difficult to refute this argument. In fact, it can be refuted in quite a number of ways. First, it is possible that he was speaking about *the final generation*, in other words, about the generation that would see his return, explaining to his disciples (and to all subsequent readers) that those who lived to see certain specific signs fulfilled would be the ones who would see his coming. (It would be as if he said, "Those of you who will be around to hear the thunder and see the lightning will be the ones who will get wet!") Second, it is possible that he was speaking to *his own generation* about the coming destruction of the Temple, informing them that it would happen in their lifetimes (which it did, just 40 years later).[275] As to his return, however, he stressed that "No one knows about that day or hour" (Matt. 24:36).[276] Thus, he was addressing both of the disciples' questions, telling them that the Temple would be destroyed in their generation and informing them that no one knew the time of his return. Third, the Greek word translated "generation" in Matthew 24:34 is *genea*, a word which normally means generation, posterity, but can sometimes mean race.[277] So, Jesus could have simply been assuring his followers that, despite terrible worldwide calamity and suffering, his own people, the Jewish race, would not pass away until all these things were fulfilled.

The fact is, all of these interpretations are viable (especially options one and two), and it would really be stretching things—actually, trying to find fault when there is none—to call Yeshua's statement here false in the least.

What about Matthew 16:27–28? Do these verses tell us that Jesus predicted that his disciples would be alive when he returned? Not at all! We read there,

> For the Son of Man [which was a Messianic title Jesus used for himself] is going to come in his Father's glory with his angels, and then he will reward each person according to what he has done. I tell you the truth, some who are standing here will not taste death before they see the Son of Man coming in his kingdom.

The problem is that many people stop reading instead of continuing on in the text:

> After six days Jesus took with him Peter, James and John the brother of James, and led them up a high mountain by themselves. There he was transfigured before them. His face shone like the sun, and his clothes became as white as the light. Just then there appeared before them Moses and Elijah, talking with Jesus.
> Peter said to Jesus, "Lord, it is good for us to be here. If you wish, I will put up three shelters—one for you, one for Moses and one for Elijah."

While he was still speaking, a bright cloud enveloped them, and a voice from the cloud said, "This is my Son, whom I love; with him I am well pleased. Listen to him!"

When the disciples heard this, they fell facedown to the ground, terrified. But Jesus came and touched them. "Get up," he said. "Don't be afraid." When they looked up, they saw no one except Jesus.

Matthew 17:1–8

It happened just as Jesus said it would! Some of those who stood there that day—namely, Peter, James, and John—got to witness firsthand a picture of Yeshua the Messiah coming in his kingdom power and royal authority. It was so overwhelming that Peter blurted out, "Let's put up three shelters" (one for Jesus, one for Moses, one for Elijah, all of whom were there at that glorious mountain scene), because he didn't know what he was saying (see Luke 9:33). It was quite a moment.

"But how do you know that's what Jesus meant? Your answer seems like a convenient way out rather than a truthful interpretation."

Not at all. The Gospel authors themselves make this perfectly clear. You see, if you study the Gospels of Matthew, Mark, and Luke, you will see that they often tell their stories with different emphases and purposes, one of them putting a particular account in its historical order, another putting that same account where it ties in better with a specific teaching or incident. This, of course, is common, and can be found in parallel accounts in the Hebrew Bible as well.[278] But in the case of the account before us here—called the transfiguration—*all three Gospel authors* give the same account in the same order, telling us clearly, "This is what Jesus said and this is what he meant!" Just read the passages in question, one after the other (Matt. 16:27–17:8; Mark 8:38–9:8; Luke 9:26–36). Their harmony here in terms of order of presentation is striking, making us know for sure that Jesus was not speaking of his future return (which we still await today) but rather of his glorification before their eyes just a few days later, giving them a foretaste of his extraordinary, end-of-days return.[279] It really is clear.

Further confirmation of this interpretation is found in some of Yeshua's parables which make reference to a master going on a long journey before returning to settle accounts. In fact, there are three consecutive, related parables in Matthew 24–25 that make the point of a delay in the Messiah's return perfectly clear. In fact, these parables begin *immediately after* his extended teaching about his return in Matthew 24:1–44.

First, in Matthew 24:45–51 (found also in Luke 12:42–48), Jesus asks, "Who then is the faithful and wise servant, whom the master has put in charge of the servants in his household to give them their food at the proper time? It will be good for that servant whose master finds him doing so *when he returns*" (24:45–46, my emphasis). "But," Jesus continues,

> suppose that servant is wicked and says to himself, "*My master is staying away a long time,*" and he then begins to beat his fellow servants and to eat and drink with drunkards. The master of that servant will come on a day when he does not expect him and at an hour he is not aware of. He will cut him to pieces and assign him a place with the hypocrites, where there will be weeping and gnashing of teeth.
>
> verses 48–51, my emphasis

Without a doubt, Jesus is stating that there is the distinct possibility that he will be a long time in returning. Indeed, this should actually be expected. The very next verses in Matthew reinforce this, in the famous parable of the bridegroom and the ten virgins (25:1–13).

> At that time the kingdom of heaven will be like ten virgins who took their lamps and went out to meet the bridegroom. Five of them were foolish and five were wise. The foolish ones took their lamps but did not take any oil with them. The wise, however, took oil in jars along with their lamps. *The bridegroom was a long time in coming*, and they all became drowsy and fell asleep.
>
> Matthew 25:1–5, my emphasis

And when did the bridegroom finally arrive? "*At midnight* the cry rang out: 'Here's the bridegroom! Come out to meet him!'" (25:6). Some of them were ready and some were not!

This parable is then followed by yet another parable, making this identical point for the third straight time (see Matt. 25:14–29). Here Yeshua states, "Again, it [namely, the kingdom of God] will be like a man going on a journey, who called his servants and entrusted his property to them. . . . *After a long time the master of those servants returned* and settled accounts with them" (25:1, 19, my emphasis). Could anything be more clear? The disciples were to live in readiness of the Messiah's return, just as traditional Jews pray for and expect the potential coming of the Messiah in every generation, but, even before his death, they were warned that he would be a long time in returning. Once again, his words have proven true!

It is not surprising, then, that he said to his disciples:

> The time is coming when you will long to see one of the days of the Son of Man, but you will not see it. Men will tell you, "There he is!" or "Here he is!" Do not go running off after them. For the Son of Man in his day

will be like the lightning, which flashes and lights up the sky from one end to the other.

Luke 17:22–24

So, his disciples were to live in expectation and readiness, but with patience as well. As Jacob (James) wrote:

Be patient, then, brothers, until the Lord's coming. See how the farmer waits for the land to yield its valuable crop and how patient he is for the autumn and spring rains. You too, be patient and stand firm, because the Lord's coming is near. Don't grumble against each other, brothers, or you will be judged. The Judge is standing at the door!

James 5:7–9

Now, let's review Yeshua's prophecies concerning the destruction of the Temple, an event that, according to Rabbinic tradition, was terribly traumatic. Just consider some of these statements, which represent a sampling from Rabbinic literature:

From the day on which the Temple was destroyed the gates of prayer have been closed. . . . But though the gates of prayer are closed, the gates of weeping are not closed. . . .

b. Ber 32b

Since the day that the Temple was destroyed, a wall of iron has intervened between Israel and their Father in Heaven.

b. Ber 32b

Since the day when the Temple was destroyed a decree has been issued against the houses of the righteous that they should become desolate.

b. Ber 58b

Since the day when the Temple was destroyed there has never been a perfectly clear sky.

b. Ber 59a

Through the crime of bloodshed the Temple was destroyed and the Shechinah departed from Israel.

b. Shab 33a

Ever since the day the Temple was destroyed the rains have become irregular.

b. Ta'an. 29a

> When [the Second] Temple was destroyed . . . men of faith disappeared from Israel. . . . Rabban Simeon b. Gamaliel says: R. Joshua testified that from the day the Temple was destroyed, there is no day without a curse, the dew has not descended for a blessing, and the flavour has departed from the fruits. R. Jose says: the fatness was also removed from the fruits. R. Simeon b. Eleazar says; [the cessation of] purity has removed taste and fragrance [from fruits]; [the cessation of] the tithes has removed the fatness of corn. But the sages say: immorality and witchcraft destroyed everything.
>
> b. Sotah 48a

> Since the day when the Temple was destroyed the south wind has not brought rain.
>
> b. B. B. 103a

According to Amos 3:7, "Surely the Sovereign LORD does nothing without revealing his plan to his servants the prophets," and we know that he sent *many* warnings through his prophets before the First Temple was destroyed, speaking of "my servants the prophets, whom I have sent to you again and again" (Jer. 26:5). In fact, Jeremiah himself warned his people about the coming destruction over a period of *forty-one years* (from 627 to 586 B.C.E.; see Jer. 1:2–3; cf. also Jer. 25:3 with 32:1). Who warned the Jewish people about the destruction of the Second Temple? Among the prominent, respected leaders in the decades leading up to this event, men like Hillel and Gamaliel and Yohanan ben Zakkai, who among them clearly prophesied and warned and wept well ahead of the event? There was only one, Rabbi Yeshua, Israel's last and greatest national Prophet. He is the one who, in his generation, fulfilled like no one else before him the role spelled out in Deuteronomy 18:18–19, which included this warning: "If anyone does not listen to my words that the prophet speaks in my name, I myself will call him to account" (Deut. 18:19). We failed to hear the warnings!

Here are some of the prophecies recorded for us by the authors of the New Testament:

> As he approached Jerusalem and saw the city, he wept over it and said, "If you, even you, had only known on this day what would bring you peace—but now it is hidden from your eyes. The days will come upon you when your enemies will build an embankment against you and encircle you and hem you in on every side. They will dash you to the ground, you and the children within your walls. They will not leave one stone on another, because you did not recognize the time of God's coming to you."
>
> Luke 19:41–44

. . . When you see Jerusalem being surrounded by armies, you will know that its desolation is near. . . . They will fall by the sword and will be taken as prisoners to all the nations. Jerusalem will be trampled on by the Gentiles until the times of the Gentiles are fulfilled.

Luke 21:20, 24

As he was leaving the temple, one of his disciples said to him, "Look, Teacher! What massive stones! What magnificent buildings!"

"Do you see all these great buildings?" replied Jesus. "Not one stone here will be left on another; every one will be thrown down."

Mark 13:1–2

Because of the extraordinary accuracy of these words, critical scholars, who do not believe in supernatural revelation or prophecy, claim that these verses can only be explained as an example of *vaticinium ex eventu*, which is,

a technical theological or historiographical term referring to a prophecy written after the author already had information about the events he was "foretelling." The text is written so as to appear that the prophecy had taken place before the event.[280]

Ironically, it is the *opposite* objection that is being raised here, namely, that the prophecies are *not* accurate, and that is what we will address here.[281] First, it should be noted that, according to the historical pattern recorded in Scripture, anyone prophesying judgment on the nation, especially of this magnitude, would be resisted and his words met with unbelief (see, e.g., Jeremiah 26). But the words of Jesus in Mark 13:1–2 (recorded also in Matt. 24:2 and Luke 21:6) seemed to go over the top. Not only was it farfetched to think that the Temple would be destroyed, but it was absolutely preposterous to claim that not one stone of the Temple building would be left in place, that "every one will be thrown down." Impossible! The stones were absolutely massive and the Temple, which had been rebuilt by Herod, was so imposing. "At the southeast corner the temple platform towered two hundred feet above the Kidron Valley."[282] How could a glorious structure like this suffer such an ignominious destruction?

According to New Testament commentator Walter W. Wessel,

Jesus' reply was startling. Great though the temple buildings were, they would be completely destroyed. This prophecy was fulfilled in A.D. 70, when Jerusalem and the temple were destroyed by the Roman general Titus. Jesus' prophecy is very specific: "Not one stone here will be left on another." Although some of the huge stones Herod's workmen used in the great walls supporting the temple platform were not battered down by Titus's soldiers, all the buildings on the temple platform, including the temple itself to which the prophecy refers, were utterly destroyed. So completely were they destroyed that no trace of them remains today. Even their exact location on the temple mount is disputed.[283]

Yet Wessel also observes that, "The massive stones used in the construction of [the retaining wall built in Herod's expansion of the Temple] may still be seen today, since part of the wall escaped the destruction of A.D. 70."[284] So then, even if not a single stone in the Temple itself was left standing, what about these other stones, since Jesus, speaking to the Roman devastation of Jerusalem as a whole, said "They will not leave one stone on another" (Luke 19:44). In light of Deuteronomy 18:22, shouldn't Jesus be classified as a false prophet, since the verse specifically says, "If what a prophet proclaims in the name of the LORD does not take place or come true, that is a message the LORD has not spoken. That prophet has spoken presumptuously. Do not be afraid of him." In other words, being "close" is not enough!

Actually, based on this interpretation of Deuteronomy 18:22, Jeremiah would have been disqualified as a prophet, since, repeatedly in his book, he prophesied that, as a result of the Babylonian onslaught in 587–586 B.C.E., the cities of Judah would be left "without inhabitant." As I noted in my commentary on Jeremiah when discussing Jeremiah 4:7, "The effects of this incursion would be devastating: The land would become desolate and its cities without inhabitant, a theme repeated throughout Jeremiah (2:15; 4:29; 9:10; 33:10; 34:22; 44:2, 22; in the oracles against the nations, see 46:19; 48:9, 50:3, 51:29, 37, 62). But did this really happen?"[285] A fair, scholarly answer would be that,

> while there is clear evidence that the cities of Benjamin escaped the Babylonian onslaught—in keeping with the call to the Benjamites to flee from Jerusalem; cf. Jer 6:1 and see Abraham Malamat, "The Last Wars of the Kingdom of Judah," *JNES* [*Journal of Near Eastern Studies*] 9 (1950), 218–27—Judah and Jerusalem were, in fact, devastated, and [B. Oded] writes that, "The archaeology of Neo-Babylonian Judah is the archaeology of destruction, reflecting the 'fury of Babylon.'"[286]

In other words, there *was* great destruction on *many* of the cities, but not *all* the cities were left desolate and without inhabitant, which *is* what Jeremiah prophesied. As I explained,

Jer 4:7, then, along with the other verses in Jeremiah cited, above, should be taken as an example of prophetic speech in which a snapshot of one, common situation becomes a graphic picture of the whole. That is to say, while one could simply take this as hyperbolic language, since a total destruction of the land and complete decimation and/or exile of its inhabitants certainly did not occur, it is better to see it as a true prediction of what would happen in a number of specific places, which then served as a vivid example of divine judgment for the nation as a whole, although this would not entirely rule out some hyperbole in the description. Judah and Jerusalem *were* devastated, and many towns and villages *were* depopulated in the judgment.[287]

With this in mind, when we reexamine Yeshua's prophecy about the devastation of the Temple and the destruction of Jerusalem, taking special note of his words, "Not one stone [of the Temple buildings] will be left on another; every one will be thrown down," we can only say, "Truly this was a prophet sent by God!" His words pass the biblical test with flying colors.[288] My colleague, professor Steve Alt, is therefore completely on target with his comments that,

it seems a little petty to admit that Jesus predicted the destruction of the temple in the lifetime of his hearers, and for the temple to be destroyed forty years later, and then to claim Jesus was a false prophet because a few stones remained on top of each other. I can imagine a Jewish survivor standing amidst the rubble of the temple, having lost his whole family to the sword or the flame, witnessing one of the most horrific events that has ever happened to the Jewish people, and bellowing, "False prophet! Jesus was a false prophet! Part of one wall remains standing." How petty is that? The point of the prophecy, not its technical accuracy to the letter, determines the validity of the prophet.[289]

In the case of the Messiah's prophecies concerning Jerusalem's fall, especially when evaluated against the grid of the biblical prophets who preceded him, his words are remarkably accurate. And who but our Messiah and King would have declared almost two thousand years ago that our people in Jerusalem would "fall by the sword and . . . be taken as prisoners to all the nations" and that "Jerusalem [would] be trampled on by the Gentiles until the times of the Gentiles are fulfilled" (Luke 21:24)? Not only were his words remarkably accurate more than 1,900 years ago, when Jerusalem fell, but they have proven true for almost twenty centuries, as it is only in recent generations that Jerusalem ceased to be "trampled on by the Gentiles" as we near the fulfilling of "the times of the Gentiles."[290] His words have stood the test of time, as he said in

Matthew 24:35 in the context of Jerusalem's coming destruction, "Heaven and earth will pass away, but my words will never pass away."

5.23. Jesus was a cruel and undisciplined man. He violated the Torah by cursing—and hence, destroying—a perfectly good fig tree for not bearing figs even though the New Testament writers tell us that it was not the time for figs. So much for your wonderful Messiah! He even called a Gentile woman a dog when she approached him for help.

Of course, this objection completely contradicts other common Jewish objections that recognize Jesus as a great teacher and exemplary rabbi but that claim that the departure from Torah devotion began with Paul (see 5.26 and 5.29). Nonetheless, to answer your objection, five points should be made: (1) During his ministry and at his trial, no such accusations were brought against Yeshua. If he was guilty of violating the Torah in these ways, surely some witness would have been found to attack him for this. (2) There is no record of any such accusations being made against him in the Rabbinic polemics against him in the first centuries of this era. (3) His cursing the fig tree was a prophetic sign and was not in violation of Torah law. (4) As for calling a Gentile woman a dog, he actually went many miles out of his way just to heal her daughter—such was his compassion!—and he did this immediately after giving an important teaching that hinted at God pronouncing the Gentiles "clean" through the Messiah. (5) There are well-known Rabbinic statements over many centuries that would make the rabbis look like proud, self-righteous haters of the Gentiles if those statements were read without further Rabbinic commentary and explanation. In comparison with the Rabbinic statements, the words and actions of Jesus are very easily explained as truly representing the loving heart of his heavenly Father. And never forget that this Jesus whom you criticize as cruel and undisciplined laid down his life for you, as well as for every Jew and Gentile in the world.

The New Testament does not offer us a fleeting glance of this man Jesus, a mere snapshot of his life. Rather, it presents us with a full-length movie of his three years in public ministry, and the picture that emerges is crystal clear: He is a man of extraordinary compassion and kindness, reaching out to the lost and hurting—to the dregs of society—while at the same time exposing religious hypocrisy and rebuking self-righteousness. No one who walked the earth has ever had more right than our Messiah to say these words: "I am the good shepherd. The good shepherd lays down his life for the sheep" (John 10:11). Is it possible that this same Jesus was cruel and undisciplined, scorning Torah laws and calling a needy Gentile woman a dog?

There is something else worth considering before addressing this objection in detail. While there is no truth to the objections that claim that the New Testament authors changed their story to make Jesus look better (or, to make it look as if he fulfilled Messianic prophecies; see above, 5.15), at least what they wrote made sense. After all, these same authors were willing to give their lives for their Messiah—some of them actually did—and they certainly wanted others to believe in him, just as they themselves had come to believe. And, it was absolutely foundational for them that the One who took away our sins was himself sinless. To present a Jesus who sinned would completely undermine their whole message, not to mention call into question why they ever followed him. As for the purpose of their writing, John was explicit: "But these are written that you may believe that Jesus is the [Messiah], the Son of God, and that by believing you may have life in his name" (John 20:31). As for their message, it was consistent:

> God made him who had no sin to be sin [or, a sin offering] for us, so that in him we might become the righteousness of God.
>
> 2 Corinthians 5:21

> He committed no sin, and no deceit was found in his mouth.
>
> 1 Peter 2:22, citing Isaiah 53:9b

> For we do not have a high priest who is unable to sympathize with our weaknesses, but we have one who has been tempted in every way, just as we are—yet was without sin.
>
> Hebrews 4:15

So, the question must be asked: Would the New Testament writers preserve and pass on instances in which Yeshua allegedly sinned? (For the historical accuracy and overall reliability of the New Testament, see above, 5.6.) Let's examine the evidence.

According to the Torah,

> When you lay siege to a city for a long time, fighting against it to capture it, do not destroy its trees by putting an ax to them, because you can eat their fruit. Do not cut them down. Are the trees of the field people, that you should besiege them? However, you may cut down trees that you know are not fruit trees and use them to build siege works until the city at war with you falls.
>
> Deuteronomy 20:19–20

Allegedly, Jesus broke this law when he cursed the fig tree only days before his death. As Mark records:

> The next day as they were leaving Bethany, Jesus was hungry. Seeing in the distance a fig tree in leaf, he went to find out if it had any fruit. When he reached it, he found nothing but leaves, because it was not the season for figs. Then he said to the tree, "May no one ever eat fruit from you again." And his disciples heard him say it. . . .
>
> In the morning, as they went along, they saw the fig tree withered from the roots. Peter remembered and said to Jesus, "Rabbi, look! The fig tree you cursed has withered!"
>
> Mark 11:12–14, 20–21

Based on a principle drawn from Deuteronomy 20:19, namely, that it is wrong to destroy needlessly a perfectly good, fruit-bearing tree, even in times of siege, it is alleged that Yeshua had absolutely no right to destroy this fig tree. In fact, according to this logic, what he did was downright cruel, since he cursed the fig tree for its failure to bear figs when it wasn't even the season for figs. Even Mark commentator Walter Wessel concedes:

> This is one of the most difficult stories in the Gospels. . . . Rawlinson (p. 154) says that it "approximates more closely than any other episode in Mk to the type of 'unreasonable' miracle characteristic of the non-canonical Gospel literature." Hunter (p. 110) comments: "With our knowledge of Jesus from other sources, we find it frankly incredible that he could have used his power to wither a fig tree because it did not yield figs two or three months before its natural time of fruitage."[291]

So then, was Jesus guilty? Before responding to this question, let's look at 2 Kings 3:19, which describes Elisha's word to Israel in the midst of a battle with Moab. By the spirit of prophecy, he declared: "You will overthrow every fortified city and every major town. You will cut down every good tree, stop up all the springs, and ruin every good field with stones." Surely this appears to be in violation of Torah law!

In response to this, Rashi comments on this verse:

> Even though it is stated (Deut. 20:19): "You shall not destroy its trees," here He permitted it for you, for this is a contemptible and insignificant nation before Him. And so [Scripture] states (Deut. 23:7): "You shall not seek their welfare and their good." These are the good trees that are among them.

So, based on the insignificance of Moab, with alleged scriptural support from Deuteronomy 23:7, Rashi declares that it was permissible to destroy all her good trees, despite the prohibition of Deuteronomy 20:19. (Cf. also the comments of Radak and Ralbag.) How interesting![292] If Elisha could be justified in his actions in calling for the destruction of every good tree in Moab—not to mention stopping up all the springs and ruining every good field with stones, is it fair to fault Jesus for cursing a single tree?

"But that's where you're wrong," you say. "The Israelites were at war with Moab, whereas Jesus simply flaunted his powers by destroying a good tree with no justification."

Actually, I could argue that if Elisha's actions could be justified, seeing that they are in apparent contradiction to Deuteronomy 20:19, Yeshua's actions could be justified. In reality, however, no such justification is needed since the tree that the Messiah cursed was *not* a good, fruit-bearing tree. As explained by New Testament commentator Craig Keener,

> At this time of year, edible figs were still about six weeks away, but the bland fruit had recently appeared on the tree in late March; they would become ripe by late May. These were the early figs that preceded the main crop of late figs, which were ripe for harvest from mid-August into October. If only leaves appeared, without the early figs, that tree would bear no figs that year—early or late. Because everyone would know that it was "not yet the season for [real] figs," Jesus is making a point about trees that only pretend to have good fruit (cf. Jeremiah 24).[293]

Did you follow that? This event took place a few days before Passover, which generally falls in late March or early April, at which time the fig trees would be in leaf and nonedible figs would be visible as well, the forerunners to the edible figs which would come about six weeks later. Yet here was a fig tree with *the appearance* of health and fruitfulness whereas, in reality, it would not bear edible fruit that year. If there was

a tree that could be cursed, this was it! And there was prophetic significance to this act as well.

As explained by F. F. Bruce in *Hard Sayings of the Bible*,

> Was it not unreasonable to curse the tree for being fruitless when, as Mark
> expressly says, "it was not the season for figs"? The problem is most satis-
> factorily cleared up in a discussion called "The Barren Fig Tree" published
> many years ago by W. M. Christie, a Church of Scotland minister in Pal-
> estine under the British mandatory regime. He pointed out first the time
> of year at which the incident is said to have occurred (if, as is probable,
> Jesus was crucified on April 6th, A.D. 30, the incident occurred during the
> first days of April). "Now," wrote Christie, "the facts connected with the
> fig tree are these. Toward the end of March the leaves begin to appear, and
> in about a week the foliage coating is complete. Coincident with [this],
> and sometimes even before, there appears quite a crop of small knobs,
> not the real figs, but a kind of early forerunner. They grow to the size of
> green almonds, in which condition they are eaten by peasants and oth-
> ers when hungry. When they come to their own indefinite maturity they
> drop off." These precursors of the true fig are called *taqsh* in Palestinian
> Arabic. Their appearance is a harbinger of the fully formed appearance
> of the true fig some six weeks later. So, as Mark says, the time for figs had
> not yet come. But if the leaves appear without any *taqsh*, that is a sign
> that there will be no figs. Since Jesus found "nothing but leaves"—leaves
> without any *taqsh*—he knew that "it was an absolutely hopeless, fruitless
> fig tree" and said as much.
>
> But if that is the true explanation of his words, why should anyone
> trouble to record the incident as though it had some special significance?
> Because it did have some special significance. As recorded by Mark, it is an
> acted parable with the same lesson as the spoken parable of the fruitless
> fig tree in Luke 13:6–9. In that spoken parable a landowner came three
> years in succession expecting fruit from a fig tree on his property, and
> when year by year it proved to be fruitless, he told the man in charge of
> his vineyard to cut it down because it was using up the ground to no good
> purpose. In both the acted parable and the spoken parable it is difficult
> to avoid the conclusion that the fig tree represents the city of Jerusalem,
> unresponsive to Jesus as he came to it with the message of God, and thereby
> incurring destruction. Elsewhere Luke records how Jesus wept over the
> city's blindness to its true well-being and foretold its ruin "because you did
> not know the time of your visitation" (Lk 19:41–44 RSV). It is because the
> incident of the cursing of the fig tree was seen to convey the same lesson
> that Mark, followed by Matthew, recorded it.[294]

So much for Jesus being cruel and undisciplined! Of course, as Messiah and Son of God, if, in obedience to his Father, he wanted to call
down fire from heaven and destroy a thousand trees in demonstration of

his power, he could have done so, and who among us would have dared question his rights? But that was not what he was about, as expressed in his comment to his disciples when two of them, like Elijah of old (see 2 Kings 1:9–12), wanted to call down fire from heaven and burn up some disrespectful Samaritans. He rebuked them saying, "Ye know not what manner of spirit ye are of. For the Son of man is not come to destroy men's lives, but to save [them]" (Luke 9:55–56 in some Greek mss., as translated in the KJV). We can safely say, albeit somewhat tongue in cheek, that he didn't come to destroy trees either.

More importantly, we should ask, "Who is this man who speaks a word and it comes to pass? What kind of rabbi is this?" For other examples of the extraordinary character of this extraordinary rabbi, see Mark 9:5, where Peter addresses him as "rabbi" on the Mount of Transfiguration; 10:51 where the blind man, about to be healed, calls him "rabbi" and requests his sight; John 1:49, where Nathanael hails him as "rabbi" and calls him "the Son of God" and "the King of Israel"; 3:2, where Nicodemus says to him, "Rabbi, we know you are a teacher who has come from God. For no one could perform the miraculous signs you are doing if God were not with him"; 6:25, when the crowd asked him, "Rabbi, when did you get here?"—after he had just *walked* across the lake; 9:2, when his disciples called him "rabbi" when asking about the cause of a man's blindness—immediately before Yeshua healed him; and 11:8, when his disciples called him "rabbi" before he traveled into Judea to raise Lazarus from the dead. What an extraordinary rabbi indeed![295]

As for his calling a Gentile woman a dog, I can demonstrate to you that he did nothing wrong but, in reality, orchestrated the whole event to demonstrate how Gentiles could be accepted into the family of God. Before developing this in more depth, I do want to ask a question to every traditional Jewish reader: In raising this objection, isn't this a classic example of the pot calling the kettle black?

What I mean is this: Isn't it hypocritical for a Jewish person—especially a traditional Jew—to accuse Jesus of being cruel and insensitive for allegedly calling a Gentile woman a dog? (Again, we *will* carefully examine this charge and look at the biblical account, but for now, it is appropriate to ask some other questions.)

At the risk of being called an anti-Semite (this, of course, is as ludicrous as calling any Jew who criticizes Jesus an anti-Semite), let me cite for you a number of Rabbinic texts that, quite overtly, speak in derogatory terms about Gentiles.[296] Should you say to me, "I know many of the texts you're going to quote, and I have an answer for each of them," then I say in reply, "Isn't it only right, then, that you approach Yeshua's words in that same spirit?"

In actual fact, I align myself with those who defend traditional Judaism from charges of bigotry, emphasizing the positive value placed on all human beings by the Talmudic rabbis (or, at least, by some of them). There are many statements that back this up (see below). But there are also many statements in the traditional sources that could easily be construed as teaching the racial superiority of the Jew and the racial inferiority of the Gentile. Here is just a tiny sampling:

- Exodus 22:31[30] says to Israel: "You are to be my holy people. So do not eat the meat of an animal torn by wild beasts; throw it to the dogs." According to Rashi, reflecting mainline Rabbinic thought, this probably refers to Gentiles: "**you shall throw it to the dog[s].** He [referring to a Gentile] is also similar to a dog, or perhaps a dog is meant literally?" So, according to Rashi, God himself in his Torah could well be referring to a Gentile as a dog, since Gentiles, like dogs, eat the meat of animals killed by wild beasts.
- According to some traditional Jewish sources, it is permitted to violate the Sabbath to save the life of a Jew but not the life of a Gentile.[297]
- According to Maimonides, "When there is no war between us and non-Jews, . . . one does not cause their death; but it is forbidden to save them if they are dying, for example if you see one of them fall into the sea you do not fish him out, as it is said, 'You shall not stand passively beside your brother's blood'—but he is not 'your brother.'"[298]
- The Mishnah legislates that "An Israelite woman should not act as midwife to a heathen woman, because she would be delivering a child for idolatry. A heathen woman, however, may act as midwife to an Israelite woman. An Israelite woman should not suckle the child of a heathen, but a heathen woman may suckle the child of an Israelite woman in her premises" (b. A. Z. 26a). While discussing these laws, the Talmud states that, "while a Jew should not lower a Gentile into a pit to kill him, he should not lift him out of the pit to help him."
- R. Johanan in the Talmud states, "A heathen who studies the Torah deserves death, for it is written, Moses commanded us a law for an inheritance [Deut. 33:4]; it is our inheritance, not theirs" (b. Sanh 59a).
- The Targum to Ezekiel 34:31 changes the Hebrew ". . . you are men" and translates, ". . . you are the house of Israel," in keeping with R. Shimon ben Yohai's interpretation of this verse in the Talmud

(b. B. M. 114b), "You are called men, but the nations of the world are not called men, but beasts."[299]

- Various editions of Tractate Soferim preserve R. Shimon ben Yohai's statement: "The best among the gentiles, in wartime—kill!"[300] Other Rabbinic texts preserve the wording as: "The best among the gentiles—kill! The best among serpents—smash their brains!"

- Based on such texts, some right-wing rabbis in Israel have gone so far as to argue that, "Although in peacetime it is forbidden to kill non-Jews, . . . *in wartime it is a* mitzvah [good deed] *to kill them.*"[301]

- Recently, the graduate of a major yeshiva in America and basing himself on rabbinic sources, wrote a book claiming that "gentiles are 'completely evil' and Jews constitute a separate, genetically superior species," as reported by the Jewish newspaper *The Forward*.[302] The book even carried glowing endorsements from leading rabbis. The author, Rabbi Saadya Grama, claimed that the "difference between the people of Israel and the nations of the world is an essential one. The Jew by his source and in his very essence is entirely good. The *goy*, by his source and in his very essence is completely evil. This is not simply a matter of religious distinction, but rather of two completely different species."[303]

- *The Forward* article also states that, "Perhaps the most extreme version of this [racial superiority] view is found in the central text of Chabad Chasidism [practiced today by the Lubavitcher Jews], Tanya, whose author, Rabbi Shneur Zalman of Lyadi, Chabad's founder, maintained that Jewish and gentile souls are fundamentally different, the former 'divine' and the latter 'animalistic.' That viewpoint has gained ground in recent decades, particularly among *charedi* [ultra-Orthodox] thinkers."[304]

Now, before you start attacking me (or the Talmud!), let me share with you what some of the top Orthodox rabbis in America had to say about the book by Rabbi Grama.

Rabbi Aryeh Malkiel Kotler, the head of the yeshiva from which he graduated, after reviewing the book more carefully, repudiated his initial endorsement (which was done primarily because the rabbi was one of his many graduates) and stated:

> In looking at the specific points allegedly contained in the *sefer* [book], I can certainly tell you that they are not reflective of normative Jewish thought and are certainly not the philosophy of our yeshivah. Our philosophy asserts that every human being is created in the image of the Lord and

the primacy of integrity and honesty in all dealings without exception. I strongly repudiate any assertions in the name of Judaism that do not represent and reflect this philosophy.[305]

The chancellor of Yeshiva University, Rabbi Dr. Norman Lamm, stated, after seeing excerpts from the book:

It is a book by someone who has obviously taken leave of his senses and adopted the kind of racism that was used against Jews since the beginning of time. I almost feel like offering a conjecture that it was written by an antisemite posing as a rabbi. . . . The passages that I have read managed to offend everyone—the Torah, the martyrs of the Holocaust, the Jewish ideals of justice and the essential divinity that inheres in every human being regardless of religion, race or ethnic origin.[306]

As for several of the earlier quotes, most of them were assembled by a well-known, Israeli Reconstructionist rabbi, Dr. Moshe Zemer, who categorically repudiated this disparaging view of Gentiles, vigorously opposing the positions taken by some bigoted, contemporary rabbis, and he did it in the name of Judaism.[307] For further support of his position, he quoted the words of Bar Ilan University professor Uriel Simon, himself an observant Jew. Simon wrote, in part, "Every word that helps cheapen human life and makes light of the sanctity of life, especially when it comes from a rabbi, works inestimable damage."[308]

What about all those harsh statements in the Rabbinical sources? It is true, to be sure, that there is a degree of legal superiority enjoyed by the Jew over the Gentile in some traditional Jewish sources, and it is also true that the moral and spiritual superiority of a Jew over a Gentile is often assumed in some Rabbinic texts. But contemporary rabbis would be quick to explain that: (1) many of these texts must be interpreted in their historical context, in which the Gentiles in question were overt idol worshipers (this does not justify the attitude behind some of the quotes, but a number of them come from the Talmudic tractate Avodah Zarah, which deals with idolatry); and (2) Judaism also teaches that the righteous of all nations have a place in the world to come. In fact, the very Talmudic text that stated that, "R. Johanan said: A heathen who studies the Torah deserves death" (b. Sanh 59a) follows this with a different opinion that states,

An objection is raised: R. Meir used to say, Whence do we know that even a heathen who studies the Torah is as a High Priest? From the verse, [Ye shall therefore keep my statutes, and my judgments:] which, if man do, he shall live in them [Leviticus 18:5]. Priests, Levites, and Israelites are not mentioned, but men: hence thou mayest learn that even a heathen who studies the Torah is as a High Priest!—That refers to their own seven laws [said in reference to studying the so-called Seven Laws of Noah].

In short, it is fair to allow the transmitters of the tradition to have the first opportunity to explain their own traditions, and they should be given a sympathetic hearing before their sacred texts are rejected out of hand.[309] (For issues that can be raised fairly in critiquing Rabbinic tradition, see vol. 5.)

The same must hold true for the words of Jesus which, upon examination, will be found to be far less inflammatory than the Rabbinic statements quoted above and, when put in context, are actually positive in the end.

To give you the bigger picture, here are some important things to know about Yeshua, the Messiah of Israel and the Savior of the whole world:

- His disciple Matthew, in recording Yeshua's ancestry through his adoptive father's royal line, makes specific mention of two Gentile women who contributed to the royal line: Rahab, who was a Canaanite by birth, and Ruth, who was a Moabite by birth (Matt. 1:5). There was no genealogical need to mention either of these women, but he did so—in his very Jewish book!—for a specific theological reason (see also 1:3a).
- In his first sermon in his hometown synagogue in Nazareth, Jesus drew attention to instances in the Tanakh in which God went out of his way to care for a Gentile widow and heal a Gentile general, thereby infuriating everyone in the synagogue (Luke 4:24–30).
- After healing the servant of a Roman soldier, Yeshua said to those following him, "I say to you that many will come from the east and the west [meaning the Gentiles!], and will take their places at the feast with Abraham, Isaac and Jacob in the kingdom of heaven. But the subjects of the kingdom [meaning the Jews who did not believe] will be thrown outside, into the darkness, where there will be weeping and gnashing of teeth" (Matt. 8:11–12; see 8:5–13; note again that the very Jewish Matthew records these words).
- In John 4, Jesus reached out to a Samaritan woman, despite the fact that the Samaritans were despised by other Jews as half-breeds, even staying in Samaria for two days to minister to the people there (John 4:42).
- In the famous parable of the Good Samaritan, Yeshua made the hero of his parable a Samaritan, in contrast with a priest and a

Levite, commending him as an example of a true neighbor (Luke 10:29–37).

- Luke also records Jesus' healing of ten lepers as they followed the Messiah's instructions and made their way to the priest, noting that only one of the men returned to give him thanks—a Samaritan, whom the Lord then commended (Luke 17:11–19).

It is true, of course, that during Jesus' lifetime, the primary, initial mission of the disciples was only to "the lost sheep of the house of Israel" and not to the Gentiles or the Samaritans (see Matt. 10:5–6 NASB). But it is equally true that, as just noted, Jesus himself *did* minister to these very people and, more importantly, John records these famous words, "For God so loved *the world* that he gave his one and only Son, that whoever believes in him shall not perish but have eternal life" (John 3:16). And after dying for that very world and then rising from the dead, he commissioned his disciples to "go and make disciples of *all nations*" (Matt. 28:19a), telling them that the Holy Spirit would come upon them to empower them to be his witnesses "in Jerusalem, and in all Judea and Samaria, and to the *ends of the earth*" (Acts 1:8). See also Luke 24:47, where he states that "repentance and forgiveness of sins will be preached in his name to *all nations*, beginning at Jerusalem" (my emphasis added to Scriptures cited above). This was hardly a bigoted man!

That's why his followers could write that "he is the atoning sacrifice for our sins, and not only for ours but also for the sins of the whole world" (1 John 2:2), and that's why the final chapter of the final book of the New Covenant Writings can state: "The Spirit and the bride say, 'Come!' And let him who hears say, 'Come!' *Whoever is thirsty*, let him come; and *whoever wishes*, let him take the free gift of the water of life" (Rev. 22:17, my emphasis). The gospel message is good news for the whole world, as former missionary and now missions professor Don Richardson once said, "God has prepared the whole world for the gospel and the gospel for the whole world." This is the spirit of Jesus the Savior, the one of whom John the Immerser said, "Look, the Lamb of God, who takes away the sin of the world!" (John 1:29). Surely this Savior who was destined to serve as a sacrificial Lamb for the salvation of Jews and Gentiles alike would not disparage a needy Gentile woman.

How then do we explain his words in Matthew 15:26? Let's read the entire account (for the parallel passage, see Mark 7:24–31):

> Leaving that place, Jesus withdrew to the region of Tyre and Sidon. A Canaanite woman from that vicinity came to him, crying out, "Lord,

Son of David, have mercy on me! My daughter is suffering terribly from demon-possession."

Jesus did not answer a word. So his disciples came to him and urged him, "Send her away, for she keeps crying out after us."

He answered, "I was sent only to the lost sheep of Israel."

The woman came and knelt before him. "Lord, help me!" she said.

He replied, "It is not right to take the children's bread and toss it to their dogs."

"Yes, Lord," she said, "but even the dogs eat the crumbs that fall from their masters' table."

Then Jesus answered, "Woman, you have great faith! Your request is granted." And her daughter was healed from that very hour.

Jesus left there and went along the Sea of Galilee.

Matthew 15:21–29

Notice the opening phrase, "Leaving that place." What place was this? That place was Gennesaret, where Jesus had been performing miraculous healings for the sick and hurting people (see Matt. 14:34–36; Mark 6:53–56). At that same time, "some Pharisees and teachers of the law came to Jesus from Jerusalem and asked, 'Why do your disciples break the tradition of the elders? They don't wash their hands before they eat!'" (Matt. 15:2). This triggered a lecture from Yeshua, including some rebuke for man-made traditions that got in the way of obedience to God's Word. He then called the crowd to him and explained, "Listen and understand. What goes into a man's mouth does not make him 'unclean,' but what comes out of his mouth, that is what makes him 'unclean'" (Matt. 15:10–11). He then expanded on this to his disciples, who seemed to have a hard time following his point:

"Are you still so dull?" Jesus asked them. "Don't you see that whatever enters the mouth goes into the stomach and then out of the body? But the things that come out of the mouth come from the heart, and these make a man 'unclean.' For out of the heart come evil thoughts, murder, adultery, sexual immorality, theft, false testimony, slander. These are what make a man 'unclean'; but eating with unwashed hands does not make him 'unclean.'"

Matthew 15:16–20

Mark 7:19b adds a further insight to this teaching. I'll quote Mark 7:18–19 (NRSV) to make the point more clear:

He said to them, "Then do you also fail to understand? Do you not see that whatever goes into a person from outside cannot defile, since it enters, not the heart but the stomach, and goes out into the sewer?" (Thus he declared all foods clean.)

Now, it is clear that Jesus did not abolish the dietary laws at that time (see below, 5.33, where an alternate rendering of the final clause is offered), but it is also clear that he was elucidating an important spiritual principle, namely that food, in and of itself—even ritually "unclean" food—could not defile our essential being, our "inner man," any more than eating with ritually unwashed hands (or, by implication, hands that were simply unwashed) could make our hearts unclean. This is then reinforced in Mark 7:20–23, which parallels Matthew 15:18–20a: "What comes out of a man is what makes him 'unclean.' . . . All these evils come from inside and make a man 'unclean'" (Mark 7:20, 23).

After this, Matthew and Mark both record that "Jesus withdrew to the region of Tyre and Sidon," ostensibly to be alone (Matt. 15:21; Mark 7:24). It was here that Jesus encountered the Gentile woman and, after having spoken a word of healing and deliverance for her daughter, Matthew records, "Jesus left there and went along the Sea of Galilee" (Matt. 15:29a; Mark 7:31, with more geographical details). This is highly significant, since, in retrospect this whole episode seemed quite intentional—we might say, the Messiah acted by divine premeditation[310]—and the end result of a round-trip journey of between 60 and 100 miles (on foot!) was the healing of this Gentile woman's daughter. What was the divine lesson in all this?

As we note, below, 5.33, when Peter received a thrice-repeated vision in Acts 10 which ordered him to kill and eat all kinds of unclean animals, God was *not* telling him to change his dietary habits. Rather, it was a visionary lesson that Peter should no longer call *the Gentiles* unclean; instead, they would now be accepted as spiritual equals through the Messiah (see below, for full discussion). In the same way here, Yeshua's teaching about "clean" and "unclean," about spiritual defilement coming from the inside and not the outside, about no food, in and of itself, being truly "unclean" (even if it carries that legal status), is now put into spiritual practice, as the Lord takes a long journey *into a Gentile region* and then reaches out in mercy to a needy "Canaanite." Was there nowhere else where Jesus could get alone for a little while?

The object lesson is indisputable: Jesus was pointing to the fact that the Gentiles were no longer to be considered "unclean" if they put their trust in him. As articulated some years later by Paul, "As the Scripture says, 'Anyone who trusts in him will never be put to shame.' For there is no difference between Jew and Gentile—the same Lord is Lord of all and richly blesses all who call on him, for, 'Everyone who calls on the name of the Lord will be saved.'" (Rom. 10:11–13, quoting Isa. 28:16 and Joel 2:32). So then, in terms of salvation, Jesus the Messiah broke down the wall of separation so that, in this respect, "there is no difference between Jew and Gentile." This was revolutionary! (In fact, it still *is* revolutionary, an object of misunderstanding and spiritual stumbling for many Jews.)

As Carson observes:

> Of greater interest is the placing of this pericope in both Gospels. It not only records Jesus' withdrawal from the opposition of the Pharisees and teachers of the law (cf. 14:13) but contrasts their approach to the Messiah with that of this woman. They belong to the covenant people but take offense at the conduct of Jesus' disciples, challenge his authority, and are so defective in understanding the Scriptures that they show themselves not to be plants the heavenly Father has planted. But this woman is a pagan, a descendant of ancient enemies, and with no claim on the God of the covenant. Yet in the end she approaches the Jewish Messiah and with great faith asks only for grace; and her request is granted (cf. 8:5–13).[311]

With this perspective in mind, we now return to the verses in question. Note first that, while Mark identifies the woman as "a Greek, born in Syrian Phoenicia" (Mark 7:26), Matthew simply calls her a "Canaanite" (Matt. 15:22), probably to elicit a negative emotional response from a biased reader. The woman, quite amazingly, acknowledges Yeshua as Messiah, calling him "Son of David," and pleading for mercy, since her daughter was "suffering terribly from demon-possession" (15:22b).[312] Jesus, however, does not answer her. This was a test! "So his disciples came to him and urged him, 'Send her away, for she keeps crying out after us.'" (15:23; Carson notes that this could either mean, "Send her away without helping her," or, as he prefers, "Send her away with her request granted," which would be supported by 15:24).[313] To this Jesus replies, "I was sent only to the lost sheep of Israel." That was the state of things for the present (as noted above), and this Gentile woman would have to acknowledge it.

Her need, however, was so great and her faith so strong that, "The woman came and knelt before him. 'Lord, help me!' she said" (15:25). It is here that Jesus uttered the controversial words, recorded by both Matthew and Mark (the latter being significant, since his intended readership was primarily Gentile), "He replied, 'It is not right to take the children's bread and toss it to their dogs,'" to which she replied, "Yes, Lord, . . . but even the dogs eat the crumbs that fall from their masters' table." In response to this extraordinary statement, "Jesus answered, 'Woman, you have great faith! Your request is granted.' And her daughter was healed from that very hour" (15:26–28). Significantly, the only other time in Mathew that the phrase "great faith" appears is in 8:10, where he says to the Roman (and therefore Gentile!) centurion, "I tell you the truth, I have not found anyone in Israel with such great faith," leading into his comments about a great ingathering of Gentiles while many Jews would not make it in (8:11–12, quoted above).

Now, there can be no question at all that: (1) Jesus put this woman through a test to draw out—and thereby demonstrate—her great faith, granting her request and, in the process, continuing to display his power to heal as the Messianic Son of David.[314] (2) He went many miles out of his way to give a practical illustration of his teaching about "clean" and "unclean." (3) Ultimately, he went many miles out of his way to heal a needy woman's daughter. (Was it her cries of desperation that got God's attention and drew Messiah there in the first place?) (4) He used the occasion to, once again, highlight "great faith" existing outside the people (or, borders) of Israel.

In light of all this, it is preposterous to think that this narrative actually highlights a negative and derogatory attitude towards Gentiles on the part of Jesus. Absolutely not!

How then do we explain his words, "It is not right to take the children's bread and toss it to their dogs"? It is true that he says, "their dogs," rather than just "dogs," and it is true that the Greek word used can refer to "household dogs" as opposed to "wild dogs," and this, to a degree, lessens the harshness. More importantly, however, it is clear that the woman grasped the spiritual point Yeshua was making by replying, "even the dogs eat the crumbs that fall from their masters' table." In other words, "I recognize that healing is the children's bread and that your people are the covenant people, God's children, to whom the promises of healing belong. And I recognize that they come first. But I can still get the leftovers!"

What great faith, and what extraordinary insight, none of which would have become evident if not for the sequence of events which unfolded. And how often does God put us to the test, delaying an answer and even appearing aloof, before demonstrating his power and love (see, e.g., John 11:1–21; for a different dimension of divine "absence," cf. 2 Chron. 32:31). Yeshua's actions are certainly in harmony with those of his Father!

As for the reference to "dogs," it obviously was not a big deal to the woman or to the disciples, who faithfully recorded these words. (As I pointed out, above, it is both Matthew and Mark who recount this, the former primarily writing to Jews, the latter primarily writing to Gentiles. It was not a problem for either of them.) This could be argued against the backdrop of the Hebrew Scriptures, as Messianic Jewish scholar David

Stern does, or against the backdrop of contemporary Jewish thought, as Jewish professor Samuel Tobias Lachs does.[315] Either way, the words of Jesus, spoken in a very specific context for a very specific purpose, should not be an occasion for stumbling, especially when it is realized that he did not say to this woman, "You lousy Gentile dog! I will never help you." Rather, he gave a vivid illustration that produced a dramatic and historic response, and I for one am blessed that this is part of the historical record. I'm sure this Gentile woman was blessed as well, as the story concludes: "And her daughter was healed from that very hour" (Matt. 15:28).

Thank God for the Son of David!

5.24. Actually, Jesus also taught that salvation came through obeying the Law. Just read Matthew 5:17–20; 7:21; 19:16–30; 25:31–46. This whole "gospel of grace" message is the invention of Paul and the other writers.

> The same Gospels that preserve teachings of Jesus that you have just quoted state categorically that he came to save us from our sins (Matt. 1:21), that he gave his life as a ransom for many (Mark 10:45), that his blood was the blood of the new covenant, poured out for us (Luke 22:20), and that the message of repentance and forgiveness of sins had to be preached in his name (Luke 24:46–47). This hardly fits the description of someone who taught that complete salvation came through obeying the Law! Rather, Jesus used the Torah as a standard of righteousness and a means of convicting us of our sins and exposing our lack of obedience before ushering in the new covenant which granted us complete and total forgiveness through his death and through which we are called to a higher level of obedience than was possible through keeping the Law.

There is no question that Yeshua pointed people to the Torah and to obedience to God's commandments, and there is no question that he instituted the new covenant through which God's laws are written on our hearts and through which we receive forgiveness of sins. It is not a matter of either–or but of both–and. And it is clear that Yeshua did not abolish the Law (see below, 5.28), that his disciples continued to obey the Law (see below, 5.33), and that he and his disciples preached the necessity of both repentance and faith (see vol. 1, 1.11). But it is equally clear that he did not teach that salvation could be attained through obedience to the Law alone, and he is the one who called people to believe in him.

Before looking briefly at the key verses involved, let's listen to some of the statements made by Yeshua himself:

- To Nicodemus, a leading Pharisee, Jesus said, "I tell you the truth, no one can see the kingdom of God unless he is born again [or, born from above]," further explaining, "Just as Moses lifted up the snake in the desert, so the Son of Man must be lifted up, that everyone who believes in him may have eternal life" (John 3:3, 14–15).
- It is also possible that Yeshua himself uttered the well-known words found in the verses that follow: "For God so loved the world that he gave his one and only Son, that whoever believes in him shall not perish but have eternal life. For God did not send his Son into the world to condemn the world, but to save the world through him. Whoever believes in him is not condemned, but whoever does not believe stands condemned already because he has not believed in the name of God's one and only Son. This is the verdict: Light has come into the world, but men loved darkness instead of light because their deeds were evil. Everyone who does evil hates the light, and will not come into the light for fear that his deeds will be exposed. But whoever lives by the truth comes into the light, so that it may be seen plainly that what he has done has been done through God" (John 3:16–21). If he did not utter them, then John wrote them as further explanation of the previous verses.
- Repeatedly, he called on his Jewish people to believe in him: "I am the bread of life. He who comes to me will never go hungry, and he who believes in me will never be thirsty" (John 6:35); "If anyone is thirsty, let him come to me and drink. Whoever believes in me, as the Scripture has said, streams of living water will flow from within him" (7:37–38); "I tell you the truth, whoever hears my word and believes him who sent me has eternal life and will not be condemned; he has crossed over from death to life" (5:24); "I am the resurrection and the life. He who believes in me will live, even though he dies; and whoever lives and believes in me will never die" (11:25–26); "When a man believes in me, he does not believe in me only, but in the one who sent me. When he looks at me, he sees the one who sent me. I have come into the world as a light, so that no one who believes in me should stay in darkness" (12:44–46).

- He stated that there were consequences for not believing in him: "You are from below; I am from above. You are of this world; I am not of this world. I told you that you would die in your sins; if you do not believe that I am [he], you will indeed die in your sins" (John 8:23–24).

- He said that it was his Father's will that all men honor him: "For just as the Father raises the dead and gives them life, even so the Son gives life to whom he is pleased to give it. Moreover, the Father judges no one, but has entrusted all judgment to the Son, that all may honor the Son just as they honor the Father. He who does not honor the Son does not honor the Father, who sent him" (John 5:21–23).

- He said that true rest was found in him: "Come to me, all you who are weary and burdened, and I will give you rest. Take my yoke upon you and learn from me, for I am gentle and humble in heart, and you will find rest for your souls. For my yoke is easy and my burden is light" (Matt. 11:28–30).

- He called on people to hear his voice and believe his words: "I tell you the truth, whoever hears my word and believes him who sent me has eternal life and will not be condemned; he has crossed over from death to life" (John 5:24).

- He said that he was the only way for the sheep: "I tell you the truth, I am the gate for the sheep. All who ever came before me were thieves and robbers, but the sheep did not listen to them. I am the gate; whoever enters through me will be saved. He will come in and go out, and find pasture. The thief comes only to steal and kill and destroy; I have come that they may have life, and have it to the full" (John 10:7–10).

- He called himself the good shepherd, since he would lay down his life for the sheep and faithfully keep the sheep: "I am the good shepherd. The good shepherd lays down his life for the sheep. . . . My sheep listen to my voice; I know them, and they follow me. I give them eternal life, and they shall never perish; no one can snatch them out of my hand. My Father, who has given them to me, is greater than all; no one can snatch them out of my Father's hand. I and the Father are one" (John 10:11, 27–30).

- He said that he was the only way to the Father: "I am the way and the truth and the life. No one comes to the Father except through me. If you really knew me, you would know my Father as well. From now on, you do know him and have seen him" (John 14:6–7).

- He said that he was the true vine and that his disciples had to remain in him in order to have spiritual life: "Remain in me, and I will remain in you. No branch can bear fruit by itself; it must remain in the vine. Neither can you bear fruit unless you remain in me. I am the vine; you are the branches. If a man remains in me and I in him, he will bear much fruit; apart from me you can do nothing. If anyone does not remain in me, he is like a branch that is thrown away and withers; such branches are picked up, thrown into the fire and burned. If you remain in me and my words remain in you, ask whatever you wish, and it will be given you" (John 15:4–7).

- He presented himself as a doctor for the sick at heart: "It is not the healthy who need a doctor, but the sick. I have not come to call the righteous, but sinners to repentance" (Luke 5:31–32).

- He called his disciples to leave everything and follow him: "If anyone would come after me, he must deny himself and take up his cross and follow me" (Mark 8:34); "Any of you who does not give up everything he has cannot be my disciple" (Luke 14:33).

- He declared that people would be judged by whether or not they confessed him without shame: "Whoever acknowledges me before men, I will also acknowledge him before my Father in heaven. But whoever disowns me before men, I will disown him before my Father in heaven" (Matt. 10:32–33). "If anyone is ashamed of me and my words in this adulterous and sinful generation, the Son of Man will be ashamed of him when he comes in his Father's glory with the holy angels" (Mark 8:38).

- He told his disciples that he was offering himself for the sins of many: "The Son of Man did not come to be served, but to serve, and to give his life as a ransom for many" (Mark 10:45).

- Immediately before his death, during his last meal with his disciples, he told them that he was giving his body and blood to institute the new covenant: "And he took bread, gave thanks and broke it, and gave it to them, saying, 'This is my body given for you; do this in remembrance of me.' In the same way, after the supper he took the cup, saying, 'This cup is the new covenant in my blood, which is poured out for you'" (Luke 22:19–20).

- After his resurrection, he called on his disciples to go and make disciples of the nations, making faith essential to salvation: "All authority in heaven and on earth has been given to me. Therefore go and make disciples of all nations, baptizing them in the name of the Father and of the Son and of the Holy Spirit, and teaching them to obey everything I have commanded you. And surely I am with you always, to the very end of the age" (Matt. 28:18–20). As expressed in the longer ending of Mark, "Go into all the world and preach the good news to all creation. Whoever believes and is baptized will be saved, but whoever does not believe will be condemned" (Mark 16:15–16). As stated in Luke, "Yes, it was written long ago that the Messiah must suffer and die and rise again from the dead on the third day. With my authority, take this message of repentance to all the nations, beginning in Jerusalem: 'There is forgiveness of sins for all who turn to me.' You are witnesses of all these things." (Luke 24:46–48 NLT).

In light of this testimony—and there are more verses that could have been cited—there can be no question whatsoever about what constituted the central issue *according to Yeshua himself*: It was believing in him, obeying him, following him, honoring him. That's why, without exception, his followers preached this very message to both Jew and Gentile, beginning with Peter's sermon on Shavuot (Pentecost) to the Jewish crowd gathered at the Temple: "Turn from sin, return to God, and each of you be immersed on the authority of Yeshua the Messiah into forgiveness of your sins, and you will receive the gift of the *Ruach HaKodesh* [Holy Spirit]!" (Acts 2:38 JNT). If you have never read through the Book of Acts, I would encourage you to do so at your earliest opportunity. You will see there that the message is consistent:

Rulers and elders of the people! . . . If we are being examined today about a good deed done for a disabled person, if you want to know how he was restored to health, then let it be known to you and to all the people of Isra'el that it is in the name of the Messiah, Yeshua from Natzeret, whom you had executed on a stake as a criminal but whom God has raised from the dead, that this man stands before you perfectly healed.

This Yeshua is the *stone rejected by* you builders which *has become the cornerstone*. There is salvation in no one else! For there is no other name under heaven given to mankind by whom we must be saved!

Acts 4:8 JNT, my emphasis

This was not something Paul dreamed up years later, nor was it something concocted by some of the other disciples. This was the only possible conclusion to draw from the teachings of Jesus himself, both before his death and after his resurrection.

How then do we explain Matthew 5:17–20? We treat that passage at length, below (5.28), but in short, we can say that Jesus was making clear that he was not coming to abolish the Law and the Prophets but to fulfill them, indicating that through him, the Law and the Prophets found their ultimate expression. Moreover, he called his followers to an even higher level of righteousness than that of the religious Jews of his day, some of whom were hypocrites but some of whom were quite sincere and godly. Then, through his death, resurrection, and sending of the Spirit, he empowered us to attain this level of obedience, also providing forgiveness for our sins through the new covenant (for more on that, see below, 5.34).

What about Matthew 7:21? There Yeshua said, "Not everyone who says to me, 'Lord, Lord,' will enter the kingdom of heaven, but only he who does the will of my Father who is in heaven," but he was certainly not teaching that salvation could be attained through our obedience to the Law. Rather, he was saying that the only proof of devotion to him was obedience to the Father and that calling him, "Lord, Lord," in and of itself, would do nothing. As others have put it, "The only proof of the new birth is the new life," something Paul preached clearly as well (cf. Acts 20:21; 26:20). It is also important to remember that he taught elsewhere that an essential part of doing the Father's will consisted in believing in him (John 6:29).

What about his interaction with the rich young ruler who asked him, "Teacher, what good thing must I do to get eternal life?" (Matt. 19:16).[316] Jesus replied to him, "If you want to enter life, obey the commandments," going on to clarify that he was referring to the Ten Commandments (specifically citing those dealing with interpersonal relationships) along with the commandment to love your neighbor as yourself (19:17–19). To this the man replied, "All these I have kept. What do I still lack?" Jesus answered him, "'If you want to be perfect, go, sell your possessions and give to the poor, and you will have treasure in heaven. Then come, follow me.' When the young man heard this, he went away sad, because he had great wealth" (19:20–22).

What was Jesus teaching here? He was hardly affirming that complete salvation could come through the Law, otherwise he would have said to the young man, "Good job! Keep it up! You can rest assured that you will enter life."[317] Instead, he pointed out that this young man, despite his alleged fidelity to the Law, was still not fulfilling God's requirements—in keeping with the teaching of the Sermon on the Mount, which calls Yeshua's disciples to a higher righteousness (see below, 5.28)—and that to really honor the Lord, he needed to sell his possessions and give to the poor. Where was this taught in the Torah? And wasn't Jesus clearly going beyond the letter of the law and calling this young man to truly love his neighbor as himself? Not only so, but Jesus also called on this rich young man to follow him, meaning, that even distributing all his goods to the poor was not enough. He had to follow Yeshua! I fail to see how anyone can possibly use this account to justify the claim that Jesus taught that salvation came through the Law. Even the disciples were staggered by the subsequent teaching Jesus gave in which he described how difficult it was for a rich man to be saved, and they asked, "Who then can be saved?" To this Jesus replied, "With man this is impossible, but with God all things are possible" (see 19:23–26). So much for teaching that salvation comes through obeying the Law!

What then should we make of the last passage raised, Matthew 25:31–36? There Jesus taught that, upon his glorious return, he would sit and judge the nations, dividing them like sheep and goats. The sheep represented those who cared for him (meaning his disciples) during times of great need, providing food, drink, clothing, and shelter, and visiting "him" when "he" was in prison; the goats represented those who failed to do this. The sheep entered into eternal life, the goats into eternal punishment.

Once again, however, it is difficult to see how this could be equated with teaching that salvation came through obedience to the Torah. First, where did the Torah explicitly require these acts? Second, where did the Torah state that one would be judged by these acts? Third, the central issue is honoring Jesus (through his disciples). Once more he is front and center! As D. A. Carson explains:

> The fate of the nations will be determined by how they respond to Jesus' followers, who, "missionaries" or not, are charged with spreading the gospel and do so in the face of hunger, thirst, illness, and imprisonment. Good deeds done to Jesus' followers, even the least of them, are not only works of compassion and morality but reflect where people stand in relation to the kingdom and to Jesus himself. Jesus identifies himself with the fate of his followers and makes compassion for them equivalent to compassion for himself.[318]

This is in keeping with his teaching to his disciples that, "He who listens to you listens to me; he who rejects you rejects me; but he who rejects me rejects him who sent me" (Luke 10:16).

In conclusion, there is no evidence whatsoever that Yeshua taught that salvation could be obtained through obedience to the Law, while the whole of the New Testament, including dozens of Yeshua's own sayings, makes plain that salvation is found in him, as the angel explained to Joseph, the husband of Miriam, "She will give birth to a son, and you are to give him the name Jesus, because he will save his people from their sins" (Matt. 1:21). That is why the angels announced at his birth, "Today in the town of David a Savior has been born to you; he is Messiah the

Lord" (Luke 2:11). That is why the Samaritans who encountered him said, "We have heard for ourselves, and we know that this man really is the Savior of the world" (John 4:42b). And that is why Peter could say of him, "God exalted him to his own right hand as Prince and Savior that he might give repentance and forgiveness of sins to Israel" (Acts 5:31; see also 2 Peter 1:1, 11; 2:20, 3:2, 18), and why Paul could call him, "the Savior Jesus" (Acts 13:23; see also Eph. 5:23; Phil. 3:20; 2 Tim. 1:10; Titus 1:4; 2:13; 3:4–6). And that's why John could write, "And we have seen and testify that the Father has sent his Son to be the Savior of the world. If anyone acknowledges that Jesus is the Son of God, God lives in him and he in God" (1 John 4:14–15). Amen!

5.25. The teachings of the New Testament may have started out Jewish, but before long, they became totally pagan. This was done intentionally, since the Jews rejected Jesus as Messiah and only the pagans would listen to the message.

> This objection is fatally flawed from beginning to end. First, modern scholars, both Jewish and Christian, are increasingly recognizing that the teachings of the New Testament can only be rightly understood when they are read against their Jewish background. Second, all the major themes of the New Testament can be traced back to Yeshua himself and, beyond that, to the Tanakh. Third, plenty of Jews did listen to the message. Fourth, by the time the message of Jesus the Messiah had fully made its way into the Gentile world, the New Testament writings were already completed.

Answers to this objection can be found throughout this section, as well as in our other volumes. See 5.26, immediately below, where we refute the idea that Jesus was a good Jew and a fine rabbi and it was Paul who messed everything up and founded Christianity; 5.28–5.29, where we counter the objections that Jesus or Paul abolished the Torah; 5.6, where we demonstrate the historical reliability of the New Testament writings, including their close proximity to the events described; 5.8, where we dismiss the notion that the Gospels portray a mythical Jesus; 5.9, where we refute the argument that the virgin birth is a pagan myth; and volume 2, 3.1–3.4, where we demonstrate that belief in God's complex unity, along with the preexistence and divine nature of the Son of God, is taught in the Tanakh.

As to Jews believing in Yeshua as Messiah after his resurrection, the New Testament records the following:

- On the first celebration of Shavuot (Weeks; Pentecost) just days after Messiah's ascension to heaven, Peter preached to the Jews assembled in Jerusalem, and "about *three thousand* were added to their number that day" after being immersed in water (Acts 2:41).
- Not many days later, as a result of a powerful demonstration of Messiah's healing power and a clear sermon from Peter, "many who heard the message believed, and the number of men grew to about *five thousand*" (Acts 4:4; the account begins in Acts 3).
- According to Acts 6:7, "So the word of God spread. The *number of disciples in Jerusalem increased rapidly*, and a *large number of priests* became obedient to the faith" (my emphasis added to Scriptures cited here and above).
- Roughly two decades later, the Jewish elders in the Jerusalem congregation could say to Paul: "You see, brother, how many thousands of Jews have believed, and all of them are zealous for the law" (Acts 21:20; note that the Greek here is literally "how many myriads" or "ten thousands" or "countless thousands").

Historian and sociologist Rodney Stark has recently argued that the number of Jews who believed in Jesus in the first centuries of this era was far higher than most have recognized—a thesis now supported in depth by an international team of scholars—while other scholars have argued that by the end of the first century, there were at least one hundred thousand Jewish believers in Yeshua.[319] Yet all the New Testament books were completed *before* the end of the first century, with many, if not most of them, completed before the destruction of the Temple in 70 c.e.[320] This fact alone undercuts the whole objection!

Note also that the same Book of Acts that records that there were countless thousands of Jewish believers in Yeshua also records the struggles that Paul often had with his own people, on several occasions telling them that he was through dealing with them and would henceforth go to the Gentiles. See, for example, Acts 13:46: "We had to speak the word of God to you first. Since you reject it and do not consider yourselves worthy of eternal life, we now turn to the Gentiles." But that had to do with the Jewish people in that particular city. Immediately thereafter, he went into the next city and began preaching in the synagogue there, with success at that! "Paul and Barnabas went as usual into the Jewish synagogue. There they spoke so effectively that a great number of Jews and Gentiles believed" (Acts 14:1; see 14:2–7 for the opposition that followed). So much for the notion that Paul forever abandoned the Jewish mission and that Jews did not come to faith in Messiah in considerable numbers.

As for the notion that the New Testament introduces a pagan "Christianity" that had already broken away from its Jewish roots, the fact is that the biblical calendar was still observed and biblical customs still followed. Just look at these casual references to the holy days on Israel's calendar:

- Speaking of Yom Kippur, Acts 27:9 records, "Much time had been lost, and sailing had already become dangerous because by now it was after the Fast." So, rather than state what month it was, Luke describes the time of the year by reference to this biblical holy day.
- Luke also describes events that took place during Passover, including the arrest of Peter, writing, "This happened during the Feast of Unleavened Bread. . . . Herod intended to bring him out for public trial after the Passover" (Acts 12:3b, 4b; the King James Version, unfortunately, translated this with "Easter," but this, of course, is without any support from the Greek, which simply reads *ta pascha*, the Passover).
- Speaking of the Feast of Weeks (Shavuot), Paul writes to the Gentiles in Corinth, "But I will stay on at Ephesus until Pentecost" (1 Cor. 16:8), meaning that not only did he make reference to the biblical calendar, but he also knew that these Gentile believers would understand his point.
- Even Hanukkah, which was instituted after the close of the Tanakh, is mentioned in the New Testament in John 10:22, although anti-missionaries frequently claim that John's Gospel is the most anti-Semitic of all! (For a refutation of this, see 5.20–5.21, and, more fully, vol. 1, 2.8.)

So, even the calendar of the New Testament authors was the biblical, Jewish calendar.

As for New Testament teaching on the ultimate fate of the nation of Israel, Paul's statement says it all as he writes to the Gentile believers in Rome:

I do not want you to be ignorant of this mystery, brothers, so that you may not be conceited: Israel has experienced a hardening in part until the full number of the Gentiles has come in. And so all Israel will be saved, as it is written:

> "The deliverer will come from Zion;
>   he will turn godlessness away from Jacob.
> And this is my covenant with them
>   when I take away their sins."

As far as the gospel is concerned, they are enemies on your account; but as far as election is concerned, they are loved on account of the patriarchs, for God's gifts and his call are irrevocable.

Romans 11:25–29

Far from writing Israel off, Paul was confident that in the end, there would be a wonderful, national turning among his people, who remained called and chosen, despite their current state of unbelief. He even told these Gentiles that one major reason for his preaching to them was to provoke his own people to envy (see Rom. 11:11–15). For him, the Jews were the "natural branches" that would be grafted back into their own olive tree (see 11:16–24) and it remained his lifelong, fervent hope that this would happen in the end.

Which New Testament writers, then, were responsible for changing the story? Certainly not Matthew, who recorded Yeshua's statement that he did not come to abolish the Law but to fulfill it (see below, 5.28), along with his statement that, at that time, the Pharisees and teachers of the Law sat in Moses' seat (see below, vol. 5, 6.15). Certainly not Mark, who scholars believe received his information mainly from Peter, whom the New Testament tells us continued to live as a Torah-observant Jew (see below, 5.33). Certainly not Luke, who, as we have just seen, used the biblical calendar to keep time and recorded how countless thousands of Jews followed Yeshua, also noting that they were also zealous for the Law. And certainly not John, who records Jesus as teaching that "salvation is of the Jews" (John 4:22). Yet these men wrote more than 95 percent of the New Testament!

There is no question that at some point during the second to fourth centuries, Jewish believers in the Messiah began to be marginalized while the number of Gentiles continued to increase. (The conventional understanding throughout most of the twentieth century was that this marginalizing happened earlier rather than later, but this view is now being challenged, as noted above.) And there is also no question that, as a result of the marginalizing of Jewish believers, the "church" began to sever itself from its Jewish, New Testament roots. But it was only at that time that some pagan traditions began to infiltrate the ranks of the believers, which is why it has been common for many years to encourage Christians to recover the Jewish roots of their faith and why, for many centuries, the cry of many Christian leaders has been *sola Scriptura*, meaning that the Scriptures alone are the ultimate authority and only sure guide for faith and practice. As for Jewish believers in Yeshua (often called Messianic Jews), recovering an authentic, New Covenant, Jewish expression of faith and practice has been of great importance to them, although they are often criticized for this very thing by the non-Messianic Jewish community (see vol. 1, 1.5).

In short, however, it can be categorically said that not an ounce of paganism made its way into the teaching of the New Testament, and it is that divinely inspired collection of books, along with the Tanakh, that is the foundation of our faith. As for later, pagan traditions, we categorically reject them as having any authority or influence in our lives in any way, shape, or form.

5.26. Jesus was really all right. He was a good Jew and a fine rabbi. It was Paul who messed everything up and founded Christianity.

> I'm glad you recognize that Jesus was a good Jew. But Paul (Saul) was a good Jew as well, faithful to Israel's Torah and faithful to Israel's Messiah. His teachings are in complete harmony with the teachings of Jesus, despite the assertions of some authors who claim that Paul deviated from the pattern established by Jesus and his disciples, founding an alien new religion called Christianity. The consistent testimony of the New Testament—which includes the things Paul said about himself as well as the things that others said about him—affirms this point. What was unique about Paul was his calling to spread the good news about Jesus to the Gentiles, but even in this, he passed on to them the truths he had received—as opposed to creating his own innovations—and always kept Israel's salvation foremost in his mind.

In the last few decades, there has been a "Jewish reclamation of Jesus," referring to an academic trend in which Jewish scholars have sought to recognize that, in short, "Jesus is one of us." Rather than viewing him in hostile, alien terms, more and more Jewish leaders have sought to reclaim him as a brother.[321] To be sure, this reclamation has fallen short of recognizing him as Messiah, let alone as the divine Son of God, but it has been positive in many ways. Evaluating this issue in 2000,[322] I wrote:

> One of the first obstacles faced by Messianic Jews is the battle to convince fellow Jews that "Jesus is one of us." He is not, Jewish believers in Jesus argue, the founder of an alien new religion called "Christianity" as much as he is the promised Jewish Messiah—and hence, the Savior of the world. Properly conveying this truth has been an ongoing struggle for more than 1,500 years, and every act of "Christian" anti-Semitism has only heightened the tension and deepened the misunderstanding. Further exacerbating the problem has been the fact that to the extent Jesus—or, Yeshu as he is commonly referred to in traditional Jewish circles—*was* known as a Jew among our people, he was primarily known as an apostate, a deceiver, a false prophet, a misguided idolater, a bastard now burning in hell.[323] So, in Jewish eyes, Jesus was either a Christian (probably of European extract, based on the prevailing religious iconography) or an apostate Jew (based on the rabbinic traditions). There was not much room for the *appreciation* of Jesus the Jew among our people, let alone his reclamation.
>
>   In light of this, it must be said unequivocally that the Jewish reclamation of Jesus is an extremely positive development. The very fact that collaborative Jewish-Christian volumes such as *Hillel and Jesus* can be written is a huge step forward, especially since such scholarship is not just the occasional research of a Jewish professor (like Joseph Klausner's work of a previous generation) but rather is reflective of mainstream trends.[324] How can it be negative when Lawrence H. Schiffman, a traditional Jew and a leading authority on the Dead Sea Scrolls, writes on "The Jewishness of Jesus: Commandments Concerning Interpersonal Relations";[325] when Professor Irving Zeitlin authors a volume entitled *Jesus and the Judaism of His Time*;[326] when Rabbi Philip Sigal discusses the halakhah of Jesus according to Matthew's Gospel;[327] when Israeli scholars such as David Flusser and Shmuel Safrai lead the Jerusalem School for the Study of the Synoptic Gospels in its efforts to recover (and thereby rediscover) the Jewish background to the Gospels?[328] All this presupposes the Jewishness of Jesus and the fact that he can only be rightly understood as a Jew among Jews—in terms of his message, his mission, and his mindset.

I listed the following positive developments[329] in this relatively recent trend:

> First, Jewish scholars, both conservative and liberal, tend to be somewhat less skeptical of the veracity of the New Testament witness of Jesus than do non-Jewish, liberal New Testament scholars.[330] Thus, the picture of Jesus

that emerges from a straightforward reading of the Gospels is generally assumed to bear some resemblance to the historical Jesus, a view that stands in stark contrast with, e.g., the nihilistic and widely-publicized views of the Jesus Seminar.[331]

Second, the *Jewishness* of Jesus is assumed, along with the necessity of reading the New Testament through Jewish eyes. Since, on *a priori* grounds, they recognize Yeshua as a kinsman after the flesh, it is only natural that they relate to him in the milieu of first-century Judaism(s). Out of the various leadership models that have been proposed for Jesus—from charismatic holy man (e.g., Geza Vermes) to innovative Pharisee (e.g., Harvey Falk)—most all of them are Jewish. . . . [332]

Third, it is commonly recognized by Jewish scholars—sometimes in contrast with Christian scholars[333]—that the New Testament sources are often more reliable than the (later) rabbinic sources. . . .

Fourth, there is a recognition of the diversity of "Judaisms" in the first century, and Jesus and his followers are placed squarely in that life context and religious milieu. Thus, the relevant texts are not read simply as "Christian" vs. "Jewish" as much as they are read as expressions of varied Jewish beliefs and systems of practice (Pharisaic, Sadduceean, Essene, Zealot, Messianic, Apocalyptic; etc.). . . .[334]

Fifth, the self-awareness of Jesus, along with his ministry, are often analyzed in the context of first-century Messianic expectations, frequently with respect to the Scriptures. While this by no means reflects a universal trend among Jewish scholars, I believe we can recognize a general movement in this direction, in contrast with the views of some liberal Christian scholars who do not believe that even a passage such as Isaiah 52:13–53:12 factored into the self-consciousness of Jesus.[335]

So, despite some of the objections that are countered in this volume that view Yeshua in very negative terms (see, e.g., 5.13; 5.23), and despite the hostility that is often directed towards him in anti-missionary and/or ultra-religious circles, other trends within Jewish scholarship reflect a much more positive assessment of the one we hail as Messiah.[336] The downside, of course, is that for some, Paul becomes the culprit, the one who turned a valid Jewish movement into a pagan religion, the one who turned a good, Jewish rabbi into the god of the Gentiles.

Typical, albeit somewhat extreme, is the rhetoric of anti-missionary Beth Moshe. Under the heading, "TAUGHT HATRED OF JEWS," she wrote that Paul "shaped the Church in a manner which stripped away all links to Judaism and cursed it at the same time."[337] She also speaks of the need to

demonstrate the unreliability of the man [i.e., Paul] who actually formulated the break away from Judaism by the early Church. We have shown that Paul contradicted Jesus in important religious matters and made himself greater than his master. Now see who he is, by his own words [referring to 1 Cor. 9:20]. He admitted using trickery and deception to gain his ends. We can wonder whether his missionary effort was flawed with fiction throughout as well.[338]

Charges such as these will cause the vast majority of students of the New Testament to shake their heads in incredulity, yet allegations of this kind are being made nonetheless.

Most recently, David Klinghoffer, in his popular, nonacademic volume, *Why the Jews Rejected Jesus*,[339] followed Hyam Maccobby's *The Mythmaker: Paul and the Invention of Christianity*, one of the more marginal works in Pauline scholarship in the last twenty years,[340] and argued that Paul: (1) was not born Jewish; (2) could not read Hebrew; and (3) turned the Jewish Jesus movement into a Gentile religion.[341] These assertions will come as quite a surprise to careful students of the life and writings of Paul, whom many Messianic Jews prefer to call Rav Shaul, and the fact that Klinghoffer's argument is marred by some serious factual gaffes does not help his cause. For example, on page 94, Klinghoffer claims, quite remarkably, that during Paul's final visit to Jerusalem (see Acts 21) he was seized and almost murdered by "Certain Jewish believers in Jesus [*sic*], apparently taking a different view of Judaism from Paul's," whereas even the most cursory reading of the text makes plain that he was mobbed by the hostile, non-Jesus-believing Jewish crowd. Then, on page 97, Klinghoffer claims that Acts admits that "the Jews regarded Paul as 'uneducated'," citing Acts 4:13. But Acts 4:13 is the charge leveled against Peter and John, long before Paul was on the scene (for a statement in Acts regarding Paul's learning, see Acts 26:24b).

Interestingly, Klinghoffer *is* fully aware that his negative assessment of Paul flies in the face of most contemporary scholarship that *sees Paul as thoroughly Jewish in thought*.[342] That is to say, it is not just the Jewishness of Jesus that has been increasingly recognized in recent decades—which, as a corollary has included the recovery of Jesus the Jew by Jewish scholars—there has been an increasing recognition of the Jewishness of Paul by Jewish scholars as well!

You might ask, "Well, then who turned this thing into a Gentile religion?"

The answer is, *It is not a Gentile religion* (although in the course of its postbiblical development, when it lost touch with its Jewish roots, it acquired many Gentile traditions and beliefs). Rather, it is the Messianic faith, the faith of Israel now expanded to accommodate the Gentiles who become fellow-heirs with those Jews who also embrace the Messiah. But it remains a faith for the Jew first, and then for the Gentile (Rom. 1:16).

What then do some *Jewish* scholars say about Paul? Here are some statements from past generations. First, we cite Joseph Klausner (1874–1958), who taught at the Hebrew University in Jerusalem. This was his verdict on Paul's Jewishness:

> It would be difficult to find more typically Talmudic expositions of Scripture than those in the Epistles of Paul. . . .[343]
>
> Even at the end of his life, after he had had many sharp conflicts with the Jews . . . after all this, he called to his place of confinement *first of all* the Jews of Rome, and assured them that he had nothing 'whereof to accuse' his people ('my nation'). . . .[344]
>
> Truly, Paul was a Jew not only in his physical appearance, but he was also a typical Jew in his thinking and in his entire inner-life. For Saul-Paul was not only 'a Pharisee, a son of Pharisees,' but also one of those disciples of the Tannaim who were brought up on the exegesis of the Torah, and did not cease to cherish it to the end of their days. It would be difficult to find more typically Talmudic expositions of Scripture than those in the Epistles of Paul. . . .[345]
>
> Paul lived by Jewish law like a proper Jew; also, he knew the Old Testament in its Hebrew original and meditated much upon it. . . . Hence there are Semitisms and Hebraisms in the language of the Epistles, in spite of the richness of their Greek. If Paul was a 'Hebrew of the Hebrews' and 'a Pharisee,' a son of Pharisees, educated in Jerusalem and able to make speeches in Hebrew (or Aramaic), obviously he was not a 'Septuagint Jew' (*Septuaginta-Jude*) only, as various Christian scholars have been accustomed to picture him.[346]

Regarding Paul's allegedly deceptive missionary practices (referring to 1 Cor. 9:20ff.; see vol. 1, 1.5), professor David Daube, the respected author of *The New Testament and Rabbinic Judaism*, argues that Paul took over his missionary methods "from Jewish teaching on the subject: the idea that you must adopt the customs and mood of the person you wish to win over, and the idea that, to be a successful maker of proselytes, you must become a servant of men and humble yourself."[347] Even here, Paul operated within a Jewish framework.

More recently, professor Alan Segal wrote:

> Without knowing about first-century Judaism, modern readers—even those committed by faith to reading him—are bound to misconstrue Paul's writing. . . . Paul is a trained Pharisee who became the apostle to the Gentiles.[348]

According to Talmudic and Aramaic scholar Daniel Boyarin:

> Paul has left us an extremely precious document for Jewish studies, the spiritual autobiography of a first-century Jew. . . . Moreover, if we take Paul at his word—and I see no a priori reason not to—he was a member of the Pharisaic wing of first-century Judaism."[349]

Rabbi Dr. Burton Visotzky, Appleman Chair of Midrash and Interreligious Studies, Jewish Theological Seminary, New York, wrote this in his endorsement of professor Brad Young's *Paul the Jewish Theologian*: "The Pharisee Saul of Tarsus is arguably one of the most influential religious figures in the history of Western culture." Yes, the Pharisee Saul of Tarsus, not the deceiver Saul of Tarsus. Even the illustrious Rabbi Jacob Emden (1679–1776), a champion of Orthodox Judaism, said that "Paul was a scholar, an attendant of Rabban Gamaliel the Elder, well-versed in the laws of the Torah"![350]

Consider also the testimony of some of the world's leading New Testament scholars, a number of whom are thoroughly conversant with the best of early Jewish scholarship:

According to Dr. Peter J. Tomson:

> As distinct from Philo, Paul had an openly avowed knowledge of Hebrew and of Pharisaic tradition. . . . Again, as opposed to Philo, Paul does not just draw on the Hebraist Jewish tradition of Midrash but proves an independent and creative master of the genre. . . . Although apparently descending from a prominent diaspora family who had acquired Roman citizenship, his mother tongue, quite probably, was not Tarsean Greek but the Hebrew and Aramaic of Jerusalem.[351]

According to critical New Testament scholar John Dominic Crossan and archeologist Jonathan L. Reed, "Paul was Jewish born and bred, understood Hebrew, was a Pharisee, and was proud of all that lineage. He identified himself as a Jew within Judaism."[352] (This assessment is all the more noteworthy given the skeptical presuppositions of the authors.)

The highly respected *Dictionary of Paul and His Letters* states:

> Paul's use of Scripture, of midrashic techniques and of contemporary exegetical traditions in Romans 9:6–29 yielded a highly sophisticated composition. It cannot have been the product of an uneducated mind. If he was not trained by Gamaliel, then he was taught by some other Jewish master. In any case, it seems clear that Paul received a formal education in the Judaism of the time.

. . . Today . . . NT scholarship finds more and more evidence for the Jewishness of Paul's life and thought. Indeed, this change is part of a general movement in Christian scholarship to rediscover the Jewish roots of Christianity. Concurrently, Jewish scholarship shows a growing interest in reclaiming the Jewishness of Jesus and Paul.[353]

Finally, I cite professor Jaroslav Pelikan, perhaps the world's foremost authority on church history. He writes that, in contrast with past scholarly views that often saw Paul as "the one chiefly responsible for the de-Judaization of the gospel and even for the transmutation of the person of Jesus from a rabbi in the Jewish sense to a divine being in the Greek sense," studies in the last few decades are seeing things much differently. Thus, "scholars have not only put the picture of Jesus back into the setting of first-century Judaism; they have also rediscovered the Jewishness of the New Testament, *and particularly of the apostle Paul*, and specifically of his Epistle to the Romans."[354] Yes, scholars are rediscovering the Jewishness of Paul![355]

Interestingly, for Dr. Julie Galambush, a former Baptist minister who converted to Judaism, the recovery of Paul's Jewishness is somewhat paradoxical, since she believes that, by the time the New Testament books were accepted as Scripture, Jews and Christians had long since parted ways. While that view can certainly be challenged as overly simplistic, her statement about Paul points to the fact that there is no denying his Jewishness:

> For much of the twentieth century, Paul of Tarsus was considered the founder of a new religion, Christianity. Jesus had been a Galilean teacher, but Paul, a hellenized Jew of Asia Minor, brought Jesus' message, both physically and philosophically, to the Gentiles. In recent years the image of the "Christian Paul" has fallen out of favor. Just as in the nineteenth and twentieth centuries scholars rediscovered the Jewishness of Jesus, so now they have begun to reclaim the Jewishness of Paul. The reality of a Jewish Paul—a Paul who never dreamed that his missionary endeavors would spread anything but a new stage in Jewish belief—carries a particular poignancy in light of later Christian history. Whatever his intentions, Paul remains the founder of Christianity as a thought system that could continue to grow with the participation of Jews; this is the use to which Paul's writings have been put. If Paul can still be said to have founded Christianity, however, it is now clear that he did so unintentionally.[356]

As for Maccobby's thesis, which, I remind you, is rarely discussed by scholars since it is not taken seriously despite Maccobby's fine scholarship in other areas, professor James D. G. Dunn writes:

Paul shows that he is as firmly located within Judaism as anyone can be; he is no first- or even tenth-generation proselyte. Maccoby's counter-suggestion (*Mythmaker*, 95–96), that Paul was a Gentile whose claim here was totally invented and fictitious, is wildly fanciful and shows no sensitivity to Paul's whole argument in Romans. . . .[357]

Note carefully that Dunn, one of the world's top scholars in his field, can only describe Maccoby's argument (which Klinghoffer followed) as "wildly fanciful and show[ing] no sensitivity to Paul's whole argument in Romans." That is saying a lot!

What about the charge that Paul didn't know Hebrew and, therefore, always cited the Septuagint (LXX)? This would certainly be quite a surprise to the Jewish scholars—cited above—most, if not all, of whom are fluent in Hebrew, Aramaic, and Greek and can recognize the Hebraic fluency of Paul. Unfortunately, Klinghoffer, through a poorly worded endnote, gave the false impression that professor E. P. Sanders, a top Pauline and early Judaica scholar, actually endorsed the view that Paul did not know Hebrew, citing Sanders for what he calls "a telling example of how Paul's Hebrew illiteracy [*sic*] shaped his understanding of the Bible," whereas in reality Sanders was simply treating Paul's use of the LXX in Galatians 3:10 without a hint that Paul did not know Hebrew.[358]

What indications, then, do we have that Paul in fact did know Hebrew and was trained as a Pharisee, as he claimed? First, there is the testimony of Jewish scholars like Klausner and Boyarin and Segal and Daube, cited above, who recognized Paul as one of their own. Second, he did not always follow the LXX, despite the fact that he was writing to Gentiles who used the LXX exclusively and who did not have access to any other translation (see above, 5.1). The most prominent example is found in his quotation of Habakkuk 2:4 (see Rom. 1:17; Gal. 3:11), a foundational text for Paul, but one where he does not follow the LXX.[359] Third, some LXX scholars have observed that, upon careful examination, in roughly half of the cases involved (approximately fifty out of a hundred) Paul does not follow the LXX exactly when he cites it, suggesting that he was involved in a revision of the text based on the Hebrew![360] So much for his alleged ignorance. Fourth, passages such as Romans 11:26–27, discussed above (5.1), which some have cited as misquotations, actually point to a careful knowledge of the biblical text.

Putting the question aside of Paul's alleged ignorance of Hebrew—and it really is a fringe question not representing top scholarship—what of the accusation that Paul started a new religion called Christianity, one that bore no resemblance to the very Jewish movement started by Rabbi Yeshua (or, by his other followers)? This too can be refuted fairly easily; since much solid work has been done on this already, I will summarize the findings of some important, recent studies.

Professor David Wenham wrote,

> Many people today have a negative view of Paul: he is often accused of not being a faithful follower of Jesus, but a freelancer who did his own thing with the Christian religion. He is accused of changing Jesus' good ideas, and of introducing all sorts of bad ideas. . . . His failure to refer to much of Jesus' earthly life and teaching in his letters has been thought to confirm that he was not really interested in the real Jesus, only in the quite different Jesus of his own theological imagination.[361]

Wenham devotes the rest of his book, which supplements an earlier, more exhaustive study, to refuting these erroneous views, pointing to the consistent testimony of Scripture that makes clear the fact that Paul was a devoted and loyal follower of Yeshua rather than the creator of a new set of religious beliefs.[362] Based on his analysis of Paul's earliest letters—Galatians, 1 and 2 Thessalonians, and 1 Corinthians—Wenham concludes:

> In [these letters] we have found evidence that Paul taught people about the death and resurrection of Jesus; he told them the story of the Last Supper, of the arrest of Jesus, of his crucifixion, his burial, and his resurrection, including the appearances of the risen Lord. We have found unmistakable evidence of Paul's familiarity with Jesus' teaching on the Second Coming, on ethical issues, such as divorce, and on ministry issues, such as apostleship. We have found unmistakable evidence that he and his churches knew about Jesus addressing God as Abba, and saw this word of Jesus as something important.[363]

In his earlier study, *Paul, Follower of Jesus or Founder of Christianity?*, which I would recommend to anyone wanting to make a thorough study of the question, Wenham divided the teachings of Jesus and Paul into key subjects, setting those teachings out clearly, one after the other. His conclusions are as follows. Concerning their teaching on the kingdom of God he wrote,

> . . . the overall similarity of Jesus' kingdom preaching to Paul's gospel is clear. Both men proclaimed the dawn of God's promised day of salvation. Both believed that God was intervening to bring righteousness, healing and reconciliation to the world. Both called on people to respond to the good news in faith. Much of what they have in common has Jewish precedent,

but the level of agreement in the broad pattern of their respective gospels is striking. . . .[364]

There is significant evidence that Paul was influenced by the Jesus-tradition, some of that being relatively strong, some much weaker.[365]

Regarding the person and nature of Jesus (called Christology), Wenham had this to say, after making room for some differences in perspective and terminology:

> That Paul was not a radical innovator in the matter of Christology may be confirmed by the evidence of Paul's letters dealing with the controversies in which he was involved. His gospel was highly controversial in some circles, but the controversy seems to have focused on his attitudes toward the Gentiles and the Jewish law, and there is no hint that his view of Jesus as Messiah, Lord, and Son of God was seen as inadequate or unorthodox. On this he was in agreement with others. . . .[366]
>
> Paul's use of *Abba* is the one unambiguous piece of evidence linking Pauline Christology and the teaching of Jesus. [See Mark 14:36; Rom 8:15; Gal 4:6.] The use of the term was derived from Jesus, and there is evidence that Paul knew that it was.[367]

As a supplement to these comments, attention should be drawn to the work of New Testament scholar Larry Hurtado in his comprehensive monograph on devotion to Jesus among the first generations of believers. He wrote that

> a veritable explosion of devotion to Jesus took place so early [among the first Jewish disciples], and was so widespread by the time of [Paul's] Gentile mission, that in the main Christological beliefs and devotional practices he advocated, Paul was not an innovator but a transmitter of tradition.[368]

Since critics have claimed that Paul was the one guilty of turning a nice Jewish rabbi named Yeshua into a pagan god come to earth, Hurtado's conclusion, the fruit of massive scholarship, must be taken seriously. Paul did not introduce new concepts when speaking of exactly who Yeshua was. Rather, he was "not an innovator but a transmitter of tradition."

As for the reason for Jesus' crucifixion, another topic of great import, Wenham, a scholar of clear intellectual integrity, concluded:

> Some particularly difficult questions are raised by the comparison of Jesus' and Paul's teachings on the cross. But if the sketches that we have offered are anywhere near correct, then they show on the one hand a

substantial gap between Jesus and Paul, with Jesus saying rather little about the cross and Paul having a much fuller and more explicit theology of the Lord's death. On the other hand, the main lines of the Pauline doctrine are in almost all cases hinted at in the Jesus-tradition. In some cases there is more than a hint: The idea of Jesus' death as a redemptive sacrifice bringing in God's salvation is quite explicit in the last supper traditions. But in other cases, notably when it comes to the idea of participation in the death of Jesus, Paul does go well beyond the hints in the Jesus-tradition, though those hints are there (e.g., the "take up your cross" saying).[369]

It is not difficult, however, to explain the differences in perspective:

> For Jesus the cross lies ahead, and is in a real sense an unknown and, as the Gospels suggest, almost impossible to explain to his followers in advance. For Paul the cross has happened and is now a massively important datum to be explained; the prominence of it in his thinking is not at all surprising.[370]

All this makes perfect sense, and it cannot be denied that: (1) Yeshua made it clear on numerous occasions that he had to go to the cross and die. This was why he came! (See, e.g., Matt. 16:21.) (2) The fact of his death and resurrection was absolutely central in all the preaching in Acts, whether it was Peter, Stephen, or Paul who was preaching (see, e.g., Acts 2:22–24; 3:13–15; 5:30–31; 7:52; 13:26–31). (3) Yeshua himself pointed to Isaiah 53 when teaching his disciples (see Luke 22:37, which helps to explain why his disciples frequently pointed back to that portion of Scripture; see Matt. 8:17; John 12:38; 1 Peter 2:22–25). (4) Paul, with full knowledge of Messiah's death and resurrection, and reflecting on the Hebrew Scriptures, gave further insight into the meaning and function and power of that act of redemption, but in doing so, he only built on the words and traditions he had already received. As he wrote to the Corinthians in a well-known passage:

> For I received from the Lord what I also passed on to you: The Lord Jesus, on the night he was betrayed, took bread, and when he had given thanks, he broke it and said, "This is my body, which is for you; do this in remembrance of me." In the same way, after supper he took the cup, saying, "This cup is the new covenant in my blood; do this, whenever you drink it, in remembrance of me." For whenever you eat this bread and drink this cup, you proclaim the Lord's death until he comes.
>
> 1 Corinthians 11:23–26

Once again, we see clearly that Paul was a transmitter of tradition rather than the creator of a new religion.

Concerning the teachings of Jesus and Paul on the important issue of community, Wenham notes some differences in thrust, such as, "for Jesus the focus of mission is on the Jews, with the Gentiles only on the horizon, for Paul the Gentiles are in the foreground and the Jews are rather problematic."[371] Yet, he explains:

> The difference is a reflection of different missionary contexts, and yet there is considerable theological continuity, with Jesus looking for a universal kingdom and Paul recognizing the priority of the Jews. Rather similarly with the temple: Jesus in his Palestinian context pays considerable attention to the Jerusalem temple (albeit largely negative attention), whereas for Paul working among Gentiles the Jerusalem temple has effectively been superseded by the church as God's spiritual house. And there is continuity with Jesus' anticipation of a new spiritual temple. . . .[372]
>
> There is very good evidence that Paul was familiar with the mission discourse traditions. . . . It is also highly probable that Paul knew Jesus' saying about the destruction and rebuilding of the temple. He uses it in a variety of ways to address a range of questions from the question of church leadership, to the Judaizing issue [i.e., the teaching that Gentile followers of Jesus had to become Jewish], to questions of sexuality and resurrection.[373]

As far as Jesus' and Paul's teaching on "living in love," Wenham concludes,

> There is much in common between Jesus' ethical teaching and Paul's. Both were critical of "Jewish" righteousness; both spoke of the fulfillment of the law and a superior righteousness; both emphasized love and had a radical social outlook. . . . Paul's and Jesus' ethics have much in common. . . .[374]

Regarding their teaching on the "future coming of the Lord," Wenham states:

> . . . We conclude that [Paul and Jesus] have a great deal in common.

- Both have a very strong sense that the last days have come. The eschatological countdown has begun, and the longed-for kingdom of God is excitingly and urgently near.
- Both see Jesus' death and resurrection as key events in the coming of the future kingdom. . . .
- Both associate the coming kingdom with the future heavenly coming of Jesus.

- Both decline to specify when the future kingdom will actually arrive, but suggest that its coming will be preceded by a period of witness, suffering, and judgment on the Jewish nation. [To this it could be added that both look forward to Israel's final salvation!][375]

Finally, regarding Paul's actual knowledge of Yeshua's life and ministry, Wenham concluded that,

> . . . Paul may well have been familiar with much of the gospel "story" as we know it. He certainly knew resurrection traditions, very probably a form of the passion narrative, and also traditions of Jesus as a miracle worker. He probably knew about Jesus' baptism, about his style of ministry and life, and (a little less certainly) about the transfiguration. He may have known the stories of Jesus' infancy similar to those found in Matthew and Luke, the story of Jesus' temptation, and possibly an ascension story.[376]

Again, those wishing to study this topic further are referred to Wenham's very useful study, one in which he simply *analyzes the evidence* rather than seeks to prove a preconceived point. Even critical scholars like Crossan and Reed, after asking, "But how could Paul, even in vision, recognize a Jesus he had never met?", could only respond in one way: "We can only imagine one answer, and it emphasizes that Paul already knew enough about the life, death, and resurrection of Jesus to persecute his followers for proclaiming its implications to their fellow Jews in Damascus."[377] There is no concrete evidence that contradicts this statement, nor is there concrete evidence that indicates that Paul broke away from the original teaching and "invented" Christianity, to use Maccobby's phrase. Indeed, the only way that Maccobby can argue his thesis is to redate—in radical fashion—when most of the foundational books of the New Testament were written, and even then, his arguments are specious.[378]

It should also be noted that for Paul to be the "inventor" of Christianity, he would have had to pull a major coup, since it was Luke who not only wrote the Book of Acts, speaking favorably of Paul there and presenting his story as part and parcel of the development of the Messianic movement, but he was also the author of the Gospel that bore his name, and no one has claimed that *Luke* was the "inventor of Christianity"!

Based on a straightforward, unbiased reading of the New Testament, we can state the following, with some reference to the previous discussion:

1. Saul of Tarsus certainly heard about Jesus and passionately persecuted his followers.

2. After his life-changing encounter on the road to Damascus, he was embraced by Yeshua's disciples.

3. He was recognized as a key player by the other key leaders in Acts 15.

4. He dispelled any doubts about his teaching and personal practices in Acts 21.

5. He consciously distinguished between his own opinions and the commands of the Lord (see, e.g., 1 Cor. 7:10; cf. also Acts 20:35).

6. He passed on what he received (1 Cor. 11:23; 15:3).

7. Other New Testament writings refer to his letters, even calling them "Scripture" (2 Peter 3:16).

8. With the exception of some heretical groups (like the Ebionites), Paul's teachings were received by the second generation of believers, including men who were disciples of the original apostles (such as Polycarp).

9. Wenham has demonstrated that the emphases of Paul agree with the emphases of Jesus, and so, rather than seeing Paul as *ignoring* the life of Jesus before his death, it is more accurate to see him *emphasizing* the Messiah's death and resurrection which formed the central core of Paul's preaching. But key passages such as Philippians 2:5–11 indicate clearly that Paul recognized the importance of Jesus' earthly life, speaking of how the Son of God took on human flesh and lived as a servant among us before suffering a criminal's death on the cross.

I leave you with Paul's words:

Now, brothers, I want to remind you of the gospel I preached to you, which you received and on which you have taken your stand. By this gospel you are saved, if you hold firmly to the word I preached to you. Otherwise, you have believed in vain.

For what I received I passed on to you as of first importance: that [Messiah] died for our sins according to the Scriptures, that he was buried, that he was raised on the third day according to the Scriptures, and that he appeared to Peter, and then to the Twelve. After that, he appeared to more than five hundred of the brothers at the same time, most of whom are still living, though some have fallen asleep. Then he appeared to James [Jacob], then to all the apostles, and last of all he appeared to me also, as to one abnormally born [meaning, born out of due time].

. . . this is what we preach, and this is what you believed.

1 Corinthians 15:1–8, 11

Yes, what he received he passed on to us as of first importance, and we are eternally indebted to him for being such a faithful witness of the Lord.[379]

5.27. If you study world religions, you will see that the teachings of Jesus borrow extensively from Hinduism and Buddhism.

> There is absolutely no substance to this argument, and it can easily be refuted. First, there are parallels that exist in all world religions, and you could just as well argue that the traditional rabbis borrowed extensively from Hinduism and Buddhism as you could argue that Jesus did. Second, there is a not a stitch of scholarly evidence that Jesus had any connection or contact with these religions. Third and most importantly, his teachings clearly contradict these religions in many foundational, irreconcilable ways.

This objection need not detain us, nor is it a specifically Jewish objection. In reality, it is so bizarre as to hardly be an objection at all, but since it has come up in anti-missionary polemics, we will address it briefly using three lines of argument.

There is some common ground that can be found in all world religions. This fact is known to any student of world religions, and it should be expected, since: (1) God has revealed truths about himself through nature (see Ps. 19:1–6; Rom. 1:19–20). (2) We are created in the image of God, and although we have fallen from that image, there remain vestiges of that nature—such as a moral conscience—within every human being (Gen. 1:26–27; 5:1–3; John 1:9). (3) There are certain traditions, like the flood or Tower of Babel, that go back to some of the earliest stages of the human race and have been passed on in varied forms around the world.[380] (4) Certain religions, like Islam, utilized portions of the Bible as well as Jewish and Christian traditions. (5) As human beings seek after God and learn to distinguish right from wrong, they will develop moral codes and wise sayings that, in many cases, will be similar in various cultures. (6) It is only natural that certain elements, such as water, would be used in similar rites (in the case of water, rites of purification, cleansing, initiation, etc.) even across different cultures and in different religions.

This list could easily be multiplied, but one simple example will suffice. New Testament scholar John Nolland notes that:

The Golden Rule has a very ancient and diverse pedigree. Though the wording is not at all fixed, versions of the rule have been found in Zoroastrianism, Confucianism, Buddhist literature, ancient Indian literature, Greek literature from the time of Herodotus, and Jewish sources at least from the time of the *Letter of Aristeas* and of the Greek versions of Sirach [meaning, from the second century B.C.E.].[381]

Does this "prove" that all these different religions borrowed the concept from each other and that, wherever such a teaching might be found in some other ancient or hitherto unknown text, it must have been borrowed? Hardly. Does it rather suggest that religious people around the world, either through practical experience or some level of spiritual insight, came to the same conclusion? Certainly. We can safely say, then, that when Yeshua taught the Golden Rule—or when Hillel taught it, for that matter—he was not quoting Confucius.

There is not one stitch of evidence that would support the notion that Jesus borrowed from Hinduism and Buddhism. First, there is no archaeological or literary evidence of any kind indicating that first-century Jews living in Judea had any ongoing, substantive contact with either of these religions—not an inscription, not a literary account, not an archaeological relic. Second, there is not a single line of a single, reliable historical document that states that Jesus visited India or any other country where he would have been able to study Hinduism or Buddhism. Therefore, since these religions did not come to him and he did not go them, there was no way that he could have borrowed from them.

What Jesus did teach completely undermines the foundations of both Hinduism and Buddhism. Here are just a few examples: (1) Whereas Hinduism believes in many gods and Buddhism does not believe in a personal god, Jesus emphatically taught that there is only one true God, and that loving him with heart, soul, mind, and strength was the first and greatest commandment. (Bear in mind that he came in fulfillment of the Tanakh, which emphasized the uniqueness of the God of Israel from cover to cover.) (2) Whereas Hinduism believes in reincarnation and Buddhism believes that the ultimate goal is the cessation of existence, Jesus made it clear that when this one life is over, each of us will enter into our eternal reward or punishment.[382] (3) Whereas Hinduism and Buddhism have a certain level of acceptance of other religious faiths, as long as they are not exclusivist, with both having respect for Jesus (indeed, Hindus would gladly say that they believe in Jesus, even as one of many divine incarnations), the teachings of Jesus were totally exclusivist, emphasizing that he alone was the way to God (John 14:6 is always quoted in this context) and that his blood was *the* payment for the sins of the world. (4) Neither Hinduism nor Buddhism have a concept of redemption from sin and transformation of life by faith in this life. Jesus taught that, through faith in him, we could be born anew and receive complete cleansing and deliverance. (Note that Buddhism does not really have a doctrine of sin.)

This list, too, could easily be multiplied, but there really is no need to do so. Those interested in further studies will benefit from the sources cited in the notes. On a more personal level, it is quite enlightening to read or hear the testimonies of former Hindus and Buddhists who have come to saving faith in Jesus. They can underscore the differences more clearly than any academic manual—and the differences are as distinct as darkness and light.[383]

5.28. Jesus abolished the Law.

> As Messiah, Yeshua was the ultimate Torah teacher, showing us how the entire Hebrew Bible reached fulfillment in him and also giving us deep spiritual insights into how the Torah could remain relevant for the Jewish people in generations to come, even when we would be scattered throughout the world, without a Temple, a sacrificial system, or a functioning (earthly) priesthood—and he did all this without the need for an endlessly growing corpus of laws and traditions. Once the Temple was destroyed in 70 c.e. only two major systems of faith remained for the Jewish people, that of the Pharisees, developing into Talmudic Judaism, and that of the Messiah, developing into the Messianic Jewish/Christian faith. Although there is much beauty and wisdom in Talmudic Judaism, Messiah has given us a better way.

In answer to the question, "Why don't Jews believe that Jesus was the messiah?", Rabbi Naftali Silberberg, writing for AskMoses.com, responds:

> In Jewish belief the messiah is one who strengthens the ways of the Torah, redeems the Jewish people from their oppression and brings peace to the world. Since Jesus did none of these things—and on the contrary, exacerbated all these problems further—there is no reason we should believe he was the messiah.[384]

As expressed by Maimonides (*Hilchot Melachim* 11:4):

Can there be a greater stumblingblock than [Christianity]? All the prophets spoke of the Messiah as the redeemer of Israel and its savior, who would gather their dispersed and strengthen their [observance] of the Mitzvot. [By contrast, Christianity] caused the Jews to be slain by the sword, their remnants to be scattered and humbled, the Torah to be altered, and the majority of the world to err and serve a god other than the Lord.[385]

Are these claims true? Certainly, there is some confusion over this issue because the great majority of Jesus' followers have been Gentiles, for whom the Torah was not originally given, and with a largely Gentile following, it could easily—but wrongly—be surmised that Jesus did away with the Law. Also, in comparison with Talmudic Judaism, which has added an almost infinite number of details to the commands of the written Torah, not to mention new laws, customs, and traditions, it could be wrongly surmised that Jesus did away with the Law. In reality, he is the fulfillment of the Law, and through his teaching and example, as well as through the help of the Spirit of God, he has made the Torah forever relevant. Let's explore this concept more fully, looking at some of the key teachings of the Messiah. And, rather than seeking to interact with all the varied approaches to this topic, we will do our best to let Yeshua speak for himself.

We begin with the Sermon on the Mount (Matthew 5–7), the first major body of Messianic teaching in the New Testament.[386] In keeping with a sermonic style attested in later Jewish literature, Yeshua begins with a prologue consisting of 5:3–16—the Beatitudes and then his teaching on his disciples being the salt of the earth and the light of the world—followed by the main subject matter, found in 5:17–7:12, before closing with his final words of exhortation and warning in 7:13–27. (In contrast with some later Rabbinic homilies, it should be noted that the prologue to Yeshua's sermon was more foundational than ornamental.)

How do we know that 5:17–7:12 represents the core of the sermon? There is a key phrase that sets this section apart. Notice the language of 5:17: "Do not think that I have come to abolish *the Law or the Prophets*; I have not come to abolish them but to fulfill them." Then compare this with 7:12: "So in everything, do to others what you would have them do to you, for this sums up *the Law and the Prophets*" (my emphasis in both quotations). Significantly the words "Law" and "Prophets" occur together in Matthew only in these verses and in 11:13 (speaking of "the Prophets and the Law") and 22:40 ("All the Law and the Prophets hang on these two commandments," namely, the commandments to love God and to love our neighbor).[387] In addition to this, the Greek word *oun*, translated "therefore" or "so," seems odd at the beginning of 7:12, since it does not sum up what has been said in the immediate context (which deals with prayer in vv. 7–11). It does, however, make perfect sense when it is understood to sum up everything that has just been taught. As professor D. A. Carson explained, it most probably "refers to the entire body of the sermon (5:17–7:12), for here there is a second reference to 'the Law and the Prophets'; and this appears to form an envelope with 5:17–20." This is of great import, as Carson notes:

> "Therefore," in the light of all I have taught about the true direction in which the OT law points, obey the Golden Rule; for this is (*estin*; NIV, "sums up") the Law and the Prophets (cf. Rom 13:9). This way of putting it provides a powerful yet flexible maxim that helps us decide moral issues in a thousand cases without the need for multiplied case law. The rule is not arbitrary, without rational support, as in radical humanism; in Jesus' mind its rationale ("for") lies in its connection with revealed truth recorded in "the Law and the Prophets." The rule embraces quantity ("in everything") and quality (*houtos kai*, "[do] even so"). And in the context of fulfilling the Scriptures, the rule provides a handy summary of the righteousness to be displayed in the kingdom.[388]

What exactly does this mean? Let's look back again to Matthew 5:17, reading through verse 20 before continuing with the rest of the sermon:

> Do not think that I have come to abolish the Law or the Prophets; I have not come to abolish them but to fulfill them. I tell you the truth, until heaven and earth disappear, not the smallest letter, not the least stroke of a pen, will by any means disappear from the Law until everything is accomplished. Anyone who breaks one of the least of these commandments and teaches others to do the same will be called least in the kingdom of heaven, but whoever practices and teaches these commands will be called great in the kingdom of heaven. For I tell you that unless your righteousness surpasses that of the Pharisees and the teachers of the law, you will certainly not enter the kingdom of heaven.

Several key observations can be made: (1) Jesus made clear that he was not coming to abolish the Law or the Prophets. Therefore, any interpretation of his words that effectively abolishes the Torah must be rejected. (2) He not only said that he would not abolish the Law but that he would not abolish the Prophets as well, indicating that the issue was not just one of legal interpretation but one that also dealt with his relationship to the Tanakh as a whole.[389] (3) He did *not* say that he came "to affirm" or "strengthen" or "enhance" or "explain" the Law and the Prophets; rather, he said that he came to *fulfill*.[390] (As noted by Carson,

"The antithesis is not between 'abolish' and 'keep' but between 'abolish' and 'fulfill.'")[391] This means that the Hebrew Bible finds its goal, its full meaning, and its completion in him, something that Matthew empha- sizes throughout his book by using this identical verb *plēroō, fulfill,* in terms of the events of Yeshua's life being the fulfillment of what was written in the prophets (see Matt. 1:23; 2:15, 17, 23; 4:14; 8:17; 12:17; 13:35; 21:4; 26:54, 56; 27:9; note also esp. Luke 24:44; for a different, but related usage, cf. Matt. 3:15; for Rom. 8:4, see below).

What does this mean on a practical level? Most obviously, it means that what he is about to teach, which, on a superficial reading might be taken to mean that he intended to annul the Law, was anything but an undoing of the Law. Rather, "until heaven and earth disappear, not the smallest letter, not the least stroke of a pen, will by any means disappear from the Law until everything is accomplished" (or, as translated in the NLT, "until its purpose is achieved"; the Greek is literally, "until it has all happened"). As New Testament scholar John Nolland observed, "In Jewish terms any attempt to annul (Gk. *kataluein*) the Law could have been viewed only with horror. . . . The Law defined the identity of the Jewish people."[392] In the strongest possible terms, Yeshua stated that his purpose was *not* to annul that Law.

Notice next that the word "until" occurs two times in the verse just quoted: "until heaven and earth disappear . . . until everything is accom- plished." So, as long as heaven and earth endure, not even the tiniest part of the Law will disappear until everything is accomplished, which also means that some aspects of the Torah could reach their comple- tion—or fulfillment—before the end of the age.

Again I ask, What does this mean on a practical level? We already brought attention to the phrase "Law or the Prophets" in 5:17, a surpris- ing combination of words in this particular context, especially since the verses that follow place little emphasis on the Prophets but rather focus primarily on the Law. Yet Jesus is reminding us that he has come to fulfill both the Law and the Prophets. Accordingly, when Philip encountered Yeshua, he said, "We have found the one Moses wrote about in the Law, and about whom the prophets also wrote—Jesus of Nazareth, the son of Joseph" (John 1:45). As expressed by Paul, "But now a righteousness from God, apart from law, has been made known, to which the Law and the Prophets testify" (Rom. 3:21). To reiterate: The entire Tanakh points forward to Yeshua and thus, as expressed by Carson, "Here Jesus presents himself as the eschatological goal of the OT, and thereby its sole authoritative interpreter, the one through whom alone the OT finds its valid continuity and significance."[393]

So to explain what this means, the Torah laws dealing with sacrifice, atonement, ritual cleansing, priesthood, and tabernacle/Temple reach their goal in the Messiah, the ultimate and final sacrifice for sins—in keeping with the Rabbinic principle that "the death of the righteous atones" (see vol. 2, 3.15)—the great High Priest, and the living embodiment of the Shekhinah, that is, the manifest presence of God on earth (see vol. 2, 3.1–3.2). The Torah was pointing to him! That's why, when the Temple was destroyed and the sacrifices ceased and the priests could no longer fulfill many of the functions, the followers of Yeshua were not set back at all. He had already fulfilled this aspect of Torah and replaced the shadow with the substance (for this imagery, see Hebrews 8–10). To underscore just how major this is, note that in the Torah, words like "offering" and "sacrifice" occur more than 500x (just those two occur 492x), whereas Sabbath, for all its importance, occurs just 37x. Yeshua gives eternal significance to this major part of the Torah!

Now, this does not mean that his disciples stopped going to the Temple or even offering various kinds of sacrifices after his death (see, below, 5.29), nor does it imply that priests who believed in him (see Acts 6:7) stopped serving at the Temple. What it does mean is that they understood that all these rites and rituals ultimately found their full expression and goal in the Messiah's atoning death and so, when the Temple was destroyed in 70 c.e.—an event that Yeshua explicitly predicted on a number of occasions (see above, 5.22)—this presented no theological problem at all, despite its traumatic nature. This part of the Torah had already reached its goal!

Now, Rabbinic Judaism also survived the crisis of the destruction of the Second Temple, thanks, in part, to the already established, decentralized, Pharisaic synagogue system, and thanks to other emerging traditions that provided alternative structures of worship and service without a functioning Temple or priesthood. Nonetheless, the Temple's destruction was far more traumatic for Pharisaic/Rabbinic Jews than for Messianic Jews (see 5.22), since: (1) Yeshua had warned his disciples about the coming destruction of the Temple and city; (2) through his atoning death, he accomplished what no amount of sacrifices and offerings could have ever accomplished (note Acts 13:38–39; Heb. 9:6–14) and what no high priest could ever have done (cf. again Hebrews 5 and 7); and (3) his teachings had already anticipated the day when there would be no Temple, sacrifice, or functioning priesthood.[394]

Jesus' words in John 4:21–24 are also relevant here. Speaking to a Samaritan woman, he said:

Believe me, woman, a time is coming when you will worship the Father neither on this mountain nor in Jerusalem. You Samaritans worship what you do not know; we worship what we do know, for salvation is from the Jews. Yet a time is coming and has now come when the true worshipers will worship the Father in spirit and truth, for they are the kind of worshipers the Father seeks. God is spirit, and his worshipers must worship in spirit and in truth.

His followers therefore understood that true worship did not ultimately depend on a location but rather on the attitude of heart before God, and this concept, coupled with the understanding that he fulfilled key Messianic prophecies—such as those pertaining to the Lord's suffering servant in Isaiah 42, 49, 50, and 52:13–53:12, along with other key passages such as Psalm 2; 22; Psalm 110; Daniel 9:24–27 (for all these passages, see vol. 3)—made the loss of the Temple a strength, rather than a weakness, for the Messiah's disciples. With the destruction of the Temple—which represented the end of at least one aspect of the former system because of the failure of the people (see Heb. 8:8)—his words and actions, and his death and resurrection now spoke all the more loudly. What he said was true, what he did was efficacious. He was both Prophet and Priest, bringing Messianic expectations to a head in one man, rather than in two or three different end-time figures, namely, an anointed High Priest, a great Prophet, and the Messianic King (see vol. 1, 2.1). Messiah is all three!

Although in many ways, Rabbinic Judaism has functioned well without a Temple, traditional Jews still pray daily for the rebuilding of the Temple and for the restoration of the sacrificial system, recognizing that, until such time, something on some level is missing, since, at the very least, they are unable to fulfill certain commandments (cf. vol. 2, 3.9) Followers of Jesus, however, experience no such lack, since he *has already fulfilled* these relevant parts of the Torah and the Prophets.[395] In saying this, I am not casting stones at Rabbinic Judaism, a system of religion that I deeply admire, despite my fundamental differences with some of its foundations and practices (see vol. 5, 6.8–6.9). However, I *am* saying that the Messiah's way is best, since: (1) his followers have experienced *no spiritual lack* because of the Temple's absence during the last two thousand years, actually coming into a richer spiritual experience *without* the Temple, and (2) Jesus explained in advance how the Torah and Prophets found their ultimate meaning in him and even prophesied the destruction of the Temple. Doesn't it make sense, then, to trust the one who predicted that all this was going to happen and who set things in motion beforehand so that, for all those who would look to him, there would be no lack in their relationship with God or service for God? (For the key prophetic role fulfilled by Yeshua, see above, 5.22.)

We also recognize that Yeshua is the fulfillment of the biblical calendar, as explained in volume 1, 2.1, with Passover pointing to his death as the Lamb of God, paving the way for a greater exodus, Firstfruits pointing to his resurrection, Shavuot (Pentecost) corresponding to the outpouring of the Spirit, and then, still in the future, Trumpets (in Jewish tradition, Rosh HaShanah) pointing to his return, Yom Kippur to national atonement for Israel, and Sukkot (Tabernacles) to the final ingathering of the nations. Even the calendar ultimately points to Messiah, and all this is part of his fulfilling the Torah and Prophets.

You might say in response, "But now you're saying that he *did* change the Law."

To the contrary, I'm saying that only through him can the Law be fully obeyed. In fact, if you go through each chapter of the Torah beginning in Exodus 12, where most Torah legislation begins, and read to the end of Deuteronomy, you will see that a large proportion of the Torah (including the majority of the laws) can only be fulfilled when our people are living in the land of Israel and there is a functioning priesthood and sacrificial system.[396] If you are a traditional Jew, you now do many things *in place of* the Jerusalem-based Temple system, such as facing towards Jerusalem in prayer and praying twice each day during the times when sacrifices would have been offered, or studying the laws of the sacrifices rather than offering them. If you are a follower of the Messiah, you rejoice in the fact that his blood atones for all our sins and that, as the great High Priest, he brings us into the Holy of Holies in God's heavenly presence. And you recognize that the people of God, indwelt by his Spirit, now constitute the spiritual Temple, the habitation of the Lord (see 1 Cor. 3:16–17; Eph. 2:21–22; 1 Peter 2:4–5).

But this is only part of the answer. Rabbinic Judaism also acknowledges that, on some level, changes in the Law are inevitable, based on changing circumstances. For traditional Judaism, these changes come through the rabbis who, it is believed, have a system in place that allows for the written Torah—which by nature is fixed—to be a living Torah. Thus, they believe that on Mount Sinai, God revealed to Moses a system of interpretation through which ongoing, relevant insights could be derived from the written Word, as well as explaining to him orally the meaning of the written code, instructing him to pass this oral tradition on through the generations, right up until our day. (For a refutation of this position, see vol. 5, 6.1.) Traditional Jews also believe that, according to Deuteronomy 17:8–13, the rabbis have authority to enact new laws (*takkanot*, enactments, and *gezerot*, decrees), recognizing the need for such developments as certain aspects of Jewish life would change and develop over the centuries. And it is believed that, beginning with the Talmudic sages, the Spirit of God that once moved on the prophets now helped the Rabbinic leaders, guiding them in their decisions for the community (see vol. 5, 6.5). Moreover, as various customs developed among the people, some of those customs became law as well, in accordance with the Rabbinic dictum that, "The custom of the people is law."

More specifically, as defined by the *Oxford Dictionary of Jewish Religion*, a *gezerah* is:

> a legal term paired with *taqqanah* referring to a halakhic directive that is not derived from scriptures or from previous legal decisions. It generally refers to a directive that obstructs a prohibited action, while a taqqanah calls for positive behavior. The power to make such decrees is derived for the former from Leviticus 18.30; for the latter, from Deuteronomy 17.11 or 30.7."[397]

Expanding on the definition of a *takkanah* (or *taqqanah*), it notes that a *takkanah* is "a regulation or an ordinance promulgated for the public welfare or for the purpose of strengthening religious and moral life and supplementing the law of the Torah."[398] Examples of *takkanot* (or *taqqanot*) and *gezerot* would include the prohibition against polygamy (instituted in the eleventh century CE) or the earlier Talmudic rulings that "communities must appoint elementary school teachers" and that "a father must support his minor children."[399]

As for *minhag*, custom, the *Oxford Dictionary of Jewish Religion* explains that

> customs not introduced by a rabbinical authority or based on biblical writ often became sacred by virtue of long usage. Accepted custom is one of the formative factors in the development of Jewish law and religious observance. This applies both to local *minhag*, that is customs that obtain in one locality only, as well as customs that have been adopted universally. *Minhagim* [pl. for customs] are less binding than formal legal enactments, though, in the event of conflict, custom can take precedence over law (Y. *Yev.* 12.1)."[400]

The rabbis, then, along with the communities as a whole, become part of the very process of developing Jewish law, and for a traditional Jew, observing Torah includes, in seamless fashion, the commandments written in the Torah, the *gezerot* and *takkanot* of the rabbis, and the customs of the communities.

In stating this, I am not stating anything that would be controversial for a traditional Jew. This is all basic knowledge, as illustrated by the comments posted under the topic "Halakhah: Jewish Law" on Judaism 101, a popular website. The website article, written by Tracey Rich, explains that Jewish Law (i.e., *halakhah*) includes commandments (*mitzvot*) which are found in the Torah, along with rabbinic *takkanot* (ordinances), *gezerot* (decrees), and *minhagim* (customs). All of these, she explains, are considered to be Jewish law and they are all "equally binding," the exceptions being that: (1) the penalties for violating Torah laws are more severe than the penalties for violating rabbinic laws and customs; and (2) in certain circumstances, rabbinic laws can be changed while Torah laws cannot. In sum, however, she emphasizes that "these 'customs' are a binding part of halakhah" just as the commandments and the ordinances and decrees are a part of Jewish law.[401]

So then, for Rabbinic Judaism, the law is a living law, subject to change and adaptation as long as certain parameters are followed.

Let me give you some examples of Rabbinic changes that were made to the *written Torah* because of (alleged) necessity. Again, my point here is not to demean Rabbinic tradition, since some things *had to change*. I am simply giving examples. Where I do have differences with traditional Judaism, I have them respectfully, and in that spirit volume 5 is written, examining the claims of the oral law.

According to Numbers 15:37–42 (see also Deut. 22:12), the people of Israel were commanded to wear blue tassels (or, fringes) on the corners of their garments which, in ancient times, had four "corners" and were worn out (as opposed to a shirt that is tucked into the pants).[402] The Hebrew word for blue is *tekhelet*, often called "royal blue," and it has been noted that this distinct color (which some scholars believe was actually closer to violet or blue-purple) and style of garment was worn by ancient Near Eastern royalty and/or priests. So, the tassels were there to remind the Israelites to keep the commandments of God, as well as to remind them that they were a kingdom of priests (see Exod. 19:4–5).

Why don't traditional Jews dress like this today? There are two principle reasons. First, the rabbis believe that the specific dye used to make this particular blue color had to come from a certain snail that is no longer obtainable.[403] The tassels are therefore white. Second, the style of clothes has changed over the centuries, so Jewish men now wear what is called a *tallit katan* (a small *tallit*) under their shirts, with the tassels hanging outside so as to be visible; while in prayer, they drape themselves with a larger *tallit*. In addition to this, Rabbinic tradition requires that these tassels must have a specific series of knots as a reminder to keep the 613 Torah commandments (this is the number of commandments according to the traditional count), although these knots are not mentioned in the written Torah at all.[404]

As described by professor Jacob Milgrom:

> Presently, the *tsitsit* are attached to the four corners of a prayer shawl *(tallit)*. Each *tsitsit* consists of four white threads, one of which is longer than the others. Holes are made in each of the four corners of the *tallit*, and the threads are inserted into them and folded over. The two collections of threads are then tied with a double knot. The long thread is wound round the others seven, eight, eleven, and thirteen times, each joint being separated from the other by a double knot. The Hebrew numerical value of the consonants of the word *tsitsit* is 600. If five (for the sets of double knots) and eight (for the number of thread ends) be added, they yield a total of 613, which, according to rabbinic tradition, represents the number of biblical commandments of which the *tsitsit* are to remind the wearer.[405]

Now, let's say that a contemporary traditional Jew said, "Actually, the written Torah doesn't tell me to wear a *tallit katan* or to pray wrapped in a *tallit*, and it doesn't tell me to wear white fringes with 613 knots, and since, with today's technology, I can produce something that looks identical to *tekhelet*, and since archaeologists can tell me what the ancient garments looked like, I'm going to do exactly what God commanded Moses and follow what is written. No knots. No white fringes. No *tallit katan*. No *tallit* when I pray. I'm just going to follow the Torah!" Such a person would be viewed as *violating the Torah*, since, for a traditional Jew, what is written cannot be separated from what the traditions teach. The comments on the Judaism 101 website illustrate this from a traditional, observant Jewish perspective:

> It is important to note that from the point of view of the practicing Jew, there is no difference between a gezeirah and a Torah mitzvah. Both are equally binding; neither can be disregarded on a whim. . . . A takkanah, like a gezeirah, is just as binding as a Torah mitzvah. . . . It is important to note that these "customs" are a binding part of halakhah, just like a mitzvah, a takkanah or a gezeirah.[406]

Or, as stated in the midst of a typical, Talmudic legal discussion in b. Ket 84a, "the Sages have imparted to their enactments the same force as that of Pentateuchal laws." It is therefore understandable that, with this mindset, Rabbinic Judaism has always been vehemently opposed to the Karaites, Jews who sought to follow the written Torah *without* the Rabbinic traditions. How dare they! (For more on this, see vol. 5, 6.5.)

Let's look at a few more examples out of the countless scores that could be examined before returning to the Sermon on the Mount and examining the implications of the Messiah's teachings. According to the Mishnah (Sotah 9:9; see also b. Sotah 47a–b),

> When murderers increased in number, the rite of breaking the heifer's neck was abolished [see Deuteronomy 21:1–9]. . . . When adulterers increased in number, the application of the waters of jealousy ceased [see Numbers 5:11–31]; R. Jochanan ben Zakkai abolished them, as it is said, *I will not punish your daughters when they commit idolatry nor your daughters-in-law when they commit adultery* [Hosea 4:14]. . . .[407]

By what authority were these changes made to the written Torah? By the authority of the Rabbinic sages! And what of the notion that the Torah is eternal and unchangeable? The answer would be that, according to the Rabbinic exegesis of these laws, they had to be abrogated—at least temporarily—or, they didn't apply to the current circumstances.[408] (The verse from Hosea, read in context, obviously has nothing to do with its use here in the Mishnah.)

Here is one more, quite famous example, called the *prosbul*. As summarized by Dr. Dan Gruber:

> Sometimes, the Rabbis were unable to read their teachings into the Scriptures by any means. So they simply annulled the decrees of Torah. The most well-known instance of this concerns the "prosbul." "The prosbul was a deed whereby a creditor transferred his debts to the Beth din, which were then regarded as though already collected from the debtor, so that the seventh year did not cancel them. This was done only if the debtor possessed land." [b. Kid. 26b, Soncino Edition, 126, n. 12]
>
> The Torah says, "At the end of every seven years you must cancel debts. This is how it is to be done: Every creditor shall cancel the loan he has made to his fellow Israelite. He shall not require payment from his fellow Israelite or brother, because the LORD's time for canceling debts has been proclaimed. . . . Be careful not to harbor this wicked thought: 'The seventh year, the year for canceling debts, is near,' so that you do not show ill will toward your needy brother and give him nothing. He may then appeal to the LORD against you, and you will be found guilty of sin." [Deut. 15:1–2, 9]
>
> "Hillel instituted the prosbul. . . . A prosbul prevents the remission of debts (in the Sabbatical year). This is one of the regulations made by Hillel the Elder. For he saw that people were unwilling to lend money to one another and disregarded the precept laid down in the Torah. Beware that there be not a base thought in thine heart saying, etc. He therefore decided to institute the prosbul." [b. Git. 36a, cf. m. Shevi'it X,3; m. Pe'ah III,6; b. Git.36b]
>
> Apparently, in the time of Hillel, poor Israelites were unable to attain needed loans before the Sabbatical year, because their better-off brothers

were not obeying the Torah, not fearing that the Lord would find them "guilty of sin." Hillel reasoned that, because of the people's disobedience, annulling the Torah would produce a greater good than following it.[409]

In volume 5, 6.1, I will return to the subject of the *prosbul*, but what has been said here is clear in and of itself.

What is my point in citing these examples which, again, could be multiplied almost endlessly? It is simply to say that even Rabbinic Judaism, which is so deeply devoted to the Torah, recognizes that certain changes must come, not just with the destruction of the Temple and dispersion of the people, but simply over the course of the development of normal life. It therefore has a massive system in place which actually empowers those changes. And because it continues to evolve, it has produced an enormous body of literature—literally, thousands of volumes of law, tradition, and explanation[410]—along with an extraordinarily detailed way of life that dictates the way a Jew lives, from the moment he rises from bed to the moment he goes to sleep, from bathroom habits to bedroom habits, from when he prays to what words he uses in prayer—just to name a few, virtually none of which are explicitly commanded in the Torah. (For more on this, see vol. 5, 6.3–6.4.)

Again, I am not saying this to disparage Rabbinic Judaism. It has many beautiful traditions and insightful interpretations. My point is simply that the written Torah, in and of itself, cannot sustain the ongoing life of a people, especially scattered around the world, not to mention without a functioning Temple. Rabbinic Judaism, which would argue that God never intended for the written Word to stand on its own, has erected one system that makes the Torah viable through the centuries, one which, in reality, makes many changes to the written Torah through additions, subtractions, and new interpretations. (Even if the rabbis claim that all these changes are *not* really changes, in actual practice, they are.)

Yeshua, through his teaching and example, and through his life, death, resurrection, and sending of the Spirit—thereby inaugurating the new covenant and the Messianic age—has provided another, better way. With this in mind, let's return to his sermon, looking as well at other key passages in which he established a pattern for implementing Torah. As stated above, the core of his sermon is found in 5:17–7:12, but we will return to 5:17–20 after looking at the rest of the sermon. It should also be noted that some of Yeshua's Torah—that is, his particular brand of Torah teaching—is included in both the prologue in 5:3–16 and the closing exhortation in 7:13–27, but it is in 5:17–7:12 in particular that he shows how he fulfills the Torah and Prophets.

Beginning in 5:21–48, he gives his own, authoritative interpretation of Torah laws, taking the moral commands to a deeper level, thereby providing a template for the interpretation of other, similar Torah laws (for a good example of this, see Matt. 19:16–26). This too is part of his "fulfilling" the Torah.[411] So, while the Torah prohibits murder, Jesus addresses murderous attitudes of the heart—specifically angry thoughts and words—urging his disciples to seek reconciliation (5:21–26). As for adultery, Jesus teaches that even to look at another woman lustfully is to commit adultery with the heart, something that could have treacherous consequences (5:27–30). Regarding divorce, he prohibits it except in the case of *porneia*, rendered "sexual immorality" in the ESV (5:31–32).[412] Regarding oaths, he calls on his disciples not to swear but rather to let their "Yes" be "Yes" and their "No" be "No" (5:33–37). As for the *lex talionis* (i.e., "eye for eye and tooth for tooth"), he states that this is not to be the governing attitude of our lives. Rather, when we are wronged and shamed, we should "turn the other cheek" and not seek retaliation—teachings which are best understood against the Jewish legal background of the day (5:38–42).[413] And rather than loving our neighbors but hating our enemies, Jesus commands his followers to love their enemies, treating even the ungodly and undeserving with kindness, just as our heavenly Father does, since being like him is our goal (5:43–48). As simple as some of this sounds, it is profoundly challenging without the help of the Spirit, not allowing us to rely on outward obedience while our hearts are unclean. If you've never read these words of the Messiah, now would be a good time to stop and take them in.

In 6:1–18, Yeshua takes up the issue of "acts of righteousness," such as giving to the needy (6:2–4), prayer (6:5–15), and fasting (6:16–18), in each case urging us not to perform these acts of righteousness for people to see, but rather in secret, seen only by our heavenly Father, who will reward us openly. Not only does he renounce hypocrisy and religious showmanship, but in a few short words (6:9–13), he provides a marvelous guideline for prayer, sufficient in itself, but also serving as a pattern for prayer that can serve as a launching pad for further devotions.[414] And in keeping with his pattern, he commands us to forgive others if we want our Father to forgive us (6:14–15). This is the way of the Messiah, calling on us to crucify human, fleshly attitudes and reactions, following in his footsteps (remember Luke 23:32–34!). Then in 6:19–27, he gives instruction on what our attitude should be towards material things, warning against storing up treasures on earth but not in heaven (6:19–21), warning against greed (6:22–23)[415] and the love of money (6:24), and encouraging us to trust in the goodness of our heavenly Father rather than giving place to worry (6:25–34), laying out an important principle of life: If we seek first God's kingdom and righteousness, everything we need will be given to us (6:33).

Now, for a traditional Jew who is used to having every detail of life spelled out, these teachings might appear profound but vague. However, once it is understood that God never intended to map out every detail of our lives with specific laws but rather to order our lives according to certain spiritual principles within the framework of general laws, then Messiah's teaching begins to make more sense. We'll return to this concept shortly.

In Matthew 7:1–5, Yeshua sets forth the principle of nonjudgmentalism, calling for self-examination rather than self-righteousness. Then, in 7:6, he warns his disciples, whom he has instructed to love even their enemies, not to "become undiscerning simpletons" (Carson). Finally, in 7:7–11, he gives strong assurances of our Father's willingness to hear and answer our prayers—as a good father would be expected to do!—before concluding this portion of the sermon with his final statement: "So in everything, do to others what you would have them do to you, for this sums up the Law and the Prophets" (Matt. 7:12). Those with spiritual eyes will recognize that this has been a major theme throughout the sermon, and here Jesus tells us that obedience to this principle, means obedience to the Scriptures as a whole, similar to Paul's words in Romans 13:10: "Love does no harm to its neighbor. Therefore love is the fulfillment of the law." (The Greek word for "fulfill" here is *plērōma*, the nominal form of the verb *plēroō*, used in Matt. 5:17b.) Traditional Jews will immediately remember the famous comment of Hillel, an older contemporary of Jesus, responding to a Gentile who wanted him to teach him the whole Torah while standing on one foot: "What is hateful to you, do not do to anyone else. This is the whole law; all the rest is commentary. Go and learn it" (b. Shab 31a).

Thus, in a few short chapters—less than a feather in weight compared to the massive volumes of Rabbinic law, but of incredible weight and value in terms of truth and spiritual penetration—Yeshua sets forth principles of Torah interpretation and clearheaded but heavenly-minded Messianic teaching "as one who had authority, and not as their teachers of the law" (Matt. 7:29b). With good reason he could say, "Therefore everyone who hears these words of mine and puts them into practice is like a wise man who built his house on the rock"—a house that would withstand the storms (see Matt. 7:24–27).

Let me challenge those of you who have never tried to govern your life by these words to read them carefully and then seek to live them out on a daily basis. You will see that they are quite inclusive. (To traditional Jewish readers I say again: It will take some level of reorientation for you, since you are accustomed to having almost every detail of life mapped out by Rabbinic tradition, which, for many of you, is considered positive rather than negative. With a renewed mindset, however, you will see how comprehensive Messiah's spiritual principles can be.)

But this is only the beginning. Throughout the Gospels, Jesus provides further guidelines about how to live before God (or, how to apply the Torah according to its true meaning and intent). Let's consider for a moment his teaching about the Sabbath, before returning to one specific teaching in the Sermon on the Mount.

What does the Torah say about the Sabbath? Traditional Jews would point out that it says very little in terms of details, seeing that it does not define what "work" is—we are to cease from "work" on the Sabbath—yet imposes the death penalty for those who do any kind of "work" on that day. In the Rabbinic mindset, God would never have done this, and the rabbis taught that there were thirty-nine subdivisions of labor given to Moses orally on Mount Sinai as well as hidden in the written text. And these thirty-nine subdivisions of labor have ultimately given place to an almost endless series of laws which continue to grow until this day. (See vol. 5, 6.3–6.4 for further discussion.)

Alfred Edersheim, in an appendix to his classic work *The Life and Times of Jesus the Messiah*, gave a sampling of Talmudic Sabbath law (which, I remind you, represents just the first stage of development; things have become infinitely more detailed through the years, as we will observe shortly). To help orient the reader, he gave the following background information which is *not* presented in terms flattering to Talmudic Judaism. Still, the facts, which are accurate, are as follows:

> The Mishnic tractate *Sabbath* stands at the head of twelve tractates which together form the second of the six sections into which the Mishnah is divided, and which treats of Festive Seasons (*Seder Moed*). Properly to understand the Sabbath regulations, it is, however, necessary also to take into account the second tractate in that section, which treats of what are called 'commixtures' or 'connections' (*Erubin*). Its object is to make the Sabbath Laws more bearable. For this purpose, it is explained how places, beyond which it would otherwise have been unlawful to carry things, may be connected together, so as, by a legal fiction, to convert them into a sort of private dwelling. Thus, supposing a number of small private houses to open into a common court, it would have been unlawful on the Sabbath to carry anything from one of these houses into the other. This difficulty is removed if all the families deposit before the Sabbath some food in the common court, when 'a connection' is established between the various houses, which makes them one dwelling. This was called the 'Erubh of Courts.' Similarly, an extension of what was allowed as a 'Sab-

bath journey' might be secured by another 'commixture,' the 'Erubh' or 'connection of boundaries.' An ordinary Sabbath day's journey extended 2,000 cubits beyond one's dwelling. But if at the boundary of that 'journey' a man deposited on the Friday food for two meals, he thereby constituted it his dwelling, and hence might go on for other 2,000 cubits. Lastly, there was another 'Erubh,' when narrow streets or blind alleys were connected into 'a private dwelling' by laying a beam over the entrance, or extending a wire or rope along such streets and alleyways. This, by a legal fiction, made them 'a private dwelling,' so that everything was lawful there which a man might do on the Sabbath in his own house.

Without discussing the possible and impossible questions about these Erubin raised by the most ingenious casuistry, let us see how Rabbinism taught Israel to observe its Sabbath. In not less than twenty-four chapters, matters are seriously discussed as of vital religious importance, which one would scarcely imagine a sane intellect would seriously entertain [I certainly do *not* concur with Edersheim's comment here and will provide a balance to it shortly]. Through 64 1/2 folio columns in the Jerusalem, and 156 double pages of folio in the Babylon Talmud does the enumeration and discussion of possible cases, drag on, almost unrelieved even by Haggadah. The Talmud itself bears witness to this, when it speaks (no doubt exaggeratedly) of a certain Rabbi who had spent no less than two and a half years in the study of only one of those twenty-four chapters! And it further bears testimony to the unprofitableness of these endless discussions and determinations. The occasion of this is so curious and characteristic, that it might here find mention. The discussion was concerning a beast of burden. An ass might not be led out on the road with its covering on, unless such had been put on the animal previous to the Sabbath, but it was lawful to lead the animal about in this fashion in one's courtyard. The same rule applied to a packsaddle, provided it were not fastened on by girth and backstrap. Upon this one of the Rabbis is reported as bursting into the declaration that this formed part of those Sabbath Laws (comp. Chag. 1:8) which were like mountains suspended by a hair! (Jer. Shabb. p. 7, col. *b*, last lines)[416]

Having provided this background, Edersheim supplies a case in point:

The tractate on the Sabbath begins with regulations extending its provisions to the close of the Friday afternoon, so as to prevent the possibility of infringing the Sabbath itself, which commenced on the Friday evening. As the most common kind of labor would be that of carrying, this is the first point discussed. The Biblical Law forbade such labor in simple terms (Exodus 36:6; comp. Jeremiah 17:22). But Rabbinism developed the prohibition into eight special ordinances, by first dividing 'the bearing of a burden' into two separate acts—lifting it up and putting it down—and then arguing, that it might be lifted up or put down from two different places, from a public into a private, or from a private into a public place. Here, of course, there are discussions as to what constituted a 'private place' . . . 'a public place' . . . ; 'a wide space,' which belongs neither to a special individual or to a community, such as the sea, a deep wide valley, or else the corner of a property leading out on the road or fields, and—lastly, a 'legally free place.' Again, a 'burden' meant, as the lowest standard of it, the weight of 'a dried fig.' But if 'half a fig' were carried at two different times—lifted or deposited from a private into a public place, or *vice versa*—were these two actions to be combined into one so as to constitute the sin of Sabbath desecration? And if so, under what conditions as to state of mind, locality, etc.? And, lastly, how many different sins might one such act involve? To give an instance of the kind of questions that were generally discussed. The standard measure for forbidden food was the size of an olive, just as that for carrying burdens was the weight of a fig. If a man swallowed forbidden food of the size of half an olive, rejected it, and again eaten of the size of half an olive, he would be guilty, because the palate had altogether tasted food to the size of a whole olive; but if one had deposited in another locality a burden of the weight of a half a fig, and removed it again, it involved no guilt, because the burden was altogether only of half a fig, nor even if the first half fig's burden had been burnt and then a second half fig introduced. Similarly, if an object that was intended to be worn or carried in front had slipped behind it involved no guilt, but if it had been intended to be worn or carried behind, and it slipped forward, this involved guilt, as involving labor.

Similar difficulties were discussed as to the reverse. Whether, if an object were thrown from a private into a public place, or the reverse. Whether, if an object was thrown into the air with the left, and caught again in the right hand, this involved sin, was a nice question, though there could be no doubt a man incurred guilt if he caught it with the same hand from which it had been thrown, but he was not guilty if he caught it in his mouth, since, after being eaten, the object no longer existed, and hence catching with the mouth was as if it had been done by a second person. Again, if it rained, and the water which fell from the sky were carried, there was no sin in it; but if the rain had run down from a wall it would involve sin. If a person were in one place, and his hand filled with fruit stretched into another, and the Sabbath overtook him in this attitude, he would have to drop the fruit, since if he withdrew his full hand from one locality into another, he would be carrying a burden on the Sabbath.[417]

Bear in mind that all this is just the tiniest sampling of Sabbath law, like a teacup drawn from an ocean, and this does not include 1,500 years of additional development. Is it possible that God intended *this* when he gave the Sabbath laws to Israel? (See again 6.3–6.4 for further discussion, and note that the Talmud claims in b. Shab 14b that it was Solomon who instituted the laws of *'erub*.)

Now, I want to be quick to say that: (1) Traditional Jews would emphasize that they find the holiness of the day *in the details* rather than *despite the details*, which become a way of life, having been raised with them since childhood. (2) Some of the most profound spiritual works on the Sabbath have been written by traditional Jews (or, those from a traditional background, like Abraham Joshua Heschel). (3) Traditional Jews, more than any other group of Jews, have been diligent to keep the Sabbath (at least, in accordance with their understanding of what the Sabbath requires), as acknowledged below, 5.32.

Having said all this, I repeat my question: Is it possible that God intended *the Rabbinic Sabbath* when he gave the Sabbath laws to Israel? In Exodus 31:13–17, God made it very clear that the penalty for breaking the Sabbath was death:

> Say to the Israelites, "You must observe my Sabbaths. This will be a sign between me and you for the generations to come, so you may know that I am the Lord, who makes you holy.
> "Observe the Sabbath, because it is holy to you. Anyone who desecrates it must be put to death; whoever does any work on that day must be cut off from his people. For six days, work is to be done, but the seventh day is a Sabbath of rest, holy to the Lord. Whoever does any work on the Sabbath day must be put to death. The Israelites are to observe the Sabbath, celebrating it for the generations to come as a lasting covenant. It will be a sign between me and the Israelites forever, for in six days the Lord made the heavens and the earth, and on the seventh day he abstained from work and rested."

If the Sabbath was to be kept in perpetuity, what about the death penalty for breaking it? (Note that the death penalty for Sabbath breaking *was* enforced in ancient Israel according to the Pentateuch; see Num. 15:32–36.) And, by extension, if the Talmudic position is true—which I say just for argument's sake—and does not represent merely additional rulings by the rabbis but also contains the very laws that God gave to Israel through Moses, should we surmise that Israelites who violated any of the laws just presented in the lengthy Edersheim quote, above, should be put to death for that? And what about Rabbinic laws today that teach that it is permissible to use a soft hairbrush on the Sabbath but not a hard hairbrush? If Rabbinic law ruled the land of Israel today, would this be enforced? If so, would other Talmudic interpretations of the Sabbath, such as carrying an item from a public to a private domain, be punishable by death?[418] Would these laws be enforced nationally?

Consider this random sampling of Sabbath laws found in a standard compendium that is widely used by religious Jews today, bearing in mind that these selections represent just a few parts of a few pages of a *three-volume* set of books:

a. It is permissible to scratch one's head or beard lightly, and one need not be afraid that one might thereby pull out some of the hairs.
b. It is also permissible to extract the remains of food stuck in one's beard, so long as one takes care not to pull out any of the hair.

a. One is allowed to remove loose dandruff from one's hair with one's hand, but
b. one must be careful not to remove dandruff which is still attached to the skin.

a. One may neither
   1) comb one's hair, **nor**
   2) brush one's hair with a hard brush. . . .

c. 1) While one is permitted to tidy one's hair a little with a soft brush which is not likely to pull out any of the hair,
   2) it is advisable to keep this brush especially for Shabbath and Yom Tov (holy days), so that there is a recognizable distinction between the way in which one brushes one's hair on a normal weekday and the way in which one does so on Shabbath and Yom Tov.

A married woman who has forgotten to comb her hair before Shabbath or Yom Tov, as is required before going to the *mikveh* (ritual bath) on Shabbath or Yom Tov, should consult a qualified rabbinical authority who will tell her how to proceed in the circumstances.[419]

a. On Shabbath and Yom Tov one is not allowed to cut, trim or file nails, whether with scissors, a nail file or any other instrument or by biting them.
b. Similarly, small pieces of skin which are peeling off around the fingernail or any other part of the body, but which are still connected, may not be pulled or cut off with an instrument, by hand or even with the teeth.
c. Nonetheless, if
   1) the end of a nail has become detached for most of its width and is, therefore, close to coming off **and**
   2) it is causing, or one is afraid that it will cause, pain, it may be removed, either by hand or with the teeth, but not with an instrument.

A married woman who has forgotten to cut her fingernails or toenails before Shabbath or Yom Tov, as is required before going to the *mikveh* (ritual bath) on Shabbath or Yom Tov, should consult a qualified rabbinical authority who will tell her how to proceed, according to the circumstances of the case.[420]

a. One is allowed, on Shabbath, to wash one's face, hands and feet or other individual parts of the body, in water which was heated before Shabbath.

b. One is generally not allowed to wash or shower the whole, or the major part, of one's body in such water, even if one does so bit by bit.

c. A person who is used to washing the whole of his body in warm water every day and will suffer extreme discomfort should he not do so, or someone who is ill, may wash the whole of his body, even on Shabbath, in warm water, provided that it was heated before Shabbath.

d. Anyone washing himself on Shabbath should take care to avoid squeezing water out of his hair.[421]

If, upon opening an electric refrigerator on Shabbath or Yom Tov, one finds that the internal light has automatically been switched on,

a. this does not make it forbidden to eat the food inside, but

b. one should consult a qualified rabbinical authority about what to do with regard to closing the door of the refrigerator again.[422]

a. No fruit may be squeezed either
   1) into an empty vessel or
   2) into a liquid.

b. This prohibition applies regardless of whether the fruit is squeezed
   1) by means of an instrument or
   2) by hand.

c. Common examples are
   1) squeezing lemons,
   2) squeezing oranges,
   3) squeezing the juice out of shredded carrots and
   4) chopping up fruit to such an extent that it becomes liquefied.

d. On the other hand, lemon may be sliced and put into a drink, such as tea or cold water, even though some of the juice will come out by itself, but
   1) it is forbidden to squeeze the lemon with one's hand or with a spoon even while it is in the drink and,
   2) on Shabbath, one must be careful that the drink should either
      a) have a temperature of less than 45 degrees centigrade (113 degrees Fahrenehit) **or**
      b) be in a k*eli sh*elishi [Lit., " a third vessel," which is defined as, "A pot or other vessel into which food is transferred from a k*eli sheini," lit., "a second vessel," which is defined as, "A pot or other vessel into which food is transferred from the vessel in which it was cooked."][423]

So, *this* is what the Lord meant when he commanded Israel not to work on the Sabbath!

A few years ago, the leader of ultra-Orthodox Sephardi Jews, Rabbi Ovadiah Yosef, hailed as a great scholar and godly man by his followers but often reviled by secular Israelis, announced that it was permitted to pick one's nose on the Sabbath, thereby putting an end to a series of halakhic questions that have been raised. Naturally, this announcement was greeted with scorn by the nonreligious (and, probably, even some religious), and I don't cite it here to add to the scorn.[424] I make reference to it simply to indicate just how far traditional Judaism has gone in prohibition of "work" on the Sabbath. (The question regarding nose-picking was whether nostril hairs would be pulled out in the process.)

With all my heart, I do not believe that these laws (from the Talmudic extensions to the hairbrush regulations to the nose-picking ruling) were what God intended when he gave the Sabbath to Israel. Not for a moment! And, given the fact that the Torah expressly forbids adding to God's laws (or taking away; see Deut. 4:2; 12:32 [13:1]), I see no way around the fact that these Rabbinic laws, however noble their intent may be, are anything less than a violation of "Do not add." (For further discussion, see again vol. 5, 6.1, 6.3–6.5.) Once more I say: Yeshua showed us a better way.

Compare also the teaching of Yeshua that nothing that enters a person's mouth can cause inner defilement—in the context of the question of whether it was permissible to eat with unwashed hands (see below, 5.33)—with a Pharisaical debate that, according to the Mishnah, would have been taking place in Jesus' day:

> **8:1** A. These are the issues [argued] by the House of Shammai and the House of Hillel, concerning the [ritual of the] dinner:
> B. The House of Shammai say, "One recites the blessing over the day [and] then one recites the blessing over the wine."
> C. But the House of Hillel say, "One recites the blessing over the wine and then one recites the blessing over the day."
> **8:2** A. The house of Shammai say, "They wash the hands and then mix the cup [of wine]."
> B. But the House of Hillel say, "They mix the cup and then wash the hands."
> **8:3** A. The House of Shammai say, "One wipes his hands on the napkin and places it on the table."
> B. But the House of Hillel say, "On the cushion."
> **8:4** A. The House of Shammai say, "[After the meal] they sweep the floor [house] and then wash the hands [required before recitation of the grace after meals]."
> B. But the House of Hillel say, "They wash the hands and then sweep the floor."

8:5 A. The House of Shammai say, "[The order of the blessings at the conclusion of the Sabbath is] lamp, meal, spices, and *habdalah* [this is the closing prayer]."
  B. But the House of Hillel says, "Lamp, spices, meal, and *habdalah*."
  C. [The blessing over the lamp—]the House of Shammai say, "Who created the light of the fire."
  D. But the House of Hillel say, "Who creates the lights of the fire."[425]

Is this really what the Lord intended? In his much-used law compilation, the Mishnah Berurah, the Chofetz Chayyim, one of the most respected and beloved rabbis of the last century, had this to say about the laws of Sabbath:

> It is absolutely impossible for one to observe Shabbos—and extradite oneself from transgressing the Shabbos prohibitions—without the diligent study and clear understanding of all of Hilchos Shabbos [the laws of Sabbath observance].
> There is, amongst the populace, a lack of knowledge and clarity with regard to Hilchos Shabbos. One of the reasons is that these halachos [laws] are very complicated. One cannot learn the Shulchan Aruch [the sixteenth century, definitive Orthodox code of law] and expect to fully understand Hilchos Shabbos. Rather, he must first thoroughly familiarize himself with the fundamentals—the relevant Gemaras [referring to the difficult, lengthy Talmudic material] and poskim [referring to the rulings in the Responsa Literature; see the glossary].
> In this day and age, most people simply do not have enough time to accomplish this task. . . .[426]

So, this ultra-Orthodox rabbi is telling us that, in his day and age, it was exceedingly difficult to devote the sufficient time and effort required for the adequate study of the laws of Sabbath—not to become a scholar, but simply to observe the Sabbath properly—and he penned these words almost a hundred years ago! Speaking of one specific subset of Sabbath laws, the laws of muktzeh—referring to objects which cannot be moved or handled on the Sabbath or holy days, or, objects which are unprepared for use on these days—a contemporary rabbi writes:

> Many advanced students, even after much study, find difficulty in conceptualizing, quantizing, and categorizing the subject material. They have even greater difficulty when trying to apply the various rules and principles to practical situations which commonly arise.[427]

More than three-hundred pages of detailed, difficult, complicated, and complex rulings then follow—and this is just one aspect of Rabbinic Sabbath law. Yeshua's way is better! No wonder the prophet Isaiah declared that "the coastlands shall await his teaching" (Isa. 42:4b NJPSV; the Hebrew for "his teaching" is "his *torah*").

Now, it is more than likely, that Yeshua himself lived within the framework of *some* of these laws, which were still in the early stages of development.[428] It is quite certain, however, that he opposed the direction in which these laws and traditions were going, categorically differing with them at times (see vol. 5, 6.15) and setting forth his ways in clear contrast to their ways. Therefore it is not surprising that most of the recorded conflicts that he had with the leaders in his day centered around Sabbath observance. Space does not permit an in-depth review of all the relevant accounts, nor can we stop here to analyze exactly what aspects of the developing traditions he differed with.[429] What we can set forth briefly are some of his key teachings and principles.[430]

The Sabbath as a day of liberation from bondage. While the Sabbath commandment in Exodus 20:8–11 calls Israel to remember God resting on the seventh day after creation, the version in Deuteronomy 5:15 states, "Remember that you were slaves in Egypt and that the LORD your God brought you out of there with a mighty hand and an outstretched arm. Therefore the LORD your God has commanded you to observe the Sabbath day."[431] In keeping with this, Jesus went out of his way to heal and deliver on the Sabbath, showing how the traditions of men had become more important to many of the leaders than the spirit and purpose of the day as established by God. First, let me explain the theology of these healings as they relate to the Sabbath, quoting from my book *Israel's Divine Healer*:[432]

> For Jesus, the Sabbath was . . . the ideal day for removing the terrible burden of sickness and demonic oppression, thereby providing true rest for the formerly enslaved (cf. Heb 4!).[433] In fact, *he went out of his way to heal on the Sabbath, in some cases healing in spite of opposition and unbelief, in contrast to his normal pattern of ministry. . . . The Sabbath was the day for doing good, and healing was a good thing (cf. Ac 4:9; 10:38; see also Jn 10:32). Thus, he challenges the religious leaders with the question: "Is it lawful to heal on the Sabbath? . . . Which is lawful on the Sabbath: to do good or to do evil, to save life or to kill?" (Mt 12:10b; Mk 3:4). Then, answering his own question, he asks rhetorically: "If any of you has a sheep and it falls into a pit on the Sabbath, will you not take hold of it and lift it out? How much more valuable is a man than a sheep! Therefore it is lawful to do good on the Sabbath" (Mt 12:11–12).[434] He then heals the man with the shriveled hand, to the consternation of the leaders (Mt 12:13–14).

In Luke 13, the two Sabbath concepts, viz., *true rest* through *emancipation*, are again combined in the healing of the crippled woman. Thus, in answer to the indignant synagogue ruler's charge to the people that, "There are six days for work. So come and be healed on those days, not on the Sabbath" (13:14), Jesus answers sternly, "You hypocrites! Doesn't each of you on the Sabbath untie his ox or donkey from the stall and lead it out to give it water? Then should not this woman, a daughter of Abraham, whom Satan has kept bound for eighteen long years, be set free on the Sabbath day from what bound her?" (13:15–16). The Sabbath was *not* the day to be bound, nor was it a time for carrying heavy loads.

It is also noteworthy that on at least five different occasions, Jesus *initiated* a healing on the Sabbath, each time, healing just one (Lk 14:1–6; Jn 5:1–14, 9:1–41; and the two instances just cited). He was thereby declaring himself Lord of the Sabbath, which includes the concept of being Lord of every word of God made into a tradition of men. The strategic positioning of these accounts in the Synoptics (in Mark and Luke, immediately after the parable of the new wineskins, coupled with the dispute concerning picking grain on the Sabbath [Mk 2:18–3:5;[435] Lk 5:33–6:11]; in Matthew, following Jesus' invitation to the weary and burdened to come to him, for his yoke was easy and his burden light [11:28–30])[436] and the legal controversies which followed the healings in John's Gospel make this emphatically clear. Jesus as Lord of the Sabbath saved, healed, and delivered, bringing to full expression the divine purpose for the day.[437]

For Yeshua, healing, deliverance, and liberation were important elements of the Sabbath, and rather than that sacred day being one of added burdens, it was to be a day for the easing of burdens and a day of doing good for those in critical need. And because it was a day of liberation, Jesus the Messiah stood in strong opposition to human traditions that brought bondage rather than freedom. Consider these differing perspectives on some of Messiah's Sabbath day healings:

- After Jesus healed the man who had been crippled for thirty-eight years, ordering him to get up and carry his mat, the religious leaders saw him and did not praise God for this incredible miracle. Instead they said to him: "It is the Sabbath; the law forbids you to carry your mat" (John 5:10b). So, what they saw was a man violating their traditions rather than a man healed by God.
- Referring to this healing later, Yeshua said to the religious leaders, "I did one miracle, and you are all astonished. Yet, because Moses gave you circumcision (though actually it did not come from Moses, but from the patriarchs), you circumcise a child on the Sabbath. Now if a child can be circumcised on the Sabbath so that the law of Moses may not be broken, why are you angry with

me for healing the whole man on the Sabbath? Stop judging by mere appearances, and make a right judgment" (John 7:21–24).

- After Jesus healed the man born blind by making dirt into mud with his spittle, then applying it to the man's eyes and telling him to go and wash, the religious leaders were not awestruck by this demonstration of divine power and mercy. Instead some of them said: "This man is not from God, for he does not keep the Sabbath" (John 9:16a).

- After Jesus healed a man with a shriveled hand, first asking those present about whether it was "lawful on the Sabbath to do good or to do evil, to save life or to kill?"—a question to which they would not reply—some Pharisees "went out and began to plot with the Herodians how they might kill Jesus" (Mark 3:1–6).

- After Jesus healed the woman who had been paralyzed for eighteen years, rebuking those who had a faulty understanding of God's intent for Sabbath, "all his opponents were humiliated, but the people were delighted with all the wonderful things he was doing" (Luke 13:10–17).

The Sabbath as a time of true spiritual rest. I drew attention, above, to the fact that Mark and Luke present Jesus' teachings about new wineskins immediately before recording the Sabbath conflicts he had with some of the leaders. This in itself is significant, suggesting that the old wineskins of human tradition could not contain the new wine of the Messiah (see Mark 2:18–3:5; Luke 5:33–6:11).[438] Matthew, however, places the wineskins teaching in a different context (see Matt. 9:16–17) and instead prefaces the Sabbath conflict with these words from the Messiah: "Come to me, all you who are weary and burdened, and I will give you rest. Take my yoke upon me and learn from me, for I am gentle and humble in heart, and you will find rest for your souls. For my yoke is easy and my burden is light" (Matt. 11:28–30). The next two verses read, "At that time Jesus went through the grainfields on the Sabbath. His disciples were hungry and began to pick some heads of grain and eat them. When the Pharisees saw this, they said to him, 'Look! Your disciples are doing what is unlawful on the Sabbath.'" The contrast is clear, and Matthew is saying that Yeshua's way, in contrast with the developing traditions, is the way to real Sabbath rest.

What exactly does this mean? Again, this answer will not satisfy those who are looking for every aspect of the Sabbath to be spelled out in minute detail, but, as emphasized, that was never God's intent. First, Yeshua as the fulfillment of the Torah brings those who follow him into true Sabbath rest, not just one day, but every day. The burden of sin is lifted off of our shoulders, the sense of guilt removed, the need to strive to somehow be accepted by the Father—this is all taken away when we turn to God through him. To be sure, there is a future rest in the world to come that we desire (cf. Heb. 4:8–11), but already, in this life, we enter a supernatural rest through our Messiah. Second, he shows us that sanctifying the Sabbath is not primarily accomplished through endless laws and customs; rather, it comes out of a heart at rest before God, as we cease from our labors and enter into God's rest.

The Son of Man (meaning, the Messiah) is Lord of the Sabbath. Matthew 12:1–14 contains what we can call "Messianic halakhic principles." Although we cannot develop them further in the context of this study, we can set some of them forth for further consideration.[439] First, the priests in the Temple did what was "unlawful" on the Sabbath, engaging in works that were forbidden to others. Temple service, however, made it lawful. Jesus states that he himself is greater than the Temple, meaning, that in his service, certain acts are permissible. Second, quoting Hosea 6:6, Jesus reiterates that God desires mercy and not sacrifice. As paraphrased in *The Message*, he was saying: "There is far more at stake here than religion. If you had any idea what this Scripture meant—'I prefer a flexible heart to an inflexible ritual'—you wouldn't be nitpicking like this" (Matt. 12:6–7). Third, not only is the Sabbath made for man, a truth that was also taught in Jewish tradition (see Mekhlita to Exod. 31:14; b. Yoma 85b)—which would explain why the disciples, when hungry on the Sabbath, could pick some heads of grain—but the Son of Man is the Lord of the Sabbath (see Mark 2:27–28, which adds an additional saying to Matt. 12:8). As explained by commentator Vincent Taylor, "Since the Sabbath was made for man, He who is man's Lord . . . has authority to determine its law and use."[440]

These are just some of the Sabbath principles presented by Yeshua, the main point being: The approach that is based on human tradition and endless legal expansion does *not* define the real meaning of the Sabbath and is *not* what God intended. Rather, following the Torah principles set forth by the Messiah brings full meaning to the day, and through him, there is healing and deliverance and freedom and rest. Not only so, but his presence in our midst is part of the meaning of that day while, through the giving of the Spirit, the principles of Sabbath rest are written on our heart.

Messiah's way would also be in keeping with the fact, noted above, that the Sabbath commandments in the Torah are quite brief with little or no explanation while the commandments having to do with subjects like sacrifices and the building of the tabernacle are incredibly detailed.

Could it be that, rather than God secretly giving Moses a massive amount of rules and regulations, the Lord never intended for so many detailed and specific rules to be developed, since to do so would actually undermine some of the divine intent for the day?[441] Messiah's halakhah points in this direction as well.

Much more could be said on this important topic, but enough has been said to rebut the objection presented. Yeshua by no means abolished the Law! (For Yeshua's teaching concerning dietary laws, see below, 5.33; for Jesus' call that his disciples "turn the other cheek," another principle of Messianic halakhah, see above, 5.19.) The comments of New Testament scholar Douglas J. Moo are certainly relevant here:

> In different ways and with different emphases, all four Gospels reflect a dominant theme in the teaching of Jesus: his divine authority with reference to the Law. Jesus was quick to clarify that his authority did not negate the role of the Law in salvation history. But he also made it clear that this authority involved the right not only to exposit, add to or deepen the Law, but to make demands of his people independent of that Law. This being the case, it is quite inadequate, and potentially misleading, to think of Jesus as 'the last great expositor of the Law.' The Law, God's great gift to Israel, anticipated and looked forward to the eschatological teaching of God's will that Jesus brought. This teaching, not the Law, is the focus of the Gospels, and the Law remains authoritative for the disciple of Jesus only insofar as it is taken up into his own teaching.[442]

That is to say, everything is ultimately filtered through the lens of the Messiah, he to whom the Law and the Prophets point. Does this mean that there is a change in our relationship to Torah as Jews? Actually, many changes had already taken place by the time of Jesus and, in fact, they had to. Consider this important data regarding the possibility of fully obeying a Torah command without living in the Land with a functioning Temple and priesthood. Could these commandments be kept "forever"? (I have used the following symbols: * = potential perpetuity, meaning that these commandments can be kept anywhere in the world, with or without a Tabernacle or Temple, with or without a Jewish government; + = temporary duration, meaning that they cannot be kept in full while exiled from the land of Israel or without a Tabernacle or Temple or without a Jewish government; ? = questionable, meaning the conclusion can be debated.) First, consider this sampling of core legal material in the Torah from Exodus 20 to Leviticus 27. While you might debate the labeling of some of the material here, the overall conclusions remain the same.

BREAKDOWN OF CHAPTERS, EXODUS 20–LEVITICUS 27

* Exod. 20:1–17—Decalogue
+ Exod. 20:22–26—building an earthen altar
? Exod. 21:1–11—laws on slaves
+ Exod. 21:12–17—laws with the death penalty
? Exod. 21:18–32—laws on bodily injuries
* Exod. 21:33—22:15—laws on property damages
+/*Exod. 22:16–31—laws on society (death penalty, etc.)
* Exod. 23:1–9—laws on justice and neighborliness
+ Exod. 23:10–19—laws on sacred seasons (only doable in the Land and with the Temple standing)
+ Exod. 23:20–33—epilogue
+ Exod. 25:1–31:11—tabernacle construction and priestly laws
* Exod. 31:12–17—Sabbath laws
+/*Exod. 34:10–26—renewal of the covenant (some of this temporary because of Land and sacrifices)
+ Exod. 35:1–40:28—building of tabernacle
+ Lev. 1:1–7:37—sacrifices and offerings
+ Lev. 8:1–9:23—ordination of Aaron and his sons
+ Lev. 10:1–19—rules of priestly conduct in the holy place
* Lev. 11:1–46—dietary laws
+ Lev. 12:1–8—ritual purification after childbirth
+ Lev. 13:1–15:33—skin diseases and bodily discharges
+ Lev. 16:1–34—day of atonement (temporary, because of the centrality of the sacrifices, high priest, and tabernacle/Temple)
+/*Lev. 17:1–22:33—laws of personal holiness
+/*Lev. 23:1–44—the annual feasts (mixed, because of the sacrifices)
+ Lev. 24:1–9—care of the lampstand and bread of the presence
+ Lev. 24:10–23—identical laws for the stranger and the Israelite
+ Lev. 25:1–55—laws of land use
* Lev. 26:1–46—blessings and curses
+ Lev. 27:1–34—laws concerning gifts and endowments (temporary because of the animal offerings and involvement of priests)

The laws set forth in the great bulk of these chapters could *not* be kept in perpetuity, as written, while the Jewish people were in exile and/or without a Temple and functioning priesthood and/or without the ability to self-govern. Is this not significant, especially when we realize that this has been the case for us for more than 1,900 years? Is this the way it was intended to be?

Consider next the commandments that were said to be "forever" or "throughout your/the generations." These too could not be kept in perpetuity with our people in exile and without a Temple and functioning priesthood:

'olam ("forever") REFERENCES[443]

1*)   Circumcision: Gen. 17:13 (note the earlier references to God's covenantal promise of the land: Gen. 17:7–8)

2*)   Passover: Exod. 12:14, 17, 24; Lev. 23:41

3?)   A lifetime slave: Exod. 21:6

4+)   Lamp burning in the tent of meeting: Exod. 27:21; Lev. 24:3

5+)   Priestly garments: Exod. 28:43; 29:9 (with other items)

6+)   Priestly portion: Exod. 29:9, 28; differently, Lev. 6:11[15], 18 [21]; 7:34, 36; 10:15

7+)   Priestly washing: Exod. 30:21

8*)   Sabbath: Exod. 31:16–17

9+)   Priesthood: Exod. 29:9

10*)   Not eating fat and blood: Lev. 3:17

11+)   Priests not drinking wine or strong drink in the tabernacle: Lev. 10:9

12*/+) Day of atonement: Lev. 16:29, 31, 34; 23:31 (mixed, because of the sacrificial rites)

13+)   Sacrifices only at the tent of meeting: Lev. 17:7

14+)   Not eating until after the firstfruits: Lev. 23:14

15+)   Solemn assembly on firstfruits: Lev. 23:21

16+)   Bread of the presence: Lev. 24:5–9

17+)   Blowing of trumpets: Num. 10:8

18+)   Same rules for foreigners: Num. 15:15

19+)   Offering covenant of salt: Num. 18:19

20+)   Role of the Levites: Num. 18:23

21+)   Ashes of the heifer: Num. 19:10, 21

22?)   Priesthood through Phinehas: Num. 25:13

"THROUGHOUT YOUR/THE GENERATIONS" REFERENCES

1*)   Circumcision: Gen. 17:9, 12

2*/+) Passover: Exod. 12:14, 17, 42 (mixed, because of the sacrificing of the lamb; note also the references to appearing in Jerusalem three times a year, which cannot be accomplished during the exile; see Exod. 23:14–17; 34:23–24; Deut. 16:16–17)

3+)   Preserving the jar of manna: Exod. 16:32, 33

4+)   Lamp burning in the tent of meeting: Exod. 27:21

5+)   Burnt offering: Exod. 29:42

6+)   Burning incense: Exod. 30:8

7+)   Day of atonement sacrifices: Exod. 30:10

8+)   Priestly washing: Exod. 30:21

9+)   Sacred anointing oil: Exod. 30:31

10*)   Sabbath: Exod. 31:13, 16 (although the death penalty has not been enforced through the generations)

11+)   Anointing of priests: Exod. 40:15

12*)   Not eating fat and blood: Lev. 3:17

13+) Priestly portion: Lev. 6:18; 7:36 (differently)
14+) Priests not drinking wine or strong drink in the tabernacle: Lev. 10:9
15+) Sacrifices only at the tent of meeting: Lev. 17:7
16?) No priests serving with defects: Lev. 21:17
17+) No priests serving with ceremonial uncleanness: Lev. 22:3
18+) Not eating until after the firstfruits: Lev. 23:14
19+) Solemn assembly on firstfruits: Lev. 23:21
20*) No work on day of atonement: Lev. 23:31
21*) Observing tabernacles: Lev. 23:41
22+) Bread of the presence: Lev. 24:5–9
23+) Blowing of trumpets: Num. 10:8
24+) Same rules for foreigners: Num. 15:14–15
25+) Firstfruits to the Lord: Num. 15:21
26+) Offering for unintentional sins: Num. 15:23
27*) Tassels: Num. 15:38
28+) Role of the Levites: Num. 18:23
29?) Homicide laws: Num. 35:23

The conclusions are striking: *Fifteen* out of the *twenty-two 'olam* ("forever") commandments are clearly temporal in duration; *only five* can be perpetual while in exile and without a Temple and priesthood. As for the "throughout your/the generations" commandments, *twenty* out of *twenty-nine* are clearly temporal in duration; *only seven* can be perpetual! So, out of these fifty-one commandments that are either said to be "forever" or "throughout our generations," for the last 1,900+ years, we have not been able to keep more than three-quarters of them as written in the Torah.

Traditional Jews say, "That's why we have the Talmud and the Law Codes and the Responsa Literature and the customs and the traditions and the rabbis!" I say in reply: That's why we have Yeshua the Messiah, the New Testament, and the Holy Spirit! Is it merely a coincidence that he was the one who prophesied that the Temple would be destroyed and that our people would be scattered and it happened just as he said? Is it merely a coincidence that, before the Temple was destroyed, he offered his own blood to usher in the new covenant? Perhaps we should listen more closely to the rest of what he said. (See further above, 5.22.)

It is so clear that so much of the Torah presupposes (and requires!) Israel to be living in the Land, with the Temple (tabernacle) standing, in a basically agricultural society. Scatter our people out of the Land, destroy the Temple—and much of the Torah becomes strangely irrelevant or outmoded or impossible. Contrast the universal nature of Yeshua's teaching and commands—which do *not* need a Talmud and Law Codes![444]

Consider also the Torah laws that called for the death penalty.[445] As noted by the *Jewish Encyclopedia*:

Warrants for the infliction of capital punishment, as opposed to private
retribution or vengeance, are found in the Pentateuchal codes for the com-
mission of any one of the following crimes: adultery (Lev. xx. 10; Deut.
xxii. 22); bestiality (Ex. xxii. 18 [A. V. 19]; Lev. xx. 15); blasphemy (Lev.
xxiv. 16); false evidence in capital cases (Deut. xix. 16–19); false prophecy
(Deut. xiii. 6, xviii. 20); idolatry, actual or virtual (Lev. xx. 2; Deut. xiii. 7–19,
xvii. 2–7); incestuous or unnatural connections (Lev. xviii. 22, xx. 11–14);
insubordination to supreme authority (Deut. xvii. 12); kidnapping (Ex.
xxi. 16; Deut. xxiv. 7); licentiousness of a priest's daughter (Lev. xxi. 9);
murder (Ex. xxi. 12; Lev. xxiv. 17; Num. xxxv. 16 *et seq.*); rape committed
on a betrothed woman (Deut. xxii. 25); striking or cursing a parent, or
otherwise rebelling against parental authority (Ex. xxi. 15, 17; Lev. xx. 9;
Deut. xxi. 18–21); Sabbath-breaking (Ex. xxxi. 14, xxxv. 2; Num. xv. 32–36);
witchcraft and augury (Ex. xxii. 17; Lev. xx. 27). . . .

As to the spirit of later rabbinic legislation, it clearly appears that
there was a tendency to reduce capital punishment to a minimum, if not
to abolish it altogether. That capital punishment was a rare occurrence
in the latter days of the Jewish commonwealth is patent from the statement in the Mishnah that a court was stigmatized as "murderous" if it
condemned to death more than one human being in the course of seven
years. Indeed, Eleazar b. Azariah applied the same epithet to a court that
executed more than one man in every seventy years; and his famous colleagues, Tryphon and Akiba, openly avowed their opposition to capital
punishment, saying, "Had we belonged to the Sanhedrin [during Judea's
independence], no man would ever have been executed," as they would
always have found some legal informalities by which to make a sentence
of death impossible (Mak. i. 7a).[446]

What an extreme contrast from Torah law! Traditional Jews would
say, "These changes were instituted by Rabbinic authority which was
given by God, and they reflect the ultimate intent of the Torah." I would
say in reply, We agree that changes had to come, but I look to the Messiah rather than the Talmudic sages, however wise they may have been.
Liberal Jews (Reform, Reconstructionist, and even some Conservatives)
look to Torah for "guidance not governance," rejecting what they consider
to be the harshness and inflexibility of contemporary Orthodoxy, finding today's version of "traditional Judaism" to be contrary to the spirit
of Talmudic law.[447] Traditional Jews, of course, strenuously disagree,
considering themselves to be the true heirs of Talmudic Judaism.[448] And
yet for a traditional Jew today, Sabbath breaking is not punished by the
death penalty (indeed, since there is no theocratic state run by traditional
Jews, traditional Judaism has no death penalty in force for any violation
of the Torah). As followers of Yeshua (especially Jewish followers), we
see the Messiah as the ultimate goal of the Law and Prophets, recogniz-

ing Torah as a gift rather than as a binding obligation, and looking for spiritual meaning and application in all the details of the Law.

We also recognize that there are hints in the prophetic books that the fulfillment of the Messianic promises would bring about changes in the application of the Torah. Thus, based on Jeremiah 33:10–11, some of the Rabbinic sages stated that in the age to come, the only sacrifices that would be offered would be thanksgiving sacrifices (see vol. 2, 3.17).[449] This is quite a change! Other rabbis speculated that verses such as Deuteronomy 15:11, calling for generosity because "there will always be poor people in the land," would not apply in the same way in the Messianic age when everyone would be rich (for discussion, see below, n. 476). As followers of Yeshua, we say that that age has already broken in, but not in its fullness, and so we are this transition state, this time of "already but not yet." It is a time of glory, but only a foretaste of what is to come. Thank God that we have his deposit already!

To sum up: Everything having to do with our approach to God (sacrifices, ritual purification, blood, priesthood, etc.) has been fulfilled in Jesus, the moral and ethical commands are deepened, the feasts and holy days reach their goal in him (some already past, the rest future), and we are given halakhic principles by which we can apply the rest of the Torah commandments. There is also a way for Gentiles to enter in alongside Jewish believers—one of the great acts of the Messianic age!—without the wall of separation being erected. And all this is done in the life and power of the Spirit, another key part of the inbreaking of the Messianic era during this age of transition (see further the comments of Risto Santala, below, 5.29). As expressed by Paul in Romans 8:3–4:

> ... For what the law was powerless to do in that it was weakened by the sinful nature [in other words, by our innate, human failure to obey it fully], God did by sending his own Son in the likeness of sinful man to be a sin offering. And so he condemned sin in sinful man, in order that the righteous requirements of the law might be fully met in us, who do not live according to the sinful nature but according to the Spirit.

That is the goal!

Interestingly, on a practical level, as multiplied thousands of Jews have come to faith in Yeshua in the last few decades, many who were secular *before* believing in him now worship on Shabbat, setting that day aside for the Lord, and celebrate the feasts, among other Torah commands, yet they do it in newness of life in the Spirit, not out of bondage or even necessity. Isn't this an example of the Messiah writing the Torah on our hearts through the new covenant? As for Jewish believers in Jesus who are not as "observant," this parallels the wide range of expressions that is also found in the non-Messianic Jewish world, ranging from Reconstructionist to Charedi. The difference, of course, with Jewish followers of Jesus is that, for all of them, there are aspects of Torah lived out every day in the deepest sense of the word, with morality and holiness instilled as core values in our innermost being, with Sabbath rest in Yeshua enjoyed on a daily basis, with the reality that we are living temples of the Spirit (individually and corporately) ingrained in our psyche, and with the consciousness of Messiah's sacrificial blood being our refuge and hope and strength. We have found the one of whom Moses and the Prophets testified and the one to whom they pointed, and in him and through him, we lack nothing.[450] The Messiah, not the Torah, is now central (for statements regarding the Messiah's centrality, see above, 5.24; cf. also Luke 16:16–17), and while the Torah continues to play an important role, its greatest function is to point us to Yeshua, Israel's Redeemer and King.[451]

5.29. Paul abolished the Law.

I understand why you hold to this position, but it is actually a serious misconception based on several factors: (1) Paul (whose Hebrew name was Saul) took the message of the Messiah to the Gentiles without requiring them to follow the Torah; (2) Paul clearly explained that we are ultimately made right with God through faith (which is followed by a pattern of good works) rather than by our good works themselves, since none of us can fully live up to the Law's requirements; (3) some of Paul's teachings are quite deep and complex and have therefore been misunderstood; (4) Paul emphasized how God had broken down the barrier that separated Jews from the Gentiles, uniting them in one spiritual family in the Messiah; and (5) Paul clearly viewed the Torah from a different perspective in light of the inbreaking of the Messianic era. But this does not mean that Paul taught that the Torah was now null and void. To the contrary, Paul lived and died as a Torah-observant Jew and never taught that Jewish believers in the Messiah should abandon the Torah, although it appears that if taking the good news of the Messiah to the Gentiles meant that he sometimes had to break a certain law or tradition—such as a dietary restriction—then he would be willing to do that for the sake of their salvation, a principle that could even be deduced from Rabbinic thinking as well.

Scores of books and hundreds of articles have been written about the relationship of Paul to the Law, and it is impossible to attempt to review them all here. (In reality, it would be difficult to review them all in one lifetime, let alone in one small section of one book!) There are even scholarly debates about exactly what Paul meant when he used the word *nomos* in Greek ("law" or "the law"; the Septuagint [LXX] used *nomos* to translate *torah*). Did he always mean the Law of Moses or did he sometimes mean "law" as in "principle" (e.g., "the law of sin and death")?[452] This much, however, is sure: He made certain statements that could easily be understood to teach that the Law of Moses was passé, something old and negative, a relic to be discarded. Here are some of the most prominent statements, which we will cite first without comment so the full force of this objection can be felt:

For he [Jesus] himself is our peace, who has made the two one and has destroyed the barrier, the dividing wall of hostility, by abolishing in his flesh the law with its commandments and regulations. His purpose was to create in himself one new man out of the two, thus making peace, and in this one body to reconcile both of them to God through the cross, by which he put to death their hostility.

Ephesians 2:14–16

Therefore no one will be declared righteous in his sight by observing the law; rather, through the law we become conscious of sin.

Romans 3:20

It was not through law that Abraham and his offspring received the promise that he would be heir of the world, but through the righteousness that comes by faith. For if those who live by law are heirs, faith has no value and the promise is worthless, because law brings wrath. And where there is no law there is no transgression.

Romans 4:13–15

For sin shall not be your master, because you are not under law, but under grace.

Romans 6:14

For when we were controlled by the sinful nature, the sinful passions aroused by the law were at work in our bodies, so that we bore fruit for death. But now, by dying to what once bound us, we have been released from the law so that we serve in the new way of the Spirit, and not in the old way of the written code.

Romans 7:5–6

For apart from law, sin is dead. Once I was alive apart from law; but when the commandment came, sin sprang to life and I died.

Romans 7:8b–9

Christ is the end of the law so that there may be righteousness for everyone who believes.

Romans 10:4

The sting of death is sin, and the power of sin is the law. But thanks be to God! He gives us the victory through our Lord Jesus Christ.

1 Corinthians 15:56–57

We who are Jews by birth and not "Gentile sinners" know that a man is not justified by observing the law, but by faith in Jesus Christ. So we, too, have put our faith in Christ Jesus that we may be justified by faith in Christ and not by observing the law, because by observing the law no one will be justified.

Galatians 2:15–16

All who rely on observing the law are under a curse, for it is written: "Cursed is everyone who does not continue to do everything written in the Book of the Law." Clearly no one is justified before God by the law, because, "The righteous will live by faith." The law is not based on faith; on the contrary, "The man who does these things will live by them." Christ redeemed us from the curse of the law by becoming a curse for us, for it is written: "Cursed is everyone who is hung on a tree."

Galatians 3:10–13

Before this faith came, we were held prisoners by the law, locked up until faith should be revealed. So the law was put in charge to lead us to Christ that we might be justified by faith. Now that faith has come, we are no longer under the supervision of the law.

Galatians 3:23–25

You who are trying to be justified by law have been alienated from Christ; you have fallen away from grace.

Galatians 5:4

But if you are led by the Spirit, you are not under law.

Galatians 5:18

These verses are also relevant:

Circumcision is nothing and uncircumcision is nothing. Keeping God's commands is what counts.

1 Corinthians 7:19

Neither circumcision nor uncircumcision means anything; what counts is a new creation.

Galatians 6:15

A man is not a Jew if he is only one outwardly, nor is circumcision merely outward and physical. No, a man is a Jew if he is one inwardly; and circumcision is circumcision of the heart, by the Spirit, not by the written code. Such a man's praise is not from men, but from God.

Romans 2:28–29

"Well then," you say, "that settles it! No observant Jew in his right mind would say such things. So, even if you were right about Jesus not abolishing the Law, it's clear that Paul did, and that's why Christianity is *not* for Jews. We don't hate the Law, like Paul did; we love it! And we don't find keeping the law burdensome. We find it to be a joy. Obviously, Paul had some personal issues with the Law and then decided to impose his own struggles on his disciples, and that's how Christianity got off track."

I can understand your sentiments. The verses just quoted seem to support the position that Paul was against the Law, that he felt that the Law was meaningless at best and destructive at worst, that he regarded it as temporary, and that he taught emphatically that believers were free from the Law. But could it be that things are not so simple? In a unique statement in the New Testament, Peter wrote that, "[Paul's] letters contain some things that are hard to understand, which ignorant and unstable people distort, as they do the other Scriptures, to their own destruction" (2 Peter 3:16b). Is this part of what Peter had in mind?

Consider first that, in some of the very contexts just quoted, Paul has some extremely positive things to say about the Law (and circumcision too):

For it is not those who hear the law who are righteous in God's sight, but it is those who obey the law who will be declared righteous.

Romans 2:13

Now you, if you call yourself a Jew; if you rely on the law and brag about your relationship to God; if you know his will and approve of what is superior because you are instructed by the law; if you are convinced that you are a guide for the blind, a light for those who are in the dark, an instructor of the foolish, a teacher of infants, because you have in the law the embodiment of knowledge and truth. . . . You who brag about the law, do you dishonor God by breaking the law?

Romans 2:17–20, 23

Circumcision has value if you observe the law, but if you break the law, you have become as though you had not been circumcised.

Romans 2:25

What advantage, then, is there in being a Jew, or what value is there in circumcision? Much in every way! First of all, they have been entrusted with the very words of God.

Romans 3:1–2

But now a righteousness from God, apart from law, has been made known, to which the Law and the Prophets testify. This righteousness from God comes through faith in Jesus Christ to all who believe. . . . Do we, then, nullify the law by this faith? Not at all! Rather, we uphold the law.

Romans 3:21–22, 31

What then? Shall we sin because we are not under law but under grace? By no means!

Romans 6:15

What shall we say, then? Is the law sin? Certainly not! Indeed I would not have known what sin was except through the law. For I would not have known what coveting really was if the law had not said, "Do not covet." . . . So then, the law is holy, and the commandment is holy, righteous and good. . . . We know that the law is spiritual; but I am unspiritual, sold as a slave to sin. . . . And if I do what I do not want to do, I agree that the law is good. . . . For in my inner being I delight in God's law . . . So then, I myself in my mind am a slave to God's law, but in the sinful nature a slave to the law of sin. . . . The sinful mind is hostile to God. It does not submit to God's law, nor can it do so.

Romans 7:7, 12, 14, 16, 22, 25b; 8:7

For what the law was powerless to do in that it was weakened by the sinful nature, God did by sending his own Son in the likeness of sinful man to be a sin offering. And so he condemned sin in sinful man, in order that the righteous requirements of the law might be fully met in us, who do not live according to the sinful nature but according to the Spirit.

Romans 8:3–4

For the goal at which the *Torah* aims is the Messiah, who offers righteousness to everyone who trusts.

Romans 10:4 JNT
(note that this verse was cited, above, from the NIV)

Let no debt remain outstanding, except the continuing debt to love one another, for he who loves his fellowman has fulfilled the law. . . . Love does no harm to its neighbor. Therefore love is the fulfillment of the law.

Romans 13:8, 10

Do I say this merely from a human point of view? Doesn't the Law say the same thing? For it is written in the Law of Moses . . .

1 Corinthians 9:8–9b

Is the law, therefore, opposed to the promises of God? Absolutely not! For if a law had been given that could impart life, then righteousness would certainly have come by the law.

Galatians 3:21

We know that the law is good if one uses it properly.

1 Timothy 1:8

Yes, the same man who had such harsh things to say about the Law—at least, at first glance—could also say that circumcision was of great value, specifically because the Word of God was entrusted to the Jewish people, that faith upholds (or, establishes) the Law, that the Law "is holy, and the commandment is holy, righteous and good," and that the Law "is spiritual." And Paul himself could say that he delighted in the Law in his inner being (indeed, in his mind, he was a slave to it—meaning, totally captive to its goals and commands), and that through the Spirit, believers now live out the righteous requirements of the Law. He even said that becoming righteous through the Messiah Jesus was the goal to which the Law pointed (this is the way a number of top scholars understand Rom. 10:4).[453]

Not only so, but the Book of Acts consistently portrays Paul (or, Saul, which was his Hebrew name) as an observant, Torah-honoring Jew. He is introduced in Acts 7:58–8:1 as a young (obviously Jewish) man who gave approval to the martyrdom of Stephen, another Jewish disciple of Yeshua. The other Jews who stoned Stephen laid their clothes at Saul's feet. Acts 8:3 then reads, "But Saul began to destroy the [community of believers]. Going from house to house, he dragged off men and women and put them in prison." This was a young zealot with flaming hatred for this new Jewish sect, and he was doing everything in his power to wipe it out, until he had a radical, life-changing encounter with the risen Messiah:

> Meanwhile, Saul was still breathing out murderous threats against the Lord's disciples. He went to the high priest and asked him for letters to the synagogues in Damascus, so that if he found any there who belonged to the Way, whether men or women, he might take them as prisoners to Jerusalem. As he neared Damascus on his journey, suddenly a light from heaven flashed around him. He fell to the ground and heard a voice say to him, "Saul, Saul, why do you persecute me?"
> "Who are you, Lord?" Saul asked.
> "I am Jesus, whom you are persecuting," he replied. "Now get up and go into the city, and you will be told what you must do."
>
> Acts 9:1–6

As related years later by Saul/Paul to a large Jewish audience in Jerusalem:

> I am a Jew, born in Tarsus of Cilicia, but brought up in this city. Under Gamaliel [who was the leading Pharisaic authority of his day] I was thoroughly trained in the law of our fathers and was just as zealous for God as any of you are today. I persecuted the followers of this Way to their death, arresting both men and women and throwing them into prison, as also the high priest and all the Council can testify. I even obtained letters from them to their brothers in Damascus, and went there to bring these people as prisoners to Jerusalem to be punished.
>
> Acts 22:3–5 (after this, Paul relates what happened when Jesus appeared to him)

Similarly, speaking to King Agrippa, before whom he was being accused by other Jews, he said:

> The Jews all know the way I have lived ever since I was a child, from the beginning of my life in my own country, and also in Jerusalem. They have known me for a long time and can testify, if they are willing, that according to the strictest sect of our religion, I lived as a Pharisee. And now it is because of my hope in what God has promised our fathers that I am on trial today. This is the promise our twelve tribes are hoping to see fulfilled as they earnestly serve God day and night. O king, it is because of this hope that the Jews are accusing me.
>
> Acts 26:4–7

And in the last chapter of Acts, he said to the Jewish leaders in Rome, "My brothers, although I have done nothing against our people or against the customs of our ancestors, I was arrested in Jerusalem and handed over to the Romans" (Acts 28:17). Was he only referring to the commotion in the Temple or was he referring to his whole life? The latter would make better sense, given the broad nature of his statement.

In his speech to Agrippa, Paul states clearly that he was a Jew of the Jews, a fact that he claims was well-known to his contemporaries. (Common sense would tell you someone would not make such public claims before a hostile audience unless that very audience knew that these parts of his story were true. This part was not in dispute; what *was* in dispute was his testimony about Yeshua, since those accusing him were not believers.) And notice carefully his opening statement: "The Jews all know the way I have lived ever since I was a child"—meaning, this is still the way I live! We will return to this shortly, but let's look at one more autobiographical account. Here is how Paul relates the story of his own experience and background to the Gentile believers in Galatia:

> For you have heard of my previous way of life in Judaism, how intensely I persecuted the church of God and tried to destroy it. I was advancing in Judaism beyond many Jews of my own age and was extremely zealous for the traditions of my fathers. But when God, who set me apart from birth and called me by his grace, was pleased to reveal his Son in me so that I might preach him among the Gentiles, I did not consult any man, nor did I go up to Jerusalem to see those who were apostles before I was, but I went immediately into Arabia and later returned to Damascus.
>
> Galatians 1:13–17

It is clear, then, that Paul had a life-transforming experience when he had a personal encounter with Yeshua. But how did he continue to live thereafter? The first thing he did was begin to preach in the synagogues, meaning, he preached as a Jew preaching to other Jews:

> And immediately he began preaching about Jesus in the synagogues, saying, "He is indeed the Son of God!"
>
> All who heard him were amazed. "Isn't this the same man who persecuted Jesus' followers with such devastation in Jerusalem?" they asked. "And we understand that he came here to arrest them and take them in chains to the leading priests."
>
> Saul's preaching became more and more powerful, and the Jews in Damascus couldn't refute his proofs that Jesus was indeed the Messiah.
>
> Acts 9:20–22 NLT

This was his regular pattern from city to city. If there was a synagogue, he would go there first and look for opportunities to speak (see, e.g., Acts 14:1, "At Iconium Paul and Barnabas went as usual into the Jewish synagogue. There they spoke so effectively that a great number of Jews and Gentiles believed"; in Philippi, "every Sabbath he reasoned in the synagogue, trying to persuade Jews and Greeks," Acts 18:4). Acts 13 provides further insight into Paul's lifestyle:

> From Paphos, Paul and his companions sailed to Perga in Pamphylia, where John left them to return to Jerusalem. From Perga they went on to Pisidian Antioch. On the Sabbath they entered the synagogue and sat down. After the reading from the Law and the Prophets, the synagogue rulers sent word to them, saying, "Brothers, if you have a message of encouragement for the people, please speak."
>
> Acts 13:13–15

Obviously, Paul and his companions were outwardly identifiable as Jews, otherwise they would not have been recognized as Jews, let alone invited to speak.[454] Paul's whole message presupposed his Jewishness (see lines such as, "We tell you the good news: What God promised *our fathers* he has fulfilled *for us, their children*, by raising up Jesus," Acts 13:32–33a).

Another important insight into Paul's lifestyle is found in Acts 18:18, which states that, "Paul stayed on in Corinth for some time. Then he left the brothers and sailed for Syria, accompanied by Priscilla and Aquila. Before he sailed, he had his hair cut off at Cenchrea because of a vow he had taken." Yes, Paul the apostle was still a Torah-practicing Jew! Several years later, when accusations began to surface against him to the effect that he taught Jews to turn away from Moses, Acts records the following account. Please take a moment to read it carefully:

> When we arrived at Jerusalem, the brothers received us warmly. The next day Paul and the rest of us went to see James, and all the elders were present. Paul greeted them and reported in detail what God had done among the Gentiles through his ministry.
>
> When they heard this, they praised God. Then they said to Paul: "You see, brother, how many thousands of Jews have believed, and all of them are zealous for the law. They have been informed that you teach all the Jews who live among the Gentiles to turn away from Moses, telling them not to circumcise their children or live according to our customs. What shall we do? They will certainly hear that you have come, so do what we tell you. There are four men with us who have made a vow. Take these men, join in their purification rites and pay their expenses, so that they

can have their heads shaved. Then everybody will know there is no truth in these reports about you, but that you yourself are living in obedience to the law. As for the Gentile believers, we have written to them our decision that they should abstain from food sacrificed to idols, from blood, from the meat of strangled animals and from sexual immorality."

The next day Paul took the men and purified himself along with them. Then he went to the temple to give notice of the date when the days of purification would end and the offering would be made for each of them.

Acts 21:18–26

Because Paul had been so successful in taking the message of the Messiah to the Gentiles, accusations arose that he taught "all the Jews who live among the Gentiles to turn away from Moses, telling them not to circumcise their children or live according to our customs" (Acts 21:21). But this was a totally false charge, which is why Paul did not hesitate to comply with the request to join in the purification rites of the Temple. (Remember: We just read that, without any outside constraint whatsoever, he shaved his head because of a vow in Acts 18.)

Acts 15 is also of great importance to our overall understanding of the issue of Paul and the Law, since the issue there was whether Gentile believers would be required to be circumcised and obey the Torah, a position that was ultimately rejected by the Messianic Jewish leadership, with clear input from Paul. But no one thought of asking whether it was fitting for *Jewish* followers of Yeshua to continue to keep the Torah. That was taken for granted!

To repeat: Paul continued to live as a Torah-observant Jew, even though his primary mission was to take the Good News to the Gentiles. This was his testimony before the Sanhedrin, the most prestigious body of Jewish leaders of his day, and one that was composed of Sadducees and Pharisees: He "looked straight at the Sanhedrin and said, 'My brothers, I have fulfilled my duty to God in all good conscience to this day'" (Acts 23:1)—a comment that earned him a slap on the face by the order of the high priest. Yet it was a comment he could make in good conscience, despite their objection to it. (Obviously, because of his faith in Yeshua, the high priest took exception to Paul's words.) What follows next is even more amazing:

Then Paul, knowing that some of them were Sadducees and the others Pharisees, called out in the Sanhedrin, "My brothers, I am a Pharisee, the son of a Pharisee. I stand on trial because of my hope in the resurrection of the dead." When he said this, a dispute broke out between the Pharisees and the Sadducees, and the assembly was divided. (The Sadducees say that there is no resurrection, and that there are neither angels nor spirits, but the Pharisees acknowledge them all.)

> There was a great uproar, and some of the teachers of the law who were Pharisees stood up and argued vigorously. "We find nothing wrong with this man," they said. "What if a spirit or an angel has spoken to him?"
>
> Acts 23:6–9

Was this a shrewd political tactic designed to expose the divided state of the Sanhedrin? Certainly. But was Paul speaking the truth about himself? In light of the consistent testimony throughout the rest of Acts, the answer is, Yes, he was. He still identified himself as a Pharisee, and at the very least, he still identified himself as a Torah-observant Jew.[455]

Since we are using the New Testament as our authority—in other words, What does the New Testament tell us about Paul and his message?—this testimony must be taken quite seriously, serving as the template through which all his other statements must be evaluated. Having laid this foundation, we will now provide an overview of Paul's theology of the Law, not seeking to interact with all possible interpretations, but seeking to present a plausible reading of his words in light of the testimony of Acts. You might differ with these interpretations, but at the least, you will see that they are plausible, even if they challenge some of your thinking (which, of course, can be healthy for any of us who love the truth).

The first question we should ask is, To whom was Paul writing? In the case of Galatians, his audience was entirely Gentile, and the problem he faced was that some teachers had negatively influenced the believers there, telling them that in order to be fully pleasing to God, they had to become circumcised and obey the Law.[456] Faith in Jesus was not enough. New life in the Messiah was not enough. They needed to be circumcised! To Paul, this was a complete denial of the gospel message, a falling from grace, a striving after the flesh (literally and figuratively), a decided step backwards, not forwards. And so he asks them,

> You foolish Galatians! Who has bewitched you? Before your very eyes Jesus Christ was clearly portrayed as crucified. I would like to learn just one thing from you: Did you receive the Spirit by observing the law, or by believing what you heard? Are you so foolish? After beginning with the Spirit, are you now trying to attain your goal by human effort? Have you suffered so much for nothing—if it really was for nothing? Does God give you his Spirit and work miracles among you because you observe the law, or because you believe what you heard?
>
> Galatians 3:1–5

While a traditional Jew might struggle with some of these concepts, put in their proper context—especially in light of Messiah's work of redemption—they make perfect sense and are not an attack on the Torah itself. Against this backdrop, we can also understand verses such as, "For in [Messiah] Jesus neither circumcision nor uncircumcision has any value. The only thing that counts is faith expressing itself through love. . . . Neither circumcision nor uncircumcision means anything; what counts is a new creation" (Gal. 5:6; 6:15; we'll look at 1 Cor. 7:17 shortly). In other words, what matters is being a new creation in the Messiah, not being Jewish or Gentile (or, more specifically, becoming circumcised). Whether you are circumcised and in right relationship with God through the Messiah or whether you are uncircumcised and in right relationship with God through the Messiah, it's all the same. This would be like saying to a Christian audience, "Being Methodist or Baptist or Presbyterian is meaningless. What matters is that you love the Lord." But he was not telling Jewish believers in Yeshua not to circumcise their children or to abandon the Law, a subject that had no relationship to his warnings to the Gentile believers in Galatia.

To explain further, let's say that black people were the chosen ones and that white people were left out, until the black redeemer came and opened the door for everyone to be included in God's family, to the great joy of the white people. (In this analogy, Paul is black and the Galatians are white.) Now let's say that some black teachers came to the white Galatians believers, all of whom had been forgiven and transformed by putting their faith in the redeemer, and these teachers said to the Galatians, "Unless you become black you are not really redeemed"—as a result of which, these white believers started tanning themselves day and night and trying to find ways to blacken their skin. Can you imagine how outraged Paul would be, especially as a black man who had devoted his life to sharing the good news with the whites? You can easily picture him saying, "Being black or white is meaningless! What matters is being a new creation in the Messiah." That's exactly what was happening with the Galatians, and Paul would not stand for it, not for a moment. But who would conclude from this analogy that Paul was now telling blacks to become white or to cast off their history or law? One does not follow from the other.

Further support for this view comes from: (1) Acts 21:20–26 (cited above), where Paul went out of his way to refute the false rumor that he taught "all the Jews who live among the Gentiles to turn away from Moses, *telling them not to circumcise their children* or live according to our customs" (my emphasis). This was simply not true! Surely, in light of his strong words to the Galatians (see esp. Gal. 1:6–10), under no circumstances would he have gone along with this show just to keep the peace unless, in fact, the rumors were false. Otherwise he would have been backing the very position he was seeking to dismantle in Galatia. (2) In 1 Corinthians 7:17–18 he writes that "each one should retain the place in life that the Lord assigned to him and to which God has called him. This is the rule I lay down in all the [congregations]. Was a man already circumcised when he was called? He should not become uncircumcised. Was a man uncircumcised when he was called? He should not be circumcised." In other words, let Jewish believers remain Jewish and let Gentile believers remain Gentile. In terms of being in right relationship with God, neither one is the determining factor, as stated in the next verse: "Circumcision is nothing and uncircumcision is nothing. Keeping God's commands is what counts" (7:19). In saying this, however, he does *not* mean that circumcision was *not* commanded by God in the Torah or was no longer a commandment for Jews. Rather, he means that being Jewish or Gentile is not the issue. The issue is obedience to God's commands. Is this such a heretical view? As he expressed it in Romans 2:25, "Circumcision has value if you observe the law, but if you break the law, you have become as though you had not been circumcised." Notice also that Paul had Timothy circumcised, apparently because his mother was Jewish (although his father was Greek), but he refused to have Titus circumcised, apparently because neither of his parents were Jews (see Acts 16:1–3; Gal. 2:1–5).[457] (3) In Romans 3:1, after explaining that what God really wants is circumcision of the heart (cf. Deut. 10:16; 30:6; Jer. 4:4), Paul asks, "What advantage, then, is there in being a Jew, or what value is there in circumcision?" His answer is very strong: "Much in every way! First of all, they have been entrusted with the very words of God" (Rom. 3:2). So then, there was a high privilege that came with being a circumcised Jew, namely, that the very words of God—meaning the Scriptures—had been entrusted to that people. But did being circumcised guarantee salvation or secure right standing with God? Absolutely not, and this was one of Paul's issues as well: Any sense of ethnic or spiritual superiority was dangerous and destructive, a theme to which we will return shortly.

Recognizing the audience to whom Paul was writing helps us to understand Colossians 2:16–17, "Therefore do not let anyone judge you by what you eat or drink, or with regard to a religious festival, a New Moon celebration or a Sabbath day. These are a shadow of the things that were to come; the reality, however, is found in Christ." Commentators point out that there were false teachers who were putting pressure on the Gentile believers in Colosse to observe the new moons and Sabbaths, as well as, possibly, the Torah's dietary laws. In keeping with this theology, Paul urged them not to succumb to this pressure, recognizing that the biblical calendar, including even the Sabbath, which had never been incumbent on the Gentiles, did not contain the full reality of God's revelation in the Messiah but was rather a shadow of that which was to come. Even the concept of the Sabbath being a foretaste of that which was to come during the Messianic kingdom—the one-thousand-year Sabbath!—would not necessarily have been an alien concept to Paul as a Jew. But once again, the audience being addressed is key, and it should be noted that, in the case of the Colossians, there were other issues involved, as pointed out by commentator Peter T. O'Brien:

> For Israel the keeping of these holy days was evidence of obedience to God's law and a sign of her election among the nations. At Colossae, however, the sacred days were to be kept for the sake of the "elemental spirits of the universe," [see Col 2:8] those astral powers who directed the course of the stars and regulated the order of the calendar. So Paul is not condemning the use of sacred days or seasons or such; it is the wrong motive involved when the observance of these days is bound up with the recognition of the elemental spirits.[458]

Context and background are key! In keeping with this principle, differing views on the identity of Paul's audience at Rome have produced differing interpretations of his letter to the Romans. So, if he was writing to believing Jews who lived alongside believing Gentiles, then verses such as Romans 14:5–6a are more readily understood: "One man considers one day more sacred than another [theoretically, a Jewish follower of Yeshua]; another man considers every day alike [theoretically, a Gentile follower of Yeshua]. Each one should be fully convinced in his own mind. He who regards one day as special, does so to the Lord." In contrast, if he was writing only to Jewish believers—which, of course, no one believes he was—then a statement such as this would seem to be more of a direct attack on the Law. (Again, I state this only to illustrate how changing the potential recipients completely changes the interpretation.) On the other hand, the radical new proposal put forth by Dr. Mark D. Nanos, turns things completely around, as he suggests that the Gentile believers were the minority community, still meeting in the synagogues along with Jews who did not believe in Yeshua. Hence, those "weak" in faith, which in Romans 14 referred to those who were more scrupulous in their eating habits (see 14:1–4), were the Jews who did not believe in Yeshua rather than the Jews who did believe in Yeshua.[459]

This being said, there are other statements in Paul's letters that seem to speak against the Torah itself such as Ephesians 2:15, where Paul apparently stated quite bluntly that Jesus abolished "in his flesh the law with its commandments and regulations." First, let's look at the overall point he was making about Jews and Gentiles coming together in the Messiah. Please take a moment to read the whole passage:

> Therefore, remember that formerly you who are Gentiles by birth and called "uncircumcised" by those who call themselves "the circumcision" (that done in the body by the hands of men)—remember that at that time you were separate from Christ, excluded from citizenship in Israel and foreigners to the covenants of the promise, without hope and without God in the world. But now in Christ Jesus you who once were far away have been brought near through the blood of Christ.
>
> For he himself is our peace, who has made the two one and has destroyed the barrier, the dividing wall of hostility, by abolishing in his flesh the law with its commandments and regulations. His purpose was to create in himself one new man out of the two, thus making peace, and in this one body to reconcile both of them to God through the cross, by which he put to death their hostility. He came and preached peace to you who were far away and peace to those who were near. For through him we both have access to the Father by one Spirit.
>
> Consequently, you are no longer foreigners and aliens, but fellow citizens with God's people and members of God's household, built on the foundation of the apostles and prophets, with Christ Jesus himself as the chief cornerstone. In him the whole building is joined together and rises to become a holy temple in the Lord. And in him you too are being built together to become a dwelling in which God lives by his Spirit.
>
> Ephesians 2:11–22

I will let professor Craig Keener give the relevant background:

2:11–13. In ancient Jewish beliefs, non-Jews could never participate in the fullness of the covenant without circumcision, although they could be saved by keeping some basic commandments. To be circumcised was to be grafted into the community of Israel, to become part of God's covenant people.

2:14–16. Paul writes this letter from prison because he has been falsely charged with taking a non-Jew inside the temple in Jerusalem (Acts 21:28). Taking a non-Jew beyond a particular dividing point in the temple was such an important breach of Jewish law that the Romans even permitted Jewish leaders to execute violators of this law. Paul's readers in Ephesus and Asia undoubtedly know why Paul is in prison (Acts 21:27, 29); thus for them, as well as for Paul, there can be no greater symbol of the barrier between Jew and non-Jew than "the dividing wall" of verse 14. But Paul says that this dividing wall is shattered in Christ. "He is our peace" might (but need not) reflect the Hebrew of Micah 5:5.

2:17–18. Isaiah 57:19 could be understood as referring to the scattered seed of Israel as those "who were far away," but not long before this passage God had promised that his house would be for foreigners too (Is 56:3–8). This text thus fittingly expresses Paul's point concerning the unity of Jew and Gentile in the new temple (cf. also Acts 2:39).

2:19–22. In the Old Testament, the only division in the temple was between priests and laity, but by Paul's day architects had added barriers for non-Jews and for women (contrast 1 Kings 8:41–43); Paul says these barriers are abolished in God's true, spiritual temple. Some other Jewish writers spoke of God's people as his temple, but only Paul and other early Christians recognized that this new temple included non-Jews. (Paul derived the image of Christ as the cornerstone from Ps 118:22, probably via Jesus' teaching; see comment on Mk 11:10.)

Around the time Paul was writing these words, arguing for racial unity in Christ, Jews and Syrians were massacring each other in the streets of Caesarea, a city where he had been not long before (Acts 23:23). Here Paul does not simply mimic a common stand against racism in his culture; he condemns racism and segregation of a religious institution even though he has to challenge his culture to do so.[460]

So, the major issue here was the breaking down of the wall of spiritual separation between Jew and Gentile and the abolishing of the enmity that kept them apart. That is Paul's primary point. But does he state in Ephesians 2:15 that Jesus actually abolished the Law? It is possible to read the verse like that, but it is also problematic since Paul himself said that faith did *not* nullify the Law (Rom. 3:31, quoted above), that he himself kept the Law, and that he was a loyal follower of Jesus (see 5.26), who stated plainly that he did not come to abolish the Law but to fulfill it. David Stern also argues that what was abolished was the enmity caused by human reaction to Torah law, rendering Ephesians 2:15a with "by destroying in his own body the enmity occasioned by the Torah, with its commands set forth in the form of ordinances" (JNT). Compare also the literal rendering of Ephesians 2:14–16 by Dan Gruber (his emphasis throughout):

> For he is our peace, who made both one and broke down the middle wall of the fence, **having annulled in his flesh the enmity of the law** of commandments in decrees, that he might create one new man, making peace; and might reconcile both in one body to God through the cross, **having slain the enmity by it**.[461]

The phrase translated literally "the law of the commandments in decrees,"[462] is also very odd and found only here in the entire New Testament, and some have taken it to refer to human extensions of the Torah or to some form of legalism, meaning that Jesus struck at the heart of the human system that was erected as an extension of Torah law, a system that put up a wall of hostility between Jew and Gentile.[463] Could *that* be what Paul was saying here? And how would it follow that by *abolishing the Torah* Jesus brought Jew and Gentile together and removed the hatred that separated them? Rather, the hatred would be removed by abolishing the human laws and commandments that grew out of the Torah, the laws that resulted in a literal wall at the Temple with the inscription that any Gentile who passed that wall would be put to death. This certainly makes good sense.

Consider also that, to this day, religious Jews in their daily prayer and practice constantly remind themselves that they have been specially chosen by God to be separated from the nations. And, although Paul was not negating Israel's special calling and role (see esp. Rom. 11:11–29), he *was* combating the spiritual separation between Jew and Gentile, stating that the wall of partition, erected through ordinances and decrees growing out of the Torah, had been torn down by the Messiah. In contrast, among traditional Jews, those ordinances of separation have only grown and increased through the centuries, to this very day, even if they have not always resulted in enmity between Jew and Gentile.

This being said, there were definitely issues that Paul had with the Torah itself, primarily because of human weakness—in other words, the problems were on our end, not God's—just as the Lord told Israel in Jeremiah 31:31–34 that he would make a new covenant with them *because they broke the Sinai covenant*. As explained in Hebrews 8:7–8, "For if there had been nothing wrong with that first covenant, no place would have been sought for another. But God found fault with the people" and declared that he would make a new covenant. So, what was wrong with the first covenant was that it depended on the people's obedience—and they were hardly obedient through the centuries.

Paul takes this up further and explains that, as a consequence of the Law's holiness and people's sinfulness, the Law produced wrath and judgment since it revealed sin rather than enabled obedience. For Paul, that's why the Messiah came into the world: to satisfy the Law's demands and enable us to fulfill the righteous requirements of the Law. And that process begins with us being justified by faith, which Paul also finds as a fundamental Torah truth (Rom. 1:16–17, citing Gen. 15:6 and Hab. 2:4; see also Gal. 3:11).[464]

To be sure, Paul has often come under attack for his statements in Galatians 3:10 and 3:13, "All who rely on observing the law are under a curse, for it is written: 'Cursed is everyone who does not continue to do everything written in the Book of the Law.' . . . [Messiah] redeemed us from the curse of the law by becoming a curse for us, for it is written: 'Cursed is everyone who is hung on a tree.'" (Paul cited Deut. 27:26 from the LXX in 3:10 and Deut. 21:23 in 3:13.)[465] Notice, however, that Paul is not calling the Law itself a cursed thing. God forbid! Rather, he is stating that, since the Law punished disobedience with a curse, and since none of us completely obeys the Law, those "who rely on observing the law are under a curse." Elsewhere Paul wrote that "it is those who obey the law who will be declared righteous," concluding, however, that, "Jews and Gentiles alike are all under sin" (Rom. 3:9b), and that, "whatever the law says, it says to those who are under the law, so that every mouth may be silenced and the whole world held accountable to God. Therefore no one will be declared righteous in his sight by observing the law; rather, through the law we become conscious of sin" (Rom. 3:19b–20).

I am aware, of course, that concepts such as these may be difficult for a traditional Jew to grasp, accustomed as he is to emphasizing the beauty and perfection of the Torah, just as the psalmist did (see, e.g., Psalms 19 and 119). Paul's point, however, is that the beauty and perfection of the Torah are the very things used by God to reveal our sinfulness and our need for grace and mercy, just as Jacob (James) later wrote that God's Word is like a mirror that shows us our true condition (James 1:22–25).

You might say, "But God never demanded perfect obedience from us, understanding that we would always fall short of his standards," and to some extent, that is true. God did pronounce people "righteous" in the Scriptures without suggesting that they were absolutely perfect (see, e.g., Gen. 6:9; Ps. 1:5–6; Prov. 2:20; and throughout Psalms and Proverbs), while the New Testament records that Zechariah and Elizabeth, the parents of John the Immerser, were "upright in the sight of God, observing all the Lord's commandments and regulations blamelessly" (Luke 1:6). In fact, Paul himself states that, before he became a believer in the Messiah, he lived this same way: "as to the righteousness which is in the Law, found blameless" (Phil. 3:6b NASB). Obviously Paul understood what it meant to be righteous according to the Law—on a certain level. But he also understood that, due to the sinful tendencies of Israel (not to mention the whole human race), the Law ultimately exposed sin and brought judgment, and this was the pattern throughout Israelite and Jewish history (see vol. 1, 103–6). To test out the accuracy of this statement, read through all of Deuteronomy 28, containing God's words of blessings and curses, and then ask yourself, "Throughout Jewish history, what is the primary national pattern we can observe, divine blessing or divine judgment?" The answer, although painful, is obvious, contradicting the claim made in b. Avod Zar 3a, put on the lips of God, that Israel (through different righteous individuals) observed the entire Torah and was thereby justified.[466]

Pauline scholar Andrew Das also points out that many scholars have failed to recognize that some Jewish literature roughly contemporary with Paul also emphasized the need to walk in perfect obedience before the Lord, stating that "Paul too finds the Law's demands for perfect obedience problematic."[467] While it is true that Rabbinic Judaism never separated God's mercy and forgiveness from his requirements to obey his laws and decrees, Paul could point to the biblical record to support his view that we all fall short (see, e.g., Gen. 8:21; Prov. 20:9; Isa. 53:6; 1 Kings 8:46; Ps. 143:2; Eccles. 7:20; Isa. 64:6), using the history of Israel and Judah to underscore his argument: Our pattern as a people has been to find ourselves under divine judgment because of our failure to adhere to God's Law. And in the centuries since Paul wrote, things have not gotten better for us on a national level, as we have suffered the lasting destruction of the Temple and many terrible scatterings and expulsions, at least some of which have to be understood as acts of judgment. To this day, there has not been a generation among us that has proved righteous—indeed, one Talmudic tradition teaches that if all Israel observed the Sabbath for a single week, the Messiah would be revealed—and there is no indication that things will change if we are left to ourselves. Yet the standards of the Jewish people are often higher than the standards of the rest of the world, especially of those who are outside of Jesus the Messiah, which means that *everybody* is in need of grace and mercy.

Traditional Jews therefore await the advent of the Messiah, increasingly putting their trust in Torah study and attempts to obey the Law, looking forward to the day when the Messiah will lead all Israel into perfect obedience and ultimately bring worldwide peace. Paul recognized that the Messiah already came and did what the Law could not do, making the way for all people—both Jew and Gentile—to receive complete forgiveness of sins and a new heart through Yeshua. By this, they are declared righteous before God by faith (in accordance with Gen. 15:6) and thereby receive empowerment to keep the righteous requirements of the Law (Rom. 8:1–4).

Does this mean, then, that Paul taught Torah-observing Jews to cast off the Law now that Messiah had come? Not at all. Rather, he taught his Jewish people that they should no longer depend on the law for their justification and righteousness, but trust rather in the Messiah's perfect life and atoning death, which puts an end to human boasting and to all forms of self-righteousness:

> Where, then, is boasting? It is excluded. On what principle? On that of observing the law? No, but on that of faith. For we maintain that a man is justified by faith apart from observing the law. Is God the God of Jews only? Is he not the God of Gentiles too? Yes, of Gentiles too, since there is only one God, who will justify the circumcised by faith and the uncircumcised through that same faith. Do we, then, nullify the law by this faith? Not at all! Rather, we uphold the law.
>
> Romans 3:27–31

And that means that our right standing with God must be seen as a gift rather than something earned:

> Now when a man works, his wages are not credited to him as a gift, but as an obligation. However, to the man who does not work but trusts God who justifies the wicked, his faith is credited as righteousness. David says the same thing when he speaks of the blessedness of the man to whom God credits righteousness apart from works:
>
> > Blessed are they
> > whose transgressions are forgiven,
> > whose sins are covered.
> > Blessed is the man
> > whose sin the Lord will never count against him.
>
> Romans 4:4–8, citing Psalm 32:1–2

A similar concept can be found in Psalm 130:

> O Lord, hear my voice.
> Let your ears be attentive
> to my cry for mercy.
>
> If you, O Lord, kept a record of sins,
> O Lord, who could stand?
> But with you there is forgiveness;
> therefore you are feared. . . .
>
> O Israel, put your hope in the Lord,
> for with the Lord is unfailing love
> and with him is full redemption.

> He himself will redeem Israel
> from all their sins.
>
> Psalm 130:2–4, 7–8

Paul saw verses such as these as fulfilled in Jesus, putting obedience to the Torah into proper perspective. As Augustine wrote: "Law was given that grace might be sought, grace was given that the law might be fulfilled."[468] It is in this light that we should also understand Romans 6:14, "For sin shall not be your master, because you are not under law, but under grace," as well as, possibly, Romans 10:4: "For Christ is the end of the law as a means of righteousness for all who believe" (as translated by James D. G. Dunn); "For Christ is the culmination of the law, so that there might be righteousness for everyone who believes" (as translated by Douglas Moo; see further, below).

That is why Paul wrote to the Galatians, "I do not set aside the grace of God, for if righteousness could be gained through the law, [Messiah] died for nothing! . . . Is the law, therefore, opposed to the promises of God? Absolutely not! For if a law had been given that could impart life, then righteousness would certainly have come by the law" (Gal. 2:21; 3:21).[469] How much more does this apply to the Gentile world, which did not even have the benefit of the Torah!

You say, "But all this sounds *very* different than traditional Judaism."

Exactly. It *is* different than traditional Judaism, but what else would you expect? Traditional Judaism has been building on both the written Word and human traditions for the last two thousand years, still longing for the coming of the Messiah. The New Testament faith has been building on the fact that the Messiah came two thousand years ago in accordance with the Scriptures. Of course the perspective is different. The key question, as always, comes back to this: Is Yeshua the promised Messiah? If so, Paul's perspective makes sense. If not, it is irrelevant.

It is in this light that we must understand other statements in Paul's writings, such as Galatians 3:23–25:

> Before this faith came, we were held prisoners by the law, locked up until faith should be revealed. So the law was put in charge to lead us to [Messiah] that we might be justified by faith. Now that faith has come, we are no longer under the supervision of the law.

Or, as rendered in the New Living Translation:

Until faith in Christ was shown to us as the way of becoming right with God, we were guarded by the law. We were kept in protective custody, so to speak, until we could put our faith in the coming Savior.

Let me put it another way. The law was our guardian and teacher to lead us until Christ came. So now, through faith in Christ, we are made right with God. But now that faith in Christ has come, we no longer need the law as our guardian.

Now, we must remember that (1) Paul himself remained Torah-observant; (2) in his letters he quoted the Torah to support his teaching (e.g., 1 Cor. 9:9; 1 Tim. 5:18, both citing Deut. 25:4); and (3) he said that faith established the Law rather than nullified it (Rom. 3:31). So then, he was not saying here that the Law had been abrogated. Instead, he was saying that our relationship to the Torah had changed and that we were no longer "under the Law," which should be understood to include: (1) We are no longer under the Law as a means of justification; (2) we are no longer under the condemnation of the Law; and (3) we are no longer under the supervision of the Law to bring us to the Messiah. That being said, the Torah remains a gift from God to his people, but not with the sense of binding obligation with the penalty of death for disobedience.

It is in this light that we should also interpret Paul's statement that "through the law I died to the law so that I might live for God" (Gal. 2:19), which is further explained by Paul's words in Romans 7:11, "For sin, seizing the opportunity afforded by the commandment, deceived me, and through the commandment put me to death," and so, "by dying to what once bound us, we have been released from the law so that we serve in the new way of the Spirit, and not in the old way of the written code" (Rom. 7:11, 6).

It is true that there are Messianic Jewish scholars, along with traditional Christian scholars, who understand Paul's primary issue to be with *legalism* rather than with the Torah itself. In keeping with this, some commentators take Paul's expression "the works of the law" to refer to legalism (see Rom. 3:20, 28; Gal. 2:16; 3:2, 5, 10, rendered in the NIV with "observing the law"), since the Greek language did not have a specific term for "legalism."[470] More broadly, David Stern has identified this concept in a number of the passages just cited, which he translates accordingly: "legalistic observance of Torah commands" (Rom. 3:20 JNT); "you are not under legalism" (Rom. 6:14 JNT); "the old way of outwardly following the letter of the law" (Rom. 7:6 JNT); "For it was through letting the *Torah* speak for itself that I died to its traditional legalistic interpretation so that I might live in a direct relationship with

God" (Gal. 2:19 JNT); "in subjection to the system which results from perverting the *Torah* into legalism" (Gal. 3:23 JNT).

In keeping with this view, Stern explains that when Paul speaks of "being dead to the Torah" in Romans 7 he refers to three aspects of the Torah: "(1) its capacity to stir up sin in him (vv. 5–14), (2) its capacity to produce irremediable guilt feelings (vv. 15–25), and (3) its penalties, punishments and curses (8:1–4)."[471] Similarly, he interprets Galatians 3:25 to mean, "Therefore, **now that the time for this** peerless example of **trusting faithfulness** which Yeshua displayed **has come**, which same trusting faithfulness we now have too because we are united with him (v. 26), **we** Jews **are no longer under** legalism of any sort, no longer **under a custodian**."[472] The argument, then, according to Paul's analogy in Romans 7:1–4 of the woman being freed from the law of marriage when her husband dies, would be as follows: We were previously married to our sinful nature; through the death of Jesus, our sinful nature died; now, in accordance with the Law, we are united with a new husband, even the Lord, and through this new union, we can now serve God and keep his commandments in the newness of the Spirit.

These interpretations are certainly plausible and, if accepted, point to a far less radical interpretation of Torah by Paul. I will leave that to the reader to decide. What is indisputable is that for Paul, the Law could only go so far in terms of being a vehicle of salvation for the Jewish and Gentile world, functioning rather to reveal our need for the Messiah and to bring us to him so that we could receive forgiveness and a new heart. Paradoxically, even though traditional Judaism would never dream of speaking of the shortcomings of the Torah (or even of the Sinaitic covenant), according to traditional Jewish belief, in the end of this age it will be the Messiah who brings the Jewish people into obedience to the Torah. That is to say, the Torah itself will not function any differently, and, left to ourselves, we would always fall short of its demands. However, by God's gracious intervention through the Messiah, we will turn back to God as a nation—and so, in that sense, it is the Messiah who makes the difference, not the Torah. Paul's view, while more radical than this, also puts its emphasis on the Messiah rather than on the Torah.

Christian scholars often refer to this as a matter of salvation history, and while those scholars sometimes fail to appreciate the continuity between Torah and Gospel,[473] they are right in emphasizing that everything changed with the coming of Jesus the Messiah into the world, and this is now the watershed event through which everything else has to be interpreted.[474]

This is in keeping with the perspective of the Finnish scholar Risto Santala who emphasizes that Paul's view of the Torah must be understood in light of the Messiah's coming. This again reminds us that the central question is not, "What does Paul say about the law?" but rather, "Is Yeshua the Messiah of Israel and the Savior of the world?"

> Here is the heart of the whole problem. *Paul's ideas can only be understood in a "post-Messianic situation."* If the Messiah has already come, all inferences must be drawn *on the basis of a theology of fulfillment.* It would be strange and ungenuine if Paul's thoughts were identical with other rabbis' assertions. . . .
>
> In order for us to understand Paul's "post-Messianic" thinking, which is based on the conviction that the Messiah has already come, there is reason *to quote in a concentrated way some words of the rabbis* which are connected with the future of the Law. . . .
>
> In these traditional sources of Judaism there appear to be *two main emphases.* On the one hand, *in the Messianic era there will be prevalent Messianic interpretation* with emphasis on the *central* message of the Law. . . .
>
> On the other hand, any of the precepts of the Torah which are considered unnecessary in the new situation are "abrogated" and "abolished" (Heb. *bittel*).[475]

In support of this last statement, Santala points out:

> The Talmud also states that *"the commandments will be abolished in the future"* [b. Nid 61b, speaking of certain commandments that will be irrelevant after the resurrection; but this is part of a debate in the Talmud]—the expression *"le-atid lavo"* usually means the Messianic future. . . . The Jewish Professor *Joseph Klausner* explains in his book "The Messianic Idea in Israel" that *"by this is meant naturally that the Torah and commandments lose their significance in the days of the Messiah."*[476]

He then explains what he understands to be Paul's perspective on the Law:

> *The new Messianic status of the Law* in Paul's thought may be expressed in his three central passages: **1.** Romans 10:4 says, *"Christ is the goal of the Law (in Greek "telos") so that there may be righteousness for everyone who believes."* Using the same concept, Paul writes in 1 Tim. 1:5, *"The goal of this command is love, which comes from a pure heart and a good conscience and a sincere faith."*
>
> **2.** Galatians 3:23–25 says, *"Before this faith came, we were held prisoners by the Law, locked up until faith should be revealed. So the Law has become for us an educator to lead us to Christ that we might be justified by faith. Now that faith has come, we are no longer under an educator."* The word 'educator' or 'director' (Gr. *paidagogos*) points to the fact that the Torah's

many "pedagogical" interpretations later lose their significance. Just as
the canes used to support plants or the scaffolding of a building are later
removed, so the *"fence of the Torah"* is meant to be only temporary. In
Jeremiah 31:31–34 God promises to his people that *"in the new covenant"*
he will place *"his Law within them and write it on their hearts."*

   3. But **this will happen only when the Messianic era has dawned**.
Galatians 4:1–5 says that we are *"as minors subject to guardians and trust-
ees until the time set by the father." "But when the time had fully come, God
sent his Son, born of a woman, born under Law, to redeem those under Law,
that we might receive the full rights of sons."*

   Paul's relation to the Law was always based, however, on the fact that,
according to the Bible, *God is holy and demands holiness.* Moses received
from time to time the command: "Be holy because I, the LORD your God,
am holy" (Lev. 11:44, 19:2, 20:26 etc.). It was the Pharisees who emphasized
this holiness. Therefore Paul wrote his hard words: "The wrath of God is
being revealed from heaven against all the godlessness and wickedness
of men . . . trouble and distress for every human being who does evil; first
for the Jew, then for the Greek"(Rom. 1:18; 2:9). "So then, *the Law is holy,
and the commandment is holy, righteous and good"* (Rom. 7:12). The Law
is similarly *"spiritual"* in essence (Rom. 7:14). *"The Law is good if one uses
it lawfully"* (1 Tim. 1:8). Paul was not thus negative in relation to the Law.
It functioned and continues to function as Christ's pedagogue. . . .

   *Paul did not have a negative attitude towards the commandments nor
even towards the Torah.* The Torah only had a determined task *"to guard"*
(Gal. 3:23) and protect the people under the Law until the Messianic era.
In its post-Messianic period the Messianic Law holds sway and the time
of the *"guardian"* is past. *This truth of salvation history also appears in the
interpretation of the Elijah tradition,* with reference to which Professor
Joseph Klausner said that two thousand years of the Torah and two thousand years of "the days of the Messiah" means *"naturally that in the days
of the Messiah the Torah and commandments lose their significance."*[477]

   Again, I leave it to the reader to sort through the issues raised here
by Santala, Stern, and others, also working through some of the studies
cited in the endnotes as well; see also our observations about changes
in the application of the Torah in the Messianic age, above, 5.28.[478] For
the sake of space, however, and recognizing that this is not the place
for a full-length study of Paul and the Torah, I will close with three final
observations.

   First, Paul stood firmly against all forms of ethnic and spiritual exclu-
sivity, and some scholars have seen this as the primary issue Paul had
with the Law. For example, Dunn explains Romans 10:4 as follows:

   The word "end" . . . is probably intended in the primary sense of "termination, cessation." What has been brought to an end by Christ's coming and

work is that stage of God's saving purpose which focused principally on Israel, is the resulting ground of Israel's presumption that God's choice of Israel had Israel as such exclusively in view, is the consequently plausible assumption that God gave the law to Israel as a means for Israel to confirm its special place within God's favor.[479]

Certainly, it is problematic to speak of the "end" of the Law, and Dunn still acknowledges that,

> It is possible that Paul intended "end" here to have also the fuller or further sense of "fulfillment, goal." Israel had after all been specially chosen by God (hence the misunderstanding), but that choice had always been wholly in terms of grace (9:6–13) and always had the extension of that grace to all the nations wholly in view from the first (4:16–18), in which case Christ is the realization of God's final purpose in choosing Israel initially.[480]

On either interpretation, however, it is clear that full access to Israel's God was not to be the sole possession of the Jewish people. Rather, through them—specifically, through the Messiah and his emissaries—the God of Israel was to become the God of all who put their trust in him, without class distinction or special favoritism.

Was this, then, a trap into which many Jewish people had fallen, namely the sense that because they were specially chosen they enjoyed a unique status to which the other peoples could not attain? Is it possible that there was some self-righteousness and even legalistic boasting? Interestingly, when John the Immerser preached at the Jordan River, calling his people to repentance, he did not say a word to the crowds about any claims to ethnic or spiritual superiority, despite the fact that all of them were Jews. Rather, it was only when he saw some of the religious leaders coming to be immersed that he rebuked them, saying, "And do not think you can say to yourselves, 'We have Abraham as our father.' I tell you that out of these stones God can raise up children for Abraham" (Matt. 3:9). It appears that Paul fought a similar battle with some of his people, as evidenced by the account in Acts 22. It was only when Paul spoke of his calling to the Gentiles that the crowd erupted. "The Lord said to me," Paul recounted, "'Go; I will send you far away to the Gentiles.' The crowd listened to Paul until he said this. Then they raised their voices and shouted, 'Rid the earth of him! He's not fit to live!'" (Acts 22:21–22). To this day, the concept that Jews and Gentiles can worship together as "one new man" in the Messiah (Eph. 2:15) is a great stumbling block to our people.[481]

As noted by Cambridge professor Markus Bockmuehl,

Paul gets into trouble not because for him the Gentiles are saved without conversion, nor because of his Noachide halakhah for them. His problem, and his ultimate undoing in Jewish eyes, lies in the attempt to forge a united body of Jewish and Gentile Christians in a fellowship of equals, in which the former continue to live by the whole Torah and the latter merely by the Noachide laws.[482]

Second, Paul clearly emphasized the surpassing greatness of God's new covenant, writing in 2 Corinthians 3:7–11:

He has made us competent as ministers of a new covenant—not of the letter but of the Spirit; for the letter kills, but the Spirit gives life.
Now if the ministry that brought death, which was engraved in letters on stone, came with glory, so that the Israelites could not look steadily at the face of Moses because of its glory, fading though it was, will not the ministry of the Spirit be even more glorious? If the ministry that condemns men is glorious, how much more glorious is the ministry that brings righteousness! For what was glorious has no glory now in comparison with the surpassing glory. And if what was fading away came with glory, how much greater is the glory of that which lasts!

2 Corinthians 3:7–11

Yes, the Sinaitic covenant was glorious, despite the fact that it brought a sentence of death to our people because of our sin. (Without question, the Torah offered us *life*; see Deut. 30:15–16, 19–20; 32:47; cf. also the many positive statements to this effect in Psalms and Proverbs. The problem, as emphasized by Paul, was our failure to live up to the terms of the glorious Sinaitic covenant.) But the new covenant was far more glorious! This is in keeping with the perspective of Hebrews, where the word "better" occurs repeatedly. See, for example, Hebrews 7:22, "Jesus has become the guarantee of a better covenant"; 8:6, "But the ministry Jesus has received is as superior to theirs as the covenant of which he is mediator is superior to the old one, and it is founded on better promises"; 9:23, "It was necessary, then, for the copies of the heavenly things to be purified with these sacrifices, but the heavenly things themselves with better sacrifices than these," referring to Yeshua's sacrifice, which cleansed the heavenly sanctuary; 11:40, "God had planned something better for us so that only together with us would they be made perfect"; 12:24, "the sprinkled blood [of Jesus] that speaks a better word than the blood of Abel" (see also 10:34; 11:4, 16, 35).

And this new and better covenant also brought about changes to the first covenant, specifically in terms of the high priest and the sacrificial system. Speaking of Israel's high priests, Hebrews states, "The former regulation is set aside because it was weak and useless (for the law made nothing perfect), and a better hope is introduced, by which we draw near to God" (7:18–19). Traditional Judaism has developed various ways to make up for the absence of a functioning high priest for more than 1,900 years. Hebrews says that God himself provided a better High Priest!

> Now there have been many of those priests, since death prevented them from continuing in office; but because Jesus lives forever, he has a permanent priesthood. Therefore he is able to save completely those who come to God through him, because he always lives to intercede for them.
>
> Hebrews 7:23–25 (see also 2:17–18; 3:1; 4:14–15; 5:5, 10; 6:20; 7:26–8:2; 9:11–14; Hebrews 7 explains that the biblical justification for this concept is found in Psalm 110)

The same can be said of the sacrificial system, as Hebrews explains:

> The law is only a shadow of the good things that are coming—not the realities themselves. For this reason it can never, by the same sacrifices repeated endlessly year after year, make perfect those who draw near to worship. If it could, would they not have stopped being offered? For the worshipers would have been cleansed once for all, and would no longer have felt guilty for their sins. But those sacrifices are an annual reminder of sins, because it is impossible for the blood of bulls and goats to take away sins.
> Therefore, when [Messiah] came into the world, he said:
>
> "Sacrifice and offering you did not desire,
>   but a body you prepared for me;
> with burnt offerings and sin offerings
>   you were not pleased.
> Then I said, 'Here I am—it is written about me in the scroll—
> I have come to do your will, O God.'"
>
> First he said, "Sacrifices and offerings, burnt offerings and sin offerings you did not desire, nor were you pleased with them" (although the law required them to be made). Then he said, "Here I am, I have come to do your will." He sets aside the first to establish the second. And by that will, we have been made holy through the sacrifice of the body of Jesus [the Messiah] once for all.
>
> Hebrews 10:1–10 (see further above, 5.5; and vol. 3, 4.27)

Naturally, with the absence of the sacrificial system for more than 1,900 years, Rabbinic Judaism has developed various traditions to make up for this lack (see vol. 2, 3.8–3.17 for discussion of a broad range of related topics). Hebrews states that God himself made up for this lack by providing something better, the atoning death of his Son in keeping with the concept that "the death of the righteous atones"—specifically, the death of the high priest atones (see again vol. 2, 3.15).

The revelation, then, of these New Testament authors is that God did not leave us in the dark all these years. Rather, the old was displaced by something better, just as the light of dawn is displaced by the full light of the noonday sun. In that sense too, the Law finds its fulfillment in Yeshua, the Sun of Righteousness, whose light illuminates everything that has come before him. With good reason he said to John, "I am the Root and the Offspring of David, and the bright Morning Star" (Rev. 22:16).[483]

Third, verses such as Isaiah 2:1–4 do not contradict the position articulated here. That is to say, it is not necessary to read Isaiah 2:3 ("The law [torah] will go out from Zion, the word of the LORD from Jerusalem") in traditional Jewish terms as if torah here meant the Pentateuch.[484] If this were true, then the teachings of Paul and Hebrews would be wrong, since they indicate that in certain ways, the Torah's function is subservient to the Messiah and with his coming, he, not the Torah, has become central. Could it be, then, that the future age will turn back to the centrality of the Torah? This would be a misconception since, in the fullness of the Messianic age, it is God and his Anointed One who will be central, rather than the Torah (see, e.g., Isa. 2:4; 11:1–9; Jer. 23:5–6; Ezek. 34:20–31). Moreover, it is clear that in the age to come, changes in our relationship with God will bring about changes in the Law or in our relationship to the Law (see the end of our discussion in 5.28, and cf. also the comments of Santala, cited above). This means that the best understanding of Isaiah 2:3 is that God's teaching will go forth from Zion, as translated in the New Jewish Publication Society Version: "For instruction shall come forth from Zion, the word of the LORD from Jerusalem," since the definite article does *not* appear before the word *torah* here—again, as if to say, *the Torah*, as in "the Pentateuch." In fact, the NJPSV's footnote to the words, "For instruction shall come forth from Zion" explains, "I.e., oracles will be obtainable," while elsewhere in the NJPSV, the translators regularly render *ha-torah* (the Torah) with the word "Teaching," which they did not use here.

So, Isaiah did not prophesy that in the Messianic age, the nations would come flocking to Jerusalem to study the Pentateuch with the Messiah—much less to learn Talmudic interpretations of the text!—but rather that divine instruction would go forth from the Lord in Mount

Zion, and the nations would come flocking to it and to him. Undoubtedly, Paul would concur with this, also explaining that through the coming of the Messiah, we already have a glimpse of what will happen on that day and of how God's laws and statutes will be written on our hearts (see further, below, 5.34; for reflections on Deuteronomy 30, see vol. 5, 6.9). Having moved forward, there is no reason to turn back.

5.30. The Torah is forever, every jot and tittle, and only traditional Jews keep it. In fact, even the so-called new covenant of Jeremiah 31 says that God will put the Torah in our hearts. Therefore, since Jesus abolished the Torah, he cannot be the Messiah.

> We addressed this in 5.28–5.29, refuting the objections that Jesus and Paul abolished the Torah. As for traditional Jews being the only ones who keep the Law, they are to be commended for their tremendous zeal and devotion to the Law, but they must be challenged as to the endless human traditions they have added in the name of the Law (see vol. 5, 6.1, 6.3–6.5), and they must be questioned as to their missing the One of whom the Law and the Prophets spoke. Regarding the new covenant, see below, 5.34.

This is certainly an important objection, but its fundamental premise has already been refuted—i.e., the notion that Jesus and Paul abolished the Law—along with other details of this objection taken up at length elsewhere in this book. And so I refer you to the following responses for full and complete answers: 5.28; 5.29; 5.32–5.34; vol. 5, 6.16.

It is also important to bear in mind that God did not stop speaking to Israel at Sinai, nor did he intend to leave our people unable to keep most of the Law's commandments for most of our history, which has been the case since the destruction of the Temple in 70 c.e. (see above, 5.22, 5.28). Rather, God continued to speak to our forefathers through the prophets, indicating that the day would come when he would make a new covenant with our people, putting his laws within our hearts and completely forgiving our sins (see below, 5.34). This was because of our repeated failures as a nation, brought to a climax in Josiah's day, when his valiant efforts at national reform failed and, in the days of his sons, the Temple was destroyed and many of the people exiled (see 2 Kings 22–25). It was at this time that the new covenant prophecies began to be introduced by Jeremiah and Ezekiel, tying in with other Messianic prophecies.

Those prophecies began to see their fulfillment when Yeshua, our appointed Redeemer, came into the world and inaugurated the new covenant with a devoted Jewish remnant, and beginning with that remnant, the knowledge of the God of Israel has been spread throughout the world in accordance with the Lord's promise to Abraham (namely, that he would bring worldwide blessing through Abraham's seed, beginning in Gen. 12:2–3).

Followers of Jesus, therefore, see the Torah and Prophets as ultimately pointing to someone (the Messiah) and something (the Messianic age), recognizing that we are now in a transition age in between Messiah's first and second comings (for more on this, see vol. 1, 2.1). And just as Rabbinic Jews see the Torah in light of their traditions—in fact, they would tell you that we only have the Torah because of those traditions—so also Messianic Jews see the Torah in light of the rest of the Tanakh and the New Testament Scriptures, that is to say, in light of the Messiah. Will this produce a varied approach to Torah among followers of Yeshua? Certainly, it will. But it will not bring about the abolition of Torah. To the contrary, it will bring lasting meaning even to those aspects of the Torah that the Jewish people have been unable to observe for almost two thousand years.

I would reiterate, however, that this is an important objection worthy of a more full response, and for that, I refer you again to the other answers already provided in this book, noted above.

5.31. Anyone who changes the Law—no matter what signs or wonders he performs—is a false prophet. That applies to Jesus!

Jesus made it very clear that he did not come to destroy the Law but to fulfill it, and that is exactly what he did (see above, 5.28, for a further explanation of this). And all his miracles drew attention to his heavenly Father, strengthening the people's faith in God and his Word (see vol. 2, 3.4). As for changing the Torah, it could be just as well argued that the Rabbinic authorities changed the Law with their modification and adjustments.

According to Moses Maimonides, Jesus (and/or Christianity) "caused
. . . the Torah to be altered" and taught that "these mitzvoth are true,
but were already superseded in the present age and are not applicable
for all time" (Hilchot Melachim, 11:4).[485] What makes this statement so
ironic is that Rabbinic Judaism has added to the Torah in many places
and taken away from the Torah in many other places (see vol. 5, 6.1,
6.5, for a more in-depth treatment of this). Now, if you are a traditional
Jew, you would say that Rabbinic Judaism has *not* changed the Torah
at all. Rather, you would argue that the rabbis are the possessors of an
unbroken oral tradition going back to Moses himself and that they are
the legitimate heirs of Moses and the prophets. Therefore, a traditional
Jew would claim, any modifications that the rabbis have made to the
Torah have been legitimate, even divinely inspired. In light of that,
Maimonides required—without a stitch of scriptural support—that the
Messiah would be "learned in Torah and observant of the mitzvoth, as
prescribed by the written law *and the oral law*" (Hilchot Melachim, 11:4,
my emphasis).[486]

What about the explicit command in the Torah not to *add* or *take
away* any of God's commands (see Deut. 4:2; 12:32 [13:1])? Rabbinic
Judaism has rendered many commandments obsolete while adding
many commandments not found in the written Torah (see above, 5.28
and vol. 5, 6.1, 6.3–6.5). An Orthodox Jew would answer that, in fact, the
rabbis did not add or take away anything from the Law of God. Rather,
as circumstances changed—such as the destruction of the Temple and
the scattering of the Jewish people worldwide—they made the Torah
adaptable for the nation. In volume 5, we will take up these claims at
length, examining them against the testimony of the Scriptures and
demonstrating where they are lacking, despite the sincere beliefs of
thousands of devoted Orthodox Jews. In volume 2 of our study, we addressed the objection that stated, "According to the Law (Deuteronomy
13), Jesus was a false prophet, because he taught us to follow other gods
(namely, the Trinity, including the god Jesus), gods our fathers have
never known or worshiped. This makes all his miracles utterly meaningless." In response, we saw that Jesus and his followers emphasized,
"Love the Lord your God with all your heart, mind, soul, and strength.
Follow him. Obey him!" Jesus pointed everyone to God his Heavenly
Father—by his miracles, by his message, and by his life. He lived, died,
and rose again for the glory of his Father. Thus Jesus was a faithful and
true prophet (see vol. 2, 3.4).

The question that remains then is, Did Jesus actually change the Law,
or did he, by a divine authority greater than that claimed by the rabbis,
bring the Torah to full expression and set in motion the new covenant,

which includes a Messianic halakhah of life in the Spirit? The answer, as we have seen clearly (above, 5.28) is emphatically "Yes, he brought the Torah to full expression and set in motion the new covenant." That is because Yeshua is the Messiah of the Jewish people and the King of Israel, the ultimate interpreter of Torah, indeed, the one to whom the Torah and Prophets ultimately point. All the miracles he performed, which were unprecedented in human history in terms of their nature and scope, were divine confirmations of his Messianic status, in keeping with the promises of Scripture (see Isa. 35:1–6; 42:6–7; 61:1–3) and in keeping with the biblical pattern of supernatural signs and wonders confirming the veracity of God's messengers (see, e.g., Exodus 4; 1 Kings 18). When the time came for Messiah to manifest himself in this world, the miracles were all the more pronounced, which is why Jesus sometimes pointed to them in no uncertain terms, saying, "The miracles I do in my Father's name speak for me. . . . Even though you do not believe me, believe the miracles, that you may know and understand that the Father is in me, and I in the Father. . . . Believe me when I say that I am in the Father and the Father is in me; or at least believe on the evidence of the miracles themselves" (John 10:25, 38; 14:11; see also 10:32; 15:24; cf. also Acts 2:22). As John (Yohanan), one of his original twelve followers wrote, "Jesus' disciples saw him do many other miraculous signs besides the ones recorded in this book. But these are written so that you may believe that Jesus is the Messiah, the Son of God, and that by believing in him you will have life" (John 20:30–31 NLT). The fact that these miracles, performed in his name by his disciples, continued after his crucifixion, demonstrated that he was alive from the grave, just as the prophets predicted (see Isa. 53:8–12; Ps. 16:8–11; 22:20–31; see further vol. 2., 3.4 and the treatment of these passages throughout vol. 3).

So, in contrast with the Rabbinic sages, against whom the charge of changing the Torah can also be raised (see again vol. 5, 6.1, 6.3–6.5), Yeshua brings the Torah to fulfillment, and he does it with divine miracles backing his claims.

Having said this, it is appropriate to point to the great contrast between Rabbinic Judaism and the New Covenant faith. Following the death of Moses, Deuteronomy 34:10–12 records:

> Since then, no prophet has risen in Israel like Moses, whom the LORD knew face to face, who did all those miraculous signs and wonders the LORD sent him to do in Egypt—to Pharaoh and to all his officials and to his whole land. For no one has ever shown the mighty power or performed the awesome deeds that Moses did in the sight of all Israel.

Followers of Yeshua can make a good case for *him* being not only equal to Moses in stature (see Deut. 18:15–22, for the well-known passage about "a prophet like Moses," and see vol. 3, 4.1), but even greater than Moses. As Hebrews states, "Moses was faithful as a servant in all God's house, testifying to what would be said in the future. But [Messiah] is faithful as a son over God's house" (Heb. 3:5–6a). And God confirmed Jesus as Messiah through outstanding signs, wonders, and miracles, culminating in Yeshua's resurrection from the dead, his visible, bodily ascension to heaven (see Acts 1:9–11), and his sending the Spirit to his disciples with supernatural signs and wonders accompanying them (in just the first five chapters of Acts, see 2:1–4, 43; 3:1–10; 4:30–31; 5:1–16). Miraculous confirmation such as this certainly lends strong support to the Messianic credentials of Jesus, putting him in the class of Moses as described in Deuteronomy 34:10–12.

What does Rabbinic Judaism say about these verses in Deuteronomy 34? Remarkably, there is a saying that goes, "From Moses to Moses, there was none like Moses"—referring to none other than Moses Maimonides, the brilliant (and rationalistic) compiler of the first Jewish law code, the Mishneh Torah, as well as the author of a commentary on the Mishnah and the influential philosophical work *Guide for the Perplexed* (titled *Moreh Nebuchim* in Hebrew). Yet he is somehow compared to the Moses of Scripture, despite the complete lack of miraculous, divine confirmation of his life and message, and despite the complete absence of signs and wonders—the very credentials described in Deuteronomy 34:10–12.

Yet it is this very contrast that underscores one of the major differences between the Messianic, New Covenant faith and the faith of traditional Judaism, which, in short, is the difference between Yeshua the Messiah and the Rambam, Moses Maimonides. Both were great rabbis and both were devoted to the Torah, but one, the Messiah, came in fulfillment of Scripture and received supernatural confirmation from heaven; the other, Rambam, was a brilliant commentator and legal analyst, but not a man accompanied by signs, wonders, and miracles. Thus, to be true to the spirit of the Tanakh, we cannot say "from Moses to Moses [Maimonides] there was none like Moses" but rather, "from Moses to the Messiah, there was none like Moses."

5.32. Observance of the Sabbath has been the hallmark of the Jewish people, separating us from other nations and identifying us with the cov-

enant of God. Since Christianity changed the Sabbath, Christianity is obviously not for the Jewish people.

> Hundreds of years after the death and resurrection of Jesus, when the official "church" had separated itself from its biblical roots, Christendom did, indeed, change the Sabbath from Saturday to Sunday. But that has absolutely nothing to do with the teachings of the New Testament, which is why it is common for Messianic Jews today to hold worship service on Saturday rather than Sunday and to celebrate Shabbat with newfound meaning through the teaching and example of the Messiah. As for Gentile Christians setting aside Sunday as a special day of rest and worship, what is wrong with this?

Without question, traditional Jews have led the way in Sabbath observance for many centuries, and they are to be commended for it. No one has developed more beautiful traditions or made more sacrifices to honor this day than observant Jews. This is in keeping with my position that Judaism is the greatest religion man has ever made, in many ways a living faith but still one that has not obtained what it has sought (see vol. 5, 6.7–6.8). "I can testify about them," Paul wrote of his own people who had rejected the Messiah, "that they are zealous for God, but their zeal is not based on knowledge" (Rom. 10:2) and that they "pursued a law of righteousness" without attaining righteousness (Rom. 9:31). And even when rebuking the hypocritical leaders among our people, Yeshua referred to their punctilious observance of certain laws (e.g., Matt. 23:23). So, often with good motives and at times with mixed motives, traditional Jews have faithfully observed the Sabbath for hundreds and hundreds of years, just as they have sought to observe many other Torah commandments. This is certainly praiseworthy, even though their very best efforts still fall short of obtaining righteousness. I would also point out that God promised that he would preserve the Jewish people as a people, regardless of our sins or shortcomings (see Jer. 31:35–37), and so, even in our dispersion from the Land—an ongoing sign of judgment—God has been at work in our midst to preserve us as a people. (It has often been stated that it is not so much that the Jews kept the Sabbath as much as it is that the Sabbath has kept the Jews.)

But the objection here is not focused on Jewish observance of the Sabbath, something we discuss at some length elsewhere in this volume and in volume 5 (see 5.29; vol. 5, 6.3), critiquing some of the traditions that developed over the centuries. Rather, this objection claims that "Christianity" changed the Sabbath and that, therefore, "Christianity" is not for the Jewish people. Is there any truth to this?

If by "Christianity" you mean the religion of the Tanakh and the New Covenant Scriptures, the religion of Yeshua and his emissaries, the answer is absolutely, categorically "No." As we demonstrated at length, above (5.28), Yeshua did not abolish the observance of the Sabbath (or change it to another day). To the contrary, he exposed faulty human traditions that took away from the meaning of the Sabbath and instead opened up the deepest, most spiritual aspects of the Sabbath. We also demonstrated that Paul himself was a Sabbath-observant Jew (5.29) and that he too did not teach Jewish believers in the Messiah to abandon the practice of the Sabbath. (At the same time, he did not require Gentile believers to observe the Sabbath, nor would he allow an issue to be made over this.) In keeping with this, for several hundred years after the New Testament period, despite the increasing hostility of the Rabbinic community and the increasing Gentilization of the church, there were Jewish believers in Yeshua who continued to observe the Sabbath, just as many do today.

On the other hand, if by "Christianity" you mean the decisions and councils of later church leaders, hundreds of years after Jesus' death and resurrection, then the answer is, "Yes," Christendom did change the Sabbath from Saturday to Sunday—but there is no scriptural mandate for this decision, as has often been demonstrated. (See, in particular, Samuele Bacchiocci, *From Sabbath to Sunday: A Historical Investigation of the Rise of Sunday Observance in Early Christianity* [Rome: Pontifical Gregorian Press, 1977], with interaction in D. A. Carson, ed., *From Sabbath to Lord's Day: A Biblical, Historical, and Theological Investigation* [Grand Rapids: Zondervan, 1982]. More recently, see Daniel Gruber's treatment of this in *The Separation of Church and Faith, Copernicus and the Jews, Volume 1* [Hanover, NH: Elijah Publishing, 2005].)

There is limited evidence that some of Yeshua's early followers celebrated his resurrection, which took place on a Sunday, in early morning gatherings for prayer or worship on that day.[487] But we must not see that through the lens of later church practice, since there was not a five-day work week in that culture, and so Jewish believers who continued to observe the Sabbath did not set aside Sunday as an additional day of worship (or change their Saturday observance to Sunday). At most, they added another time of worship and prayer to their weekly schedule on Sunday mornings (or, possibly, evenings). But, to repeat: These Jewish followers of Yeshua did *not* change the Sabbath to Sunday.

Eventually, due to the massive influx of Gentiles into Messiah's community, followed by the institutionalizing of the church and the eventual severing of some of its biblical and Jewish roots, it was decreed in the fourth century that the Sabbath had now been changed to Sunday, but this was *not* what Yeshua taught, and it is not found anywhere in the New Testament.

Is it wrong, then, for Gentile Christians around the world to worship on Sunday and to set this day aside as a Sabbath to the Lord? Certainly not, since the seventh-day Sabbath was something specifically given as a sign to Israel (see, e.g., Ezek. 20:12–21), although some groups, such as Seventh Day Adventists (or many Messianic Jews), would argue that since the seventh-day Sabbath was instituted at creation (Gen. 2:1–3), given to Israel before Sinai (Exod. 16:22–30), offered to Gentiles through the prophets (Isa. 56:4–7), and spoken of in the still-to-come millennial kingdom (Isa. 66:22–24), it should be observed by all.

This much is sure: There is no question that observance of the Sabbath was strongly emphasized in the Hebrew Scriptures, beginning with God's "Sabbath rest" after creation, and continuing through the rest of the Torah, historical books, and prophets. Yeshua emphasized it as well! But, to repeat, if you as a traditional Jew believe that the seventh-day Sabbath was specifically given to the Jewish people, why should it be an issue to you if Christians around the world from a Gentile background set aside Sunday as a day of Sabbath rest and worship of the Lord? How does this disprove the Messiahship of Jesus?

As for Jewish believers in Jesus who feel no obligation to observe the seventh-day Sabbath, numerous perspectives and convictions exist: some Messianic Jews would argue that these other believers are missing out on a divine blessing; others would argue that they are falling short of their covenantal obligations as Jews; certain others would argue that, to the contrary, with the coming of Messiah, their relationship to the Torah has changed and they are no longer under its obligation (e.g., there is no death penalty today for failure to keep the Sabbath); others would argue that many of them should be treated as though they were Gentiles (the Rabbinic term for Jews who were not raised in traditional homes is *tinoq shenishbah*, a child that was born in captivity) for whom the Sabbath has different significance, since they were not raised in observant homes; yet others would argue that engaging in ministry to and for the Lord is the best expression of the Sabbath, and still others would argue that they have now entered into the meaning of Sabbath through Yeshua, and that is greater than the day itself. (You will find almost as much diversity in beliefs about this subject among Jewish believers in Jesus as you will among Jews who do not believe in him—ranging from the most nontraditional to the most traditional—although it could be argued that Messianic Jewish congregations take the Sabbath more seriously than their Reform or Conservative Jewish counterparts.)[488]

On the other hand, if you are a traditional Jew and you come to faith in Yeshua as Messiah, you will step forward into an even greater experience of Sabbath rest, something that transcends just one day a week. As for your weekly Sabbath observance, you will probably keep some of your old traditions while casting off others and adding some new expressions before the Lord. For good reason Yeshua said,

> Come to me, all you who are weary and burdened, and I will give you rest. Take my yoke upon you and learn from me, for I am gentle and humble in heart, and you will find rest for your souls. For my yoke is easy and my burden is light.
>
> Matthew 11:28–30

In him we find ultimate Sabbath rest (see Heb. 4:8–11).

5.33. According to Mark 7:19, Jesus abolished the dietary laws.

Did you ever read this chapter, along with the parallel account in Matthew 15? Jesus was exposing the error of being scrupulous in terms of outward, ritual purity (specifically, practicing ritual handwashing before eating) while having filthy hearts and minds. As he explained: "What goes into a man's mouth does not make him 'unclean,' but what comes out of his mouth, that is what makes him 'unclean'" (Matt. 15:11). It is the thoughts of the heart that defile someone, not whether or not they follow the Rabbinic traditions and wash their hands before they eat. In principle, then, this makes all foods "clean"—in other words, no food can make you spiritually impure, which is the point of Mark 7:19. But there is no evidence that the disciples of Jesus heard these words and threw out the dietary laws. Rather, they grasped the meaning of Jesus' words and continued to live as Torah-observant Jews. However, because they understood the spiritual principles the Messiah was teaching, they would be willing to be in an environment where they ate nonkosher food in order to teach Gentiles about the one true God. Doesn't this seem right to you? Over time, they also realized another spiritual principle based on Yeshua's words, namely, "If God pronounces someone 'clean'—in this case, meaning, if he accepts the Gentiles as his own people through faith in the Messiah—then we have no right to call them 'unclean,' rejecting them as fellow-heirs of our heavenly Father and as spiritual brothers and sisters." Having said all this, I'm fully aware that many Christian scholars would argue that Jesus did, in fact, change the dietary laws, but even if this were the case, there are Rabbinic traditions stating that in the world to come (and/or the Messianic era), some of the dietary laws will be changed.

Acts 10 records an important event in the development of the first decade after Yeshua's resurrection. An angel of the Lord appeared to Cornelius, who was a God-fearing Gentile, telling him that his "prayers and gifts to the poor [had] come up as a memorial offering before God" (v. 4). Cornelius was then instructed to send for Simon Peter, who was one of the original disciples of Jesus (see Acts 10:1–8). Cornelius promptly complied, sending two of his trusted servants to Joppa to find Peter. The narrative continues:

> About noon the following day as they were on their journey and approaching the city, Peter went up on the roof to pray. He became hungry and wanted something to eat, and while the meal was being prepared, he fell into a trance. He saw heaven opened and something like a large sheet being let down to earth by its four corners. It contained all kinds of four-footed animals, as well as reptiles of the earth and birds of the air. Then a voice told him, "Get up, Peter. Kill and eat."
>
> "Surely not, Lord!" Peter replied. "I have never eaten anything impure or unclean."
>
> The voice spoke to him a second time, "Do not call anything impure that God has made clean."
>
> This happened three times, and immediately the sheet was taken back to heaven.
>
> Acts 10:9–16

Now, this has often been interpreted as a divine command for Peter to eat treif (i.e., unclean food), but the text says nothing of the kind. Rather, as Peter was soon to understand upon receiving the invitation to accept the invitation of Cornelius and actually go into this Gentile man's house, "God has shown me that I should not call any man impure or unclean" (Acts 10:28b). But that is not the point I want to emphasize here. Rather, it is Peter's earlier response to the visionary command to kill and eat all kinds of unclean animals. "'Surely not, Lord!' Peter replied. 'I have never eaten anything impure or unclean'" (Acts 10:14). How interesting! Several years after the resurrection of the Messiah, Peter still had "never eaten anything impure or unclean," and the command to do so was shocking to him. Yet many scholars believe that Peter was a key source of information for Mark's Gospel.[489] If his Master and Teacher had revoked the dietary laws, as some have understood Mark 7:19, surely Peter would have understood, especially if Peter had been a primary source of Mark's information!

What then is the meaning of Mark 7:19? Let's briefly review the debate that took place in Mark 7 (paralleled in Matthew 15). According to Mark 6:53–56, after Jesus arrived in Gennesaret and was recognized by the people, "They ran throughout that whole region and carried the sick on mats to wherever they heard he was"—and he healed them all, throughout the villages and countryside. This, however, was not what caught the eye of some Pharisees who had come from Jerusalem. Rather, they noticed that Yeshua's disciples were eating with (ritually) unwashed hands (and therefore "unclean" hands), contrary to the Pharisaic traditions of the elders, prompting them to ask, "Why don't your disciples live according to the tradition of the elders instead of eating their food with 'unclean' hands?" (see Mark 7:1–5). To this Yeshua responded with a rebuke, charging them with hypocrisy (i.e., looking pious on the outside but being far from God on the inside) and with making void God's commands with their traditions (7:6–13). He then proceeded to explain to the crowd that, "Nothing outside a man can make him 'unclean' by going into him. Rather, it is what comes out of a man that makes him 'unclean'" (v. 15), going into further detail with his disciples (7:14–23). He said to them, "Are you so dull? Don't you see that nothing that enters a man from the outside can make him 'unclean'? For it doesn't go into his heart but into his stomach, and then out of his body," after which Mark inserts the parenthetical comment: "In saying this, Jesus declared all foods 'clean'" (7:17–19). After Mark records the rest of Jesus' teaching, he records how the Messiah then demonstrated a major spiritual implication of his teaching, extending healing mercy to a Gentile woman in a Gentile land—the epitome of someone who was "unclean" in the eyes of many (see above, 5.23, for further discussion).

What exactly did Mark have in mind with his parenthetical comment? The Greek is more concise than the NIV would indicate, not containing the words "In saying this, Jesus declared," but rather, "Thus he declared clean [or, made clean] all foods" (cf. RSV; for a very different understanding of the Greek, see below). The meaning, however, seems relatively clear, especially since the comment follows Yeshua's teaching that "nothing that enters a man from the outside can make him 'unclean'" (7:18), and the Greek verb used in 7:19b, *katharizō*, is also used in a very similar context in Acts 10:15 when the voice said to Peter, "Do not call anything impure that God has *made clean*." So then, was Jesus actually abrogating the dietary laws?

If he was, his disciples certainly didn't get it—and I don't mean just Peter. In Acts 21, perhaps more than two decades after Messiah's resurrection, it is recorded that there were multiplied thousands of Jewish followers of Yeshua, all of whom were "zealous for the Law," including Paul himself (see Acts 21:20). Messianic Jewish scholar John Fischer also notes:

> Many have interpreted the next section, Mark 7:17–19, to mean that Yeshua set aside the food laws. But by doing so he would have contradicted himself. His detractors had just accused him of not observing their traditions, and he had responded that they did far worse; they did not observe the commandments of the Torah (vv. 9–13). To choose this time to set aside other commandments of the Torah would have undercut his whole response. It would have left him open to the charge they made, and which he implicitly denied. It would also have shown him to be inconsistent.[490]

So, we ask again, what exactly did Jesus mean? Here are several interpretations that have been offered:

1. His teaching did, in fact, by clear implication, render all foods, in and of themselves, "clean," meaning, "Nothing that you eat can actually defile you on the inside. No food, in itself, is actually 'unclean.'" In saying this, however, he was not encouraging his followers to go out and get a pork sandwich, he was simply opening their eyes to an important spiritual principle, one which would be extremely important in their ministry to the Gentiles in the coming years. Possible support for this view is also found in Romans 14:1–23; 1 Corinthians 8:1–13; 10:25–33; and 1 Timothy 4:4 (see further, below, for discussion of these verses).
2. He was simply saying that food eaten with unwashed hands—and thereby rendered "unclean" according to the Pharisaic traditions—was not actually unclean at all, and to eat such food could not defile the inner being. The closing comment in Matthew's account lends support to this view: "These [namely, the defilements that proceed from our hearts] are what make a man 'unclean'; but eating with unwashed hands does not make him 'unclean'" (Matt. 15:20). This would also be supported by the specific issue being

addressed.[491] (A further argument raised to support this view is that Mark 7:19b speaks of "all *foods*," which, by implication would supposedly mean "only clean foods," since nothing unclean could be considered a "food." This, however, seems forced, since: first, Mark was writing for a Gentile audience who would not have been expected to grasp this concept; second, the Greek word *broma* used here, according to all major lexicons, simply means, "that which is eaten, food"; third, even in Rabbinic literature, the word *ma'akal*, food, can sometimes be used with reference to "unclean food"; fourth, this would undermine the force of Jesus' words in 7:18 that, "*nothing* that enters a man from the outside can make him 'unclean.'")

3. Jesus was, in fact, pronouncing all foods clean, but this was only significant for Mark's Gentile readership. This is the position adopted, for example, by Dr. Mark Kinzer in his *Postmissionary Messianic Judaism* (cited below, n. 495).[492]

4. Although Jesus rebuked the Pharisees for making void the Word of God through their traditions, he, as Messiah and by the Spirit, did, in fact, change these laws, which, until now, had served the purpose of helping to keep Israel separate from the nations. But now, with the inbreaking of the Messianic age and the inclusion of the Gentiles in the kingdom of God by faith, those laws were no longer necessary. In support of this, attention is sometimes drawn to some Rabbinic traditions that state that in the world to come, the dietary laws would be abolished (see Midrash Tehillim 146:4, discussed below at the end of this objection). Against this, however, are the points mentioned above, first, that the disciples, for many years after this teaching, continued to follow the Torah and second, that changing the law would contradict Yeshua's rebuke of the Pharisees. In defense of this interpretation, Carson writes (speaking of Matthew 15):

The only way to explain these phenomena is the one Matthew has already developed (see esp. 5:21–48): Jesus insists that the true direction in which the OT law points is precisely what he teaches, what he is, and what he inaugurates. He has fulfilled the law; therefore whatever prescriptive force it continues to have is determined by its relationship to him, not vice versa. It is within this framework that Jesus' teaching in this pericope theologically anticipates Romans 14:14–18; 1 Corinthians 10:31; 1 Timothy 4:4; Titus 1:15, and that historically it took some time for the ramifications of Jesus' teaching to be thoroughly grasped, even by his own disciples. Once again it is a mark of Matthew's fidelity to the historical facts that he does not overstate Jesus' teaching, and a mark of his literary skill that he does not find it necessary to draw Mark's parenthetical conclusion (Mark 7:19b), even though he obviously shares it.[493]

5. A very different view is that the verb *katharizō* here means "purge" rather than declare clean, with the subject of the verb being the just-mentioned "toilet, latrine, sewer" (NIV's "out of his body" is literally, "out into the sewer"; cf. NRSV). The meaning would then be that the food a man eats doesn't enter into his heart, but his stomach, and from there out into the sewer, thereby purging the food from the body" (see KJV). This is argued at length by professor Fischer:

But then, what <u>did</u> he mean here? As [professor David] Flusser aptly notes:

"The passage about the washing of hands does not justify the assumption that Jesus opposed the Jewish legal practice of this time; but by the third century, Origen understood it as signifying the rejection of Jewish dietary laws by Jesus. The overwhelming majority of modern translators thoughtlessly accept Origen's interpretation when they take Mark 7:19b to mean 'Thus he declared all foods clean,' although the Greek original can hardly be read in this sense."

As Flusser pointed out, "the Greek original can hardly be read in this sense." The nominative participle (<u>katharizon</u>) modifies "drain" or "latrine" (accusative). This is just one example of a construction "in which the grammatical object of the sentence is regarded as the logical subject." Or, it is quite possible that since the entire process of digestion and elimination is in view as the subject of consideration, the participle takes on the nominative case to indicate this. What Yeshua stated, then, is what is physically true: the latrine removes that part of the food which cannot be used for nourishment and in this way "purges" the food. As Alford goes on to note:

"The <u>aphedron</u> (latrine, drain) is that which, by the removal of the part carried off, purifies the meat; the portion available for nourishment being in its passage converted into chyle, and the remainder being cast out."

The passage should then read: "Do you not understand that whatever enters a man from without cannot defile him because it does not enter his heart but his stomach, and then passes out of it, thus purging (i.e., 'eliminating') the food." Yeshua's lesson here is directly stated in Matthew's rendition (Mt. 15:17-20):

"Don't you see that whatever enters the mouth goes into the stomach and then out of the body? But the things that come out of the mouth come from the heart, and these make a man 'unclean'. . . eating with unwashed hands does not make him 'unclean.'"

The issue Yeshua addressed is not kosher or non-kosher food, but eating with unwashed hands. . . .

Further, if the disciples had understood Yeshua to mean he had set aside the dietary laws, why did Peter—who put the question to Yeshua and received the answer (Mt. 15:15f.)—react so strongly against the possibility of eating non-kosher food when he saw the vision (Acts 10)? He expressed great indignation and shock. And why did he not later say, especially when explaining these events (Acts 11), "Now, I remember the words of the Lord, making all foods clean"? He said nothing of the sort, because Yeshua had not in fact set aside the dietary laws.

As Phillip Sigal rightly reflected:

"It is apparent that Jesus did not abolish the dietary practices."[494]

Against this view it can be argued that, first, it too fails to grasp the implications of Yeshua's teachings and second, it does not explain the other passages in the New Testament that could be interpreted to speak of the abrogation of the dietary laws (although Fischer, as a serious Messianic Jewish scholar, addresses these concerns in other writings).

What then should be our final conclusion to the question at hand? Although a good case can be made for the last position (although some of the arguments seem overstated, such as, "modern translators thoughtlessly accept Origen's interpretation," and, "the Greek original can hardly be read in this sense"), I believe that an even better case can be made for the first position, in keeping with some related passages in the New Testament. To reiterate: This did *not* mean that Yeshua was abrogating the dietary laws. If he had, surely he would have been accused of this at some point, but he was not. And surely, as emphasized above, this would have been reflected somewhere in Acts, but it was not.

But something *did* change, and that was the disciples' *relationship* to these laws, meaning that, with the understanding that nothing we ate would actually render us spiritually unclean—that is to say, unclean on the inside—under certain circumstances, it was better to eat ritually unclean food than to ostracize a Gentile believer or to miss the opportunity of bringing the message of the Messiah into an environment where ritually clean food was not available. Can you see the spiritual sense of this? It is similar to the teaching that "the Sabbath was made for man, not man for the Sabbath" (see above, 5.28), which means that, even in traditional Jewish law, it is appropriate for an Orthodox Jewish doctor to practice medicine on the Sabbath in order to save a life. It is concepts like these that were emphasized by Yeshua, concepts that also emphasized the spiritual unity and equality of all believers, Jew and Gentile alike, albeit with certain distinctives still in force.

This understanding of Yeshua's teachings, over against the growing Pharisaic traditions, would also be in harmony with the subsequent development of the Messianic faith and the Rabbinic faith: The former did not develop an elaborate system of dietary restrictions (going far beyond anything that was written in the Torah), while the latter did; the former created an environment in which Gentiles were received into full and equal spiritual fellowship (as Gentiles!), side by side with their Jewish brothers and sisters, while the latter did not. In defense of Rabbinic Judaism, it can be said that, while being open to the charge of having added to the Torah laws and needlessly increasing all kinds of unnecessary burdens, it has produced a people who have been careful to keep those laws (and many others!); in criticism of the traditional Jewish position, it can be argued that the over-and-above observance of the dietary laws has continued to erect a wall that keeps Gentiles out—the very wall that Messiah broke down. This, however, is not the place to work out the details of what should and should not be practiced by Jewish and Gentile followers of the Messiah. Rather, it is to respond to the objection raised, and I believe that has been done.

What then should we make of key, related passages in the New Testament? I will cite each passage and offer varied interpretations. While these passages *could* be interpreted to mean that the dietary laws had been forever changed, other, plausible interpretations can be offered to the contrary.

- In Romans 14:14, Paul wrote: "As one who is in the Lord Jesus, I am fully convinced that no food [in the Greek, "nothing"] is un-clean in itself. But if anyone regards something as unclean, then for him it is unclean." Here are three possible interpretations: (1) Paul is simply making a spiritual observation, his major emphasis throughout the chapter being that we should not judge one another. (2) In keeping with that emphasis, Paul was addressing a problem occurring between Jewish and Gentile believers. As he wrote in 14:2–3, "One man's faith allows him to eat everything, but another man, whose faith is weak, eats only vegetables. The man who eats everything must not look down on him who does not, and the man who does not eat everything must not condemn the man who does, for God has accepted him." (3) Recognizing that certain changes did occur with the inbreaking of the Messianic age and that Jesus had rendered the dietary laws obsolete, he was stating that it didn't matter what we ate.[495]

- In 1 Corinthians 10:25–26, Paul instructed the Corinthians, "Eat anything sold in the meat market without raising questions of

conscience, for, 'The earth is the Lord's, and everything in it.'"
Although this passage could, in fact, be tied in with the idea that
Jesus abrogated the dietary laws, the context in these chapters
has to do with food that was sacrificed to idols, and the recipients
of Paul's letter were Gentile believers. The problem for them was
that the meat that was sold in the marketplace had, in many cases,
been sacrificed first in an idol temple, and their question was, "Was
it acceptable to eat such food?" While the New Testament does,
in fact, teach against intentionally eating food that was sacrificed
to idols (see Acts 15:20, 29; Rev. 2:14, 20), Paul, in harmony with
our interpretation of Yeshua's words in Mark 7 and Matthew 15,
emphasizes that "food does not bring us near to God; we are no
worse if we do not eat, and no better if we do" (1 Cor. 8:8; cf. also
1 Cor. 6:12–13). In other words, it's not a spiritual issue unless it
causes someone else to stumble. The bottom line here, of course,
is that the Corinthians were Gentiles for whom the Mosaic dietary
laws had never been applicable, so that was not the issue. The
overall point, however, remains the same: What goes into your
mouth cannot defile your heart.

- In 1 Timothy 4, Paul warned Timothy to watch out for certain
deceptive and demonic teachings that would be put forth by teachers who "forbid people to marry and order them to abstain from
certain foods, which God created to be received with thanksgiving
by those who believe and who know the truth" (1 Tim. 4:3). Paul
refuted this erroneous teaching by stating that "everything God
created is good, and nothing is to be rejected if it is received with
thanksgiving, because it is consecrated by the word of God and
prayer" (4:4–5). Although these verses are commonly understood to
mean that all foods, including those forbidden in the Torah, should
be received with thanksgiving (since, after all, they were created
by God and "consecrated by the word of God and prayer"), they
are taken here to mean, "consecrated by the teaching of Jesus in
Mark 7 and Matthew 15 and by the prayer offered over the meal."
Another view would be that the foods "which God created to be
received with thanksgiving by those who believe and who know the
truth" are those which are "consecrated by the word of God and
prayer"—meaning, those permitted by the Torah (and, of course,
consecrated in conjunction with the mealtime prayers). The error,
then, of the false teachers was to call people to abstain from foods
that were perfectly acceptable according to the Torah, just as they
forbade people from marriage. In the debate between Protestant-
ism and Catholicism, some Protestants have accused Catholics of

being guilty of these very errors, historically by forbidding priests to marry and, in the twentieth century, forbidding the eating of meat on Fridays. (I cite this only as a potential example of how Paul's words can be applied.)

Having examined the key passages, it can be said with confidence that a good case can be made that Yeshua did not abolish the dietary laws, although he did change our perspective on those laws in many important ways and, to a degree, our relationship to those laws.[496]

For those, however, who believe that the right interpretation of these New Testament texts is that Jesus did abolish the dietary laws, I would point out that the Midrash to Psalm 146:7 (Midrash Tehillim 146:4) asks, "What is meant by '[the LORD] frees the prisoners'?" The answer given is, "Some say that every creature that is considered unclean in the present world, the Holy One blessed be He will declare clean in the age to come." (The connection between this statement and the words in Psalm 146 is based on the fact that the root *h-t-r*, here used in the sense "set free" is also used in Rabbinic literature in the legal sense of "permit," while the word for prisoner, '*asir*, is closely related to the word '*asur*, used in Rabbinic legal language to mean "forbidden, prohibited." Hence, the Midrash states that in the future, God will permit what is now prohibited.)[497] So then, it could also be argued that Yeshua, in a foretaste of the age to come—indeed, we believe as his followers that we are already experiencing *in part* some of the realities of the coming age (cf., e.g., Heb. 6:5)—declared "clean" that which was previously "unclean." As the Messiah and Son of God, he would have had this authority and this reference in the Midrash indicates that the idea of an eventual change in the food laws was not considered so impossible that it could not be stated. So, turning this whole objection around, if, in fact, he was the Messiah of Israel—and there is no reason to doubt that, indeed, he was!—then his changing of the dietary laws would be something praiseworthy and acceptable. But, to reiterate, I do *not* believe that this is the only way to read the relevant texts in the New Testament, as we have indicated in the preceding discussion.

5.34. If the death of Jesus really inaugurated the new covenant spoken of by Jeremiah the prophet, then why hasn't it been fulfilled?

It is clear that we are living in a transition age, a time that can be characterized as "already but not yet," a time in which the Messianic era has been inaugurated but not fully consummated. Not only are there Rabbinic traditions that point to this transition age (see vol. 1, 2.1), but many of the major prophecies of the Tanakh can only be explained in this way. In short, the new covenant was established two thousand years ago in incipient form and it continues to advance towards its ultimate fulfillment.

In volume 1, 2.1, we addressed the objection, "If Jesus is really the Messiah, why isn't there peace on earth?" The answer we provided was: "According to the biblical timetable, things are right on schedule, and Jesus is doing everything the Messiah was to expected to do up until this point. The problem is that you have an incomplete understanding of the biblical picture of the Messiah. According to the prophet Malachi, the Messiah would bring purification and purging before he brought peace. He would execute judgment before he established justice. Many would not be able to endure the consequences of his coming. This is written in our Hebrew Bible! For many of our people, his coming would be bad news not good news. Our Scriptures also teach that the Messiah was to be a *priestly King*, like David [my emphasis]. As a royal Priest, he came to make atonement for sins and offer forgiveness and reconciliation to Israel and the nations. As King, his dominion expands every day, as he rules over those who embrace him as Messiah. Soon he will return and establish his kingdom on the earth, destroying the wicked and bringing worldwide peace. So, what you expected to be the *first act* of the play will actually be the *final act*"!

As additional support for this biblical position, we pointed to the Talmudic tradition that stated that, "The world will exist six thousand years. Two thousand years of desolation [meaning from Adam to Abraham]; two thousand years of Torah [meaning from Abraham to somewhere around the beginning of the Common Era]; and two thousand years of the Messianic era [roughly the last two thousand years]; but because our iniquities were many, all this has been lost" (i.e., the Messiah did not come at the expected time; Sanhedrin 97a–b). We also noted that, "according to this well-known Jewish tradition, the Messiah *was supposed to come* about two thousand years ago! As explained by Rashi, 'After the 2,000 years of Torah, it was God's decree that the Messiah would come and the wicked kingdom would come to an end and the subjugation of Israel would be destroyed.' Instead, because Israel's sins were many, 'the Messiah has not come to this very day'—now 2,000 years later."

As for the Rabbinic chronology itself (called *Seder Olam Rabbah*), if it was used by the author of the statement just quoted, that would place the expected beginning of the Messianic era at approximately 240 C.E., but given the fact that there is a well-documented error of between 159 and 170 years in the Seder Olam chronology, when the years are properly adjusted it dates the expected beginning of the Messianic era to somewhere around the year 70 C.E.—in other words, the very century in which Yeshua lived, very close to the time the Second Temple was destroyed, and about forty years from the Messiah's death and resurrection. How fascinating![498] We further cited the Vilna Gaon's explanation of a difficult statement in the Talmud by the second-century rabbi Yehoshua ben Chananyah to mean that, "although the Jews had not merited Mashiach's coming by their deeds, nevertheless the Era of Mashiach had indeed arrived at its appointed time. At 'the midpoint of the world' God began turning the wheels of history to insure the ultimate arrival of the scion of David."[499]

Quite oddly, Chasidic rabbi and anti-missionary Moshe Shulman writes:

> Now the correct understanding of this teaching [i.e., the tradition quoted in Sanhedrin 97a] is NOT that the Messiah comes in the year 4000, just like the Torah was not given in the year 2000 which was when Avraham lived. It means, just as the Vilna Goan [*sic*] indicates, that this is when the time leading to the coming of the Messiah starts. Similarly the year 2000, when Avraham was alive, was the start of the period leading up to the giving of the Torah.[500]

To the contrary, Talmudic tradition claims that Abraham was in full possession of both the oral and written Torah (see vol. 5, 6.1) and that he brought others into the knowledge of the Torah, so that, in a real sense, the era of Torah began with him. More importantly, Rashi explicitly states, "After the 2,000 years of Torah, it was God's decree that the Messiah would come and the wicked kingdom would come to an end and the subjugation of Israel would be destroyed." As explained in the Schottenstein Talmud, which reflects staunchly Orthodox thought, according to Rashi, "Because of our sins the Messiah did not come at the end of the fourth millennium. The final two millennia, *which were supposed to have been the Messianic era*, have turned out differently, for the Messiah still has not come" (97b[1], n. 1, my emphasis). What then happened? According to the Talmudic statement, "because our iniquities were many, all this has been lost." So, not only does Rashi understand the era of Torah to span two thousand years, he understood that the Messiah *was expected* at the end of this period, but things did not happen as originally scheduled because of Israel's sins, leading the Vilna Gaon to explain that the Messianic era actually *did* begin, but in a different way than expected (namely, ushering in ultimate apostasy before the final redemption).[501] Further support for this interpretation of the Talmudic text is found in other traditional commentaries.[502]

Even if Rabbi Shulman's interpretation were correct—which is *not* the case—why then was the Torah given on Mount Sinai roughly 600 years after Abraham (according to the Rabbinic chronology) whereas the traditional Jewish Messiah still has not come almost 1,800 years after the expected time (again, following the Rabbinic chronology)? And, more importantly, how could the Talmud, compiled in its present form in the sixth century C.E., already bemoan the fact that "because our iniquities were many, all this has been lost"? It is absolutely clear from this statement that the Messiah was expected to arrive and establish his kingdom *at the beginning of the Messianic age* rather than at the end of the Messianic age, otherwise, what is the Talmud bemoaning? If Rabbi Shulman were correct, the statement should have said, "And everything is right on schedule!"

Could it be that the obvious interpretation of the Talmudic tradition supports the Messianic Jewish view of redemption and the Messianic era rather than the traditional Jewish view? Could it be that we really are in an age of transition? To quote the Vilna Gaon once again:

> Mankind will realize that the only way to convert himself back into a true human, a God-like being filled with wisdom, love, kindness, and an exalted spirit, is by the acceptance of God's dominion. And when God demonstrates all this and man recognizes it, Mashiach will finally come.[503]

And when did this process begin? It was "with the advent of the last third of human history: the Era of Mashiach may not be apparent, but it is 'here.'"[504] Yes, even though the Messiah himself has not come, the Messianic era began right on schedule, only not in the way that most were expecting. (Does this sound vaguely familiar?)

As I stated in volume 1:

> I remind you, of course, that the Vilna Gaon did not believe in Jesus anymore than he believed that Muhammad was the first Pope (note also that, in all probability, the Gaon did not have an accurate picture at all of who Yeshua was and what he did). But it is striking that this great Jewish scholar recognized that the Messianic era actually began at its appointed time and that this era was first a time of transition. Shades of "Christianity"! The biggest differences between our positions are these: (1) The Gaon saw the present, transition age as one of universal, increasing darkness and apostasy. We see it as an age of ever-increasing awareness of the Messiah

in the midst of great darkness and apostasy. (2) He believed that the Messianic era began without the coming of the Messiah. We believe it began with his coming! Which position seems more reasonable to you?[505]

With this in mind, let's return to the question of the inauguration of the new covenant, quoting Jeremiah's passage in full:

> "The time is coming," declares the Lord,
>   "when I will make a new covenant
> with the house of Israel
>   and with the house of Judah.
> It will not be like the covenant
>   I made with their forefathers
> when I took them by the hand
>   to lead them out of Egypt,
> because they broke my covenant,
>   though I was a husband to them,"
>   declares the Lord.
> "This is the covenant I will make with the house of Israel
>   after that time," declares the Lord.
> "I will put my law in their minds
>   and write it on their hearts.
> I will be their God,
>   and they will be my people.
> No longer will a man teach his neighbor,
>   or a man his brother, saying, 'Know the Lord,'
> because they will all know me,
>   from the least of them to the greatest,"
>   declares the Lord.
> "For I will forgive their wickedness
>   and will remember their sins no more."
>
> Jeremiah 31:31–34

The obvious (and very fair) question that must be asked is: Has this really happened? The author of Hebrews had no hesitation in answering with an emphatic yes, also quoting the passage in full, something that is quite striking for a passage of this length (see Heb. 8:7–12). Other verses in the New Covenant Scriptures point to this understanding (see the listing of New Testament "new" verses below). We also know that the authors of some of the Dead Sea Scrolls frequently took up this new covenant terminology as well.[506]

But none of this responds to the objection being raised and the question remains: How can we claim that the new covenant was inaugurated by Jesus if universal forgiveness for sins has still not come to Israel, if complete, automatic obedience to God's laws still does not exist (either in Israel or the church), and if teachers are still needed to exhort people to "know the LORD"? The answer to all this is very important, since it provides the template through which many prophecies in the Tanakh are to be interpreted. I had the joy of investigating this in depth when writing a commentary on the Book of Jeremiah from 2002 to 2004, and I will share here some of the insights I gleaned.[507]

What the anti-missionaries often miss is that both Jeremiah and Ezekiel prophesied that the return from exile would be glorious—both physically and spiritually—and their prophecies concerning the restoration from Babylonian exile included: (1) the physical return of the exiles to the Land; (2) their blessed resettlement there; (3) their spiritual renewal and restoration; and (4) the glorious reign of the Messianic king. Each of these promises has a historic, partial fulfillment, beginning in the 530s B.C.E., when the first wave of exiles returned home and when Jerusalem was initially rebuilt, and each of these promises has a future, ultimate fulfillment which awaits the end of the age.

The Jews for Judaism website states concerning the Messiah:

> **He will rule at a time when the Jewish people will observe G-d's commandments**—"My servant David shall be king over them; and they shall all have one shepherd. They shall follow My ordinances and be careful to observe My statutes." (Ezek. 37:24)
> The Torah is the Jewish guide to life, and its commandments are the ones referred to here. Do all Jews observe all the commandments? Christianity, in fact, often *discourages* observance of the commandments in Torah, in complete opposition to this prophecy. . . .
> . . . All of these criteria are best stated in the book of Ezekiel Chapter 37 verses 24–28:
> And David my servant shall be king over them; and they shall all have one shepherd. They shall also follow My judgments and observe My statutes, and do them. And they shall dwell in the land that I have given to Yaakov my servant, in which your fathers have dwelt and they shall dwell there, they and their children, and their children's children forever; and my servant David shall be their prince forever. Moreover, I will make a covenant of peace with them, it shall be an everlasting covenant with them, which I will give them; and I will multiply them and I will set my sanctuary in the midst of them forevermore. And my tabernacle shall be with them: and I will be their G-d and they will be my people. Then the nations shall know that I am the L-rd who sanctifies Israel, when My sanctuary will be in the midst of them forevermore.[508]

Therefore, Jews for Judaism concludes, Jesus cannot be the Messiah.

What Jews for Judaism fails to note, however, is that these promises in Ezekiel, which parallel the new covenant promises in Jeremiah,
should have been fulfilled after the Babylonian exile. Note the summary
of Jeremiah's expectations by the critical Old Testament scholar S. R.
Driver, writing a hundred years ago:

> Not only does he promise what actually came to pass: the return of the
> exiles to the territories of Benjamin and Judah, and the resumption there
> of the interrupted social state, in which again, as of old, the sounds of joy
> and life would be heard in the villages (xxx. 18f.; xxxiii. 10f.), shepherds
> would again tend their flocks (xxxiii. 12f.), and houses and fields would
> again be bought and sold by the restored exiles (xxxii. 15, 44); but he invests
> the future with ideal colours. The exiles of the Northern Kingdom will
> share in the restoration (iii. 18; xxxi. 4ff.); the hills of Ephraim will again
> resound with happy throngs, and be clad with cornfields and vineyards;
> a great company will return from the furthest corners of the earth (xxxi.
> 4–9, cf. vv. 10–17, 21f.); the wants of all will be abundantly satisfied (xxxi.
> 12–14, 25; cf. l. 19). The national life will be re-established (xxx.18–21);
> Jerusalem will be rebuilt, and will be entirely holy to Yahweh (xxxi. 23,
> 38–40). . . . The restored nation is pictured as returning to Yahweh 'with
> it[s] whole heart' (xxiv. 7; cf. xxix. 13); words of confession and penitence
> are put into the mouth of both Judah (iii. 22b–25) and Ephraim (xxxi.
> 18–19; cf. also l. 4f.); the iniquity of Israel will be forgiven and remem-
> bered no more (xxxi. 34b, xxxiii. 8; cf. l. 20); one heart, and one way, even
> the way of Yahweh's fear, will be given to them (xxiv. 7, xxxii. 39f.); Israel
> will be Yahweh's people, and He will be their God (xxiv. 7, xxx. 22, xxxi.
> 1, 11, xxxii. 38). More than this, a 'new' and spiritual 'covenant' will be
> established with the house of Israel, and the nation will be ruled, not by
> a system of observances imposed from without, but by a law written in
> the heart, filling all with the knowledge of Yahweh, and prompting all to
> ready and perfect obedience (xxxi. 31–34). There will be no ark; nor will
> the ark be either needed or missed (iii. 16). The people will be governed
> by upright, disinterested 'shepherds' (i.e. judges and princes), after God's
> own heart (iii. 15, xxiii. 4); and a perfect king of David's line, supreme over
> all, will maintain judgement and righteousness in the land, and ensure
> peace for its inhabitants (xxiii. 5f; cf. xxxiii. 15f., xxx. 8, 9). The ruler of the
> future will be of native birth, and enjoy the priestly privilege of access to
> Yahweh (xxx. 21). Israel has but to turn loyally to Yahweh for the nations
> to be moved by the spectacle of its blessedness to own Him as their God
> (iv. 1f.); elsewhere in the books the nations are depicted as in the future
> discarding their idols, confessing that Yahweh alone is God (xvi. 19b; cf.
> the conditional promise, xii. 16), making pilgrimages to Jerusalem (iii. 17),
> and looking with awe and wonder at the restored Zion (xxxiii. 9). Israel
> will never be cast off by Yahweh, or cease from being a nation before Him
> (xxxi. 36f.; cf. xxxiii. 23–26). . . . Egypt, Moab, Ammon, and Elam, after

their expected desolation by Nebuchadnezzar, will be restored (xlvi. 26b, xlviii. 47, xlix. 6, 39 . . .)."[509]

Do you understand the significance of this? Jeremiah (much like Ezekiel) expected that the return of the exiles from Babylon would be so glorious that it would be followed by the transformation of the nation—through the inauguration of the new covenant (see also Ezek. 36:24–32) and the reign of the Messiah—leading ultimately to the transformation of the whole world. Were Jeremiah and Ezekiel false prophets? God forbid! Rather, what they prophesied did happen, only not in the expected measure or scope. In other words, in the same way that the prophesied return of the exiles did happen, but not in the expected measure or scope, and in the same way that the prophesied rebuilding of the Temple did take place, but not with the expected glory (see esp. Ezekiel 40–48, and cf. vol. 2, 3.17), in the very same way the Messiah did come and inaugurate the new covenant—just as was prophesied!—but not with the expected glory or scope. As I wrote in my commentary to Jeremiah:

> So then, just as the return from exile did take place after seventy years, as prophesied, although not with the expected glory, so also the Messianic era began and the new covenant was established, only not with the expected glory. But the historic event serves as the deposit and down payment of the future event, the former guaranteeing the latter, with the return from Babylon in the late sixth century BC serving as the "first coming home," while the final, eschatological return will serve as the "second coming home," similar to the Messiah's first and second comings. So also with the establishing of the new covenant: It did begin, as promised—the "days are coming" oracles cannot be pushed into the eschaton in their entirety—but touching a much smaller group of people than expected and still not in its full force. When the Messiah returns, the promise will reach its ultimate fulfillment (see Zec 12:10–13:2). Thus the realization of the new covenant will follow the same pattern outlined in Zec 9:9–10, growing from humble beginnings (the Messianic king begins his reign "gentle and riding on a donkey") until in the end, it encompasses the entire world ("His rule will extend from sea to sea and from the River to the ends of the earth").[510]

The significance of all this cannot be overstated, since it is impossible to separate the Messianic prophecies from the prophecies speaking of the return from exile, and it is exegetically unacceptable to use one method of interpretation on one set of prophecies and an entirely different method of interpretation on another set of related, intertwined prophecies; placing the return from exile prophecies into their historical context while wrenching the Messianic prophecies from their historical context would put the former into the distant past and the latter into the distant future. Doing this completely undermines the integrity of the biblical text.

So, the real question that must be asked is not whether the new covenant has been inaugurated but rather whether Jeremiah and Ezekiel were false prophets. Since this is not an option for followers of Yeshua or for traditional Jews, we must then use a consistent method of interpretation throughout these books, one which recognizes that what they prophesied did take place—beginning with the destruction of Jerusalem and the exiling of thousands of Judeans and continuing with the return from exile and the eventual inauguration of the new covenant—although the prophecies were not initially fulfilled to the degree that was expected. However, since we have the first installment in place, we can be confident that the rest will come to pass as well; and, quite strikingly, we are living in what appears to be major days of ongoing restoration and fulfillment, with the reestablishment of the state of Israel in 1948, the massive return of Jewish exiles from around the world in the second half of the twentieth century, the exponential spreading of the Messianic faith throughout the world in this same century, and an ever-growing remnant of Jewish followers of Jesus, especially within Israel itself.

To quote again from my Jeremiah commentary:

> The question that must be asked is: Were these verses fulfilled in any sense with the return of the exiles from Babylon? [Professor Walter] Brueggemann, who rightly rejects a supersessionist reading of the text (i.e., applying these verses to the church at the expense of and to the exclusion of Israel; see further, below), speaks of "the community formed anew by God among exiles who are now transformed into a community of glad obedience," contrasting "the recalcitrant Jews prior to 587" with the "transformed Jews after 587 who embrace the covenant newly offered by God." But when did this community of transformed Jews exist in post-exilic Judah, especially on a national level? (Citing Brueggemann again, "All inclination to resist, refuse, or disobey will have evaporated, because the members of the new community of covenant are transformed people who have rightly inclined hearts." See also his comments to 32:38–41 and 50:4–5.) What do the books of Ezra, Nehemiah, and Malachi say of this? Certainly, there is some degree of covenant renewal and repentance in these books, but it hardly resembles what is prophesied here, nor does there seem to be any consciousness of a "new covenant" being ratified in Ezra or Nehemiah, nor do Malachi's oracles suggest such a renewed community. At what point, then, did God say to the exiles, "I have forgiven and forgotten your sins once and for all?" Forgiveness is offered, to be sure (cf. also the sentiments of Ne 8:9–10), but not on such a comprehensive level. . . . And, if this new covenant was

established with all Israel at that time, why then were both Jerusalem and the second temple destroyed 600 years later, with a dispersion more severe than the Babylonian exile taking place in the succeeding centuries? Simply stated, the new covenant oracle was *not* fulfilled when the exiles returned home in the 530s BC, a reality not addressed in the comments in *The Jewish Study Bible*: "The *new covenant* has been interpreted by Christians as a prophecy of the new covenant through Jesus (New Testament means new covenant), but here it refers to the restoration of Israel after the Babylonian exile and the reconstruction of the Temple." (Rashi does not comment on these verses at all, for no evident reason.)

Should these verses then be interpreted in wholly eschatological terms, with their fulfillment, even in an incipient sense—if such a sense is permitted by the text—postponed until the end of the age? Certainly not, since to do so would completely remove these promises from their context, without exegetical justification. Moreover, a consistent hermeneutic would also demand the removal of *all* unfulfilled prophecies of a glorious return from exile, in effect, making Jeremiah into a false prophet (or, at the least, making him into a true prophet of doom but a false prophet of hope).

What then of the Christological reading of the text that interprets these verses in light of the coming of Jesus into the world? It is actually this reading that provides the template for interpreting *all the restoration from exile promises* in Jer, promises which include: (1) the physical return of the exiles to the land; (2) their blessed resettlement there; (3) their spiritual renewal and restoration; (4) the glorious reign of the Messianic king. Each of these promises has a *historic, partial fulfillment*, beginning in the 530s BC, when the first wave of exiles returned home and when Jerusalem was initially rebuilt, and each of these promises has a *future, ultimate fulfillment* which awaits the end of the age. . . . At that time—at the eschaton—there will be a final, supernatural regathering of Israel's remaining exiles, a Jewish return to God of national proportions, the Messiah's second coming, the establishing of God's kingdom on the earth, and the final, glorious rebuilding of Jerusalem. The promises in the late sixth century BC would have the quality of "already/not yet"—to borrow George Eldon Ladd's terminology—signifying that the time of redemption had begun but its final consummation was still to come. (See in particular Ladd's work *The Presence of the Future: The Eschatology of Biblical Realism* [repr. Grand Rapids: Eerdmans, 1996].) As noted in the discussion of several key passages (see 23:5–8; 24:5–7; 30:8–9; 31:38–40; 32:37–42; 50:4–5), it is clear that something monumental was expected in the aftermath of the Babylonian exile, something of even greater proportion than the destruction itself, yet those hopes, articulated by Jeremiah, Ezekiel, and Isaiah, among others, were not fully realized. And since it is impossible to dismiss these oracles as extreme examples of prophetic hyperbole, while readers who accept the Scriptures as inspired must recognize some level of historic fulfillment of the time-related prophecies (in other words, prophecies that had to come to pass within a certain historical framework), it is the

Christological reading alone, a reading that recognizes that we have been in a "transition age" for two millennia, that satisfies the criteria. . . .

Followers of Jesus, then, whether Jewish or Gentile, do well to remember Paul's words in 1Co 11:26: "For whenever you eat this bread and drink this cup, you proclaim the Lord's death until he comes." Thus, living in this transition age, this time period of already/not yet, believers look back to the sacred and costly inauguration of Yahweh's new covenant with Israel through the cross, recognizing this as the very fountainhead of their hope and salvation, while they look ahead with great anticipation to its glorious culmination, also described by Paul, and ending with the people with whom it began: "Israel has experienced a hardening in part until the full number of the Gentiles has come in. And so all Israel will be saved, as it is written: 'The deliverer will come from Zion; he will turn godlessness away from Jacob. And this is my covenant with them when I take away their sins.' [Isa 59:20]" (Ro 11:25b–27).[511]

It is true, of course, that the New Testament writers did not always make explicit reference to the new covenant promise of Jeremiah and Ezekiel, but the concepts of new life through the Messiah, of new birth from above, of God's laws being written on our hearts, are found throughout the New Testament. The emphasis on something "new" is a constant theme, and quite understandably, this collection of books ultimately became known as *the* New Covenant (or, Testament). Consider these "new" concepts:

- *New wine* requiring *new wineskins* (Matt. 9:17).
- The enlightened teacher of the law who "brings out of his storeroom *new treasures* as well as old" (Matt. 13:52).
- A *new command*, to love one another as the Messiah loved us (John 13:34; see also 1 John 2:7–8; 2 John 1:5).
- The message of this *new life* (Acts 5:20; for other "new life" references, see Rom. 6:4).
- The *new way of the Spirit* (Rom. 7:6).
- We are called to be a *new batch of dough* without yeast (1 Cor. 5:7).
- ". . . if anyone is in [Messiah], he is a *new creation*; the old has gone, *the new has come!*" (2 Cor. 5:17; see also Gal. 6:15).
- Believing Jews and Gentiles become *one new man* (Eph. 2:15).
- We are called "to be *made new* in the attitude of [our] minds; and to put on the *new self*, created to be like God in true righteousness and holiness" (Eph. 4:23–24; see also Col. 3:10).
- The time of the *new order* (Heb. 9:10).

- A *new and living way* (Heb. 10:20).
- In God's "great mercy he has given us *new birth* into a living hope through the resurrection of Jesus the [Messiah] from the dead" (1 Peter 1:3).
- Yeshua is even buried in a *new tomb*! (See Matt. 27:60; John 19:41.)

Still for the future, "we are looking forward to a new heaven and a new earth, the home of righteousness" (2 Peter 3:13; see Rev. 21:1–2), including a new Jerusalem (Rev. 3:12) in keeping with the word of the One who says, "I am making everything new!" (Rev. 21:5). At that time, overcomers will receive a new name (Rev. 2:17; 3:12), and in heaven a new song is sung (Rev. 5:9; 14:3). But even now, in this present age, we have entered into new life in Yeshua and we presently enjoy the firstfruits of that new life while still enduring the pains, struggles, and challenges of the present age (for a deeply spiritual statement concerning this, see Rom. 8:18–27). And that new life is characterized by the very things Jeremiah prophesied: God's Word has been written on our hearts, and whereas it was our nature to do wrong before we were born anew, it is now our nature to do right, although we have not yet been fully redeemed.[512] Some of us tried with all our might to change our ways before meeting Yeshua—not all of us who believe in him today used to live in boldfaced immorality and sin!—but without success. Some can relate to the words of John Wesley who sailed from England to America *as a missionary* to the native Americans *before* he had experienced personal conversion. Yet he was a deeply religious man, of extraordinary piety. (Perhaps some of you reading this who are quite religious but yet still outside of the Messiah can relate well to his words, despite the Christian terminology and his extensive quotes from Paul's words in Romans 7.)

All the time I was at Savannah [Georgia] I was thus beating the air. Being ignorant of the righteousness of Christ, which, by a living faith in Him, bringeth salvation "to every one that believeth," I sought to establish my own righteousness; and so labored in the fire all my days. I was now properly "under the law;" I knew that "the law" of God was "spiritual; I consented to it that it was good." Yea, "I delighted in it, after the inner man." Yet was I "carnal, sold under sin." Everyday was I constrained to cry out, "What I do, I allow not: For what I would, I do not; but what I hate, that I do. To will is "indeed" present with me: But how to perform that which is good, I find not. For the good which I would, I do not; but the evil which I would not, that I do. I find a law, that when I would do good, evil is present with me:" Even "the law in my members, warring against the law of my mind," and still "bringing me into captivity to the law of sin."

In this vile, abject state of bondage to sin, I was indeed fighting continually, but not conquering. Before, I had willingly served sin; now it was unwillingly; but still I served it. I fell, and rose, and fell again. Sometimes I was overcome, and in heaviness: Sometimes I overcame, and was in joy. For as in the former state I had some foretastes of the terrors of the law, so had I in this, of the comforts of the Gospel. During this whole struggle between nature and grace, which had now continued above ten years, I had many remarkable returns to prayer; especially when I was in trouble: I had many sensible comforts; which are indeed no other than short anticipations of the life of faith. But I was still "under the law," not "under grace:" (The state most who are called Christians are content to live and die in:) For I was only striving with, not freed from, sin. Neither had I the witness of the Spirit with my spirit, and indeed could not; for I "sought it not by faith, but as it were by the works of the law."[513]

Can you relate to this?

And then, after much more internal struggle, deep searchings of the heart and mind, and many more efforts to try harder and harder to please God, something extraordinary happened to Wesley on May 24, 1738. This is how he described that transforming experience as he sat at a meeting and listened as a commentary was being read to Romans which

was describing the change which God works in the heart through faith in Christ, I felt my heart strangely warmed. I felt I did trust in Christ, Christ alone for salvation: And an assurance was given me, that he had taken away my sins, even mine, and saved me from the law of sin and death. . . .

After my return home, I was much buffeted with temptations; but cried out, and they fled away. They returned again and again. I as often lifted up my eyes, and He "sent me help from his holy place." And herein I found the difference between this and my former state chiefly consisted. I was striving, yea, fighting with all my might under the law, as well as under grace. But then I was sometimes, if not often, conquered; now, I was always conqueror.[514]

The transformation was real and lasting, and Wesley ended up changing the course of British history.[515] His brother Charles, who became a famous hymn writer, described in verse what happened to him when he was born anew:

Long my imprison'd spirit lay,
Fast bound in sin and nature's night:

Thine eye diffused a quickening ray;
   I woke; the dungeon flamed with light;
My chains fell off, my heart was free,
I rose, went forth, and follow'd Thee.

No condemnation now I dread,
   Jesus, and all in Him, is mine:
Alive in Him, my living Head,
   And clothed in righteousness Divine,
Bold I approach th' eternal throne,
And claim the crown, through Christ, my own.[516]

There *is* such a thing as new birth in the Messiah; there *is* a new life. You *can* receive a new heart and have God's Spirit put within you (Ezek. 36:26–27). And even though you will still experience the frustrations and struggles of living in this transition age, still clothed in mortal, human flesh (1 Corinthians 15) and still awaiting ultimate redemption, you will understand what it means to be an overcomer: "This is love for God: to obey his commands. And his commands are not burdensome, for everyone born of God overcomes the world. This is the victory that has overcome the world, even our faith" (1 John 5:3–4).

Allow me to share my own story of transformation. I remember well the night of December 17, 1971, when, in a moment of time, all the guilt left my heart. For six weeks I had been trying, at long last, to reform my profligate ways and wishing I could find a way to get rid of that miserable internal stain, when I received a revelation of God's love for me through Jesus, and everything changed. That instant, I promised the Lord that I would never put a needle in my arm again (having been virtually "addicted to the needle" in terms of my craving to inject heroin or other drugs into my veins), and from that day on, it was done. In a moment of time, the guilt was replaced with joy—inexpressible joy—and my heart was fully cleansed, as I received the gift of eternal life through faith in Jesus. And it was that faith that empowered me to repent. I can personally attest to the reality of the new covenant! My desires radically changed—and continued to change radically for many months; my morals did a complete about-face; my whole life-orientation experienced a dramatic upheaval. I now lived to do the will of God, and whatever he said was what I wanted to do and continue to want to do.

A dear Indian colleague of mine, Bro. P. Yesupadam, was raised in an untouchable home and became a staunch atheist, an alcoholic, and a violent communist, a hardened man who had not shed a tear in years—until he had a vision of Jesus with his hands outstretched saying to him, "I love you this much!" From that day on he was transformed, and thirty years later he is a spiritual pioneer in his city, housing and educating hundreds of orphans, caring for the elderly, training the handicapped, building hospitals, starting colleges, planting churches among unreached tribal peoples, unflinchingly enduring hardship and persecution, being stoned for his faith, and then winning to the Lord those who stoned him. . . . This is just a small part of his story. And he who virtually never cried before meeting Jesus has become a man of tears and compassion, deeply burdened for the hurting and the helpless. He too, along with countless other Indian believers, can attest to the realities of the new covenant! The same can be said for hundreds of millions of people from every nation—and almost every tribe and tongue—around the world. The new covenant has been inaugurated!

And even though we have not yet seen the full realization of the words, "No longer will a man teach his neighbor, or a man his brother, saying, 'Know the Lord,' because they will all know me, from the least of them to the greatest" (Jer. 31:34a), without a doubt, we have experienced the deposit and down payment, and we understand the words of 1 John 2:27 which states, "As for you, the anointing you received from him remains in you, and you do not need anyone to teach you. But as his anointing teaches you about all things and as that anointing is real, not counterfeit—just as it has taught you, remain in him." As Yeshua taught, "It is written in the Prophets: 'They will all be taught by God.' Everyone who listens to the Father and learns from him comes to me" (John 6:45, quoting Isa. 54:13). In a very real way, although we have teachers in Messiah's community to help deepen our understanding, and although we go into the world to make God known, we know what it is to be "taught by God," and we can truly say, "We know the Lord!"

We understand, with all of our hearts and souls and minds, what the Lord meant when he said through Jeremiah, "For I will forgive their wickedness and will remember their sins no more" (Jer. 31:34b). And we understand what Paul meant when he wrote, "In [Jesus] we have redemption through his blood, the forgiveness of sins, in accordance with the riches of God's grace" (Eph. 1:7). The new covenant has been inaugurated! God's promise to Ezekiel is something we understand: "I will give you a new heart and put a new spirit in you; I will remove from you your heart of stone and give you a heart of flesh. And I will put my Spirit in you and move you to follow my decrees and be careful to keep my laws" (Ezek. 36:26–27). And it makes perfect sense to us that we enjoy these covenant benefits during this transition age, but not in full measure.[517] That will only happen at the end of this age when the promises are realized for our people as a whole, at which time there will be mass repentance—the likes of which the world has never seen (see Zech. 12:10–13:1)—and all Israel will be saved (Rom. 11:26).

I am aware, of course, of the argument that for the new covenant to be real, God must put *the Torah* in our hearts, by which traditional Jews think of the Talmudic interpretation of the Torah. But that is quite a stretch from what is written in the text—in fact, it could be argued that all the Talmudic extensions and interpretations were put in place precisely because the new covenant was *not* in place—and the meaning is much more simple than that. In keeping with this understanding is the fact that the Septuagint did not translate *torah* here with *law* (Greek *nomos*) but with *laws* (*nomous*), promising to write *them* (not "it") on the hearts of God's people (see also Ezek. 36:27).

As I explain in the Jeremiah commentary:

> It is commonly pointed out that the new covenant oracle did not envisage a change in the *content* of the divine law (*tôrâ*, rendered "Teaching" by NJPSV here and in verses such as Jos 1:8); see, e.g., the note to 31:31 in *The Jewish Study Bible*: "According to this passage, it is not the content of the new covenant which will be different, but how it is learned." Rather, the difference between the Sinaitic covenant and the new covenant would be in the response of the people, obedient by nature rather than recalcitrant. Certainly, the text itself does not state that there will be a new Torah, nor would other passages in Jeremiah explicitly point to such a change. However, three observations should be borne in mind: First, it is unlikely that those hearing or reading this oracle over the centuries would have even raised the question of, "Will this be the same law/teaching or a different law/teaching?" The sweeping, wonderful nature of the promises would overshadow any such thought. In fact, it is probable that the question would never have been raised if not for Jewish-Christian polemics about the perpetuity of the Torah. Second, the radical newness described here and in the previous oracles is so comprehensive that it would be fair to ask whether there would be any changes in the way the people of Israel would live and the way they would relate to God. If those changes could be countenanced, then a change in the law could be countenanced as well. (For example, if the Israelites no longer sinned, would they need all the laws dealing with sin and uncleanness?) Moreover, both Jews and Christians would agree that in the age to come, some aspects of the Torah would no longer apply. (If there is no more death, then surely there is no more defilement from touching a corpse!) The question then would be *when*, not *if*, such changes would begin. Third, it follows then, with the destruction of the temple in AD 70 and the banishing of the Jews from Jerusalem

in AD 135, that many Torah texts had to be reinterpreted and/or reapplied, as a result of which Jewish observance in the fifth century BC looked very different than Jewish observance in the fifth century AD, the latter heavily influenced by the developing Talmudic traditions. Yet this was not an intentional deviation from the Torah on the part of the rabbinic sages but rather an attempt to maintain allegiance to the Torah despite national upheaval. In the same way, the NT Scriptures offer a different way to maintain allegiance to the Torah (specifically, for the Jewish people, while providing a way for Gentile believers to relate to God's law), claiming that radical changes *were intended by God* with the coming of the new covenant, changes, however, that may not have been fully implemented or even realized by Yeshua's Jewish followers until the temple was destroyed (cf. Ac 21:20 for a good summary of Messianic Jewish allegiance to the Torah; Heb 8:13, then, anticipates the destruction of the temple and the end of the sacrificial system: "By calling this covenant 'new,' he has made the first one obsolete; and what is obsolete and aging will soon disappear.")[518]

It could also be argued that with the internalizing of the commandments, certain laws would become redundant, such as the wearing of tassels as a reminder to keep the commandments. (As stated in Num. 15:39, "You will have these tassels to look at and so you will remember all the commands of the LORD, that you may obey them and not prostitute yourselves by going after the lusts of your own hearts and eyes.")[519] This, however, could hardly mean that the law was abolished; rather, in a very real sense, it would have been fulfilled. (For further discussion of these concepts, see above, 5.28–5.29.)

Having said this, it is common for Jews who were secular and nonobservant to find a new love for the Torah upon coming to faith in Yeshua, incorporating Shabbat and the biblical calendar into their lives, while Gentiles who had no interest in the Bible at all often feel a deep identification with Israel upon their conversion and a real sense of solidarity with the biblical calendar, having special appreciation for the feasts and holy days, not to mention a fundamental change of heart and life through their new birth in the Messiah.

In short, the new covenant *has* been inaugurated, and if it was not done by Yeshua almost two thousand years ago, it will never be done by anyone. Thankfully, he started the process in earnest, he is moving it forward around the world to this hour, and in the future—may it be soon!—he will bring his work of redemption to completion. This is why, as his followers, we can look ahead with absolute confidence because of what Messiah *has already done.*

The Spirit and the bride [speaking of Messiah's spiritual community] say, "Come!" And let him who hears say, "Come!" Whoever is thirsty, let him come; and whoever wishes, let him take the free gift of the water of life.

Revelation 22:17

You don't need to wait and hope and pray for the new covenant to come. It is already here.

Notes

1. Roger Nicole, "New Testament Use of the Old Testament," in *Revelation and the Bible*, ed. C. F. H. Henry (Grand Rapids: Baker, 1958), 138.

2. In contrast with this, the Mishnah, the first foundational document of Rabbinic Judaism, rarely quotes its scriptural sources—indeed, in many cases, there *are* no scriptural sources for the Mishnaic discussions—and one of the purposes of the discussions in the Talmud was to connect the rulings of the Mishnah with the text of the Tanakh. According to Jacob Neusner, "By the end of the composition of those components of the oral Torah that would be complete in ancient times—from the Mishnah through the Bavli—the consenus had been reached that statements in the oral Torah could be shown to derive from, to rest upon the authority of, the written Torah. Hence, a systematic effort to locate warrant or proof in the written Torah for propositions first surfacing in the oral Torah would follow." See the anthology edited and translated by Jacob Neusner, *The Scriptures of the Oral Torah: Sanctification and Salvation in the Sacred Books of Judaism* (San Francisco: Harper & Row, 1987), 230. See also Samuel Rosenblatt, *The Interpretation of the Bible in the Mishnah* (Baltimore: Johns Hopkins Press, 1935), and note that the entire book, which consists mainly of endnotes, totals just 93 pages.

3. Craig A. Evans, "From Prophecy to Testament: An Introduction," in idem and J. A. Sanders, eds., *From Prophecy to Testament: The Function of the Old Testament in the New* (Peabody, MA: Hendrickson, 2004), 1–2, with bibliography on 1.

4. Joseph A. Fitzmyer, S.J., *Essays on the Semitic Background of the New Testament* (Missoula, MT: Scholar Press, 1974), 17–18.

5. Ibid., 21–22.

6. Ibid., 22.

7. Ibid., 31.

8. Ibid., 33.

9. Ibid., 46.

10. Ibid., 52.

11. The verbal root *t-h-r* occurs 43x in Leviticus, and in each case, the clear, unambiguous meaning of the root is "to be clean, pure"; elsewhere in the Torah, it occurs 1x in Genesis and 10x in Numbers, and in each case, the meaning remains the same. This is not a matter of dispute! The only different usage of *t-h-r* is found in Job 37:21, where it means "to clear" the sky (apparently, of clouds; cf. NJPSV). This, however, is not cited in

the Talmudic discussion and, in fact, neither provides an exact parallel to the Talmudic interpretation of Leviticus 22:7 nor negates the fact that the plain, contextual meaning of the verb in Leviticus 22:7 has been abandoned in favor of a farfetched interpretation.

12. Soncino Talmud, with footnote 23. Footnote 24 simply references "I Chron. XXVII, 34." The rendering of 2 Sam. 20:23 is, "And Joab was in command of all the army of Israel; and Benaiah the son of Jehoiada was over the Kerethites and over the Pelethites." Cf. e.g., 2 Sam. 8:18; 23:20, 22; 1 Kings 1:8; 2:25; 1 Chron. 11:22.

13. When I say that the Talmud got this confused, I mean that either the Talmudic rabbi who quoted the verse got it wrong, or later editors or copyists transmitted it incorrectly to the point that it became the "standard" text, not to be changed by subsequent editors. Amazingly, some later Talmudic commentators sought to defend the Talmudic text here. See further, below, 5.16.

14. Sometimes, the Talmudic rabbis do make explicit reference to the "literal" meaning of the text (often referred to as *kemashma'o*, according to its sense, or *legupheyh*, according to its own meaning) in contrast with a more homiletical meaning. In keeping with this, the Talmud states that "the scriptural verse does not depart from its plain meaning" (b. Shab 63a; b. Yev 11b; 24a), although the Talmud also states that "whoever translates a verse according to its literal sense [lit., form] is a liar" (b. Kid 49a, which footnote 17 in the Soncino Talmud explains to mean, "This refers to the public translations in the synagogue alongside the Reading of the Law, which was also a feature of ancient times."). For a very useful orientation into the wider subject of Talmudic dialectology, cf. Louis Jacobs, *The Talmudic Argument: A Study in Talmudic Reasoning and Methodology* (Cambridge: Cambridge University Press, 1984).

15. Generally speaking, traditional Jews do not recognize the Qumran Jews as holding to a legitimate form of Judaism and, therefore, they do not recognize the Qumran literature as preserving a "Jewish" method of biblical interpretation. In reality, however, biblical interpretation in the Dead Sea Scrolls was every bit as "Jewish" as the later methods of biblical interpretation of the Rabbinic literature, as most scholars, both Jewish and Christian, would recognize. For a summary of Qumran hermeneutics, see Fitzmyer, *Essays on the Semitic Background*, cited in note 4; for a focused, recent study, see Julie A. Hughes, *Scriptural Allusions and Exegesis in the Hodayot* (Studies on the Texts of the Desert of Judah 59; Leiden: Brill, 2006); for a useful, wide-ranging survey, cf. Richard N. Longenecker, *Biblical Exegesis in the Apostolic Period*, 2nd ed. (Grand Rapids: Eerdmans, 1999).

16. Robert H. Gundry, *The Use of the Old Testament in St. Matthew's Gospel, with Special Reference to the Messianic Hope* (Supplements to Novum Testamentum 18; Leiden: Brill, 1967), xiii.

17. David Klinghoffer, *Why the Jews Rejected Jesus: The Turning Point in Western History* (New York: Doubleday, 2005), 66.

18. Most recently, cf. John Nolland, *The Gospel of Matthew: A Commentary on the Greek Text*, New International Greek Testament Commentary (Grand Rapids: Eerdmans, 2005), 29–37.

19. W. D. Davies and Dale C. Allison Jr., *A Critical and Exegetical Commentary on the Gospel according to Saint Matthew: Matthew 1–7*, vol. 1, International Critical Commentary (Edinburgh: T & T Clark, 1988), 279, with reference to R. T. France (henceforth cited as *Matthew 1–7*).

20. If you come to the text with a presupposition that Matthew was ignorant of the Scriptures, you will find your view confirmed by a citation like this. On the flip side, if you come to the text with a presupposition that Matthew had a tremendous handle on the Scriptures, you will find that view confirmed by a citation like this. In the same way, if you come to the Talmud with the presupposition that the rabbis played footloose and

fancy-free with the Scriptures, or with the presupposition that they were masters of the Scriptures, you will find either of those views confirmed by what you read. So, my goal here is not to persuade you that "Matthew got it right." My goal is to seek to understand what text or texts he had in mind and why he chose to use them, since I am convinced that there is ample evidence to support the belief that he had a firm grasp on the Scriptures.

21. A number of objections listed in this volume deal with some specific New Testament verses in question; for further treatment of the Rabbinic use of the Hebrew Bible, see vol. 5, 6.1–4.

22. Rabbi Tovia Singer, "A Lutheran Doesn't Understand Why Rabbi Singer Doesn't Believe in Jesus: A Closer Look at the 'Crucifixion Psalm'," Outreach Judaism, http://www.outreachjudaism.org/like-a-lion.html.

23. For a vigorous critique of the concept of *the* Masoretic text as opposed to the Masoretic textual tradition, see Harry M. Orlinsky, Prolegomenon to Christian D. Ginsburg, *Introduction to the Masoretico-Critical Edition of the Hebrew Bible* (New York: Ktav, 1966), I–XLV; see further Barry Levy, *Fixing God's Torah* (Oxford: Oxford University Press, 2001).

24. For a convenient summary with bibliography, see Evans, "From Prophecy to Testament," 4–8. For the different Hebrew text forms found in the Dead Sea Scrolls, cf. E. Tov, "Scriptures: Texts," in L. H. Schiffman and J. C. VanderKam, eds., *Encyclopedia of the Dead Sea Scrolls* (Oxford: Oxford University Press, 2002), 2:832–36; E. Ulrich, "Pluriformity in the Biblical Text, Text Groups, and Questions of Canon," in J. Trebolle and L. Vegas Montaner, eds., *The Madrid Qumran Congress: Proceedings of the International Congress on the Dead Sea Scrolls, Madrid, 18–21 March 1991* (Studies on the Texts of the Desert of Judah 11; Leiden: E. J. Brill, 1991), 23–41.

25. According to some early Christian traditions, primarily based on the testimony of Papias, Matthew originally wrote his Gospel (or, a collection of Yeshua's sayings) in Hebrew (or, Aramaic; or, a heavily Semitized Greek); for recent discussion, cf. Nolland, *Gospel of Matthew*, 2–4, who, like most Matthew scholars, does not believe there is any direct connection between our current, Greek Matthew, and the alleged Hebrew Matthew; cf. further S. McKnight, "Matthew, Gospel of," in *Dictionary of Jesus and the Gospels*, ed. Joel G. Green; Scot McKnight; I. Howard Marshall (Downers Grove, IL: InterVarsity, 1992), specifically, "The Origin of Matthew," 526–27. He states, "In conclusion, the most recent scholarship on the Papias logion suggests that the traditional rendering is insufficient and should be understood now in the following manner: In contrast to Mark's unordered, chreia-style Gospel, Papias contends, Matthew composed a more Jewish, orderly styled Gospel. The original language, then, is of no concern to Papias. . . . In all likelihood our Gospel of Matthew was composed originally in Greek and in a Jewish style." Some, however, have argued that a medieval copy of Matthew in Hebrew preserves some of Matthew's alleged original Hebrew text. See George Howard, *The Gospel of Matthew according to a Primitive Hebrew Text* (Macon, GA: Mercer University Press, 1987); see further, vol. 5, 6.15. For refutation of the claim that the whole New Testament—or, at least, the text of the four Gospels—was originally written in Hebrew, see Michael L. Brown, "Recovering the Inspired Text? An Assessment of the Work of the Jerusalem School in the Light of *Understanding the Difficult Words of Jesus*," *Mishkan* 17/18 (1993): 38–64.

26. Abraham Ibn Ezra, *The Secret of the Torah: A Translation of Abraham Ibn Ezra's Sefer Yesod Mora Ve-Sod Ha-Torah*, trans. Norman Strickman (Northvale, NJ: Jason Aronson, 1995), 27–28. When he refers to the second version of the Decalogue, he means Deuteronomy 5:1–21, as compared to Exodus 20:1–17, the first version of the Decalogue. Even a casual comparison between the two demonstrates that there are a number of important differences between the texts, yet we are talking about the Ten Commandments here.

Still, there are differences between the two versions! See further the relevant discussion in the appendix to vol. 5.

27. There is even a fascinating Talmudic tradition that when two prophets bring an identical message, it is to be rejected for this very reason. See b. Sanh 89a and note the further discussion in Michael L. Brown, "Jeremiah," *Expositor's Bible Commentary*, rev. ed., vol. 7 (Grand Rapids: Zondervan, forthcoming) to Jer. 49:16 (henceforth cited as *EBC*[2]); my appreciation to Zondervan for allowing me to excerpt some of my forthcoming commentary from the unedited manuscript later in this volume.

28. Evans, "From Prophecy to Testament," 5.

29. For further discussion, see Michael L. Brown, *Israel's Divine Healer*, Studies in Old Testament Biblical Theology (Grand Rapids: Zondervan, 1995), 196.

30. For further discussion and analysis, see Bruce Chilton, "From Aramaic Paraphrase to Greek Testament," in Evans and Sanders, *From Prophecy to Testament*, 23–43.

31. It has also been observed that Matthew's citation here points to the vicarious nature of Yeshua's earthly ministry, as he entered into human suffering and took it on himself—by bearing it and removing it—until he ultimately bore our sins on the cross. As D. A. Carson rightly noted, "Jesus' healing ministry is itself a function of his substitutionary death, by which he lays the foundation for destroying sickness" "Matthew," *Expositor's Bible Commentary* (Grand Rapids: Zondervan, 1984), 8:205 (henceforth cited as *EBC*); for further details, see Brown, *Israel's Divine Healer*, 196–98.

32. See Martin Hengel, *The Septuagint as Christian Scripture: Its Prehistory and the Problem of Its Canon* (Grand Rapids: Baker, 2002).

33. For a detailed study of the intentional reinterpretation of the Hebrew text in the LXX, see Ashley Crane, "Ezekiel 36–39: The Restoration of Israel in Early Jewish Interpretation," (Ph.D. diss., submitted to Murdoch University, Australia).

34. As translated by Fitzmyer, *Semitic Background*, 34, with further explanation on 35–36.

35. Joseph Klausner, *From Jesus to Paul*, trans. William F. Stinespring (New York: Macmilian, 1943), 453–454.

36. Walter C. Kaiser Jr., Peter H. Davids, F. F. Bruce, and Manfred T. Brauch, *Hard Sayings of the Bible* (Downers Grove, IL: InterVarsity, 1997), 77.

37. Ibid, 78.

38. John Wenham, *Christ and the Bible* (Grand Rapids: Baker, 1994), 107.

39. The second part of the citation is also different, with Paul writing in Romans 11:26, "he will turn godlessness away from Jacob," whereas the Hebrew reads, "to those in Jacob who repent of their sins," but there is clearly no difference in substance here, and this point is not generally raised as an issue by anti-missionaries.

40. See C. H. Gordon, *Ugaritic Textbook* (Rome: Pontifical Biblical Institute, 1965), 92; Wallis proffered this suggestion while a graduate student of Gordon's.

41. For a detailed study of Paul's use of the book of Isaiah in his citations (especially in Romans 9–11), see now J. Ross Wagner, *Heralds of the Good News: Isaiah and Paul "in Concert" in the Letter to the Romans* (Novum Testamentum Supplements 101; Leiden: Brill, 2002). Wagner believes that Paul had the Greek translation of Isaiah committed to memory, helping to explain the depth of understanding he brought to his interpretations.

42. In the words of professor James Kugel, Hebrew parallelism is best explained as, "'A' is this, and what's more, 'B'." See his *The Idea of Biblical Poetry: Parallelism and Its History* (New Haven: Yale University Press, 1981), in which he argued for the Rabbinic understanding of parallelism in contrast with the widely accepted approach to parallelism popularized by Archbishop Robert Lowth in the nineteenth century.

43. Carson, "Matthew," *EBC*, 8:438. Note that only Matthew makes reference to the two animals; the other Gospel accounts speak only of one; see Mark 11:1–3; Luke 19:28–31; John 12:14–15.

44. Ibid.

45. Ibid.

46. Cf. above, n. 25.

47. According to W. D. Davies and Dale C. Allison Jr., *A Critical and Exegetical Commentary on the Gospel according to Saint Matthew: Matthew 19–28*, vol. 3, International Critical Commentary (Edinburgh: T & T Clark, 1997), 316, "rabbinic texts contain numerous tendentious renderings of Scripture which ignore the rules of poetry in favor of excessively literal interpretation . . . [and] some rabbis found two animals in Zech 9.9."

48. For Zechariah 9:9 as a clearly understood Messianic prophecy in Rabbinic literature, cf., e.g., b. Sanh 99a.

49. For a critical analysis of the antiquity of the Shema in Jewish prayer, see Paul Foster, "Why Did Matthew Get the *Shema* Wrong? A Study of Matthew 22:37," *Journal of Biblical Literature* 122 (2003): 321–31.

50. For discussion and refutation of the rare claim that Matthew was a Gentile, cf. Foster, "Why Did Matthew Get the *Shema* Wrong?", 309–13. See further Davies and Allison, *Matthew 1–7*, 10–11.

51. See Foster, "Why Did Matthew Get the *Shema* Wrong?", 313–16, for discussion and dismissal of other reasons why Matthew might have used the preposition *en*.

52. Ibid., 327. Interestingly, the oldest preserved copy of a Hebrew text including Deuteronomy 6:5, the famous Nash papyrus from the second century B.C.E., does not agree exactly with the MT. Cf. ibid., 327–28.

53. Privately, an ultra-Orthodox rabbi informed me that it would have been acceptable to quote Deuteronomy 6:5 in different languages, even paraphrastically, meaning that Matthew 22:37 would not have been considered an error in popular Jewish usage. Note also that in Deuteronomy there is often a *twofold* emphasis on *heart and soul*—without *strength*—rather than the threefold emphasis found in Deuteronomy 6:5, and the context frequently refers to loving the Lord with one's heart and soul. This too could be a factor in Matthew's citation; see Deut. 4:29; 10:12; 11:13, 18; 13:4; 26:16; 30:2, 6, 10.

54. Cf. Nolland, *Gospel of Matthew*, 911, commenting on Matthew 22:37: "The addition of *dianoia* to the list is likely to be related to its occurrence as a variant to *kardia* ['heart'] in the LXX of Dt. 6:5 and other texts."

55. Ibid., 333.

56. I believe that some of these wrong anti-missionary concepts are based on contemporary ignorance of the Tanakh, hence leading them to think that Matthew was misleading and disingenuous. In other words, if his readers really didn't know their Bibles (just as many Jews and Christians today don't know the Scriptures well), he could "pull a fast one" on them by taking a verse totally out of context, slicing it in half so as to alter radically its meaning, and then using it to "prove" that it referred to Jesus.

57. Craig S. Keener, *A Commentary on the Gospel of Matthew* (Grand Rapids: Eerdmans, 1999), 109, my emphasis. See ibid. for further parallels in Matthew between Israel and the Messiah, including the important observation: "Matthew emphasizes Jesus' solidarity with Israel elsewhere as well (cf. 1:1; 4:2); like the Messianic servant (Is 49:5–7; 52:13–53:12) who fulfills the mission Israel had failed (Is 42:18–22), Jesus fulfills Israel's call (cf. Is 42:1–4; 43:10; 49:1–3). But like Stephen in Acts 7, Matthew emphasizes another point as well: God declares Jesus' sonship in his return from Egypt, i.e., outside the Promised Land (Patte 1987: 38). Jesus is not for Judea alone, but for all peoples."

58. As noted by Keener, *Matthew*, 108. Bruce Chilton also points out that the Targum renders Hosea 11:1 with, "Out of Egypt I have called *them* sons," which, he notes, "corrects the passage away from the singular application of 'Out of Egypt I have called to my son,'" as cited correctly by Matthew. See Chilton, "From Aramaic Paraphrase to Greek Testament," in Evans and Sanders, *From Prophecy to Testament*, 38. Cf. further, below, 5.4.

59. As noted by Craig S. Keener, *The IVP Bible Background Commentary, New Testament* (Downers Grove, IL: InterVarsity, 1993), 50 (henceforth cited as *IVPNT*).

60. Ibid.

61. Michoel Drazin, *Their Hollow Inheritance: A Comprehensive Refutation of the New Testament and Its Missionaries* (Jerusalem: Gefen, 1990), 41. Cf. also Eric V. Snow, *A Zeal for God Not according to Knowledge: A Refutation of Judaism's Arguments Against Christianity* (Lincoln, NE: Writers Club Press, 2003), 337–343, for refutation.

62. In a private email, Craig Keener also brought to my attention the larger context of Hosea 11, which culminates in verses 10–11 with the promise of a future, new exodus, suggesting that this also may have been a factor in Matthew's citation of Hosea 11:1.

63. For some of the philological issues involved in the Greek term *nazōraios*, cf. M. O. Wise, "Nazarene," in Joel B. Green and Scot McKnight, eds., *Dictionary of Jesus and the Gospels*, 571–74. He understands the term to mean, "the man from Nazareth."

64. Making no attempt to understand Matthew here, Drazin, *Their Hollow Inheritance*, 41, lists Matthew 2:23 as proof that the New Testament "resorts to imaginary quotations," citing also Matthew 27:9–10 (see immediately below, 5.4); John 7:37–38; and James 4:5. For the latter two, see the standard commentaries.

65. Richard Longenecker (in his *Biblical Exegesis in the Apostolic Period*), among others, raised some philological strictures against this identification, but these have been countered fairly by the Aramaic scholar Michael Wise (in his article "Nazarene," cited above, n. 63); among Matthew commentaries that address this issue, see especially Davies and Allison.

66. For the Talmudic account, cf. b. Sanh 43a; for *netser* as a title of the Messiah in ancient Jewish literature, see the references collected in S-B, 1:94; Testament of Judah 24:6; 4QpIsᵃ 3:15–26; cf. further Davies and Allison, *Matthew 1–7*, 277–78.

67. As noted by George R. Beasley-Murray, *John*, Word Biblical Commentary (Dallas: Word, 1987), 27, "Nathanael's expostulation at the idea that the Messiah could come from Nazareth is comprehensible, for Nazareth was utterly insignificant; it has no mention in the OT, the Talmud or Midrash, or in any contemporary pagan writings ([Strack-Billerbeck] cite one reference to Nazareth from a Jewish writer ca. A.D. 800). The residence of Jesus in Nazareth is akin to his birth in a stable; it is part of the offense of the incarnation. Philip therefore can only reply, 'Come and see'; the answer to the offense of the incarnation is Jesus himself."

68. For other possible verses and/or concepts that Matthew may have had in mind, cf. Davies and Allison, *Matthew 1–7*, 274–81 (their first choice is for the association with *nazir*, Nazarite, holy person, with special reference to Isa 4:3; they see the *netser* reference as secondary); Keener, *Matthew*, 113–15; Nolland, *Gospel of Matthew*, 128–31. According to Carson, "Matthew," *EBC*, 8:97, "[Matthew] is not saying that a particular OT prophet foretold that the Messiah would live in Nazareth; he is saying that the OT prophets foretold that the Messiah would be despised (cf. Pss 22:6–8, 13; 69:8, 20–21; Isa 11:1; 49:7; 53:2–3, 8; Dan 9:26). The theme is repeatedly picked up by Matthew (e.g., 8:20; 11:16–19; 15:7–8). In other words Matthew gives us the substance of several OT passages, not a direct quotation. . . . It is possible that at the same time there is a discreet allusion to the *neṣer* ('branch') of Isaiah 11:1, which received a messianic interpretation in the Targum's rabbinic literature, and the Dead Sea Scrolls (cf. Gundry, *Use of Old Testament*, 104); for

here too it is affirmed that David's son would emerge from humble obscurity and low state. Jesus is King Messiah, Son of God, Son of David; but he was a branch from a royal line hacked down to a stump and reared in surroundings guaranteed to win him scorn. Jesus the Messiah, Matthew is telling us, did not introduce his kingdom with outward show or present himself with the pomp of an earthly monarch. In accord with prophecy he came as the despised Servant of the Lord."

69. It should be noted that there are plays on words—but stated as if they were linguistically accurate—within the Tanakh itself, such as *babel* (Babylon) being derived from *b-l-l*, to confuse (see Gen. 11:9), whereas it is derived from Akkadian *bab ilani*, gate of the gods.

70. Davies and Allison, *Matthew 1–7*, 279, with reference to R. T. France.

71. In addition to the Matthew commentaries of Carson, Keener, Davies and Allison, Luz, and Nolland, all of which provide further bibliographical details, see the monograph of Michael Knowles, *Jeremiah in Matthew's Gospel: The Rejected Prophet Motif in Matthean Redaction* (Journal for the Study of the New Testament: Supplement Series 68; Sheffield: JSOT Press, 1993). Most recently, see Clay Alan Ham, *The Coming King and the Rejected Shepherd: Matthew's Reading of Zechariah's Messianic Hope* (Sheffield: Sheffield Phoenix Press, 2006)

72. D. P. Senior, "The Passion Narrative in the Gospel of Matthew," quoted in Knowles, *Jeremiah in Matthew's Gospel*, 61.

73. Carson, "Matthew," *EBC*, 8:563.

74. Knowles, *Jeremiah in Matthew's Gospel*, 70–71, where he conveniently lists six "close parallels" between Jeremiah 19 and Matthew 27, with reference on 70, n. 1 to the observation of Senior that Matthew 27:8 in the Greek is very close to the LXX of Jeremiah 19:6.

75. It is also possible that there are allusions to other texts in Jeremiah, including Jeremiah 32:14; there is also some close verbal similarity between key phrases in Matthew 27:9 and Lamentations 4:2. Cf. ibid., 74–77.

76. Senior, "The Passion Narrative," 369, cited in Knowles, *Jeremiah in Matthew's Gospel*, 76.

77. Knowles, *Jeremiah in Matthew's Gospel*, 77.

78. *The Jewish Study Bible*, ed. Adele Berlin and Marc Zvi Brettler (New York: Oxford University Press, 2004), 1250.

79. Yaakov Elman, ed. and trans., *The Living Nach: Later Prophets, Isaiah, Jeremiah, Ezekiel, Twelve Prophets. A New Translation based on Traditional Sources* (New York: Moznaim, 1995), 803.

80. *Living Nach*, 812. Interestingly, the footnotes point out that the "shepherd" and "colleague" are taken by the Rabbinic commentators to refer to gentile kings (fighting against Israel during the Messianic era of the Messiah ben Joseph), Esau, the nations' archangels, or even Muhammad, with Ibn Ezra and Malbim claiming that "My colleague" means that, "because of his considerable power, he will consider himself equal to God"! But when is *'amit*, colleague, neighbor (here, "the man who is my colleague/neighbor") ever used in this hostile way? See Lev. 5:21 (2x); 18:20; 19:11, 15, 17; 24:19; 25:14 (2x), 15, 17, the only other times the word is used in the Tanakh. Who could it be that God calls his colleague? The answer is found in Matt. 26:31; Mark 14:27.

81. Chilton, "From Aramaic Paraphrase to Greek Testament," 39.

82. Carson, "Matthew," *EBC*, 8:563.

83. We should also note that he was not just trying to spread the Good News to those who had never heard it. His book was also a training manual for disciples who were already convinced that Jesus was the Messiah and King (cf. Matt. 28:19), and so, in his

writing, he had several goals to accomplish. For evidence of this, note, e.g., the fivefold division of Matthew, marked by the phrase, "When Jesus had finished saying these things" (see Matt. 7:28; 13:53; 19:1; 26:1).

84. Carson, "Matthew," *EBC*, 8:566.

85. Rabbi Tovia Singer, "Outreach Judaism Responds to Jews for Jesus," Outreach Judaism, http://www.outreachjudaism.org/response.html#rfn6.

86. As Snow points out in *Zeal for God*, 74, "Had they quoted literally from the Hebrew Old Testament, but translated it into Greek, what might have happened when those they evangelized checked out their claims for Jesus (as the Bereans did)? As [Gleason] Archer remarks: 'The readers would have noticed the discrepancies at once—minor though they may have been—and would with one voice have objected, "But that isn't the way I read it in my Bible!"'" The Archer citation is from Gleason L. Archer, *Encyclopedia of Bible Difficulties* (Grand Rapids: Zondervan, 1982), 307–8.

87. Bentzion Kravitz, "'Hebrew Christians': Biblical Paradox or Religious Reality," in *The Jewish Response to Missionaries*, 4th ed. (Los Angeles: Jews for Judaism, 2001), http://www.jewsforjudaism.org/web/handbook/s_hebrew_christian.html.

88. Martin S. Rozenberg and Bernard M. Zlotowitz, *The Book of Psalms: A New Translation and Commentary* (Northvale, NJ: Aronson, 1999), 244.

89. See also Midrash Tehilim 40:4 (*k-r-h* is always an expression of digging, as in Exod 21:33); 116:2 (speaking of God's ears being *keruyot*), followed in Gevurot Yhwh 294:64, citing Yalkut Shimoni = Midr. Teh. 116:2, and then explaining the text.

90. Many scholars believe that the Septuagint followed the principle here of metonymy or, more precisely, *pars pro toto*, meaning, "the part for the whole." In other words, the Septuagint understood the Hebrew text to mean that God prepared not only (hearing?) ears, but a whole (obedient?) body, for him. (Note that the Hebrew does *not* say that God dug out *his* ears but rather that God dug out ears *for him*—"you dug out ears for me"). Or, as explained by Franz Delitzsch, since the Hebrew phrase meant, "given me the sense and faculty of obedience to Thy recognised will," this "notion of an inborn capacity of recognising and obeying the divine will is expanded into that of a body given and prepared for self-surrender to that will." Franz Delitzsch, *Commentary on the Epistle to the Hebrews, Vol. 2*, trans. Thomas L. Kingsbury (repr., Minneapolis: Klock & Klock, 1978), 151, 153. Cf. also the interpretation of Malbim.

91. For discussion of some variants in the manuscripts of the Septuagint here, cf. William L. Lane, *Hebrews 9–13*, Word Biblical Commentary (Dallas: Word, 1991), 255, note m.

92. Delitzsch, *Commentary on the Epistle to the Hebrews, Vol. 2*, 153.

93. See above, n. 26.

94. For the Messianic interpretation of Psalm 40, cf. vol. 3, 4.27. According to professor Ashley Crane, the LXX is far more interpretive than some scholars have recognized, for the most part, presuming that the readers also understood the Hebrew. See Crane, "Ezekiel 36–39: The Restoration of Israel in Early Jewish Interpretation."

95. For a summary of his work, see W. W. Ward Gasque, *Sir William Ramsay, Archeologist and New Testament Scholar: A Survey of his Contribution to the Study of the New Testament* (Grand Rapids: Baker, 1966).

96. W. M. Ramsay, *The Bearing of Recent Discovery on the Trustworthiness of the New Testament* (Grand Rapids: Baker, 1953), 222, cited in Snow, *Zeal for God*, 91.

97. Ibid., 239, cited in Snow, *Zeal for God*, 90.

98. See Snow, *Zeal for God*, 19–21, for the summary; much of his book is devoted to using these tests on the biblical evidence. On a more popular, nontechnical level, see Josh McDowell, *Evidence that Demands a Verdict* (Nashville: Thomas Nelson, 1979), 39–74.

99. Snow, *Zeal for God*, 20.

100. Note that by "the Catholic Church" Bruce is referring to all true believers at that time rather than the Roman Catholic Church as we know it today.

101. Sir Frederic Kenyon, quoted in F. F. Bruce, *The New Testament Documents: Are They Reliable?*, 6th ed. (Grand Rapids: Eerdmans, 1981), 9–15, emphasis mine. See online version of Bruce's work at http://www.worldinvisible.com/library/ffbruce/ntdocrli/nt docc02.htm.

102. Snow, *Zeal for God*, 20.

103. Keener, *IVPNT*, 39–40.

104. "The Resurrection of Jesus Christ," *Christianity Today*, 29 March 1968, 6, cited in Snow, *Zeal for God*, 76. Cf. also Craig L. Blomberg, *The Historical Reliability of the Gospels* (Downers Grove, IL: InterVarsity, 1987), 73–112.

105. As noted on a Messianic Jewish website, "Professor Simon Greenleaf of Harvard Law School, an author of an influential treatise on evidence, studied the consistency among the four Gospel writers. He offered this evaluation: 'There is enough of a discrepancy to show that there could have been no previous concert among them; and at the same time such substantial agreement as to show that they all were independent narrators of the same great transaction.' From the perspective of a classical historian, German scholar Hans Stier has concurred that agreement over basic data and divergence of details suggest credibility, because fabricated accounts tend to be fully consistent and harmonized. This is why we find four Gospels (with discrepancies), and not one." See "Challenging the Anti-Missionaries," The Refiner's Fire, http://www.therefinersfire.org/traditional_jew ish_assertions.htm.

106. Blomberg, *Historical Reliability of the Gospels*, 152; see further 113–52; for John's Gospel, see 153–89.

107. The internal evidence test is commonly utilized in popular, nontechnical defenses of the reliability of the Scriptures, such as Josh McDowell's, *The New Evidence that Demands a Verdict: Evidence I and II*, revised, updated, and expanded ed. (Nashville: Nelson Reference, 1999).

108. Snow, *Zeal for God*, 20–21.

109. Ibid., 90, with references.

110. Bruce, *The New Testament Documents*, 86–88. See online version of Bruce's work at http://www.worldinvisible.com/library/ffbruce/ntdocrli/ntdocc07.htm.

111. As noted above, n. 107, with reference to the internal evidence test, the external evidence test is commonly utilized in popular, nontechnical defenses of the reliability of the Scriptures; see again McDowell, *The New Evidence that Demands a Verdict*, for a widely-used example.

112. From the transcription of our debate of February 10, 2004, prepared by Tomi Kaiser. For the actual debate on video or DVD from ICN Ministries, see http://www.icnministries.org/resources/video.htm.

113. Ibid.

114. Carson, "Matthew," *EBC*, 8:559.

115. Ibid., 8:560.

116. Boteach-Brown debate, February 10, 2004. See above, n. 112.

117. Richard N. Longenecker, "Acts," *EBC* (Grand Rapids: Zondervan, 1981), 9:341.

118. Ibid.

119. James L. Kugel, "Stephen's Speech (Acts 7) in Its Exegetical Context," in Evans and Sanders, *From Prophecy to Testament*, 206–18.

120. Ibid., 218.

121. Ibid., 216.

122. The Tannaim were the Rabbinic scholars of the first two centuries of this era.

123. 7:216. For convenient summaries, see the articles on him in *Encyclopedia Judaica* and the *Jewish Encyclopedia*, along with Gershom Bader, *The Encyclopedia of Talmudic Sages*, trans. Solomon Katz (Northvale, NJ: Jason Aronson, 1988), 152–63. For a more full, critical study, see Jacob Neusner, *A Life of Yohanan ben Zakkai, ca. 1–80 C.E.*, rev. ed. (Studia Post Biblica; Leiden: E. J. Brill, 1970); idem, *First Century Judaism in Crisis: Yohanan ben Zakkai and the Renaissance of Tora* (Nashville, Abingdon, 1975); cf. also Amram Tropper, "Yohanan ben Zakkai, Amicus Caesaris: A Jewish Hero in Rabbinic Eyes," *Jewish Studies, an Internet Journal* 4 (2005): 1–17.

124. Interestingly, not one of the primary Rabbinic sources mentions Josephus! Perhaps we should conclude from this that Josephus didn't exist? And Philo, the great first century c.e. Jewish philosopher, did not mention by name any of the most influential Pharisaical leaders of his day. What does this prove?

125. Cf. also Gary Habermas, *The Historical Jesus: Ancient Evidence for the Life of Christ* (Joplin, MO: College Press, 1996).

126. See Robert E. Van Voorst, *Jesus Outside the New Testament: An Introduction to the Ancient Evidence* (Grand Rapids: Eerdmans, 2000), 20.

127. Ibid., 25.

128. Ibid., 30.

129. For discussion and refutation of the argument that this Chrestus was not Christ, see ibid., 32–38.

130. Ibid., 41–42. For discussion of the authenticity of this text, see ibid., 42–44.

131. Ibid., 53.

132. Ibid., 59.

133. Ibid., 66–67.

134. Ibid., 68.

135. Ibid., 70

136. Ibid.

137. Ibid.

138. Ibid., 71. Van Voorst also notes (ibid.) that even the Gospels were not written contemporaneously with Jesus—at the least, in their written form they are to be dated to two to three decades after his death and resurrection—and so it should not surprise us that Roman historians, who decidedly were *not* disciples of Jesus, would take some time to write about him.

139. Ibid., 83.

140. Ibid., 93. For full discussion of this text, see ibid., 84–104, with substantial bibliographical references.

141. See again ibid., 86–88.

142. For refutations of the totally negative position, see ibid., 88–102.

143. Cf. ibid., 104–21, again with substantial bibliographical references.

144. For philological comments on the name Yeshu, see below, n. 220.

145. For further discussion, with recent bibliography, cf. Van Voorst, *Jesus Outside the New Testament*, 104–21.

146. Note that a number of the Talmudic texts, along with later legends, were compiled in a scandalous work called *Toledot Yeshu* (The Story [or, History] of Jesus). For more on this, see below, 5.26.

147. This was noted in a candid editorial by David Klinghoffer published in the *Los Angeles Times* on January 1, 2004, shortly before Mel Gibson's film *The Passion of the Christ* was released. He stated, "It's unfair of Jewish critics to defame Gibson for saying what

the Talmud and Maimonides say, and what many historians say." See further Klinghoffer, *Why the Jews Rejected Jesus*, 73.

148. John P. Meier, *A Marginal Jew: Rethinking the Historical Jesus. Volume One: The Roots of the Problem and the Person* (Garden City, NY: Doubleday, 1991).

149. According to Graham Pockett's website, http://www.anointedlinks.com/one_soli tary_life.html, this essay was adapted from a sermon by Dr. James Allan Francis in *The Real Jesus and Other Sermons* (Philadelphia: Judson Press, 1926), 123–24, titled "Arise Sir Knight!" For the original text, see "One Solitary Life," http://www.anointedlinks .com/one_solitary_life_original.html.

150. Luke Timothy Johnson, *The Real Jesus: The Misguided Quest for the Historical Jesus and the Truth of the Traditional Gospels* (San Francisco: HarperSanFrancisco, 1996), 3.

151. Ibid., 4.

152. Ibid., 6.

153. Ibid.

154. Here is a representative quote from professor John Dominic Crossan, co-chair of the Jesus Seminar: ". . . I cannot find any detailed historical information about the crucifixion of Jesus. Every item we looked at was prophecy historicized rather than history recalled. There was one glaring exception. The one time the narrative passion broke away from its base in the prophetic passion, that is, from the single, composite trial in Psalm 2, was to assert Jewish responsibility and Roman innocence. But those motifs were neither prophecy nor history but Christian propaganda, a daring act of public relations faith in the destiny of Christianity not within Judaism but within the Roman Empire," *Who Killed Jesus? Exposing the Roots of Anti-Semitism in the Gospel Story of the Death of Jesus* (San Francisco: HarperSan Francisco, 1995), 159. Christian propaganda indeed!

155. Blomberg, *Historical Reliability of the Gospels*, 256.

156. Ibid., 256–57.

157. For the question of whether the Talmud forbids the study of the New Testament, see vol. 5, 6.4.

158. As Jeffery Tigay explains, "The evidence, as indicated in verse 17, is a garment or cloth that was spotted with the girl's blood when her hymen was perforated on the wedding night. The bride's parents would save it as evidence of her virginity. This custom is well known in the Middle East and has been practiced among various Jewish and Arab communities until recent times; in some places the cloth is displayed by the proud parents. They save it because their daughter, their reputation, and the bride-price they receive all depend on it. As Ramban notes, the mother joins the father here, though only the father speaks, because it was women who kept the cloth after the consummation of the marriage." See *Deuteronomy: The Traditional Hebrew Text With the New JPS Translation*, JPS Torah Commentary (Philadelphia: Jewish Publication Society of America, 1996), 266, with documentation in n. 47.

159. Someone might argue that medically speaking, a woman might lose her virginity and yet still preserve the physical signs of virginity, or, on the other hand, she might really be a virgin but not bleed when she loses her virginity. While this is possible, the issue here is Torah law, not medical possibility. Also, note that the Talmud deals with cases of women whose hymen was broken when they were young girls, through an accident or unusual occurrence of some kind. They are referred to as those "broken by a stick" or "injured by wood" see b. Yev. 59a–b; Ket. 10a, 11a. In the same context, the Talmud discusses cases of little girls who were sexually abused, but whose hymen was still intact and thus, technically speaking, are still to be regarded as virgins. Amazingly, anti-Semites have quoted the Talmud here, as if the rabbis said that it was no problem for a man to abuse a little girl! Of course, what it was saying was that, should such an event take place, when the

little girl grew up she was still to be regarded as a virgin, something which makes perfect sense. See further Michael L. Brown, *Our Hands Are Stained with Blood: The Tragic Story of the "Church" and the Jewish People* (Shippensburg, PA: Destiny Image Publishers, 1992), 68–69, with additional references on 199–200, 236.

160. The fact that at times, Jesus' immediate family seemed to have trouble with some of his actions during his ministry years (see, e.g., Mark 3:20–21) is no reason for surprise. The Bible is full of examples of people (from Abraham to Moses to Elijah) who had a *very* supernatural experience with God and then became either discouraged or unbelieving. Such is human nature!

161. The name of the Roman soldier is found in the Talmud as either Pandera or Panthera, apparently a play on words on the Greek word for virgin, *parthenos*; see Rashi to Sanhedrin 104b, who explains that he (i.e., Jesus) was called Ben Pandera after the name of his father, even though he was an illegitimate child; for a recent adaptation of this myth, see James D. Tabor, *The Jesus Dynasty: The Hidden History of Jesus, His Royal Family, and the Birth of Christianity* (New York: Simon and Schuster, 2006). Of course, modern Jewish scholars, with the exception of some ultra-Orthodox, would be among the first to point out that the myth of Miriam's adultery was nothing more than an ugly, polemical attack against Jesus, a mere fable of no historical value at all.

162. Bruce Chilton, *Rabbi Jesus: An Intimate Biography* (New York: Doubleday, 2000), 6. Note that this chapter (3–22) is called, "A *Mamzer* from Nazareth."

163. For an excellent, well-researched, and highly readable survey of modern cults, see Ruth A. Tucker, *Another Gospel: Alternative Religions and the New Age Movement* (Grand Rapids: Zondervan, 1989).

164. Davies and Allison, *Matthew 1–7*, 215–16.

165. It is unfortunate that Gerald Sigal, *The Jew and the Christian Missionary: A Jewish Response to Missionary Christianity* (New York: Ktav, 1981), 283, claims that according to the New Testament, God seduced Mary and committed adultery with her. Not only do such ludicrous statements insult the thoughtful reader, but they also undermine any attempt by Sigal to be taken seriously.

166. Keener, *Matthew*, 83–84.

167. After reviewing the evidence for alleged pagan parallels to the virgin birth of Jesus, D. Moody, "Virgin Birth," G. A. Buttrick, ed., *Interpreters Dictionary of the Bible* (Nashville: Abingdon, 1962), 4:791, noted that, "The yawning chasm between these pagan myths of polytheistic promiscuity and the lofty monotheism of the virgin birth of Jesus is too wide for careful research to cross."

168. R. E. Brown, "Virgin Birth," in Keith R. Crim, ed., *Interpreters Dictionary of the Bible Supplementary Volume* (Nashville: Abingdon, 1976), 942.

169. See, e.g., Singer's bizarre claim that, "at the time Paul penned the Book of Romans, he was completely unaware that Christendom would eventually claim that Jesus was born of a virgin birth"! (See "Mary's Genealogy," Outreach Judaism, http://www.out reachjudaism.org/mary.html.) That would be like saying, "At the time Abraham Lincoln penned the Emancipation Proclamation, he was completely unaware the United States would eventually claim that there had been a terrible Civil War that divided the nation." How ironic it is that the anti-missionaries frequently accuse Jewish believers in Jesus of making outlandish and completely unfounded claims.

170. As an interesting historical sidelight, in the first four centuries of this era, there were different groups of Jewish followers of Jesus, some of them "kosher" in terms of their basic beliefs being in harmony with the New Testament, and some being heretical. One of those heretical groups, the Ebionites, rejected both the writings of Paul and the virgin birth, along with the doctrine of Messiah's divine nature. This separated them from other

Jewish believers who accepted the clear testimony of their Scriptures. The point of this is that it was only a fringe Jewish-Messianic group that denied the virgin birth.

171. Carson, "Matthew," *EBC*, 8:63, rightly notes, "Actually, Matthew's chief aims in including the genealogy are hinted at in the first verse—viz., to show that Jesus Messiah is truly in the kingly line of David, heir to the messianic promises, the one who brings divine blessings to all nations."

172. Kaiser, *Hard Sayings of the Bible*, 50.

173. Glen Miller, "Problems in the Genealogies of Jesus," A Christian Thinktank, http://www.christian-thinktank.com/fabprof4.html.

174. Walter L. Liefield, "Luke," *EBC* (Grand Rapids: Zondervan, 1984), 8:861.

175. Kaiser, *Hard Sayings of the Bible*, 49–50.

176. C. F. Keil, *1 Chronicles*, in C. F. Keil and F. Delitzsch, *Biblical Commentary on the Old Testament*, vol. 3, trans. Andrew Harper, CD-ROM ed. (repr., Grand Rapids: Eerdmans, 1980; Albany, OR: AGES Software, 1997), 2:49–50.

177. Some have argued that Paul's exhortation in Titus 3:9 is relevant: "But avoid foolish controversies and genealogies and arguments and quarrels about the law, because these are unprofitable and useless." That, however, is unlikely; cf. the commentary of William D. Mounce, *Pastoral Epistles*, Word Biblical Commentary (Dallas: Word, 2000).

178. Carson, "Matthew," *EBC*, 8:63.

179. For purported DNA evidence supporting Davidic descent, see Davidic Dynasty, http://www.davidicdynasty.org/dna.php.

180. Cf. the similar claim of Uri Yosef on the Messiah Truth website: "Thus, the Jewish Messiah may emerge from **ANY** royal branch that leads to Solomon" (his emphasis); "Genealogical Scams and Flimflams," Messiah Truth Project, http://www.messiahtruth.com/genealogy.html.

181. "Jewish Belief in Messiah: The Jewish Concept of Messiah and the Jewish Response to Christian Claims," Jews for Judaism, http://www.jewsforjudaism.org/web/faq/general-messiah-jewishresponse.html.

182. Keener also notes that, ". . . Matthew probably believes this to be Jesus' legal rather than blood line (1:18–25), but such an observation in no way detracts from the importance of that line; Matthew lived in a world where adoption lines were significant and frequently qualified sons for royalty (e.g., Augustus with Tiberius, Suet. *Tib.* 23)." *Matthew*, 80.

183. According to Rashi, the phrase "with the clouds of heaven" means "swiftly" (*bimhirut*). But that is certainly not what the phrase means in Daniel 7:13–14, and we cannot be certain that such a meaning was intended by the Talmudic rabbi (named Alexandri) who raised the point in the text under discussion in Sanhedrin.

184. It is possible, of course, that some of these Rabbinic passages are merely figurative, while others point to the Messiah's *spiritual* preexistence. On the other hand, it is fair to ask: Where are such references *to* a preexistent David *in the* Rabbinic literature? This is not to say for a moment that these Rabbinic traditions about the Messiah point to his divinity. But they do point to his greatness, to say the least, and possibly, to some aspects of his transcendence.

185. For further details, see vol. 2, 3.22.

186. Gerald Sigal bluntly states, "There is no verse in the Gospel of Luke that makes the claim that Mary is a descendant of King David. In fact, there is no New Testament verse that makes this claim." See Jews for Judaism, http://www.jewsforjudaism.org/web/faq/faq003.html.

187. Keener, *Matthew*, 75.

188. As is often noted, Matthew's grouping of 14s is meant to be general, primarily for mnemonic purposes, although there may be some theological significance as well.; see Keener, *IVPNT*, 46–47.

189. There are many New Testament scholars who believe that both Matthew and Luke give genealogies of Joseph, not finding this to be contradictory to the concept of Davidic descent (see, e.g., the discussion in Carson, "Matthew," *EBC*, 8:60–65). I am not convinced, however, that Yeshua's Davidic descent can be maintained without Miriam herself also descending from that line, and so, if both Matthew and Luke record genealogies of Joseph, then we would have to look for other evidence for Miriam's lineage, either in other New Testament books or outside sources. If that evidence exists, I am not aware of it.

190. David H. Stern, *Jewish New Testament Commentary: A Companion Volume to the Jewish New Testament* (Clarksville, MD: Jewish New Testament Publications, 1995), 112, notes: "A literal translation of the Greek text starting at v. 23 would be: 'And Yeshua himself was beginning about thirty years, being son, as was supposed, of Yosef, of the Eli, of the Mattat, of the L'vi,' etc." Understanding that "Luke gives the genealogy of Yeshua through his mother Miryam, the daughter of Eli," then, "Yeshua is 'of the Eli' in the sense of being his grandson; while Yeshua's relationship with Yosef is portrayed in the words, 'son, as supposed'—implying not actually. . . ." (This work is henceforth cited as *JNTC*.)

191. See above, n. 181.

192. For ancient Near Eastern parallels, cf. Jacob Milgrom, *Numbers: The Traditional Hebrew Text with the New JPS Translation* (Philadelphia: Jewish Publication Society, 1990), 416, who notes, "Ancient Sumerian law ordains that an unmarried daughter may inherit when there are no sons, and so also do decrees of Gudea (ca. 2150 B.C.E.), ruler of Lagash. Thus, the concession made by the Bible to Zelophehad's daughters was anticipated in Mesopotamia by a millennium. It is also clear from documents of Nuzi and Ugarit (i.e., in places as far apart as the Tigris River and the Mediterranean coast during the middle and second half of the second millennium) that daughters inherited in the absence of sons." See ibid., 416–418, for discussion of the application of this principle in Rabbinic law (m. B. B. 8:1–2).

193. Sigal notes that, "Biblically, the right of lineal privilege, that is, kingship and priesthood, are exclusively passed on through the male line. The incident regarding the inheritance of the daughters of Zelophehad (Numbers, chapters 27 and 36) does not apply here since it concerns the transference of physical property and not privileges of lineage." See Jews for Judaism, http://www.jewsforjudaism.org/web/faq/faq013.html. Of course, he fails to observe that these two concepts are related—in fact, there is a principle to be deduced from this legislation regarding inheritance—and he does not deal at all with the genealogical evidence of 1 Chronicles 2:34–35 which we also discuss here.

194. Some would argue that 1 Chron. 2:21–22 is also relevant, where it is stated that "Hezron lay with the daughter of Makir the father of Gilead (he had married her when he was sixty years old), and she bore him Segub. Segub was the father of Jair, who controlled twenty-three towns in Gilead." So, the association with Gilead comes through the mother, identified only as "the daughter of Makir the father of Gilead."

195. U. Holzmeister, "Ein Erklärungsversuch der Lk-Geneaologie (3,23–38)," *Zeitschrift für Theologie und Kirche* 47 (1923): 184–218.

196. Nolland, *Luke 1–9:20*, 170.

197. Some scholars argue that this points to the *adoption* of Jarha by Sheshan (who, presumably, became a worshiper of Yahweh), rather than pointing to the genealogy being traced through the daughter. As noted in the *Jewish Encyclopedia*, "The Adoption of the slave as son and heir, as indicated in the Bible in the words of Abraham, 'One born in my house is mine heir' (Gen. xv. 3), was probably practised frequently in the manner described

in I Chron. ii. 34 *et seq.*, where Sheshan is mentioned as having given his daughter as wife to his servant and adopted their sons as his own" ("Adoption," 1:208). Either way, however, it supports the validity of the New Testament genealogies of Jesus: If Sheshan's genealogy continues through his daughter, this would serve as a direct parallel to the Messiah's genealogy coming through his mother; if Sheshan adopted Jarha into his line of descent, this would be parallel to Joseph adopting Jesus into his line. Rabbinic commentaries point to 2:31, speaking of Sheshan's son Ahlai, stating that he became sick and died without children. Wouldn't this underscore the fact that Jarha was given to Sheshan's daughter to continue his line? Note Rashi to 2:35: "From here they derived that if your daughter has matured, free your slave and give him to her (*Pes.* 113a), and from here the Sages derived in the Palestinian Talmud, Tractate *Yebamoth* (source unknown): 'Do not trust a proselyte until fifteen generations, and fifteen generations are from Ittai the Egyptian until Ishmael, and some say sixteen generations, including Jarha.' The midrash states the following: 'Is it possible that he was of the royal descent (*mizzera' hamelukah*) [as in Jeremiah 41:1]? Now was not Ishmael of the seed of Jerahmeel and not from Ram? But rather it means that he passed his seed to the molech.'" (See also Malbim to 1 Chron. 2:34; he claims that Sheshan's son was born after he gave Jarha to his daughter.)

198. Gerald Sigal, Jews for Judaism, http://www.jewsforjudaism.org/web/faq/faq030.html.

199. *Jewish Study Bible*, 694, to 1 Kings 9:4–9. Ziony Zevit writes there, "Reaffirming the conditionality of the promise to David and his dynasty, God denies Solomon's request of 8.25–26 for a guarantee. For emphasis, God states also that the existence of the Temple itself depends on the proper behavior of Israel."

200. David Rothstein, ibid., 1746, to 1 Chronicles 17:13, raises the larger issue of the conditional or unconditional nature of the promises to David, noting different scholarly views on the subject. For further discussion, cf. the standard commentaries to 1 Chronicles and 2 Samuel.

201. See, e.g., 1 Kings 11:39, with reference to God punishing David's seed, not Solomon's; Jeremiah 33:22, a promise to multiply David's seed; note also 2 Chronicles 23:3b, "Jehoiada said to them, 'The king's son shall reign, as the LORD promised concerning the descendants of David'"—not the descendants of Solomon; cf. also the reference to the "Root of Jesse" in Isaiah 11:10. This, of course, is just a sampling.

202. See further Greg Herrick, "Conceptions of Davidic Hope in Psalms 89, 110, and 132," Bible.org, http://www.bible.org/page.asp?page_id=1573.

203. Commenting on 2 Samuel 7:14, Ronald F. Youngblood, "1, 2 Samuel," *EBC* (Grand Rapids: Zondervan, 1992), 3:891, notes: "The formula 'provides both the judicial basis for the gift of the eternal dynasty (compare Pss 2:7–8; 89) and the qualification that disloyal sons will lose YHWH's protection (compare 1 Kings 6:12–13; 9:4, 6–7)' (Waltke, 'The Phenomenon of Conditionality,' p. 131; cf. Weinfeld, 'The Covenant of Grant,' p. 190)."

204. According to J. Barton Payne, "1, 2 Chronicles," *EBC* (Grand Rapids: Zondervan, 1988), 4:436, commenting on 1 Chron. 28:6–7, "That is, the fulfillment of true sonship to God the 'Father' was not achieved by Solomon (cf. comment on [1 Chron.] 22:10); it was 'an ideal that actualized only in Christ' (Payne, *Prophecy*, p. 226)."

205. See Malbim's commentary to 1 Chronicles 28:7 and Psalm 132:11–12.

206. There is now an organization seeking to reunite all descendants of David. According to the Davidic Dynasty website, "Descent from David Hamelech is more than just a shared strand of DNA; it is an inheritance of responsibility for the welfare of the Jewish people. At this crucial juncture in our people's history we face as grave a danger from within as from without. Our enemies still seek to destroy us physically and spiritually. The perils from within, assimilation, intermarriage and those who wish to forfeit their

Jewish identity and our birthright, are also threatening our very existence." Once again, the emphasis is simply on Davidic descent, not Davidic descent through Solomon. See http://www.davidicdynasty.org.

207. See Maimonides, *Sefer HaMitzvot*, Negative Commandments, 362.

208. There are *some* Rabbinic traditions that argue for Solomonic descent; see, e.g., the comments in the Schottenstein Talmud to b. Sanh 95b (95b¹), n. 12, with reference to 2 Kings 11:1: "*Yad David* points out that not *all* descendants of David were in Asaliah's [i.e., Queen Athaliah's] reach. Rather, the verse means that she killed all the descendants of Solomon, for they alone were heirs to the throne, and they were thus the ones affected by the punishment due David's heirs. See also *Margaliyos HaYam* §6." The fact, however, that it is even a subject of discussion indicates that Solomonic descent may not have been foremost in the minds of the Talmudic commentators; it does not seem to be Rashi's opinion either, as seen in his comments to 2 Chron. 22:10: "for David foresaw with the holy spirit that in the eighth generation [of his dynasty] all his descendants would be slain by Athaliah, for there are eight generations from Solomon till here." More importantly, the alleged requirement of Solomonic descent for the Messiah was *not* an issue in the Scriptures.

209. A corollary objection that could be raised would be that Athaliah only tried to kill the descendants of Solomon, who were considered the legitimate heirs to the throne and not all descendants of David; cf. immediately above, n. 208. This argument, however, carries little weight since: (1) The text does not state explicitly that she only tried to kill the sons of Solomon, simply "the whole royal family," which, if it did not refer to the descendants of David in general referred specifically to the sons and siblings of Ahaziah, rather than to all descendants of Solomon, as suggested in the previous note by some Talmudic commentators. (2) Even if she did only kill Solomon's sons—which is highly unlikely—her purposes were entirely pragmatic, as stated, seeking to eliminate any sons or siblings of the king. (3) What if she had succeeded in destroying every descendant of Solomon, thereby wiping out the "royal" line? Do you think for a moment that another son of David would not have been produced as the next possible successor? Do you think that the children of Israel would have then considered all the promises to David null and void even if other descendants of David were alive? Hardly! This, of course, is just theoretical, since Athaliah did not kill one of the king's sons; but the point remains clear.

210. For the claim that Talmudic laws regarding inheritance rights for adopted sons are relevant here, cf. Stern, *JNTC*, 8.

211. John McTernan and Lou Ruggiero, *Jesus of Nazareth: The King Messiah* (Oklahoma City, OK: Hearthstone Publishing, 2002), 183. Further support for this position is allegedly found in Jeremiah 52:10 which states that the rest of Zedekiah's sons (Zedekiah was Jehoiachin's uncle and the last king of Judah) were killed by the Babylonians, and therefore the Messiah had to come through Jehoiachin's line, which was cursed—and therefore there had to be a virgin birth. Again, these arguments are not compelling, especially when one realizes that the Messiah simply had to be a descendant of David, not a descendant of the line of Davidic kings. See also immediately below, n. 212.

212. It was also noted earlier (above, 5.11) that the Scriptures do not require the Messianic line to proceed through Solomon, meaning that the Messiah did not have to be a descendant of Jehoiachin.

213. Brown, "Jeremiah," *EBC*² (vol. 7) to Jer. 22:28–30.

214. Kaiser, *Hard Sayings of the Bible*, 310.

215. John Bright, *Jeremiah* (Anchor Bible; New York: Doubleday, 1965).

216. According to Archer, *Encyclopedia of Bible Difficulties*, commenting on Jer. 36:30, "When the Heb. verb *yašab* ["sit enthroned"] is used of a king, it implies a certain degree of permanence rather than so short a time as ninety days."

217. Parts of this text are also found in Midrash Rabbah to Song of Solomon 8:5; Midrash Rabbah Leviticus, Margoliot 10:5; cf. also Otsar Midrashim, Maasiyot Keta b; Orchot Tzadikim, Gate 26, Repentance; Shelah to Yoma 16; in the Zohar—as well as in other Rabbinic sources—Jeconiah's repentance explains the genealogy in 1 Chron. 3:17; see Zohar with additions, part b, 106a.

218. This is the standard translation of William G. Braude, *Pesikta de-Rab Kahana: R. Kahana's Compilation of Discourses for Sabbaths and Festal Days*, 2nd ed., trans. William G. (Gershon Zev) Braude and Israel J. Kapstein (1975; repr., Philadelphia: Jewish Publication Society, 2002), 316.

219. Note that Uri Yosef, writing for the Messiah Truth website, is aware of these traditions but then makes the amazing statement, "This is a rather curious position, since it is consistent with the opinion of the Sages of the Talmud, that Jeconiah repented while in exile, and that exile atones for all sins (e.g., Babylonian Talmud, Tractate Sanhedrin 37b–38a). In this case, these Christian apologists and missionaries actually admit, perhaps unwittingly, that the shedding of blood is not required to bring about the remission of sins!" (Uri Yosef, "Genealogical Scams and Flimflams," Messiah Truth Project, http://www.messiahtruth.com/genealogy.html, n. 6.). But which "Christian apologist or missionary" thinks that every single time someone repented, an animal sacrifice had to be offered for atonement? If this were the case, there would not have been a sacrificial animal left in Israel within a few days of the setting up of the first altar, nor would anyone have had time to do anything except offer sacrifices at the Tabernacle/Temple. For a refutation of this strange notion, cf. vol. 1, 1.11; vol. 2, 3.8–3.9.

220. While some Hebrew scholars claim that the Talmudic *yešu* reflects a natural philological development (from *yešu'a* > *yešu'* > *yešu*) rather than a polemical one (*yešu* standing for *yimaḥ šemô wezikrô*, "may his name and memory be obliterated"), there is no question that, at some point in time, the polemical usage became prevalent in Rabbinic circles. The widespread nature of this pronunciation through the years is seen most clearly in modern Hebrew usage, where Israelis are familiar with Jesus as Yeshu rather than Yeshua. Interestingly, the Koran uses a mistaken name for Jesus (Arabic *'isa* instead of *yasu'a*), apparently based on the fact that Mohammed learned the pronunciation of Jesus' name from Jewish sources, not realizing that these Jews referred to Jesus disparagingly as "Esau" (Arabic *'isa*). Thus, throughout the Talmud and the Koran, the name of Jesus is incorrectly rendered in Hebrew/Aramaic and Arabic. Does this reflect a spiritual battle over "the name" (cf., e.g., Acts 4:7; Phil. 2:9–11)? With regard to Jews, this is not simply a matter of pronunciation, since a Hebrew speaker or religious Jew reading the Tanakh will not realize that the strange name "Yeshu," which he has heard for years, is actually *yešu'a*, found as a proper name 27x in the Tanakh (most notably, in the person of the postexilic High Priest, Joshua/Yeshua, a Messianic prototype; see, e.g., Zech. 3:1–10; 6:9–15; Ezra 3:1–9). Regarding the pronunciation and spelling of Yeshua's name that would have been current in his day, there is evidence of the mutation of gutturals in Mishnaic Hebrew (cf. M. H. Segal, *A Grammar of Mishnaic Hebrew* [1927; repr., Oxford: Clarendon, 1978], 23), along with evidence of the confusion and even loss of gutturals in later Samaritan Hebrew (cf. Angel Sáenz-Badillos, *A History of the Hebrew Language*, trans. John Elwolde [Cambridge: Cambridge University Press, 1993], 153ff., with reference especially to the work of Z. Ben-Hayyim). However, it is very difficult to prove that *orthographic*, final *'ayyin* completely dropped out (even in a proper name) as early as the first to second century. Note also that in Syriac, the name is spelled *yešu'*, preserving the final *'ayyin* without the

nonsyllabic glide vowel (called *pataḥ furtivum*) which developed in Hebrew morphology when case endings disappeared.

221. Reference is then made to R. Travis Herford, *Christianity in Talmud and Midrash* (London: Williams & Northgate, 1903), 51ff., where the passage is discussed at length.

222. Solomon Schecther, quoted in Van Voorst, *Jesus Outside the New Testament*, 122; for discussion of the *Toledot*, which, thankfully, are totally ignored by almost all Jews today, cf. ibid., 122–28. For a modern resurrection of this scurrilous work in a book containing a bizarre mix of scholarship and nonsense, see Frank R. Zindler, *The Jesus the Jews Never Knew*: Sepher Todoth Yeshu *and the Quest of the Historical Jesus in Jewish Sources* (Cranford, NJ: American Atheist Press, 2003). He prints the text, with comments, on pages 423–50. Note well that this book was published by the American Atheist Press!

223. Brown, *Israel's Divine Healer*, 222–23; I have removed internal cross-references and the endnote references from the quote here. The interested reader will find a comprehensive study of the subject of God as Healer in this volume, along with discussion of the theology of miracles. Relevant to our discussion here is the comment of Morton T. Kelsey, *Healing and Christianity* (New York: Harper & Row, 1973), 89: "The healing ministry of Jesus is the logical result of the incarnation: God so loved the world that he gave his only begotten Son; Jesus so loved that he healed. His healings were the authentication of his mission and his person. They flowed naturally from him because he was what he was."

224. Cf. George Soares-Prabhu, *The Formula Quotations in the Infancy Narrative of Matthew: An Enquiry into the Tradition History of Matthew 1–2* (Rome: Biblical Institute Press, 1976). My appreciation to professor Scot McKnight for referring me to this volume.

225. Nolland, *Gospel of Matthew*, 947, notes that, "The dying words of the priest Zechariah in 2 Ch. 24:22 ('May Yahweh hear and avenge') make a good fit for Mt. 23 and match the blood of Abel crying out from the ground (Gen 4:10 [with further reference made in the footnote to b. Giṭ 57b]). If the right Zechariah has been identified, then the Gospel tradition is probably the earliest indication that, as was true later, 2 Chronicles was placed last in the Hebrew Bible."

226. For discussion and rejection of other views, see Carson, "Matthew," *EBC*, 8:485–86. For further discussion, cf. Martin McNamara, "Zechariah the Son of Barachiah: Mat 23:35 and Tg. Lam. 2:20," in his *The New Testament and Palestinian Targum to the Pentateuch* (Rome: Pontifical Biblical Institute, 1966), 160–63, and the works cited in Nolland, *Gospel of Matthew*, 943–44.

227. Already in the nineteenth century, Alfred Edersheim pointed out this Targumic citation; see *The Life and Times of Jesus the Messiah*, software ed. (Albany, OR: AGES Software, 1999), 2:760, n. 2230. The prophet is also called Zechariah son of Iddo in other Rabbinic writings; cf., e.g, b. Yoma 39b; b. Eruv 21a; Leviticus Rabbah 6:6.

228. Michael Knowles, *Jeremiah in Matthew's Gospel*, 138, n. 2, notes that Sheldon H. Blank, in his important study, "The Death of Zechariah in Rabbinic Literature," *Hebrew Union College Annual* 12–13 (1937–1938): 327–46, "has shown that the two Zechariahs were often confused in rabbinic exegesis."

229. It could also be argued, as some have done, albeit without any real evidence, that Berechiah was another name for Jehoiada; cf. the commentary to Matt. 23:35 by Peter of Laodicea, who states, "For he was of two names."

230. For the biblical texts, see, e.g., Ernst Würthwein, *The Text of the Old Testament: An Introduction to Biblia Hebraica*, rev. ed., trans. Errol F. Rhodes (Grand Rapids: Eerdmans, 1995); Bruce M. Metzger, *The Text of the New Testament: Its Transmission, Corruption, and Restoration*, 4th ed. (New York: Oxford University Press, 2005). This is commonly called "lower criticism" and is practiced by conservative biblical scholars, while some of

the greatest rabbis in Jewish history, such as the Vilna Gaon (1720–1797) also posited corrections to the extant Talmudic and Rabbinic texts.

231. For other explanations, see, e.g., Carson, "Matthew," *EBC*, 8:485–86; Keener, *Matthew*, 556–57; Nolland, *Gospel of Matthew*, 946–47.

232. See, e.g., Sigal, *The Jew and the Christian Missionary*, 220–21, where he claims that, "Matthew's Jesus made an egregious error which illustrates the inaccuracy of the evangelical account."

233. Soncino Talmud, with footnote 23. Footnote 24 simply references "I Chron. XXVII, 34." The rendering of 2 Sam. 20:23 is, "And Joab was in command of all the army of Israel; and Benaiah the son of Jehoiada was over the Kerethites and over the Pelethites." Cf., e.g., 2 Sam. 8:18; 23:20, 22; 1 Kings 1:8; 2:25; 1 Chron. 11:22.

234. Note that while Tosafot emends the Talmudic text to be in harmony with the biblical citation, Rashi supports the standard reading. See further the comments in the Schottenstein Talmud to Berachot, 3b[4].

235. See also the appendix to vol. 5, with n. 45 there.

236. For a response to anti-missionary rabbi Moshe Shulman's *defense* of using different weights and measures (see his online article "Just Weights and Measures," Messiah Truth Project, http://www.messiahtruth.com/weights.html), see n. 54 to the appendix to vol. 5.

237. Isidore Singer, "Gentile," *Jewish Encyclopedia*, 5:615.

238. Carson, "Matthew," *EBC*, 8:562.

239. It was in the 1970s that I first heard the claim that scientists had "discovered" a lost hour in world history as they somehow managed to go back through time, attributing this lost hour to this very text in Joshua. Although the report caused excitement in some circles, I do not think it has many serious defenders today. See, e.g., Robert C. Newman, "Joshua's Long Day and the NASA Computers," Interdisciplinary Biblical Research Institute, http://www.ibri.org/Tracts/longdtct.htm.

240. For some of these noncanonical stories, see, e.g., W. Schneemelcher, ed., *New Testament Apocrypha*, vols. 1–2, rev. ed., trans. R. McL. Wilson (Louisville: Westminster/ John Knox, 1991–1992).

241. Samuel Tobias Lachs, *Rabbinic Commentary on the New Testament: The Gospels of Matthew, Mark, and Luke* (Hoboken, NJ: Ktav, 1987), 435.

242. Nolland, *Gospel of Matthew*, 1214.

243. Rabbi Mendy Hecht, "What Are the 613 Mitzvot?" AskMoses.com, http://www .askmoses.com/article.html?h=411&o=91.

244. Because traditional Jews do not accept (or, often, do not understand) Messianic beliefs in God's complex unity and his divine revelation through Yeshua, they consider those beliefs to be idolatrous for Jews. For refutation of this viewpoint, see vol. 2, 3.1–3.4.

245. This was the title of a chapter in my book *It's Time to Rock the Boat: A Call to God's People to Rise and Preach a Confrontational Gospel* (Shippensburg, PA: Destiny Image, 1993), 154–66, where these principles were fleshed out for contemporary followers of Jesus.

246. Dan Harman; I do not have the original source of this insightful quote.

247. Stern, *JNTC*, 129.

248. Tigay, *Deuteronomy*, 256, with n. 39.

249. To listen to a message entitled "Consumers or Disciples?" go to http://www.icn ministries.org/revolution/audio.htm.

250. It could also be added that it is Luke who provides this teaching, and that Luke above all the Gospel authors is careful to show how inclusive Jesus was to women and foreigners (see, e.g., Luke 8:1–3; 17:11–19; his perspective is sometimes called "cosmopolitan"). This should also be taken into consideration, indicating that neither Luke nor his intended readers would hear Jesus' words in an ugly and completely offensive way.

251. For the level of sacrifice made by the disciples, see Peter's comment in Mark 10:28–30, in light of Matt. 8:14–15.

252. Liefield, "Luke," *EBC*, 8:936, following Joachim Jeremias and E. E. Bishop.

253. Lachs, *Rabbinic Commentary on the New Testament*, 159.

254. See B. R. McCane, "'Let the Dead Bury Their Own Dead': Secondary Burial and Matt. 8:21–22," *Harvard Theological Review* 83 (1990): 31–43.

255. Nolland, *Gospel of Matthew*, 367, with reference to Davies and Allison.

256. Nolland, ibid., 368. As for the phrase, "Let the dead bury their own dead," Nolland notes that, ultimately, "The force of the words is: 'Let other arrangements be made; you have more pressing duties.'"

257. *The Rosh Yeshivah Remembers: Stories that Inspire the Yeshivah World, as Retold by Rabbi Elazar Menachem Man Shach, Shilta*, compiled by Rabbi Asher Bergman (Brooklyn: Mesorah, 1999), 50–51. As an illustration of how passionately Rav Shach was committed to keeping his mind clear for study, consider the following: "In his late 80s, Rabbi Shach required surgery to remove a growth on his leg. The surgeon told him that general anesthesia would be required. Rabbi Shach would not agree because the anesthesia would cloud his thinking, and he could not afford that. He told the surgeon that he could deal with the pain. Students pinioned his leg to prevent any involuntary movement when the surgeon cut into his flesh." (See Jonathan Rosenbaum, "We Have Lost a Father," *Jerusalem Post*, November 11, 2001, http://www.aish.com/jewishissues/jewishsociety/We_Have_Lost_A_Father.asp (posted on Aish.com December 6, 2005).

258. Hayim Nahman Bilalik and Yehoshua Hana Ravnitzky, eds., *The Book of Legends: Sefer Ha-Aggadah: Legends from the Talmud and Midrash*, trans. William G. Braude (New York: Schocken, 1992), 235, citing m. Semahot 8:13; see also b. M.K. 21b.

259. Dan Cohn-Sherbok, *On Earth as It Is in Heaven: Jews, Christians, and Liberation Theology* (Maryknoll, NY: Orbis Books, 1987), 17–18, cited in Walter Riggans, *Yeshua ben David: Why Do the Jewish People Reject Jesus as Their Messiah?* (Crowborough, England: Marc, 1995, 196.

260. Beth Moshe [pseud.], *Judaism's Truth Answers the Missionaries*, 252, cited in Riggans, *Yeshua ben David*, 197.

261. Beth Moshe, *Judaism's Truth Answers the Missionaries*, 199.

262. Janet Aviad, *Return to Judaism: Religious Renewal in Israel* (Chicago: University of Chicago Press, 1985), 116, 117, cited in Riggans, *Yeshua ben David*, 199–200.

263. Riggans, *Yeshua ben David*, 200.

264. Cf. Steinsaltz, II, 194–96 = B. M. 33a, esp. with ref. to R. Meir's words cited on 196.

265. As summarized by Nolland, *Gospel of Matthew*, 258, n. 235. Stern points to m. B. K. 8:1 for further, related examples, see Stern, *JNTC*, 29.

266. For a point for point treatment of the relevant passages in Matthew 5–7, see Stern, *JNTC*, with interaction with Rabbinic parallels where relevant; see also below, 5.28, for broader discussion. For the spiritual application and challenge of these chapters, see Oswald Chambers, *Studies in the Sermon on the Mount* (repr., Fort Washington, PA: Christian Literature Crusade, 1985).

267. Carson, "Matthew," *EBC*, 8:151.

268. Michael L. Brown, *Go and Sin No More: A Call to Holiness* (Ventura, CA: Renew, 1999), 198–200.

269. Finding a stray person who has attempted to mutilate himself because of this teaching only proves the point. If such a person exists, he or she is one in multiplied hundreds of millions.

270. Bruce, *Hard Sayings of the Bible*, 360–61.

271. b. Shab. 108b.

272. Since that volume was published in 2000, anti-missionary author Gerald Sigal has written a 340-page study entitled *Anti-Judaism in the New Testament* (Philadelphia: self-published, Xlibris, 2004). While this is a much more substantial and serious work than his earlier work, *The Jew and the Christian Missionary: A Jewish Response to Missionary Christianity* (New York: Ktav, 1981), it does not bring much new material to the table nor does it interact directly with the material I presented in the first volume in this series, even though volume 1 was published in 2000.

273. Merrill C. Tenney, "John," *EBC* (Grand Rapids: Zondervan, 1981), 9:155.

274. For a summary of the various interpretations of what is commonly called the Olivet Discourse, since it was spoken on the Mount of Olives, see any of the major commentaries on the Synoptic Gospels.

275. In this sense, some commentators also believe that he was speaking about his coming *in judgment*—just as God sometimes referred to his own coming in acts of judgment in the Hebrew Scriptures, rather than to a real, physical appearing.

276. See *Hard Sayings of the Bible*, 445–48. In favor of this view is the common usage of the phrase "this generation," always with reference to Yeshua's current generation.

277. For the meanings of *genea*, cf. Frederick William Danker, ed., *A Greek-English Lexicon of the New Testament and Other Early Christian Literature*, 3rd ed. (Chicago: University of Chicago Press, 2000), 191–92 (henceforth cited as BDAG). This argument, however, should not be pressed too strongly, since the nuance of "race" would have been much clearer had the Greek word *genos*, as opposed to *genea*, been used here; cf. ibid., 194–95.

278. Note also the Rabbinic claim that "there is no early or late in the Torah" (*'en muqdam we'en me'uhar battorah*), i.e., the Torah is not written in chronological order.

279. For a discussion of different views, along with comments on the minor variation of six days or eight days, see, e.g., Carson, "Matthew," *EBC*, 8:380–84.

280. *Dictionary*, Labor Law Talk, http://encyclopedia.laborlawtalk.com/Vaticinium%20ex%20eventu.

281. For a fair review of the dating of the Olivet Discourse, cf. Keener, *Matthew*, 559–73.

282. Walter W. Wessel, "Mark," *EBC* (Grand Rapids: Zondervan, 1984), 8:743.

283. Ibid.

284. Ibid.

285. Brown, "Jeremiah," *EBC*² (vol. 7) to Jer. 4:7.

286. Ibid., citing B. Oded, "Where Is the 'Myth of the Empty Land' to Be Found? History versus Myth," in Oded Lipschits and Joseph Blenkinsopp, eds., *Judah and the Judeans in the Neo-Babylonian Period* (Winona Lake, IN: Eisenbrauns, 2003), 66, with ref. to Lawrence E. Stager, "The Fury of Babylon: The Archaeology of Destruction," *Biblical Archeology Review* 22 (1996): 56–69, 76–77.

287. Brown, ibid.

288. Should you argue that Jeremiah's prophecies are *still to be fulfilled* in the future, then, quite obviously, the same argument could be made for the prophecies of Jesus. A more serious question, however, has to do with the apparent nonfulfillment of Jeremiah's prophecies against Babylon (see Jeremiah 50–51), since he declared that it would be utterly demolished, whereas, in reality, the city surrendered without a fight. For discussion of this, see my discussion following Jer. 51:64 in Brown, "Jeremiah," *EBC*² (vol. 7), "Excursus on Prophetic Expectation, the Return from Exile, and the Fall of Babylon."

289. Professor Steve Alt, one of my colleagues at FIRE School of Ministry, in a private email to the author.

290. As noted by James D. G. Dunn, *Romans 9–16*, Word Biblical Commentary (Dallas: Word, 1988), 680, "[Paul's] conviction is simply of a mounting climax with the incoming of the Gentiles as the trigger for the final end in which Israel's conversion, Christ's Parousia, and the final resurrection (v 15) would all be involved. The thought once again is characteristically apocalyptic, expressive of the certainty that events on earth are following a schedule predetermined by God (e.g., Dan 11:36; *Jub.* 1.29; *2 Apoc. Bar.* 48.2–3, 6; see further Russell, *Apocalyptic*, 230–34). In particular, the idea of the number of the elect as planned by God and awaiting completion was one which came strongly to the surface in the second half of the first century A.D. (see particularly *2 Apoc. Bar.* 23.4; 30.2; 75.6; *4 Ezra* 4.36–37; *Apoc. Abr.* 29.17; Rev 6:11; 7:4; 14:1; *1 Clem* 2.4; 59.2; *4 Ezra* 2.40–41; Stuhlmann, chap. 3). That such an emphasis need not and should not serve as any excuse for human indolence and passivity is sufficiently indicated by the example of Paul himself (11:13–14; 15:14–15; 16:25–26)."

291. Wessel, "Mark," *EBC*, 8:725–26. The verdict of T. W. Manson was even more extreme: "It is a tale of miraculous power wasted in the service of ill temper (for the supernatural energy employed to blast the unfortunate tree might have been more usefully expended in forcing a crop of figs out of season); and as it stands it is simply incredible" (T. W. Manson, "The Cleansing of the Temple," *Bulletin of the John Rylands Library* 33 [1951]: 259), cited in ibid.

292. The view of C. F. Keil is similar: "In the announcement of the devastation of the land there is an allusion to Deut 20:19–20, according to which the Israelites were ordered to spare the fruit-trees when Canaan was taken. These instructions were not to apply to Moab, because the Moabites themselves as the arch-foes of Israel would not act in any other way with the land of Israel if they should gain the victory." C. F. Keil, *The Books of the Kings*, in C. F. Keil and F. Delitzsch, *Biblical Commentary on the Old Testament*, vol. 3, trans. James Martin, CD-ROM ed. (repr., Grand Rapids: Eerdmans, 1980; Albany, OR: AGES Software, 1997), 1:305, to 2 Kings 3:19.

293. Keener, *IVPNT*, 165.

294. Bruce, *Hard Sayings of the Bible*, 442. According to Wessel, "Mark," *EBC*, 8:726, "The best explanation is to see the miracle as an acted-out parable. Jesus' hunger provides the occasion for his use of this teaching device. The fig tree represents Israel (cf. Hos 9:10; Nah 3:12; Zech 10:2). The tree is fully leafed out, and in such a state one would normally expect to find fruit. This symbolizes the hypocrisy and sham of the nation of Israel, which made her ripe for the judgment of God. 'A people which honoured God with their lips but whose heart was all the time far from him (7:6) was like a tree with abundance of leaves but no fruit. The best commentary on vv. 12–14 and 20 f. is to be found in the narrative which these verses enframe' (Cranfield, *Gospel of Mark*, pp. 356–57)." While there is some truth to this description, it paints with too broad a brush, because of which some readers have wrongly concluded that Yeshua's words in Mark 11:14, "May no one ever eat fruit from you again," meaning that Israel was being rejected and cursed forever, a completely unscriptural position if ever there was one. For a refutation of this very wrong interpretation of Scripture, cf. Brown, *Our Hands Are Stained with Blood*, 117–53. (In reality, I could simply say, For a refutation of this very wrong interpretation of Scripture just read the rest of the Bible! For convenience sake, a reading of Romans 11 will suffice, with verses such as Romans 11:11–29 virtually jumping off the page.)

295. The significance of these verses being found in conjunction with the title "rabbi" was pointed out to me in a conversation with the Messianic Jewish leader Harvey (Yosef) Koellner almost twenty years ago, based on a sermon he had just preached to his congregation, Temple Aron Kodesh in Fort Lauderdale, Florida.

296. Of course, anyone who has followed my work through the years is fully aware that I have devoted much time and energy to *combating* anti-Semitism; for more on this, see *Our Hands Are Stained with Blood*, which remains the most translated work that I have written.

297. For related sources, see b. A. Z. 27a; Maimonides, *Hilkhot Shabbat* 2:12; Shulchan Arukh, Orach Hayyim 330.

298. Laws of Murderers and Preserving Life, 4:11, as cited by Rabbi Dr. Moshe Zemer, *Evolving Halakhah: A Progressive Approach to Traditional Jewish Law* (Woodstock, VT: Jewish Lights Publishing, 1999), 212–13; note that Rabbinic teachings such as these are commonly exploited on anti-Semitic (or, at the very least, anti-Zionist) websites; see, e.g., Radio Islam, http://www.radioislam.org/historia/zionism/zionrac15.html; or, Church of the Sons of YHVH/Legion of Saints, http://www.churchofthesonsofyhvh.org.

299. Cited in Leivy Smolar and Moses Aberbach, *Studies in Targum Jonathan to the Prophets*, printed with Pinkhos Churgin, *Targum Jonathan to the Prophets* (New York: Ktav, 1983), 3–4; note that "although the statement is designed for halachic purposes, namely to exclude Gentiles from the rules of levitical impurity, its spirit reflects R. Simeon's bitterness against the pagan persecutors of the Jews. For other dicta by R. Simeon expressing similar sentiments, cf. Mekhilta on Exod. 14:7 (edit. Lauterbach I, 201); T. Y. Kid. IV, 11 66c; Soferim XV, 9; Lev. R. XIII, 2; Esther R. Proem 3" (ibid., 4, n. 19).

300. Soferim 15:7; see Zemer, *Evolving Halakhah*, 212.

301. Mekhilta on Exodus 14:7 (edit. Lauterbach I, 201); see above, n. 299.

302. Allan Nadler, "Charedi Rabbis Rush to Disavow Anti-Gentile Book," *The Forward*, December 19, 2003, http://www.forward.com/issues/2003/03.12.19/news4a.html.

303. Rabbi Saadya Grama, *Romemut Yisrael Ufarashat Hagalut* [The Grandeur (or Superiority) of Israel and the Question of Exile] (self-published), cited in ibid.

304. For the *refusal* of Agudath Israel of America to condemn the book, see Steven I. Weiss, "Ultra-Orthodox Officials Go to Bat for Anti-Gentile Book," in *The Forward*, January 16, 2004, http://www.forward.com/issues/2004/04.01.16/news9.lakewood.html. Agudath Israel of America is one of the nation's largest ultra-Orthodox groups.

305. Rabbi Aryeh Malkiel Kotler, cited in ibid.

306. Rabbi Dr. Norman Lamm, cited in ibid. In a letter to *The Forward*, which sought to bridge the gap between *The Forward*'s less-Orthodox readers and the ultra-Orthodox world, Rabbi Yosef Blau, a spiritual counselor to Yeshiva University students, explained that Grama's book "is a call for a superior people to withdraw from the world and live in isolation while submitting to its enemies and placing trust in God," and therefore is not "in the category of racist tracts that call for the superior race to rule the world." See "Context Is Key to Grasping Grama's Book," in *The Forward*, January 16, 2004, http://www.forward.com/issues/2004/04.01.16/oped4.html. Rabbi Blau's intent was not to defend the book but to put it in its cultural milieu. Rabbi Blau also writes, "The vast majority of Jewish thinkers posit that all humans are created in God's image and do not see all non-Jews as a definable category. But the possibility exists that one who is unaware of the marginality of Grama's sources might draw misleading and dangerous conclusions from this book. In Israel, where there is an ongoing conflict between Jews and Arabs and there is an activist element within Orthodoxy, the viewpoint of the author could be used to justify horrendous behavior. There is an unquestioned principle of *darchei shalom* (paths of peace) that governs Jewish behavior with non-Jews. Maimonides sees this principle as being a fulfillment of the commandment to emulate God's mercy on all of His creation (*Hilkhot Melakhim*, 10:12)."

307. See his chapter "The Attitude Toward the Enemy," in *Evolving Halakhah*, 205–24. Rabbi Zemer's point, of course, is that the ultra-Orthodox approach to Jewish law is wrong

and that there should be a progressive, modernist approach, more humanistic in spirit, a position branded as heretical by the ultra-Orthodox.

308. Ibid., 209.

309. For a related discussion, see the appendix to vol. 5.

310. By this I mean either that he felt "led" to make the trip (by the ultimate direction of the Father, of course) without knowing exactly what would transpire there or, more likely, that he knew exactly what was about to happen and went there for that very reason (cf. John 5:19).

311. Carson, "Matthew," *EBC*, 8:353.

312. In fact, some have argued that the fact that she identifies Jesus as the healing Messiah, possibly demonstrating some familiarity with the Psalms, indicates that she herself was a proselyte. According to Glenna Jackson, in her monograph devoted just to the pericope under discussion, "The story of Jesus' encounter with the Canaanite woman was not included in Matthew's Gospel for the purpose of recording the evangelizing of Gentiles, but for the purpose of supporting the Jewish tradition of gaining entrance into the community as a proselyte," *"Have Mercy on Me": The Story of the Canaanite Woman in Matthew 15.21–28* (Sheffield: Sheffield Academic Press, 2002), 143. While her thesis, which has been advanced before, is well-argued and sensitive to some feminist insights, it does not seem to fit the larger message of the New Testament.

313. Carson, "Matthew," *EBC*, 8:354.

314. Cf. also Lidija Novakovic, *Messiah, the Healer of the Sick: A Study of Jesus as the Son of David in the Gospel of Matthew* (Tübingen: Mohr Siebeck, 2003).

315. Stern, *JNTC*, 53, points out that the word for dog here is *kunarion*, referring to "small dogs kept as house pets. . . . Yet even if Gentiles are not here compared with wild snarling beasts, are they still not being insulted? The answer can only be: no more than in the *Tanakh* itself, where the people of Israel are taken by God in a special way as his children." Lachs, *Rabbinic Commentary on the New Testament*, 249, n. 8, makes reference to b. A. Z. 54b, "where R. Joshua b. Levi compares the righteous to the guests invited to the king's table, and the wicked heathen to the dogs who obtain the crumbs that fall therefrom."

316. For discussion of the variants in the Gospel parallels to this account, see the standard evangelical commentaries to the Synoptic Gospels. As to the anti-missionary objection that Jesus refused to be called "good teacher" because he was not divine (see Mark 10:17–18), two comments are in order: First, elsewhere *he referred to himself* as the "Good Shepherd" (see John 10:11, 14); second, he could simply have been rebuking the inquirer for his superficiality, as if to say, "You have no idea what you mean by 'good,' nor do you have any idea who you are really talking to."

317. For discussion of Lev. 18:5 and eternal life in ancient Judaism, see Simon J. Gathercole, "Torah, Life, and Salvation: Leviticus 18:5 in Early Judaism and the New Testament," in Evans and Sanders, *From Prophecy to Testament*, 131–50; Walter C. Kaiser, "Leviticus 18:5 and Paul: Do This and You Shall Live (Eternally?)," *Journal for the Evangelical Theological Society* 14 (1971): 19–28.

318. Carson, "Matthew," *EBC*, 8:520.

319. More broadly, cf. Rodney Stark, *The Rise of Christianity: How the Obscure, Marginal Jesus Movement Became the Dominant Religious Force in the Western World in a Few Centuries* (San Francisco: HarperSanFrancisco, 1997), 49–72; for an important, major new study, cf. Oskar Skarsaune and Raidar Hvlavik, eds., *Jewish Believers in Jesus: The Early Centuries* (Peabody, MA: Hendrickson, 2006).

320. For a fair and balanced discussion, see D. A. Carson and Douglas Moo, *An Introduction to the New Testament*, 2nd ed. (Grand Rapids: Zondervan, 2005).

321. Cf. the title of the volume of Jewish scholar Schalom Ben-Horin, *Brother Jesus: The Nazarene through Jewish Eyes*, trans. and ed. Jared S. Klein and Max Reinhart (Athens, GA: University of Georgia Press, 2001). For a good survey of this trend through the early 1980s, see Donald A. Hagner, *The Jewish Reclamation of Jesus* (Grand Rapids: Zondervan, 1984). For a more recent update and evaluation, cf. Michael L. Brown, "Messianic Judaism and Jewish Jesus Research," *Mishkan* 33 (2000): 36–48.

322. Brown, ibid., 37–38.

323. The classic, medieval collation of these legends is *Toledot Yeshu* (the complete Hebrew title is *Sefer Toledot Yeshu HaMashiah* or *Sefer Toledot Yeshu HaNotsri*; cf. further Kaufmann, *Christianity and Judaism*, 49–50, n. 3; for all the major versions, cf. Samuel Krauss, *Das Leben Jesu nach judischen Quellen*, 2nd ed. [1902, 1977; repr., Hildesheim: Olms, 1994]). See further above, 5.7.

324. J. H. Charlesworth and Loren L. Johns, eds., *Hillel and Jesus: Comparative Studies of Two Major Religious Leaders* (Minneapolis: Fortress, 1997); Joseph Klausner, *Jesus of Nazareth: His Life, Times, and Teaching*, trans. Herbert Danby (New York: Macmillan, 1925).

325. In Arthur E. Zannoni, ed., *Jews and Christians Speak of Jesus* (Minneapolis: Fortress, 1994), 37–53.

326. Irving M. Zeitlin, *Jesus and the Judaism of His Time* (New York: Basil Blackwell/Polity Press, 1988).

327. Rabbi Philip Sigal, *The Halakah of Jesus of Nazareth According to the Gospel of Matthew* (Lanham, MD: University Press of America, 1986). Unique to Sigal's approach is the fact that he accepts Matthew's picture of the Pharisees but distances them from the "proto-rabbis." In other words, in his judgment these *perushim* are not the Tannaitic forerunners of the prominent Talmudic leaders.

328. Key works by David Flusser include *Judaism and the Origins of Christianity* (1988; repr., Winona Lake, IN: Eisenbrauns, 1995); Flusser, *Jesus* (1969; repr., Winona Lake, IN: Eisenbrauns, 1997); Flusser, *Jewish Sources in Early Christianity* (Tel Aviv: MOD, 1995). For an introduction to the work of Shmuel Safrai, see his articles in Flusser, ed., *The Literature of the Sages: Oral Law, Halakha, Mishna, Tosefta, Talmud, External Tractates* (Philadelphia: Fortress, 1987), 35–210. For a representative application of their methodology, cf. Brad H. Young, *Jesus the Jewish Theologian* (Peabody, NH: Hendrickson, 1995).

329. Brown, "Messianic Judaism and Jewish Jesus Research," 38–42; for the negative issues, see ibid., 42–48.

330. Interestingly, this is the flip side of the coin in which non-Jewish scholars who are highly critical of the reliability of the New Testament literature often treat *rabbinic* literature as though it were historically far more reliable. Thus they are more critical of the literature with which they have greater familiarity—and which they studied through the eyes of liberal professors—and less critical of literature with which they have less familiarity. Cf. on this the older article of Phillip S. Alexander, "Rabbinic Judaism and the New Testament," *Zeitschrift für die Neutestamentliche Wissenschaft* 74 (1983): 237–46.

331. For a trenchant critique of the methodology of the Jesus Seminar, cf. the works cited above, 5.8.

332. Cf. Geza Vermes, *Jesus the Jew: A Historian's Reading of the Gospels* (Philadelphia: Fortress, 1973); see also idem, *The Gospel of Jesus the Jew* (Philadelphia: Fortress, 1981); idem, *Jesus and the World of Judaism* (Philadelphia: Fortress, 1983); Harvey Falk, *Jesus the Pharisee: A New Look at the Jewishness of Jesus* (Mahwah, NJ: Paulist Press, 1985). Most recently, see Hyam Maccobby, *Jesus the Pharisee* (London: SCM Press, 2003), with not even a reference to Falk's identically titled volume.

333. See again Alexander, "Rabbinic Judaism and the New Testament."

334. As far back as 1983, Geza Vermes pointed to the need for a new "Schürer-type *religious* history of the Jews from the Maccabees to AD 500 that fully incorporates the New Testament data" (*Jesus and the World of Judaism*, 87–88). In 1987, Jacob Neusner, William S. Green, and Ernest Frerichs edited a volume entitled *Judaisms and Their Messiahs at the Turn of the Christian Era* (Cambridge: Cambridge University Press, 1987). Although the title seemed somewhat novel at the time, the concept of first-century "Judaisms" has become increasingly commonplace in scholarly literature.

335. Cf. the classic expression of Morna D. Hooker, *Jesus and the Servant: The Influence of the Servant Concept of Deutero-Isaiah in the New Testament* (London: SPCK, 1959), reaffirmed now in her essay, "Did the Use of Isaiah 53 to Interpret His Mission Begin with Jesus?," in William H. Bellinger and William R. Farmer, eds., *Jesus and the Suffering Servant: Isaiah 53 and Christian Origins* (Harrisburg, PA: Trinity, 1998), 88–103.

336. This objection, of course, is not new. What *is* new is the wider trend towards re-embracing Yeshua as a faithful Jew.

337. Beth Moshe, *Judaism's Truth Answers the Missionaries*, 3.

338. Ibid., 212, cited also in vol. 1, 216–17, n. 13, where I note some of the more bizarre anti-missionary claims that Paul engaged in deceit and duplicity in his attempts to trick his prospective converts.

339. For a review of David Klinghoffer, *Why the Jews Rejected Jesus: The Turning Point of Western History* (New York: Doubleday, 2005), see Michael L. Brown, "Fascinating but Fundamentally and Fatally Flawed," *Mishkan* 44 (September 2005), http://www.realmessiah.org/klinghoffer.htm.

340. Hyam Maccobby, *The Mythmaker: Paul and the Invention of Christianity* (New York: Harper & Row, 1986); note that Maccobby's views are normally not even treated in comprehensive, multifaceted reviews of Pauline interpretation and scholarship, such as surveys by Stephen Westerholm, *Perspectives Old and New on Paul: The "Lutheran" Paul and His Critics* (Grand Rapids: Eerdmans, 2003); idem, *Israel's Law and the Church's Faith: Paul and His Recent Interpreters* (1988; repr., Eugene, OR: Wipf & Stock, 1998).

341. Ironically, Maccobby's volume *Jesus the Pharisee* undermines one of the major premises of Klinghoffer's book, but evidently Klinghoffer was not aware of the existence of this Maccobby volume.

342. It is understood, of course, that Klinghoffer's book is that of an interested, well-read journalist, rather than that of a biblical or Judaica scholar. Still, given the magnitude of his thesis (see again my review of his book, cited above in n. 339), there is really no excuse for his failure to interact with the Pauline scholarship that he rejects.

343. Klausner, *From Jesus to Paul*, 453–54.

344. Ibid., 452

345. Ibid., 453–54, with examples on 454–58.

346. Ibid., 458; as to why he quoted the LXX, see ibid; Klausner also notes, "But sometimes he quotes precisely according to the Hebrew text," with ref. to the Finnish scholar Antti F. Puuko.

347. David Daube, *The New Testament and Rabbinic Judaism* (1956; repr., Salem, NH: Ayer, 1984), 336ff.

348. Alan F. Segal, *Paul the Convert: The Apostolate and Apostasy of Saul the Pharisee* (New Haven: Yale University Press, 1990), xi–xii.

349. Daniel Boyarin, *A Radical Jew: Paul and the Politics of Identity* (Berkeley: University of California Press, 1994), 2.

350. Rabbi Jacob Emden, cited by Falk, *Jesus the Pharisee*, 18.

351. Peter J. Tomson, *Paul and the Jewish Law: Halakha in the Letters of the Apostle to the Gentiles* (Minneapolis: Fortress, 1990), 52–53.

352. John Dominic Crossan and Jonathan L. Reed, *In Search of Paul: How Jesus's Apostle Opposed Rome's Empire with God's Kingdom. A New Vision of Paul's Words and World* (San Francisco: HarperSanFrancisco, 2004), 4.

353. W. R. Stegner, "Paul the Jew," in Gerald F. Hawthorne and Ralph P. Martin, eds., *Dictionary of Paul and His Letters* (Downers Grove, IL: InterVarsity, 1993), 506, 500.

354. Jaroslav Pelikan, *Jesus through the Centuries* (1985; repr., New Haven, CT: Yale University Press, 1999), 18, my emphasis.

355. See also Risto Santala, *Paul the Man and the Teacher: In Light of the Jewish Sources*, trans. Michael G. Cox (Jerusalem: Keren Ahvah Meshihit, 1995); the entire book can be accessed online at http://www.kolumbus.fi/hjussila/rsla/Paul/paul01.html. For ancient church testimony as to Paul's fluency in Hebrew, cf. Jerome, *Lives of Illustrious Men, Book V*; Eusebius, *Ecclesiastical History* 6:14:2, citing Clement of Alexandria, who claimed that Paul wrote the Letter to the Hebrews in Hebrew and that Luke translated it into Greek; cf. also *Ecclesiastical History* 3:38:2–3).

356. Julie Galambush, *The Reluctant Parting: How the New Testament's Jewish Writers Created a Christian Book* (San Francisco: HarperSanFranciso, 2005), 115. I would agree with the final sentence in this quote if it had read, "If Paul can still be said to have founded Christianity—in terms of what it became over the centuries, severed from its Jewish roots and persecuting the Jews—it is now clear that he did so unintentionally." In vol. 1, I followed other writers who preferred to use the term "Christendom" when speaking of this false form of "Christianity."

357. Dunn, *Romans 9–16*, 635–36.

358. Klinghoffer, *Why the Jews Rejected Jesus*, 230, n. 19, citing E. P. Sanders, *Paul and Palestinian Judaism* (Philadelphia: Fortress, 1977), 137.

359. For discussion and analysis, see the standard evangelical commentaries on Romans and Galatians.

360. Cf. Hengel, *The Septuagint as Christian Scripture*.

361. David Wenham, *Paul and Jesus: The True Story* (London: SPCK, 2002), ix. For a more full treatment of this subject, cf. idem, *Paul: Follower of Jesus or Founder of Christianity?* (Grand Rapids: Eerdmans, 1994).

362. See also Wenham, *Paul, Follower of Jesus or Founder of Christianity?*

363. Wenham, *Paul and Jesus*, 181.

364. Wenham, *Paul, Follower of Jesus or Founder of Christianity?*, 70, with discussion of their differences in terminology.

365. Ibid., 97, with further details.

366. Ibid., 124; his conclusion to this section begins on 123.

367. Ibid., 137, again with further details.

368. Larry W. Hurtado, *Lord Jesus Christ: Devotion to Jesus in Earliest Christianity* (Grand Rapids: Eerdmans, 2003), 216. Hurtado cites Bengt Holmberg who noted that, "when Paul visited Jerusalem three years after his conversion (or perhaps about five years after Jesus' execution), 'he there encountered a religious group which had reached a fairly high degree of development in doctrinal tradition, teaching, cultic practice, common life and internal organization,'" ibid., 215–16, with reference to Holmberg, *Paul and Power* (Philadelphia: Fortress, 1978), 180.

369. Wenham, *Paul, Follower of Jesus or Founder of Christianity?*, 155. He notes on 164, "The last supper narrative is a particularly convincing example of a Jesus tradition known to Paul."

370. Ibid.

371. Ibid., 190.

372. Ibid. Although Wenham finds Paul's "in Christ" and "body of Christ" terminology to "represent something quite new" (ibid.), these concepts are also anticipated in teaching such as that found in John 15:1–8 (where the believers are depicted as branches that must remain in the true vine, which is Jesus); 17:21b, where Jesus prays for all who would believe in him that "they also be in us so that the world may believe that you have sent me" (cf. also 17:23a, "I in them and you in me"); and 6:51 (and the surrounding verses) where Jesus says, "I am the living bread that came down from heaven. If anyone eats of this bread, he will live forever. This bread is my flesh, which I will give for the life of the world."

373. Ibid., 213.

374. Ibid., 241. As for the differences, Wenham explains that they "probably reflect their respective contexts, with Paul writing after the cross and Pentecost in a largely urban and Gentile church setting, as well as in the light of his own conversion experience" (ibid.).

375. Ibid., 304. See further Ben Witherington III, *Jesus, Paul and the End of the World: A Comparative Study in New Testament Eschatology* (Downers Grove, IL: InterVarsity, 1992).

376. Wenham, *Paul, Follower of Jesus or Founder of Christianity*, 371.

377. Crossan and Reed, *In Search of Paul*, 8.

378. As I noted earlier, Maccobby's *Mythmaker* is rarely treated by top Pauline scholars, regardless of their presuppositions (in other words, regardless of whether they are conservative or liberal).

379. For a good historical study of Paul, see Ben Witherington III, *The Paul Quest: The Renewed Search for the Jew of Tarsus* (Downers Grove, IL: InterVarsity, 2001); for a highly individualistic approach, see Bruce Chilton, *Rabbi Paul: An Intellectual Biography*, (New York: Doubleday, 2004).

380. FIRE International, the full-time missionary sending arm of our FIRE School of Ministry, has missionaries working in Irian Jaya among the Fayu people, tribes whose existence was entirely unknown until less than fifty years ago when they were discovered in the jungles, naked and quite primitive. Our missionaries recounted to us how the Fayus had a story about the flood and about the scattering of the human race!

381. Nolland, *Gospel of Matthew*, 329.

382. Some Hindus have argued that John 9:1–2 points to reincarnation, since the disciples asked Jesus about the man *blind from birth*, "Rabbi, who sinned, this man or his parents, that he was born blind?" The inference, of course, is that he must have sinned in a *previous incarnation* in order to have been born blind. The answer is that, according to some Jewish thought, it was possible to sin in the womb, leading to problems upon birth; see Craig S. Keener, *The Gospel of John: A Commentary* (Peabody, MA: Hendrickson, 2003), 1:778.

383. A more relevant objection would actually be: Did the mystery religions or paganism influence the New Testament? For a useful discussion of this in the context of Jewish apologetics, cf. Snow, *Zeal for God*, 226–346. For an example of a comparative study involving Buddha and Moses, see Vanessa Rebecca Sasson, *The Birth of Moses and the Buddha: A Paradigm for the Comparative Study of Religions*, Hebrew Bible Monographs (Sheffield, England: Phoenix Press, 2006).

384. Rabbi Naftali Silberberg, "Why don't Jews believe that Jesus was the messiah?", AskMoses.com, http://www.askmoses.com/qa_detail.html?h=227&o=350.

385. Moses Maimonides, *Mishneh Torah: Hilchos Melachim U'Milchamoteihem, The Laws of Kings and Their Wars*, ed. and trans. Eliyahu Touger (Brooklyn, NY: Maznaim, 1987), 236.

386. For a recent, stylistic analysis of Matthew 5:21–7:12, cf. Glen H. Stassen, "The Fourteen Triads of the Sermon on the Mount (Matthew 5:21–7:12)," *Journal of Biblical Literature* 122 (2003): 267–308. Stassen claims that "the Sermon on the Mount is not high ideals or antitheses. The Sermon on the Mount from 5:21 through 7:12 is structured as fourteen triads, each a transforming initiative of grace-based deliverance" (308).

387. Elsewhere in the New Testament, the phrase is found in Luke 16:16; 24:24; John 1:45; Acts 13:15; 24:14; 28:23; Rom. 3:21.

388. Carson, "Matthew," *EBC*, 8:188.

389. For "Law and Prophets" as a way of referring to the Hebrew Scriptures as a whole, cf. Andrew Steinmann, *The Oracles of God: The Old Testament Canon* (St. Louis: Concordia, 1999), and note the verses cited above, n. 387.

390. For other interpretations of the words "abolish" and "fulfill," see the major Matthew commentaries.

391. "Matthew," 144.

392. Nolland, *Gospel of Matthew*, 217–18.

393. Carson, "Matthew," *EBC*, 8:144.

394. For Rabbinic statements regarding the consequences of the destruction of the Temple, see, e.g., m. Sotah 9:12, "From the day when the Temple was destroyed there has been no day wherein there was no curse, and the dew had not come down in blessing and the flavour of the fruit has been taken away" (Blackman, 3:379). There are many Rabbinic statements beginning with this same Hebrew phrase, "From the day when the Temple was destroyed." Cf. also above, 157–58.

395. Regarding the question of whether there will be a Third (and/or Messianic) Temple in the future, along with the question of whether or not there will be sacrifices for sin in this Temple, see vol. 2, 3.17.

396. It is for this reason that traditional Judaism recognizes that the majority of the so-called 613 commandments cannot be observed by Jews living outside the Land and without the Temple standing. For discussion of the history and origin of the concept of the 613 commandments, see Abraham Hirsch Rabinowitz, *TaRYaG: A Study of the Tradition That the Written Torah Contains 613 Mitzvot* (Northvale, NJ: Jason Aronson, 1996). According to the Chafetz Chayim, Rabbi Yisrael Meir haKohen, *The Concise Book of Mitzvoth: The Commandments Which Can Be Observed Today*, English adaptation and notes Charles Wengrov (Jerusalem; New York: Feldheim, 1990), Jews today can observe 77 out of the 365 positive commandments (i.e., "You shall" commandments) and 194 out of 248 negative commandments (i.e., "You shall not" commandments).

397. "Gezerah," *The Oxford Dictionary of Jewish Religion*, (New York: Oxford University Press, 1997), 271.

398. "Taqqanah," ibid., 675

399. Ibid.

400. "Minhag," ibid., 465.

401. Tracey R. Rich, "Halakhah: Jewish Law," Judaism 101, http://www.jewfaq.org/halakhah.htm.

402. Commenting on Numbers 15:38, Milgrom, *Numbers*, 160–61, notes that, "The rendering 'corners' is really inappropriate here since, in ancient days, men wore closed robes or skirts just as did women. The term may, however, refer to the scalloped hems resembling wings or to the embroidered threads that hung from the hem at quarter points."

403. For recent challenges to this position, which claim that the dye has been found, cf. P'til Tekhelet, the Association for the Promotion and Distribution of Tekhelet, Jerusalem, Israel, www.tekhelet.com. Milgrom, *Numbers*, 161, explains that, "The violet, or blue-purple, dye was extracted from the gland of the *Murex trunculus* snail found in shallow

waters off the coast of northern Israel and Lebanon. Since it has been shown that 12,000 snails yield only 1.4 grams of dye, it can be readily understood why only royalty could afford it; and hence the term 'royal blue or purple.'"

404. Cf. further Michael L. Brown, *100 Questions Christians Ask About Jews, Judaism, and Jewish Practice* (Grand Rapids: Chosen, forthcoming).

405. Milgrom, *Numbers*, 160.

406. Rich, "Halakah: Jewish Law."

407. As translated by Blackman, 3:377–78. Cf. also m. Shevi'it 4:1; m. Sanh 3:3.

408. As explained in b. Sotah 47b, "Our Rabbis taught: When murderers multiplied the ceremony of breaking a heifer's neck was discontinued, because it is only performed in a case of doubt; but when murderers multiplied openly, the ceremony of breaking a heifer's neck was discontinued. . . . Our Rabbis taught: And the man shall be free from iniquity [Num. 5:15]—at the time when the man is free from iniquity, the water proves his wife; but when the man is not free from iniquity, the water does not prove his wife. Why, then, [was it necessary for the Mishnah to add]: AS IT IS SAID, 'I WILL NOT PUNISH YOUR DAUGHTERS WHEN THEY COMMIT WHOREDOM etc'? Should you say that his own iniquity [prevents the water from proving his wife] but the iniquity of his sons and daughters does not, come and hear: 'I WILL NOT PUNISH YOUR DAUGHTERS WHEN THEY COMMIT WHOREDOM, NOR YOUR BRIDES WHEN THEY COMMIT ADULTERY'. And should you say that his sin with a married woman [prevents the water from proving his wife] but not if it was with an unmarried woman, come and hear: FOR THEY THEM-SELVES GO ASIDE WITH WHORES AND WITH THE HARLOTS etc.' What means And the people that doth not understand shall be overthrown? R. Eleazar said: The prophet spoke to Israel, If you are scrupulous with yourselves, the water will prove your wives; otherwise the water will not prove your wives." According to this Talmudic interpretation, because the men were not sufficiently free from iniquity—a tendentious interpretation of Numbers 5:31, to say the least!—the waters could not test the accused wife..

409. Dan Gruber, *Rabbi Akiva's Messiah: The Origins of Rabbinic Authority* (Hanover, NH: Elijah Publishing, 1999), 80. See online version of Gruber's work at www.elijahnet .net. For a Rabbinic attempt to prove that Hillel was *not* actually creating a legal fiction, see H. Chaim Schimmel, *The Oral Law: A Study of the Rabbinic Contribution to Torah She-be-al-peh*, rev. ed. (Jerusalem; New York: Feldheim, 1996), 127–29.

410. On the most basic level, the fundamental law books would include the Mishnah, the Talmud, the Law Codes, and the Responsa literature, which itself has grown into a massive number of tomes through the centuries. For an introduction to Jewish law, see Menachem Elon, *Jewish Law: History, Sources, Principles*, vols. 1–4, trans. Bernard Auerbach and Melvin J. Sykes (Philadelphia: Jewish Publication Society, 1994).

411. There are, of course, Rabbinic parallels to some of Jesus' teaching; for examples, see vol. 5, 6.14.

412. For discussion of this, see the standard Matthew commentaries.

413. I noted, above, 5.19, that the meaning of "Give to him who asks you," is best understood against the backdrop of Hillel's *prosbul*. However, it is also possible to interpret this based on simple, common sense as well, understanding Jesus to mean, "If someone comes to you with a legitimate need and you have the ability to help that person, then share freely." See some of the practical comments on this as found in the Didache, the so-called "Teaching of the Twelve Apostles," see esp. Didache 1:5–6, and cf. Huub van de Sandt and David Flusser, *The Didache: Its Jewish Sources and its Place in Early Judaism and Christianity*, Compendia Rerum Iudaicarum ad Novum Testamentum (Assen, Netherlands: Royal Van Gorcum; Minneapolis: Fortress, 2002).

414. For Rabbinic parallels to what is commonly called "the Lord's Prayer," cf. especially Keener's commentary on Matthew, along with Lachs, *Rabbinic Commentary on the New Testament*, and Stern, *JNTC*.

415. This is one possible interpretation of Matt. 6:22–23; for other interpretations, cf., e.g., Robert A. Guelich, *The Sermon on the Mount. A Foundation for Understanding* (Waco: Word, 1982), 329ff.; Davies and Allison, *Matthew 1–7*, 635–41, with bibliography on 665–66; Nolland, *Gospel of Matthew*, 300–302, with key bibliography. Nolland renders the verses, "The eye is the lamp of the body. If then your eye is health, your whole body will be illuminated. But if your eye is diseased, your whole body will be darkened. If then the 'light' which is in you is darkness, how great is the darkness" (300).

416. Edersheim, *Life and Times of Jesus the Messiah*, 2:680–81.

417. Ibid., 2:681–82.

418. This is not mere speculation; see Zemer, *Evolving Halakhah*, 283–91, for reference to violent actions by ultra-Orthodox Jews against Jewish Sabbath breakers passing through their community. According to Orthodox Judaism, laws concerning carrying items from public to private domains are considered biblical, whereas laws concerning (e.g.) not tearing toilet paper on the Sabbath but rather having pre-ripped paper are Rabbinic.

419. Rav Yehoshua Y. Neuwirth, *Shemirath Shabbath: A Guide for the Practical Observance of Shabbath*, 3rd ed., trans. W. Grangewood (Jerusalem; New York: Feldheim, 1995), 1:160–61.

420. Ibid., 162.

421. Ibid., 150.

422. Ibid., 103.

423. Ibid., 66.

424. For a mocking reference, see Ami Isseroff, "Some Are More Equal," *PeaceWatch* 1, no. 30 (February 23, 1999), http://www.ariga.com/peacewatch/pv1n30.htm.

425. M. Ber 8:1–5, as rendered by Jacob Neusner, *The Mishnah: A New Translation*, electronic ed. (New Haven: Yale University Press, 1988; Oak Harbor, WA: Logos Research Systems, 1988).

426. The Chofetz Chayyim as cited in Rabbi Yisroel Pinchos Bodner, *The Halachos of Muktza* (Jerusalem; New York: Feldheim, 1981), xiii.

427. Broder, ibid., xiii–xiv.

428. Of course, traditional Jews believe that many of these laws go back to Sinai, but that opinion is only held today by right-wing Orthodox and ultra-Orthodox Jews.

429. For more on this, see John Fischer, "Jesus through Jewish Eyes: A Rabbi Examines the Life and Teachings of Jesus," Menorah Ministries, http://www.menorahministries .com/Scriptorium/JesusThruJewishEyes.htm.

430. See also Henry Sturcke, *Encountering the Rest of God: How Jesus Came to Personify the Sabbath* (Zurich: Theologischer Verlag, 2005).

431. Cf., e.g., Moshe Weinfeld, *Deuteronomy 1–11: A New Translation with Introduction and Commentary*, Anchor Bible (New York: Doubleday, 1991), 301–9.

432. See 221–22. Representative studies with discussion and bibliography relevant to the subject at hand include (through the early 1990s): S. Westerholm, "Sabbath," *Dictionary of Jesus and the Gospels*, 716–19; E. P. Sanders, *Jewish Law from Jesus to the Mishnah* (London/Philadelphia: SCM/Trinity, 1990), 6–23 (for methodological differences contrast J. Neusner, *Judaic Law from Jesus to the Mishnah: A Systematic Reply to Professor E. P. Sanders* [Atlanta: Scholars Press, 1993]); J. D. G. Dunn, *Jesus, Paul, and the Law* (Louisville: Westminster/John Knox, 1990), 10–36; Zeitlin, *Jesus and the Judaism of His Time*, 73–77; Sigal, *The Halakha of Jesus of Nazareth According to the Gospel of Matthew*, esp. 119–53; D. A. Carson, "Jesus and the Sabbath in the Four Gospels," in Carson, ed., *From*

Sabbath to Lord's Day: A Biblical, Historical, and Theological Investigation (Grand Rapids: Zondervan, 1982), 57–97; R. Banks, *Jesus and the Law in the Synoptic Tradition* (SNTSMS 28; Cambridge: Cambridge University Press, 1975); Daube, *The New Testament and Rabbinic Judaism*, 67–71; cf. also the relevant sections of Lachs, *Rabbinic Commentary on the New Testament*, and cf., in popular form, J. Neusner, *A Rabbi Talks with Jesus: An Intermillennial, Interfaith Exchange* (New York: Doubleday, 1993), 58–74. For further discussion of the Jewish legal background, cf. E. P. Sanders, *Judaism: Practice and Belief 63 BCE–66 CE* (London/Philadelphia: SCM/Trinity, 1992), 208–11; Schürer, Vermes, Miller, and Black, *History of the Jewish People* 2:424–27, 447–54, 467–75; L. H. Schiffman, *The Halakhah at Qumran* (SJLA; Leiden: E. J. Brill, 1975); for more recent studies, cf. the relevant literature cited throughout Keener, *Gospel of John*, especially to John 5 and 9. For specific studies on the healings of Jesus and the Sabbath, cf. the works cited in J. Nolland, *Luke 9:21–18:34*, Word Biblical Commentary (Dallas: Word, 1993), 721, Robert A. Guelich, *Mark 1–8:26*, Word Biblical Commentary (Dallas: Word, 1989) 130–31, and Keener, *Gospel of John*.

433. For the connection between Sabbath, Sabbatical year, and jubilee, cf. C. H. H. Wright, "Sabbatical Year," *Anchor Bible Dictionary* 5:857–61, with literature.

434. For legal analysis cf. Sigal, *The Halakah of Jesus of Nazareth*, 119–53 (although his identification of the Pharisees is not convincing); see also Str.-B., 1:610–30 for an uncritical, but useful gathering of later sources, and note also Dunn, "Pharisees, Sinners, and Jesus," in *Jesus, Paul, and the Law*, 61–88; see also Schiffman, *The Halakhah at Qumran*.

435. Cf. Dunn, *Jesus, Paul, and the Law*, 27–29.

436. On the religious meaning of "yoke" in rabbinic literature, cf. Lachs, *Rabbinic Commentary on the New Testament*, 196; note also the works cited in Donald A. Hagner, *Matthew 1–13*, Word Biblical Commentary (Dallas: Word, 1993), 322.

437. Brown, *Israel's Divine Healer*, 221–22.

438. For a different view of the wineskins teaching cf. Fischer, "Jesus through Jewish Eyes." According to John Nolland, *Luke 1:9–20*, Word Biblical Commentary (Dallas: Word, 1989), 249, "For Luke, this is not a rejection of any particular elements within the old. He does not see the two as fundamentally incompatible. . . . Luke stresses the continuity between Judaism and Christianity (see especially Luke 1 and 2 passim and Acts 2) and even between Pharisaism and Christianity (see at 5:17), and the Christian movement absorbs the baptism of John (now linked to Jesus) into its own practices (see at 3:6). The need for the new to be allowed to have its own integrity shows for Luke rather in the issues raised in Acts 11:2–3 and 15:1."

439. These principles are the subject of constant dialogue and discussion among Messianic Jewish theologians and teachers; for a good introduction, see issue 22 of *Mishkan* (1995), devoted entirely to the question of the Sabbath.

440. Cited in Wessel, "Mark," *EBC*, 8:638. Stern, *JNTC*, 89, posits that what Jesus might be saying here is, "people control *Shabbat*" and not the other way around, as if "Son of Man" simply meant here "man, person," but this is less likely.

441. See further vol. 5, 6.1–6.6.

442. Douglas J. Moo, "Law," in *Dictionary of Jesus and the Gospels*, 461.

443. Note also *huqqat 'olam* ("lasting statute") 23x in Torah (MT): Exod. 12:14, 17; 27:21; 28:43; 29:9; Lev. 3:17; 7:36; 10:9; 16:29, 16:31, 16:34; 17:7; 23:14, 23:21, 23:31, 23:41; 24:3; Num. 10:8; 15:15; 18:23; 19:10, 21.

444. Cf. also above, n. 396, on the "613 commandments."

445. For the phrase *mot yumat*, "he shall surely be put to death," see: Exod. 19:12; 21:12, 25; 21:15–17, 29; 22:18; 31:14–15; 35:2; Lev. 20:2, 9–10, 15; 24:16–17, 21; 27:29; Num. 1:51; 3:10, 38; 15:35; 18:7; 35:16–18, 21, 31; Deut. 13:6[9]; 17:6. For other capital offenses, cf. Lev. 20:2; 20:14; 21:9; 24:14, 16, 23; Num. 15:35–36; Deut. 17:5; 21:21; 22:21, 24.

446. Marcus Jastrow and S. Mendelsohn, "Capital Punishment," *Jewish Encyclopedia*, http://www.jewishencyclopedia.com/view.jsp?artid=128&letter=C&search=capital%20punishment.

447. Cf., e.g., Zemer, *Evolving Halakhah*.

448. For a Reform claim to this, see Jacob J. Petuchowski, *Heirs of the Pharisees* (New York: Basic Books, 1970).

449. For the benefit of the reader, I reproduce here the quote from the former chief rabbi of the United Kingdom, Rabbi J. H. H. Hertz, found in vol. 2, 182: "The Rabbis . . . hoped that with the progress of time, human conduct would advance to higher standards, so that there would no longer be any need for expiatory sacrifices. Only the feeling of gratitude to God would remain. 'In the Messianic era, all offerings will cease, except the thanksgiving offering, which will continue forever.'" The source of this last quote is Leviticus Rabbah 9:7 (see also Midrash Psalms 56:4, with reference to Neh. 12:40). Hertz continues, "R. Phinehas and R. Levi and R. Johanan said in the name of R. Menahem of Gallia: In the Time to Come all sacrifices will be annulled, but that of thanksgiving will not be annulled, and all prayers will be annulled, but [that of] Thanksgiving will not be annulled. This is [indicated by] what is written, The voice of joy and the voice of gladness, the voice of the bridegroom and the voice of the bride, the voice of them that say: Give thanks to the Lord of hosts' (Jer. XXXIII, II)—this refers to Thanksgiving; 'That bring offerings of thanksgiving into the house of the Lord' refers to the sacrifice of thanksgiving. So too did David say: 'Thy vows are upon me, O God; I will render thanksgivings unto Thee' (Ps. LVI, 13). It is written here not 'a thanksgiving' but 'thanksgivings', meaning Thanksgiving [in prayer] and the sacrifice of thanksgiving." J. H. Hertz, *Pentateuch and Haftorahs*, 2nd ed. (London: Soncino, 1981), 562.

450. Note Carson to Matthew 5:19: "The entire Law and the Prophets are not scrapped by Jesus' coming but fulfilled. Therefore the commandments of these Scriptures—even the least of them (on distinctions in the law, see on 22:36; 23:23)—must be practiced. But the nature of the practicing has already been affected by vv. 17–18. The law pointed forward to Jesus and his teaching; so it is properly obeyed by conforming to his word. As it points to him, so he, in fulfilling it, establishes what continuity it has, the true direction to which it points and the way it is to be obeyed. Thus ranking in the kingdom turns on the degree of conformity to Jesus' teaching as that teaching fulfills OT revelation. His teaching, toward which the OT pointed, must be obeyed." "Matthew," *EBC*, 8:146.

451. It is in this sense also that Rom. 10:4 is best understood, along with 3:31. See further, below, 5.29.

452. For a convenient summary, see A. Andrew Das, *Paul and the Jews* (Peabody, MA: Hendrickson, 2003), 155–65. More fully, cf. Westerholm, *Perspectives Old and New on Paul*, 297–340. Paul used the word *nomos* more than 120 times in his letters (i.e., all letters attributed to Paul in the New Testament), the majority being in Romans (74x) and Galatians (32x).

453. Note that Derek Leman, *Paul Didn't Eat Pork: Reappraising Paul the Pharisee* (Stone Mountain, GA: Mt. Olive Press, 2005), 14–16, also follows the not uncommon practice of providing two separate lists of law-related verses in Paul, those that appear to be positive and those that appear to be negative, ultimately viewing Paul as being strongly pro-Torah. For an insightful review of Leman's work, which is nontechnical in nature, see Rich Robinson, *Mishkan* 44 (2005): 80–82. Stegner, "Paul the Jew," has a useful section entitled, "Paul and the Torah," 509–11, where he writes, "The dilemma for scholarship is posed by Paul's apparently contradictory statements about the Law. On the one hand, Paul appears to have had a positive view of the Law: 'So the Law is holy, and the commandment is holy and just and good' (Rom 7:12). 'Do we then overthrow

the Law by this faith? By no means! On the contrary we uphold the Law' (Rom 3:31). On the other hand, Paul wrote negatively about the Law and appears to have attacked the Law itself: 'By works of the Law shall no one be justified' (Gal 2:16). 'For Christ is the end (in the sense of termination) of the Law, that every one who has faith may be justified' (Rom 10:4). Did Paul contradict himself?" (509). Stegner, who does not find Paul to be contradictory and who finds Paul's Jewish background as the key to understanding his statements on the Torah, also makes reference to the work of Peter Tomson, *Paul and the Jewish Law: Halakha in the Letters of the Apostle to the Gentiles* (Minneapolis: Fortress, 1990), who demonstrates that Paul recognized the authority of Torah even when dealing with the Gentile believers.

454. Longenecker, "Acts," 423, notes, "Perhaps Paul's dress proclaimed him a Pharisee and thereby opened the way for an invitation to speak." F. F. Bruce, *The Book of Acts*, rev. ed., New International Commentary on the New Testament (Grand Rapids: Eerdmans, 1988), 252, notes that, "It was part of the duties of the ruler or rulers of the synagogue to appoint someone to deliver the address" after the reading from the Prophets.

455. For Pharisees who believed in Jesus but continued to be identified as Pharisees, see Acts 15:5.

456. For a recent study that heavily emphasizes the relevant background, cf. Vincent M. Smiles, *The Gospel and the Law in Galatia: Paul's Response to Jewish-Christian Separatism and the Threat of Galatian Apostasy* (Collegeville, MN: Liturgical Press, 1998). For a very different view, cf. Mark D. Nanos, *The Irony of Galatians: Paul's Letter in First-Century Context* (Philadelphia: Fortress, 2001).

457. See further Shaye D. Cohen, "Was Timothy Jewish (Acts 16:1–3)? Patristic Exegesis, Rabbinic Law, and. Matrilineal Descent," *Journal of Biblical Literature* 105 (1986): 251–68.

458. Peter T. O'Brien, *Colossians, Philemon*, Word Biblical Commentary (Waco: Word, 1982), 139. Some have misunderstood Col. 2:13b–14 to state that Jesus nailed the law to the cross: "He forgave us all our sins, having canceled the written code, with its regulations, that was against us and that stood opposed to us; he took it away, nailing it to the cross." Rather, what was nailed to the cross was the "record of debt" (so ESV) or the "IOU" that stood against us (cf. O'Brien, ibid., 125). That is how God forgave us (see the end of v. 13) and that is what was nailed to the cross, as many commentators and translators recognize. The conclusion, therefore, of Curtis Vaughan, "Colossians," *EBC* (Grand Rapids: Zondervan, 1978), 11:201, does not logically follow: "Either way, the reference is to the Mosaic law; and whether it is interpreted as an official indictment or as a bond of indebtedness, the thought is that God has blotted it out so that it no longer stands against us."

459. Mark D. Nanos, *The Mystery of Romans: The Jewish Context of Paul's Letter* (Philadelphia: Fortress, 1996). The approach of Nanos has been widely followed in some Messianic Jewish circles, as reflected in Mark S. Kinzer, *Postmissionary Messianic Judaism: Redefining Christian Engagement with the Jewish People* (Grand Rapids: Brazos, 2005). There are, however, serious criticisms that can be lodged against his approach; see, e.g., Das, *Paul and the Jews*, 69–74. Nonetheless, his proposal deserves ongoing discussion.

460. Keener, *IVPNT*, 544.

461. Daniel Gruber, *Torah and the New Covenant: An Introduction* (Hanover, NH: Elijah Publishing, 1998), 125.

462. Cf. Stern, *JNTC*, 585.

463. See, e.g., Stern, *JNTC*. According to Santala, "Paul's Teaching on the Jewish Law," in *Paul the Man and the Teacher*, http://www.kolumbus.fi/hjussila/rsla/Paul/paul01.html, "Paul does indeed distinguish between oral and written Law when he says in Ephesians 2:14–15 that Christ 'destroyed the barrier, the dividing wall' and 'made inoperative (Gr.

katargesas, i.e. made powerless) the Law with its commandments and regulations'—this presupposes a knowledge of the written and oral Law and the so-called 'fence around the Law' (Heb. *seyag ha-Torah*), that is the extra protective regulations of the Law."

464. See further C. Thomas Rhyne, *Faith Establishes the Law* (Chico, CA: Scholars, 1981).

465. For discussion on the differences between the LXX and MT here, cf. Ronald Y. K. Fung, *The Epistle to the Galatians*, New International Commentary (Grand Rapids: Eerdmans, 1988), 141–43.

466. It is noteworthy that the Talmud speaks of Israel *upholding all the Torah* (using the verb *qum*, just as in Deut. 27:26, which Paul quotes in Gal. 3:10 in the LXX, but then adding the word "all" as in the LXX of Deut. 27:26) in the specific context of being *justified* (*ts-d-q*), making one wonder if this was a pointed polemic against Paul's statement in Galatians 3:10.

467. See Andrew Das, *Paul and the Jews*, 142–46, here quoting 146.

468. Augustine, *On the Spirit and the Letter*, 19, cited in Douglas J. Moo, *Romans*, New International Commentary on the New Testament (Grand Rapids: Eerdmans, 1996), 482.

469. For a discussion of Deut. 6:25, see vol. 2, 62–63; note also that many Jewish interpreters understand the word *tsedaqah*, righteousness, in Deut. 6:25 to mean "merit," as they also understand it in Gen. 15:6.

470. This was argued, in particular, by C. E. B. Cranfield in his heralded, two-volume commentary on Romans in the International Critical Commentary series.

471. Stern, *JNTC*, 375.

472. Ibid., 553; the bold words represent Stern's translation in the *Jewish New Testament* (JNT).

473. For an important corrective, see Daniel P. Fuller, *Gospel and Law: Contrast or Continuum* (Grand Rapids: Eerdmans, 1980). See also David Baker, *Two Testaments, One Bible: A Study of the Theological Relationship between the Old and New Testaments* (Downers Grove, IL: InterVarsity, 1992).

474. Cf. the comments of Douglas Moo to Rom. 10:4, *Romans*, 641–42: "These considerations require that *telos* have a temporal nuance: with the coming of Christ the authority of the law of Moses is, in some basic sense, at an end. At the same time, a teleological nuance is also present. . . . The analogy of a race course (which many scholars think *telos* is meant to convey) is helpful: the finish line is both the 'termination' of the race (the race is over when it is reached) and the 'goal' of the race (the race is run for the sake of reaching the finish life). Likewise, we suggest, Paul is implying that Christ is the 'end' of the law (he brings its era to a close) and its 'goal' (he is what the law anticipated and pointed toward. The English word 'end' perfectly captures this nuance; but, it is thought that it implies too temporal a meaning, we might also use the words 'culmination,' 'consummation,' or, 'climax.'

"As Christ consummates one era of salvation history, so he inaugurates a new one. In this new era, God's eschatological righteousness is available to those who *believe*; and it is available to *everyone* who believes. . . . Because the Jews have not understood that Christ has brought the law to its culmination, they have not responded in faith to Christ; and they have therefore missed the righteousness of God, available only in Christ on the basis of faith. At the same time, Christ, by ending the era of the law, during which God dealt mainly with Israel, has made righteousness more readily available to the Gentiles. Verse 4 is, then, the hinge on which the entire section 9:30–10:13 turns. It justifies Paul's claim that the Jews, by their preoccupation with the law, have missed God's righteousness (9:30–10:3): for righteousness is now found only in Christ and only through faith in Christ, the one who has brought the law to its climax and thereby ended its reign."

475. Santala, *Paul the Man and the Teacher*, ibid.

476. Ibid.; the notes in the brackets are mine; the references are Santala's. Santala also states, "Similarly, the *Midrash Mekhilta* from the first two centuries states that '*at the end the Torah will be forgotten.*'" [Masekhet Pischa, 2] Also Rabbi Shimon Ben Elazar, who lived and worked ca. A.D. 170–200, points out: "*This is how it will be in the days of the Messiah—then there will be no 'do'- and 'do not'-commandments (zekhut ve-hova).*" [b. Shab 130a–b]. I have, however, omitted this material because I have not been able to locate the source of the first quote, while the second quote, which actually comes from b. Shab 151b, is better understood to say, "this refers to the Messianic era, wherein there is neither merit [*zekhut*] nor guilt [*hova*]." The statement in question reads, "It was further taught, R. Simeon b. Eleazar said: Perform [righteousness and charity] whilst thou canst find [an object for thy charity], hast the opportunity, and it is yet in thy power, and Solomon in his wisdom too said: 'Remember also thy creator in the days of thy youth, or ever the evil days come'—this refers to the days of old age; 'and the years draw nigh, when thou shalt say, I have no pleasure in them' [Eccles. 12:1]—this refers to the Messianic era, wherein there is neither merit nor guilt. Now he disagrees with Samuel, who said: The only difference between this world and the Messianic era is in respect of servitude to [foreign] powers, for it is said, 'For the poor shall never cease out of the land' [Deut. 15:11]." Rashi interprets "neither merit nor guilt" in the context of generosity to the poor: Since everyone will be rich in the Messianic age, there will not be the opportunity to be generous or to be tightfisted.

477. Ibid., his emphasis.

478. In addition to relevant volumes cited thus far, see the works cited in vol. 3, 233–34, n. 356; for an excellent, very full, online resource, see Mark M. Mattison, The Paul Page, www.thepaulpage.com. See further Timothy J. Hegg, *The Letter Writer: Paul's Background and Torah Perspective* (Littleton, CO: First Fruits of Zion, 2003); D. A. Carson, Peter T. O'Brien, and Mark A. Seifrid, eds., *Justification and Variegated Nomism: The Paradoxes of Paul* (Grand Rapids: Baker, 2004).

479. Dunn, *Romans 9–16*, 597.

480. Ibid. This, however, is not Dunn's primary view.

481. I am not stating here that there should be no distinctives in our congregations or that Messianic Jewish congregations do not play a vital and important role. Rather, I am saying that the fact that redeemed Jews and Gentiles can and do worship side by side as joint heirs of the Messiah runs contrary to the traditional Jewish mindset. For a healthy discussion of the issues involved, see Louis Goldberg, ed., *How Jewish Is Christianity? Two Views on the Messianic Movement* (Grand Rapids: Zondervan, 2003).

482. Markus Bockmuehl, *Jewish Law in Gentile Churches: Halakha and the Beginning of Christian Public Ethics* (Grand Rapids: Baker, 2003), 172.

483. In a private communication, professor Scot McKnight expressed his understanding of Jesus' teaching in the Sermon on the Mount as follows: "I don't think Jesus abrogates, but consummates what the Torah was teaching. I compare it to a typewriter and computer, with the typewriter being the preliminary form of the computer. Jesus cut a special circle in the ice here, and there is no getting around it. Mark 7:1–20 is along the same lines. The implication is this: followers of Yeshua go to his teachings first and read the Tanakh in light of his hermeneutic, which is defined in Mark 12:28–34 (love of God, love of others). This is nothing if it is not Jewish; he would be like other rabbis who offered 'hermeneutical clues' on how to read Tanakh." The "typewriter and computer" comment is relevant here.

484. In point of fact, traditional Jews understand *torah* here to mean both the written and oral Law, hence, the Pentateuch in its Talmudic expression (cf., possibly, Metsudat David, who speaks of "the true" or "authentic" Torah), a position that we address in vol. 5, 6.1 and

that is certainly out of place in the context of Isa. 2:1–4. In the fullness of the Messianic age, why would Talmudic dialectics be necessary? Malbim interprets *torah* to mean "the Torah," but understands "the word of the LORD" to refer to prophecy. Cf. also the Targum which translates with "the Law," expanding on this in the earlier part of the verse.

485. Maimonides, *Hilchos Melachim*, 236, 238.

486. Ibid., 232.

487. See the relevant studies in Carson, *From Sabbath to Lord's Day*; cf. also J. C. Laansma, "Lord's Day," in Ralph P. Martin and Peter H. Davids, eds., *Dictionary of the Later New Testament and Its Developments* (Downers Grove, IL: InterVarsity, 1997), 679–87, with further bibliography. Laansma notes that, "From a very early point, at least some believers recognized the 'first day of the week' as a special day for the celebration of the Eucharist. . . . There is no indication in the NT evidence that the day displaced or rivaled the sabbath, that it was a day of rest, that it had anything to do with the Fourth Commandment or that it involved any sort of transfer theology. If the NT evidence for it gives any explanation for the fact of the day's observance and of its significance, it is in the resurrection" (683).

488. See David J. Rudolph, "Messianic Jews and Christian Theology: Restoring an Historical Voice to the Contemporary Discussion," *Pro Ecclesia* 14.1 (2005): 58–84.

489. This is largely based on the testimony of the second-century Christian leader Papias, who called Mark "Peter's interpreter" (this is according to the third-century leader Eusebius, who cited these words of Papias in his *Ecclesiastical History* 3.39.15).

490. Fischer, "Jesus through Jewish Eyes."

491. Against this view, Carson, "Matthew," *EBC*, 8:351, notes that: "Because v. 20b does not occur in Mark, many have thought it to be Matthew's way of limiting the application of the controversy to the single question of eating food with unwashed hands. Two things militate against this view: (1) Jesus deals with a broad principle touching *all* foods and applies it to this situation, but the application can be no more valid than the broader principle on which it is based; and (2) Matthew frequently ends his pericopes by referring back to the questions that precipitate them (see on 12:45; 14:12; 16:11–12; 17:13); so v. 20b requires no more explanation than that."

492. As stated above, I find this argument too nuanced and not really addressing the implications of Yeshua's whole point.

493. Carson, "Matthew," *EBC*, 8:352.

494. Fischer, "Jesus through Jewish Eyes," with reference to Flusser, "Son of Man," in Arnold Toynbee, ed., *The Crucible of Christianity* (London: Thames and Hudson, 1969), 225; see Fischer, "Jesus through Jewish Eyes," for documentation of all sources quoted and further useful discussion in the appendix to his article. Cf. further Gruber, *Torah and New Covenant*, 109–10, who states concerning the NIV's rendering: "These words are actually not in the Bible. . . . The translators changed the verb 'purifying' to the adjective 'clean,' and dropped the definite article 'the'. The resulting translation turns the text into a doctrinal pronouncement on clean and unclean animals. There is no basis for it in the text. It is unrelated to the language and the context."

495. For discussion, cf. Kinzer, *Postmissionary Messianic Judaism*, 75–82.

496. For recent, nontechnical studies related to this point, see Hope Egan, *Holy Cow! Does God Care about What We Eat?* (Littleton, CO: First Fruits of Zion, 2005); Leman, *Paul Didn't Eat Pork*. For the incident between Paul and Peter recorded in Galatians 2, a variety of views can be seen in the standard Galatians commentaries; see also Stern, *JNTC*; Nanos, *The Irony of Galatians*. It should be noted that it is increasingly common today for Gentile Christians to abstain from foods prohibited by the Torah, generally for health-related reasons, believing that God's laws were given for good reason.

497. For a similar statement—but one that is debated in the Talmud, see b. Kid 72b, "Our Rabbis taught: Mamzerim [i.e., bastards] and Nethinim will become pure in the future: this is R. Jose's view. R. Meir said: They will not become pure. Said R. Jose to him: But was it not already stated: 'And I will sprinkle clean water upon you, and ye shall be clean' [Ezek. 36:25]? R. Meir replied. When it is added, 'from all your filthiness and from all your idols,' [it implies] but not from bastardy. Said R. Jose to him: When it is [further] said, will 'I cleanse you,' you must say: From bastardy too."

498. For details and documentation, see vol. 1, 71. My appreciation goes to anti-missionary rabbi Moshe Shulman who pointed out to me that my original wording in volume 1 was potentially misleading. I had written there, using very rough dates for simplicity, that, according to Rabbinic sources, "'the expected time of the Messiah's arrival is roughly 200 C.E.' . . . When you make the adjustment for [Rashi's] error in chronology (as pointed out above with regards to Rashi's calculation) he is telling us in effect that the Messianic age began at the time of Jesus." This has been corrected in the new Russian edition of volume 1 as well as in new printings of volume 1 in English and it now reads, "Most traditional Jews follow Rashi's dating, putting the expected time of the Messiah's arrival at roughly 240 C.E. . . . So, adjusting Rashi's calculations by roughly 180 years, we find ourselves in the very century in which Yeshua lived on the earth. What do you know! *He* was the one who came in the very century the Messiah was expected to come, and this according to a *Rabbinic* tradition." Of course, my only "error" was in failing to be more precise—my point stands intact and unaffected by the sharpening of my language—since I simply wanted to demonstrate that the Talmud contained a tradition that, when adjusted for proper chronology, indicated that the Messiah was expected roughly twenty centuries ago, but because of our sins, the Messianic era did not begin when it was expected to begin. (Note also that in vol. 1, 222, n. 2, I observed that many scholars date Abraham's birth to roughly 2000 B.C.E., which would further support my chronological argument. It is also quite possible that the Seder Olam chronology was unknown to the author of the statement under discussion from Sanhedrin—a view that would be entertained by many scholars who are not ultra-Orthodox Jews—and he was speaking in sweeping terms of large, significant eras in the dealings of God, which also supports my argument.) Rabbi Shulman has enabled me to make my case more precisely, and for this help, as stated above, I am appreciative. Unfortunately, in keeping with common anti-missionary practices, he appeared to accuse me of lying when dealing with this section of my book in his Internet article, "Lies Damned Lies and What the Missionaries Claim the Rabbis Say" Messiah Truth Project, http://www.messiahtruth.com/lies.html. See also my refutation in the text here of Rabbi Shulman's position regarding the proper interpretation of b. Sanh 97a.

499. See vol. 1, 72, for further discussion; the citation is from Aharon Feldman, *The Juggler and the King: The Jew and the Conquest of Evil. An Elaboration of the Vilna Gaon's Insights Into the Hidden Wisdom of the Sages* (Jerusalem; New York: Feldheim), 146.

500. Shulman, "Lies Damned Lies."

501. See again vol. 1, 71–72.

502. This is reflected in the explanatory comment in the Steinsaltz edition.

503. Vilna Gaon, cited in Feldman, *The Juggler and the King*, 150.

504. See vol. 1, 72, citing Feldman, ibid. 149–50.

505. Vol. 1, 73.

506. This is reflected in the title of a collective volume edited by Eugene Ulrich and James VanderKam, *The Community of the Renewed Covenant: The Notre Dame Symposium on the Dead Sea Scrolls* (Notre Dame, IN: University of Notre Dame Press, 1994).

507. See more fully, Brown, "Jeremiah," *EBC*[2] (vol. 7), "Excursus on the Fulfillment of the New Covenant (31:31–34)"; once again, my appreciation to Zondervan for allowing

me to excerpt some of my forthcoming commentary from the unedited manuscript here and earlier in this volume.

508. "Messiah: The Criteria," Jews for Judaism, http://www.jewsforjudaism.com/jews-jesus/jews-jesus-index.html.

509. S. R. Driver, *The Book of the Prophet Jeremiah* (London: Hodder and Stoughton, 1906), xxxix–xli. Driver's conclusion, which reflects his somewhat rationalistic interpretation of biblical prophecy, was that, "It must be evident that many of these promises have not been fulfilled, and that now circumstances have so changed that they never can be fulfilled; but, like the similar pictures drawn by other prophets, they remain as inspiring ideals of the future which God would fain see realized by or for His people, and of the goal which man, with God's help, should ever strive to attain (xxxix–xli)." For my response to this, see Brown, "Jeremiah," *EBC*² (vol. 7), "Excursus on the Fulfillment of the New Covenant (31:31–34)."

510. Brown, ibid.

511. Ibid. See ibid. for further discussion, including answers to the questions: (1) How then was the new covenant inaugurated? (2) Why then was the second temple still destroyed in 70 C.E. if the new covenant was, in fact, inaugurated by Jesus? (3) What is the difference between a delay of more than 2,500 years (and still counting) and a delay of roughly 500 years in the Messianic fulfillment of the Jeremianic promises? (4) Isn't it a complete violation of the biblical text, which is addressed to Israel and Judah, to steal the new covenant from its rightful recipients and apply it to the (primarily) Gentile church instead?

512. See Carl B. Hoch Jr., *All Things New: The Significance of Newness For New Testament Biblical Theology* (Grand Rapids: Baker, 1995). My appreciation to my editor Paul Brinkerhoff for bringing this study to my attention.

513. John Wesley, *The Works of John Wesley*, software ed. (Albany, OR: AGES Software, 1997), 1:117.

514. Ibid., 119–20.

515. For a useful study, see J. Wesley Bready, *This Freedom Whence* (Winona Lake: IN: Light and Life Press, 1950), later published as, *England, Before and After Wesley*.

516. Charles Wesley, "And Can It Be?", *Psalms and Hymns* (1738).

517. I am fully aware that, on the one hand, other religious groups attest to certain conversion experiences while, on the other hand, followers of Jesus are not yet perfect (obviously!). I am simply sharing the truth about our own experiences, experiences which totally confirm to us the reality of God's new covenant promise. So, we can support our beliefs by the written Word which is confirmed by our experience.

518. Brown, "Jeremiah," *EBC*² (vol. 7), "Excursus on the Fulfillment of the New Covenant (31:31–34)."

519. Gruber, *Torah and New Covenant*, 79–80, after commenting on *tzitzit*, makes an apposite observation concerning *tefillin* (phylacteries): "The Rabbis say of tefillin, however, that since they are a sign to remind Israel of the commandments of God, they are not worn on Shabbat or the holy days because these days are a sufficient reminder in themselves" (cf. Eruvin 96a). Gruber continues, "The very Sabbath day itself and the very festival itself is intended to serve as an everpresent reminder of God's Presence and of His commandments. . . . To add the observance of tefilling in the context of its meaning and purpose would not only be superfluous but would imply downgrading the Sabbath," citing Hayim Donin, *To Be a Jew* (New York: Basic Books, 1991), 146. Gruber adds, "Unfortunately, although the symbols themselves remind us, as do Shabbat and the festivals, they do not give us the power to keep the commandments, and they cannot produce submission in our hearts. That is why, in the New Covenant, God puts His law in our minds and writes it on our hearts. The reminder comes from within."

Glossary

Babylonian Talmud. The foundational text for Jewish religious study, it consists of 2,500,000 words of Hebrew and Aramaic commentary and expansion on the **Mishnah**. It includes much **Halakha** as well as **Haggada**, and thus it touches on virtually every area of life, religion, custom, folklore, and law. It reached its final form between 500 and 600 C.E., and it is mainly the product of the Babylonian sages. *See also* **Palestinian Talmud**.

Dead Sea Scrolls (DSS). The popular name given to the manuscripts found primarily in the ruins of Khirbet Qumran, near the Dead Sea, beginning in 1947. The manuscripts date from the middle of the third century B.C.E. to the first century C.E. and contain copies of portions of almost all the books of the Tanakh—predating all other Tanakh manuscripts by more than one thousand years—along with commentaries on sections of the Tanakh and independent writings of the Qumran community (generally identified with the Essenes).

Five Scrolls. Hamesh Megillot (pronounced kha-MESH me-gi-LOT). The biblical books of Song of Songs (Song of Solomon), Ruth, Lamentations, Ecclesiastes, and Esther. They were read in the synagogues on special holidays. *See also* **Ketuvim**.

Haggada. (sometimes spelled Aggada) Nonlegal (i.e., nonbinding) Rabbinic stories, sermons, and commentaries relating to the **Tanakh** and Jewish life. *See also* **Halakha** and **Midrash**.

Halakha. A specific legal ruling ("What is the Halakha in this case?") or Rabbinic legal material in general. The word Halakha is interpreted as meaning "the way to go." *See also* **Haggada**.

Humash. (pronounced KHU-mash) Another name for the Five Books of Moses. *See also* **Written Torah**.

Ibn Ezra. Abraham Ibn Ezra (1089–1164). One of the three greatest Jewish medieval biblical commentators, especially famous for his careful attention to Hebrew grammar. *See also* **Radak** and **Rashi**.

Jerusalem Talmud. *See* **Palestinian Talmud**.

Kabbalah. The general term for Jewish mystical writings and traditions. It literally means "that which has been received." *See also* **Zohar**.

Ketuvim. Writings. This refers to the third division of the Hebrew Bible (*see* **Tanakh**) and includes Psalms, Proverbs, Job, the **Five Scrolls**, Daniel, Ezra-Nehemiah, and 1 and 2 Chronicles.

Masoretic Text (MT). The term for the closely related Hebrew text editions of the **Tanakh** transmitted by the Masoretes ("transmitters") from the sixth to the eleventh centuries. All translations of the **Tanakh** (including the King James and *all* modern versions) are primarily based on this text. (*Note:* There is not one Masoretic Bible; there are thousands of Masoretic manuscripts with almost identical texts.)

Midrash. Rabbinic commentaries on a verse, chapter, or entire book of the **Tanakh**, marked by creativity and interpretive skill. The best-known collection is called Midrash Rabbah, covering the Five Books of Moses as well as the **Five Scrolls**.

Mishnah. The first written collection of legal material relating to the laws of the **Torah** and the ordinances of the sages. It provides the starting point for all subsequent **Halakha**. It was compiled approximately 200 c.e. by Rabbi Judah HaNasi (the Prince) and especially emphasizes the traditions of the rabbis who flourished from 70 to 200 c.e. *See also* **Babylonian Talmud**, **Palestinian Talmud**, and **Halakha**.

Mishneh Torah. Systematic compilation of all Jewish law by Moses Maimonides (also called Rambam; 1135–1204). It remains a standard legal text to this day. *See also* **Shulkhan Arukh**.

Mitzvah. Commandment. The foundation of Jewish observance consists of keeping the so-called 613 commandments of the **Torah**.

Nevi'im. Prophets. This refers to the second division of the Hebrew Bible (*see* **Tanakh**) and consists of Joshua, Judges, 1 and 2 Samuel, 1 and 2 Kings (together called the Former Prophets), and Isaiah, Jeremiah, Ezekiel, and the Twelve Minor Prophets (together called the Latter Prophets).

Oral Torah. All Rabbinic traditions relating to the **Written Torah** and various legal aspects of Jewish life. The traditions were first passed on orally before they were written down.

Palestinian Talmud. Similar to the **Babylonian Talmud** but based primarily on the work of the sages in Israel. It is shorter in scope, less authoritative, and therefore, studied less than the **Babylonian Talmud**. It reached its final form in the Land of Israel approximately 400 c.e.

Radak. Acronym for *R*abbi *D*avid *K*imchi (pronounced kim-KHEE; 1160–1235). He wrote important commentaries on much of the **Tanakh**. *See also* **Ibn Ezra** and **Rashi**.

Rashi. Acronym for *R*abbi *Sh*lomo *Y*itschaki (pronounced yits-KHA-ki; 1040–1105), the foremost Jewish commentator on the **Tanakh** and **Babylonian Talmud**. Traditional Jews always begin their studies in Bible and **Talmud** with Rashi's commentaries as their main guide. *See also* **Ibn Ezra** and **Radak**.

Responsa Literature. She'elot u-Teshuvot (pronounced she-ey-LOT u-te-shu-VOT, "Questions and Answers"). A major source of **Halakha** from 600 c.e. until today, it consists of the answers to specific legal questions posed to leading Rabbinic authorities in every generation. *See also* **Oral Torah**.

Septuagint (LXX). The Greek translation of the Tanakh completed over a period of roughly two centuries (from the third to the first centuries b.c.e.). The Torah was translated first (according to a popular legend, by seventy-two Jewish scholars who were supernaturally aided in their work, hence the name Septuagint, meaning "seventy" in Latin), followed by the other biblical books, along with what is today called the Apocrypha or Deutero-canonicals (and included as Scripture in Roman Catholic and Orthodox Bibles). Although the LXX translation of the Tanakh became "the Bible" of the Greek-speaking followers of Yeshua, it was, in fact, a pre-Christian work translated entirely by Jews.

Shulkhan Arukh. The standard and most authoritative Jewish law code, compiled by Rabbi Joseph Karo (1488–1575). *See also* **Mishneh Torah**.

Siddur. The traditional Jewish prayer book, containing selections from the **Tanakh** as well as prayers composed by the rabbis.

Talmud. *See* **Babylonian Talmud** and **Palestinian Talmud** (Jerusalem Talmud).

Tanakh. Acronym for **Torah, Nevi'im, Ketuvim**, the Jewish name for the Old Covenant in its entirety. Although the order of the books is different from that of the Christian Old Testament, the contents are the same.

Targum. Literally, "translation." This refers to the expansive Aramaic translations of the Hebrew Bible that were read in the synagogues where biblical Hebrew was no longer understood. They were put in written form between 300 and 1200 c.e. The most important Targums are Targum Onkelos to the Five Books of Moses, and Targum Jonathan to the **Nevi'im** (Prophets).

Torah. Literally, "teaching, instruction, law." It can refer to: (1) the **Written Torah** (the first division of the Hebrew Bible; *see* **Tanakh**); or (2) the **Oral Torah** in its entirety (this of course includes the **Written Torah** as well).

Torah She-be-al-peh. *See* **Oral Torah**.

Torah She-bikhtav. *See* **Written Torah**.

Tosephtah. An early collection of Rabbinic laws following the division and order of the **Mishnah** but containing parallel legal traditions not found in the **Mishnah**.

Written Torah. The Five Books of Moses (the Pentateuch). *See also* **Humash**.

Zohar. The foundational book of Jewish mysticism. It was composed in the thirteenth century, although mystical tradition dates it to the second century. *See also* **Kabbalah**.

Subject Index

345

Pentateuch, 264
Pentecost. *See* Shavuot
pesharim, 5
Peter
  on Paul, 239
  sermon on Shavuot, 181, 185
  on unclean animals, 174
  use of Scripture, 14
Pharisees, 56, 129, 148, 208, 224, 245,
  260, 334 n. 455
  on food laws, 275, 276, 280
Philo, 53, 193, 310 n. 124
Pilate, Pontius, 53–55
Pliny the Younger, 61, 62
Polycarp, 46, 201
potter's field, 29–31, 34
prayer, 216
priesthood, 231
prophecies, fulfillment of, 25–27, 35–36
prophets, 25–26, 265–66
prosbul, 214–15

Quirinius, 52
Qumran, 4, 5, 6, 7, 302 n. 15

Rabbinic chronology, 283–85
Rabbinic Judaism, 208–15
  and changes to Torah, 212–15, 267
  and dietary laws, 280
  on law, 211–12
  on Messiah, 269
  on Sabbath, 218–26
  use of Scripture, 9
Rabbinic literature, 4, 7–8, 22, 60
  apparent contradictions, 115–16, 117
  on Gentiles, 162, 168–71
  as historically reliable, 325 n. 330
  references to Jesus, 63–64
Rabbinic Midrash, 19
rabbis, authority, 210–11, 214–15, 234
Rahab, 171
Rambam. *See* Maimonides, Moses
Ramsay, William M., 41–42, 51, 52
Rashi, 33, 81, 91, 165, 168, 283, 284, 313
  n. 183, 338 n. 498
redemption, 204
Reed, Jonathan L., 193, 200
reincarnation, 203, 328 n. 382
rest, 179, 228–29, 272
resurrection of the dead, 119–22

retaliation, 141–42
Richardson, Don, 172
Rich, Tracey, 212
rich young ruler, 182
Riggans, Walter, 136–37
righteousness, 216, 255
Roman historians, 61–62
Rosh HaShanah, 210
Rothstein, David, 315 n. 200
Rozenberg, Martin S., 39
Ruggiero, Lou, 97
Ruth, 171
Rylands papyrus, 45

Sabbath, 126–27, 208, 236, 279
  change in, 270–72
  as day of liberation from bondage,
    226–28
  as hallmark of Judaism, 269–73
  Paul on, 248–49
  in Rabbinic Judaism, 218–26
  as true spiritual rest, 228–29
sacrificial giving, 141
sacrificial system, 208, 210, 235, 263
Sadducees, 56, 245
Safrai, Shmuel, 189
salvation, through obeying Law, 177–84
salvation history, 258
Samaritan woman, 171, 208–9
Samaritans, 167, 171–72, 184
Sanders, E. P., 195
Sanhedrin, 55, 245–46
Santala, Risto, 235, 258–60, 336 n. 476
Saul (king), 80–81
Saul of Tarsus, 57, 193, 200, 236, 241. *See also* Paul
Schechter, Solomon, 104
Schiffman, Lawrence H., 189
Schneerson, Menachem, 95
Second Temple, 208
Seder Olam Rabbah, 283–84
Segal, Alan, 192, 195
self-examination, 217
selfishness, 141
self-mutilation, 143–44
self-righteousness, 255
Senior, D. P., 31
Septuagint, 10, 11, 12–13, 16, 20, 38, 40,
  195, 308 n. 90

Index of Scripture and Other Ancient Writings